Videogames and Metareference

Videogames and Metareference is the first edited collection to investigate the rise of metareference in videogames from an interdisciplinary perspective.

Bringing together a group of distinguished scholars from various geographic and disciplinary backgrounds, the book combines in-depth theoretical reflection with a diverse selection of case studies in order to explore how metareference manifests itself in and around a broad range of videogames (from indie to AAA), while also asking what cultural work the videogames in question accomplish in the process. The carefully curated chapters not only provide much-needed expansions and revisions of a concept that was at least initially derived mainly from literary studies but also cover a broad range of videogame genres, discuss the evolution of metareference across videogame history as well as the functions it fulfills in different sociocultural contexts, and scrutinize metareferential elements and examples that have hitherto received little attention.

This book with its interdisciplinary scope will appeal to scholars and students within game studies and game design as well as, more broadly, scholars and students within literary studies, media studies, popular culture studies, and digital culture studies.

Theresa Krampe is a Postdoctoral Research Associate at the International Center for Ethics in the Sciences and Humanities (IZEW) at the University of Tübingen, Germany, and a Guest Researcher in Media Studies at Osnabrück University, Germany.

Jan-Noël Thon is Professor and Chair of Media Studies and Media Education at Osnabrück University, Germany.

Routledge Advances in Game Studies

Traveling through Video Games
Tom van Nuenen

Metagames: Games about Games
Agata Waszkiewicz

On Soulsring Worlds
Narrative Complexity, Digital Communities, and Interpretation in *Dark Souls* and *Elden Ring*
Marco Caracciolo

Asian Histories and Heritages in Video Games
Edited by Yowei Kang, Kenneth C.C. Yang, Michał Mochocki, Jakub Majewski, and Paweł Schreiber

Central and Eastern European Histories and Heritages in Video Games
Edited by Michał Mochocki, Paweł Schreiber, Jakub Majewski, and Yaraslau I. Kot

Zombies, Consumption, and Satire in Capcom's Dead Rising
Connor Jackson

Videogames and Metareference
Mapping the Margins of an Interdisciplinary Field
Edited by Theresa Krampe and Jan-Noël Thon

Metareference in Videogames
Theresa Krampe

For more information about this series, please visit: Routledge Advances in Game Studies - Book Series - Routledge & CRC Press

Videogames and Metareference

Mapping the Margins of an Interdisciplinary Field

Edited by Theresa Krampe and Jan-Noël Thon

Routledge
Taylor & Francis Group
LONDON AND NEW YORK

First published 2025
by Routledge
4 Park Square, Milton Park, Abingdon, Oxon OX14 4RN

and by Routledge
605 Third Avenue, New York, NY 10158

Routledge is an imprint of the Taylor & Francis Group, an informa business

The Open Access publication of this book was generously supported by Osnabrück University and the publication fund NiedersachsenOPEN as part of zukunft.niedersachsen, a joint funding program of the Ministry for Science and Culture of Lower Saxony and the Volkswagen Foundation.

British Library Cataloguing-in-Publication Data
A catalogue record for this book is available from the British Library

ISBN: 978-1-032-88294-9 (hbk)
ISBN: 978-1-032-88591-9 (pbk)
ISBN: 978-1-003-53859-2 (ebk)

DOI: 10.4324/9781003538592

Typeset in Times New Roman
by Newgen Publishing UK

Contents

Figures

Contributors

Kübra Aksay is a lecturer and PhD student in American Studies at the University of Freiburg, Germany. Her doctoral thesis focuses on recording objects within videogames, such as in-game diaries. She is an associated member of DiGRA and DAS|LAB (University of Regensburg, Germany), and has been convening the monthly meetings of the colloquium Reading Games in Freiburg since 2019.

Hans-Joachim Backe is Associate Professor at the Center for Digital Play of IT University, Copenhagen, Denmark. His research revolves around the aesthetics of digital games and comic books. He has published extensively on strategies of self-referentiality and discourses of alterity in these media, as well as on their relation to each other. Other research interests include game analysis, ecocriticism, and narrative theory. He has participated in and chaired numerous research committees on digital culture and comics within the frameworks of the International Comparative Literature Association, the German Association for Comic Studies (ComFor e.V.), and the German Association for Media Studies.

Simone Blessing is currently studying English and Spanish language and literature as part of the Teacher Training Program at the University of Regensburg, Germany. She is a member of DAS|LAB and works as a research assistant at the University of Regensburg's Department of Interdisciplinary and Multiscalar Area Studies (DIMAS).

Kieron Brown is a PhD student currently completing his PhD thesis on playfulness in comics at Osnabrück University, Germany. Before that, he received a BA (Hons) in Communication and Media at Bournemouth University and an MA in Literary Studies: Literature and Culture at the University of Amsterdam. His primary research interests to date include play and playfulness, comics studies, game studies, and intermediality.

Marco Caracciolo is Associate Professor of English and Literary Theory at Ghent University, Belgium. Drawing inspiration from cognitive science, the philosophy of mind, and the environmental humanities, his work explores the forms of experience afforded by narrative in literary fiction and other media (especially videogames). He is the author of several books, including most recently *Contemporary Fiction and Climate Uncertainty: Narrating Unstable Futures* (2022) and *Contemporary Narrative and the Spectrum of Materiality* (2023).

Astrid Ensslin is Professor of Digital Cultures and Communication and Director of the Digital Area Studies Lab (DAS|LAB) at the University of Regensburg, Germany. Recent book publications include *The Language of Gaming* (2012), *Literary Gaming* (2014), *Digital Fiction and the Unnatural* (2021), and *Reading Digital Fiction: Narrative, Cognition, Mediality* (2024).

Martin Hennig is a Postdoctoral Research Associate and Team Leader in the Field of Media and Digitalization at the International Center for Ethics in the Sciences and Humanities (IZEW) of the University of Tübingen, Germany. He received his PhD with the thesis *Spielräume als Weltentwürfe: Kultursemiotik des Videospiels* (2017). He previously worked as a Postdoctoral Research Associate at the DFG Research Training Group "Privacy and Digitalization" and substituted the Chair of Media and Cultural Studies (focus: Digital Cultures) at the University of Passau, Germany. His research interests include semiotics, digital cultures, media ethics, AI imaginaries, narratology, culture, and mentalities.

Dominik Hübschmann is a PhD student in German Studies at the University of Münster, Germany. His PhD thesis examines markers of metareferentiality in videogames. He holds an MA in History and German Studies from the University of Münster. Since 2021, he has edited the digital journal *Textpraxis*. In 2022, he published "'My imagination is as real as my body': Realitätssystemische Unsicherheit in *What Remains of Edith Finch*" (2022).

Theresa Krampe is a Postdoctoral Research Associate at the International Center for Ethics in the Sciences and Humanities (IZEW) at the University of Tübingen, Germany, and a Guest Researcher in Media Studies at Osnabrück University, Germany. Her research interests include game studies, gender and queer studies, surveillance studies, and transmedial narratology. Recent publications include "Rewriting Rules, Changing Worlds: Diegetic and Ludic Forms of Metareference in *The Magic Circle*" (*Frontiers of Narrative Studies* 2023) and "Playful Poetics: Metareferential Interfaces in Recent Indie Games" (with Stephanie Lotzow and Jan-Noël Thon, *Poetics Today* 2022).

Sebastian R. Richter is a Research Associate at the Department for Interdisciplinary and Multiscalar Area Studies (DIMAS) of the University of Regensburg, Germany, and an associated researcher of DAS|LAB. He experiments with digital theater as a music theater director.

Fiona S. Schönberg holds a BA in Film and English Literary Studies and an MA in Mediendramaturgie (Media Dramaturgy) from the University of Mainz, Germany. She is a novelist, script writer, and (narrative) game designer as well as a PhD student and an associated researcher of DAS|LAB at the University of Regensburg, Germany.

Regina Seiwald is a Teaching Fellow in German and the Deputy Director of Languages for All at the University of Birmingham (UoB), UK. She obtained her PhD on metafiction in contemporary British fiction from Birmingham City University (BCU) in 2018, which was followed by a postdoctoral research fellowship in the Faculty of Media and English at BCU between 2019 and 2021. She has published on videogame narratology, Cold War narratives, paratextuality, and transmedia narration. She is a researcher for the EU-funded COST Action GRADE (Grassroots of Digital Europe) and co-editor of *(Not) In the Game: History, Paratexts, and Games* (2023).

Jan-Noël Thon is Professor and Chair of Media Studies and Media Education at Osnabrück University, Germany. He has previously held tenured positions at the University of Nottingham, UK, and NTNU Trondheim, Norway. His research interests focus on aesthetics, narrativity, and postdigitality across media as well as on film studies, comics studies, and game studies. Recent book publications include *From Comic Strips to Graphic Novels* (2013), *Storyworlds across Media* (2014), *Game Studies* (2015), *Transmedial Narratology and Contemporary Media Culture* (2016), *Subjectivity across Media* (2017), *Ästhetik des Gemachten* (2018), *Comicanalyse* (2019), *Comics and Videogames* (2021), *Comics and Agency* (2022), and *Bildmedien* (2023).

Sarah Thorne is an Associate Professor of Communication and Media Studies at Memorial University of Newfoundland and Labrador, Canada, where her research and teaching focus on critical media theory, creativity, video games, and artificial intelligence. Her current research project, "Between Theory and Play," examines the use of video games to encourage critical reflection. As a part of this project, she is also developing experimental games that critically investigate the implementation of AI in society.

Agata Waszkiewicz is an Assistant Professor at The John Paul II Catholic University of Lublin, Poland. Their research focuses on metagames, intersections between food and game studies, and cozy games. They are the author of two books: *Delicious Pixels: Food in Video Games* (2022) and *Metagames: Games about Games* (2024). They currently hold the position of Secretary of the Central Eastern Europe Chapter of DiGRA.

1 Videogames and Metareference

Introduction

Theresa Krampe and Jan-Noël Thon

In addition to presenting the present volume's main aims and areas of interest, this introduction offers a detailed theoretical reconstruction of and reflection on metareference. It traces the concept's history from the study of literary metafiction via transmedial narratology to its contemporary use in game studies, thus establishing a shared understanding of a multifaceted concept in an interdisciplinary research field as well as offering brief chapter summaries.

In recent years, metareference has become a rather ubiquitous phenomenon in popular media culture. Commercial television series such as *House of Cards* (2013–2018), *Fleabag* (2016–2019), *Never Have I Ever* (2020–present), or *My Lady Jane* (2024) address their audiences directly by means of voice-over narration or various characters' humorous asides; self-reflexive films such as *The Cabin in the Woods* (2012), *What We Do In the Shadows* (2014), *Birdman* (2014), or *Barbie* (2023) playfully foreground familiar genre conventions and processes of filmmaking; and comics heroes such as Deadpool, Animal Man, She-Hulk, or Gwenpool regularly break the fourth wall separating them from their readership. Conceptualized as a marked form of medial self-reflexivity that originates from a metalevel and draws the recipients' attention to aspects of a given media text's mediality, materiality, or aesthetic form, metareference can essentially be described as those moments in which media texts comment on themselves and flaunt their own artifice. The prefix "meta" indicates the presence of a logically higher level on which utterances, signs, or media texts become themselves objects of reflection (see, e.g., Hauthal et al. 2007a, 4; Wolf 2009a, 3). While metareference thus remains closely related to the perhaps more broadly established concept of "metafiction" (see, e.g., Hutcheon 1980; Waugh 2001 [1984]), it is increasingly employed as an umbrella term that emphasizes the transmedial nature of the phenomenon (see, e.g., Wolf 2009a; 2011a) or at least acknowledges that metareferential strategies can be employed in a wide variety of media forms.

Not coincidentally, videogames are certainly among the most dynamic media forms when it comes to the appearance of new and often medium-specific metareferential strategies. Early text adventures such as *Zork* (1977) already responded to certain player prompts with self-reflexive humor, arguably with the

DOI: 10.4324/9781003538592-1

double function of closing the divide between the player and the gameworld and/or storyworld, while also disguising the technological limitations of the text parser (see also, e.g., Harpold 2007; Neitzel 2007; Rapp 2007). In the 1980s and 1990s, metareference soon became a trademark of witty point-and-click adventures such as *The Secret of Monkey Island* (1990), whereas in the late 1990s and throughout the 2000s, highly visible mainstream titles such as *Metal Gear Solid* (1998), *Bioshock* (2007), or *Spec Ops: The Line* (2012) used audiovisual, ludic, and narrative elements to offer decidedly more critical comments on genre conventions and player expectations. The rise of indie games, finally, brought with it not only a wave of thoroughly metareferential videogames—including, for example, *The Stanley Parable* (2013), *The Beginner's Guide* (2015), *Undertale* (2015), or *Pony Island* (2016)—but also popularized the use of an "independent style" that strives for emancipation from the mainstream (see Juul 2019, 31; as well as, e.g., Garda and Grabarczyk 2016; Thon 2019). Associated with the use of pixelated retro graphics and supposedly 8-bit sound (see, e.g., Braguinski 2018; Lee 2020), intertextual and intermedial references, and other types of remediation (see, e.g., Kirkland 2011; Sloan 2015), independent style thus evidently creates a favorable environment for videogames to draw attention to and comment on aspects of their mediality, as demonstrated by a range of indie games such as *Terraria* (2011), *Stardew Valley* (2016), *What Remains of Edith Finch* (2017), or *Pentiment* (2022).

However, these diverse forms of metareference in videogames have thus far not been analyzed in much detail. It is certainly true that a productive body of research is currently emerging in and beyond game studies (see, e.g., Ensslin 2014b; Fest 2016; Krampe et al. 2022; Krampe 2025; Waszkiewicz 2024), and canonical examples such as *Metal Gear Solid* or *The Stanley Parable* are particularly well-studied by now (see, e.g., Backe and Thon 2019; Herte 2016; Jannidis 2009; Ryan 2004). Yet, many other phenomena and potential case studies remain entirely unexplored. Moreover, while there seems to be some agreement among scholars that metareference in videogames shares the characteristics of self-reflexivity, metaization, and medium awareness familiar from other media forms, it is less clear how these phenomena are to be delineated, what their functions are, or how they fit with the overall design of the videogame in question. There remains, in other words, an important theoretical and analytical gap in the study of metareference in videogames that the following chapters aim to fill.

Given its particularly productive role in conceptualizing meta phenomena across media forms, our starting point in presenting the present volume's theoretical trajectory will be the insights gained from the study of literary metafiction. As is well known, the term "metafiction" was coined in the 1970s, when William Gass (1970) and Robert Scholes (1995 [1970]), respectively, used it to describe the forms of textual self-reflection that emerged in the context of postmodern literature. The novels in question employed strategies and devices such as metalepsis, *mise en abyme*, fragmentation, intertextuality, unreliable narration, or impossible loops, thereby drawing attention to their own artifice (see also, e.g., Hutcheon 1980; Waugh 2001 [1984]). According to Linda Hutcheon, metafiction "includes within itself a commentary on its own narrative and/or linguistic identity" (1980,

1). This definition remains essentially applicable to videogames, though we may add that, due to their multimodality, the semiotic repertoire available to them also includes audiovisual, ludic, and haptic semiotic resources. With a view to the close temporal and conceptual connections between postmodernism and metafiction, it is often difficult to draw a clear line between the two; a terminological fuzziness that carries over to the present day and across media. Several videogame reviews, articles, and research papers, for example, refer to videogames that use metareferential strategies as "postmodern" (see, e.g., Stanton 2015; Wong 2013). While analyzing videogames within the framework of a postmodern aesthetic can certainly be productive, then, it seems problematic to conflate the two terms. Not only can metafiction be traced back well beyond postmodernism to the very beginnings of the novel (see, e.g., Alter 1975; Hutcheon 1980; Scheffel 1997) but it also describes a very specific phenomenon, namely one that is characterized by the presence of a self-commentary that seems to originate from a higher level within the text.

Patricia Waugh (2001 [1984]), whose work is commonly cited as both a staple of research on metafiction and on postmodernism (see, e.g., Lewis 2011, 170), goes to some lengths to delineate the specifics of metafiction that distinguish it from postmodern and experimental fiction in both form and function. Postmodern texts, she suggests, exhibit features that may seem random, excessive, even pointless, such as the "surrealistic juxtaposition of extremely disparate images and objects" (Waugh 2001 [1984], 141; see also Waugh 2001 [1984], 137–140; as well as Lewis 2011, 171). Metafictional texts, by contrast, are taken to depend on a carefully structured tension of opposition (see Waugh 2001 [1984], 137). Like Scholes before her (see Scholes 1995 [1970], 106–107), Waugh understands metafiction as a hybrid genre that balances the fictional mode with an intellectual (and often self-critical) perspective that certainly finds its echoes in many if not most of the case studies of metareference in videogames that the chapters collected in the present volume present. Or, as she puts it: "*Metafiction* is a term given to fictional writing which self-consciously and systematically draws attention to its status as an artefact in order to pose questions about the relationship between fiction and reality" (Waugh 2001 [1984], 2; original emphasis).

The functional component entailed in Waugh's definition is interesting insofar as it sheds some light on the cultural work of meta phenomena. Noting the prominence of metafictional literary texts in the 1960s and 1970s, Waugh hypothesizes that metafiction provided an outlet for one of the central anxieties of postmodernism, namely, the increasing awareness that history and reality are provisional and constructed (see also, e.g., Ryan 1997; Zipfel 2020 on the related issue of panfictionalism). As metafictional literary texts "explore the possible fictionality of the world outside the literary fictional text" (Waugh 2001 [1984], 2), they in fact become rather accurate representations of experiencing the actual world as artifice. To capture the spirit of metafiction thus delineated, Waugh draws productive analogies between metafiction and certain forms of play. Many metafictional novels choose play as a subject of reflection or emulate modes of play, for example by presenting multiple endings or deliberately subverting the rules and conventions associated with a specific genre (see Waugh 2001 [1984], 43). Drawing on the work of Waugh, Yaël Schlick (2023,

70–92) has recently used the term "ludic metafiction" to describe literary texts (novels, poetry, drama) that play language games to make literary conventions visible to the recipients, "keep [recipients] from simply accepting the rules [...], and in many instances foster creative engagement with lived experience beyond the text" (Schlick 2023, 71). When considering metafiction's concern with breaking free from established rules and conventions, the notion of playfulness indeed seems relevant (see, e.g., Bateson and Martin 2013; Lieberman 1977; Sutton-Smith 1997; as well as Sicart 2014; Stenros 2015; and the contributions in Thon 2021). Like many of the games we play, metafiction creates rule-governed spaces of make-believe which, though set off from the actual world, nevertheless retain considerable value for actual-world contexts in that they help us understand the role of rules and fictions in life (see also, once more, Waugh 2001 [1984], 35).

While these outward-looking, critical functions of metareference may seem obvious in hindsight, this was nowhere near as evident in the 1970s and 1980s, when authors and scholars of literary metafiction felt the need to fend off (real or imagined) accusations of self-centeredness and lack of artistic ambition (see, e.g., the quotes collected in Hutcheon 1980, 2). It is worth mentioning, at this point, that the relevant research is generally quite optimistic about the critical and innovative potential of metafiction. Hutcheon (1980, 18), though the title *Narcissistic Narrative* might suggest otherwise, stresses that metafiction usually entails a parodic intent to unmask tired conventions and find new forms of artistic expression. It is thus better understood as a sign of the genre's maturation as well as of a "renewed sense of language, formal craft, and aesthetic design" (Hutcheon 1980, 14). The optimistic view seems to have prevailed in contemporary assessments of postmodern metafiction, with Yaël Schlick (2023, 3) still proposing quite recently that it was precisely the self-reflexive engagement with its own form that allowed literary fiction to renew itself in the 1960s and 1970s and that, arguably, allows different media forms to push against and move beyond tired forms and conventions today. Ilona Mader (2017) makes a similar point when she connects metafiction to deconstruction and to the idea of the frame break. Metafiction, she suggests, operates at and through the frame of a literary text, i.e., "the boundary that encloses and delimits a work of fiction, distinguishing it from reality as well as from other fictions" (Mader 2017, 42; our translation; see also, e.g., Malina 2002; Wolf 2006 on the concept of the frame in the context of metalepsis, metareference, and representational works/media texts more generally). If such boundaries are transgressed or destroyed, if the frame is relocated or expanded, or if the distinction between inside and outside is blurred, this not only reveals the constructedness of (fictional) texts but also unsettles our perception of reality (see Mader 2017, 12, 18, 43–45).

As noted before, these observations are aimed at metafictional literary texts written around the mid-20th century, but we can certainly also observe some intriguing parallels to the present moment. While we do not want to overemphasize these parallels and certainly do not aim to conflate videogames with literary texts (though do also see, e.g., Ensslin 2014a; Mukherjee 2015 for explorations of videogames' "literariness"), videogames' maturation alongside their media-savvy players seems a plausible explanation for the increase of meta phenomena that serve the purpose of exploring new forms of expression. What is more, metaization in the (post)digital age seems symptomatic of anxieties around the erosion of traditional knowledges and certainties that are quite similar to those we find in postmodern novels. Contemporary media forms in general and videogames in particular appear increasingly concerned with what we might describe either as a renewed crisis of reference, exacerbated by the loss of trust in (digital) images, or a new form of creativity, accompanied by an increased critical consciousness (see also, e.g., Fest 2016; Nöth 2007b, 7; Wolf 2011a, 29–31). Put in a nutshell, technological advancements (from photorealistic simulations to generative AI), the emergence of hybrid realities (from alternate reality games to the metaverse), and a general erosion of trust in software and data in the post-Snowden era has made "reality" increasingly hard to pin down.

In the second half of the 20th century and well into the 21st, metafiction research continued to thrive in literary studies and narratology, with similar concepts also being developed in other medial contexts, including theater (see, e.g., Abel 1963; Hauthal 2009; Schmeling 1977), film, TV, and animation (see, e.g., Feyersinger 2011; 2017; Gymnich 2007; Roche 2022), comics (see, e.g., Kukkonen 2009; Nöth 2007a; Thoss 2011), and even music (see, e.g., Bernhart and Wolf 2010). Yet, it was only in the 2000s that scholars began to consolidate these approaches under explicitly transmedial frameworks. Winfried Nöth and Nina Bishara's edited collection *Self-Reference in the* Media (2007), for instance, explores self-reference in different media forms from a semiotic perspective. This creates several areas of overlap to our present interests, including extended discussions of devices such as metalepsis, *mise en abyme*, or intertextual references, all of which can frequently be found in metareferential videogames as well. In fact, Nöth and Bishara's anthology contains a dedicated section with a total of four chapters on games and play (see Neitzel 2007; Rapp 2007; Santaella 2007; Walther 2007). Among other questions, these chapters discuss now canonical videogame examples such as *Zork*, *Metal Gear Solid*, *Monkey Island 4: Escape from Monkey Island* (2000), and *Max Payne* (2001). Yet, the concept of "self-reference," understood as signs that refer to themselves rather than to something external to themselves, is invariably broader than metareference in that it encompasses accidental effects or loops created by the very mediality of the media text in question or the materiality of its underlying "apparatus." In the case of videogames as well as other ludic and/or digital-born media forms, we would therefore need to attest self-referentiality to any and all works—as the chapters in *Self-Reference in the Media* in fact seem to do (see Rapp 2007, 255; Santaella 2007, 209; Walther 2007, 219)—simply by virtue of their ludic and/or procedural nature. After all, ludic and algorithmic rules necessarily refer back to the sign system in which they occur (see also Bell 2016; Ensslin and Bell 2021, 41–82, on the related concept of "interactional metalepsis," which we discuss in more detail below). What we are interested in here, however, are those self-references that we might describe as "non-accidental" (Wolf 2009a, 26) or "intentional" (though we would conceptualize this "intentionality" within the framework of hypothetical intentionalism; see, e.g., Kindt and Müller 2006 for a historical reconstruction; Thon 2016 for transmedial applications).

This narrower focus is also adopted by the German-language collection *Metaisierung in der Literatur und anderen Medien* (see Hauthal et al. 2007b), the title of which translates to "Metaization in Literature and Other Media" and which explicitly defines its scope as referring to textual phenomena that "contain a logically higher level, a level of cognitive reflection from whence phenomena on the object level are described or commented on" (Hauthal et al. 2007a, 4; our translation), arguing that this typically leads to reflections on questions of mediality in the media texts as well as the recipient. Heavily influenced by the theoretical work of Werner Wolf (see, e.g., Wolf 1993; 2001), this definition is not medium-specific in that it hinges not on verbal comments or exclusively on the foregrounding of linguistic and/or fictional elements but rather on the presence of a metalevel in the media text. Nevertheless, most chapters continue to focus on literary texts, albeit including poetry and drama, while two branch out to film and TV (see Butler and Sepp 2007; Gymnich 2007). A considerably broader range of media appear in the collection *Metareference across Media* (see Wolf 2009b) and its sequel *The Metareferential Turn in Contemporary Arts and Media* (see Wolf 2011b). Taken together, the two collections cover literature, theater, cinema, TV, photography, visual art, animation, comics, dance, and music, with several chapters covering more than one medium. Fotis Jannidis's "Metareference in Computer Games" (2009) is worth highlighting here as an early engagement with the different forms of metareference that occur in videogames. Of equal importance is Wolf's detailed conceptualization of the phenomenon and its main functions in the comprehensive introductions to the two collections. Metareference, in Wolf's definition, is

> a special, transmedial form of usually non-accidental self-reference produced by signs or sign configurations which are (felt to be) located on a logically higher level, a "meta-level," within an artefact or performance; this self-reference, which can extend from this artefact to the entire system of the media, forms or implies a statement about an object-level, namely on (aspects of) the medium/system referred to. Where metareference is properly understood, an at least minimal corresponding "meta-awareness" is elicited in the recipient, who thus becomes conscious of both the medial (or "fictional" in the sense of artificial and, sometimes in addition, "invented") status of the work under discussion and the fact that media-related phenomena are at issue, rather than (hetero-) references to the world outside the media.
>
> (Wolf 2009a, 31)

In short, metareference describes a form of medial self-reflexivity characterized by the presence of a metalevel from whence the media text comments on itself and draws the recipients' attention to its own mediality. As an umbrella term, metareference thus seems particularly suitable because it limits the scope to phenomena of a semiotic nature (excluding, e.g., meta terms from fields such as physics) while remaining open to non-linguistic media forms. It is therefore readily applicable to videogames despite their multimodality, or indeed the fact that not all videogames are built around verbal narrative.

It comes as no surprise, then, that the concept of "metareference" can and has been productively employed in game studies. Hans-Joachim Backe, for example, applies the term "metareference" to the study of videogames within videogames (see Backe 2016) as well as in-game images (see Backe 2018). Theresa Krampe (2025), meanwhile, uses it as a starting point for developing an analytical model that captures the transmedial as well as medium-specific dimensions of metareference in videogames. Other scholars have preferred to coin new terms to describe specific phenomena that occur in videogames, though these phenomena are often contained within or at least partially overlap with what we would consider the set of metareferential phenomena. In her analysis of the indie game *The Path* (2009), for example, Astrid Ensslin introduces the concept of "metaludicity" to capture "aspects of a game whose purpose it is to make players reflect critically upon game mechanics and gameplay" (2014b, 84). Being much more specific than "metareference," the term "metaludicity" thus describes a medium-specific form of self-reference that takes conventional game rules and mechanics as its main object of reflection and critique. Bradley Fest, in turn, refers back to debates that arose in the context of postmodern metafiction (as discussed above), when he interprets videogames' increasing "metaproceduralism" as a sign of the medium's maturity and its responsiveness to an overall shift toward an "informatic, algorithmic logic of cultural production in the digital age" (2016, 3). Formally, these concerns manifest in the way not only videogames' narrative elements but also their ludic processes reflect on themselves—which Fest (2016, 9) considers the main feature that distinguishes meta*procedural* videogames from meta*fictional* novels.

Moreover, in recent years, papers and entire panels dedicated to metareferential videogames were presented at high-profile conferences. The "meta-panel," organized by the Italian *GAME* journal and presented at DiGRA 2013, is a case in point (see Caruso et al. 2013). The panel later evolved into the *GAME* special issue *Games on Games: Game Design as Critical Reflexive Practice* (see Caruso et al. 2016), the main interest of which lies in exploring the possibilities of using videogames as a means of doing and communicating research. In addition to several articles broadly following the conventions of the written academic essay, the issue consequently also includes examples of what has been referred to as "playable theory" (Ferri et al. 2016, 6), namely videogames that can in themselves be considered forms of research in that they offer interpretations or otherwise generate knowledge about videogames. In the German-speaking context, Bernhard Rapp's (2008) doctoral dissertation on self-reflexivity in videogames is worth mentioning as an early milestone (on self-reflexivity, see also Gualeni 2016). Recent research has furthermore probed the metareferential potential of glitches (see, e.g., Gualeni 2019), interfaces (see, e.g., Krampe et al. 2022), and ludic forms (see, e.g., Krampe 2023). The first more extensive, book-length studies of metareferential videogames have just been published, offering a discussion of a variety of different metareferential devices (see Waszkiewicz 2024) and an analytical framework for the systematic analysis of metareferential elements (see Krampe 2025), respectively.

Not coincidentally, a similar increase in scholarly attention can be observed when considering closely related terms and concepts such as metalepsis (see, e.g., Bell 2016; Ensslin 2023; Ensslin and Bell 2021; Harpold 2007) as well as its close relative, the fourth-wall break (see, e.g., Conway 2010; Waszkiewicz 2020). Research on different forms of metalepsis has been immensely productive in analyzing phenomena that are also of interest to the study of metareference. The use of the term "metalepsis" to describe transgressions between ontological boundaries within a literary (or, indeed, media) text goes back to Gérard Genette, who conceptualizes it as "any intrusion by the extradiegetic narrator or narratee into the diegetic universe (or by diegetic characters into a metadiegetic universe, etc.), or the inverse" (1983 [1980], 234–235). In more recent publications, the reliance on narrators is typically substituted with an understanding that hinges on the crossing of or confusion between different diegetic levels or sub-worlds (see, e.g., Kukkonen 2011; Thon 2016; Thoss 2015; Wolf 2005, 91). This makes the concept productive not only beyond the relatively specific cases addressed by Genette but also beyond the application to verbal narrative. On the one hand, quite a few mainstream videogames including *The Secret of Monkey Island*, *Metal Gear Solid*, *Max Payne*, and *Deadpool* (2013) have been using a variety of verbal as well as audiovisual strategies and ludic elements to break the so-called fourth wall (i.e., the boundary between the represented storyworld and the actual world of the player). Meanwhile, indie games such as *The Magic Circle* (2015; see also Krampe 2023), *OneShot* (2016; see also Krampe et al. 2022), *Doki Doki Literature Club!* (2017; see also Barkman 2021), or *There Is No Game: Wrong Dimension* (2020; see also Thorne 2021) showcase an even broader range of metaleptic forms that in some cases transgress all levels of their respective diegetic hierarchies.

The correlations between metafiction and metalepsis are quite strong; so strong, in fact, that the latter is occasionally described as a sub-form or specific technique of the former (see, e.g., Malina 2002, 1–2; Wolf 2005, 103). Yet, scholars such as Sonja Klimek (2009) or Werner Wolf (in his later works; e.g., Wolf 2009a) have convincingly argued that metalepsis can, at least temporarily, stabilize or intensify the aesthetic illusion, making it less likely to draw attention to the mediality of the media text that is representing it. In children's fantasy novels, for instance, a character's movement to a lower diegetic level is an established means for introducing readers to and immersing them in a (fictional) storyworld (see, once more, Klimek 2009). Karin Kukkonen even suggests that metalepsis might be "inherent to the entire communicative situation of fiction" (2011, 11) by virtue of the actual-world knowledge that readers bring to the storyworld. According to Kukkonen, reality and fiction are always already enmeshed so that marked cases of metalepsis merely highlight processes that are part of all fictions anyways (which is, of course, a standard position within the theory of fiction; see, e.g., Blume 2004; Köppe 2008; Ryan 1991; Walton 1990). Similar arguments can be found in the narratological sub-field of unnatural narratology (see also the broader accounts of "unnatural narrative" in Alber 2016; Richardson 2015), where Alice Bell and Astrid Ensslin identify what they call "interactional metalepsis" as an inherent part of the gaming situation (see Bell 2016; as well as Ensslin and Bell 2021, 41–82). More specifically, Bell argues, "[t]hat navigation in ergodic digital fiction produces a visual and ontological manifestation of the reader in the storyworld," which in turn "means that this non-trivial form of reading necessitates interactional metalepsis because the reader, or rather a representation of her/him, crosses the ontological boundary between the actual world and storyworld" (2016, 297). "Interactional metalepsis" thus occurs as soon as the media text affords some kind of interactive agency and hence creates a feedback loop between player and videogame (on agency in the context of videogames, see also, e.g., Bódi 2023; Bódi and Thon 2020; Murray 2017; Nguyen 2020). When employing such a conceptualization of the term, metalepsis thus becomes the default case in videogames and digital fictions, making it unlikely to elicit medium awareness except in marked cases.

Even without following Bell's and Ensslin's argument for framing metalepsis as a baseline condition of the gameplay experience, however, videogames seem to be particularly prone to offer metaleptic experiences to their players. Marie-Laure Ryan, for example, while maintaining that neither the "narrative stack" of multilayered media texts nor the "stratified architecture of the computer" (2004, 451) are in themselves metaleptic, nevertheless argues that computers create favorable conditions for metalepses of at least two kinds: technological and artistic. The former includes "viruses [and] programs that operate on themselves" (Ryan 2004, 451), the latter aesthetically motivated techniques for exhibiting the mediality of a media text. Among other examples, Ryan cites the by-now canonical *Metal Gear Solid 2: Sons of Liberty* (2001), in which one of the characters spells out the fact that this "is just a game" (quoted in Ryan 2004, 460) and then proceeds to directly address the player. Perhaps most interestingly, Ryan also discusses the possibility for metalepsis to "*really* spill into the real world and affect it *physically*" (2006, 226; original emphases), a potential that videogames share with dramatic acting and alternate reality games. As Ryan puts it, "it would be fairly easy to write a computer game that destroys the user's system" (2004, 461), and while she did not think this likely to happen two decades ago, current developments suggest otherwise. Recent indie games such as *Imscared: A Pixelated Nightmare* (2016), *OneShot*, or *Doki Doki Literature Club!*, for instance, manipulate files on the actual computer, thus cutting across the divide between the videogame and what is outside it (see also Krampe et al. 2022). The experimental art game *Lose/Lose* (2009), meanwhile, introduces real-life consequences by deleting data on the player's computer. Intended as an artistic intervention in contemporary computer-related anxieties, *Lose/Lose* foregrounds the pervasiveness of data and our precarious dependency on it (see Gage 2009).

Yet, Ryan (2006, 224) also notes that many of the metaleptic techniques that occur in videogames are actually used to increase or preserve the player's immersion in the videogame, for instance by integrating instructions into the gameworld and/or the storyworld, or through operations of "recapture" (Harpold 2007, n.pag.) that hide the videogame's technological foundations. If an adventure game text parser directly addresses the player in a humorous manner, this might simply serve to hide its own technological limitations (see, once more, Harpold 2007). In fact, just like the basic feedback loop that Bell and Ensslin describe as "interactional metalepsis" (see Bell 2016; Ensslin and Bell 2021, 41–82), the player is unlikely to particularly notice these operations even though they may be technically metaleptic in that they cross the boundary between the actual world and that of the videogame. In light of this rather broad spectrum of videogames' metaleptic functions, it is helpful to distinguish between forms of metalepsis that are metareferential in the sense that they draw attention to the mediality, materiality, and aesthetic form of the media text, and those that serve the opposite effect or are mere expressions of the communicative situation in which they are embedded. In this sense, metalepsis emerges as a rhetorical figure that holds a particularly high "metareferential *potential*" (Wolf 2009a, 55; original emphasis) but is *not* automatically metareferential in the sense in which the concept is used in the present volume. In any case, videogame-specific forms of metalepsis constitute an important part of the videogame-specific forms of metareference that the following chapters aim to explore. What follows is an overview of the volume's chapters.

Lamenting that the concept of "poetics" has largely been marginalized by the concepts of "rhetoric" and "aesthetics" within game studies and game design, Hans-Joachim Backe's chapter "Metareferentiality as an Indicator of Procedural Poetics" proposes a descriptive, analytical poetics of videogames. Backe argues that the concept of "metareference" (or "metareferentiality") is central for such a "procedural poetics," since the metareferential reflection on a videogame's features make visible its immanent "poetics." Against this background, Backe considers "procedural poetics" as a particularly promising area of application of the concept of "metareferentiality," which he demonstrates through analyses of the first-person shooter *Wolfenstein II: The New Colossus* (2017) and a selection of videogames commonly referred to as immersive sims.

Martin Hennig's chapter "Orders of Anti-Illusion: An Analytical Framework for Metareference from a Semiotic Perspective" then offers an extended discussion of the semiotic foundations of a conceptualization of "metareference" in videogames that emphasizes the basic distinction between object language and metalanguage from the philosophy of language, on the one hand, and the question whether non-linguistic media forms may exhibit structures that function analogously to metalanguage, on the other. Having explored the theoretical implications of this semiotic perspective in some detail, Hennig proceeds to analyze Daniel Mullins's indie game *The Hex* (2018), highlighting occurrences of metareference in its game mechanics, its narrative layer, and the visual representation of both.

Further pursuing a semiotic account of metareference in videogames that likewise explores the question of videogame-specific "metasigns," but also extensively discusses Lotman's influential account of artistic language, Dominik Hübschmann's chapter "Not Salient Enough? Videogame-Specific Marker Failure of Implicit Metareference in *Far Cry 2* and *Far Cry 3*" zooms in on the question of when (or under which conditions) markers of metareference "fail." Hübschmann identifies the saliency of metareference as a problem that is particularly central in videogames, which also leads him to focus his comparative analysis of *Far Cry 2* (2008) and *Far Cry 3* (2012) on implicit forms of metareference (or "metacomments") that require players to "read" the relevant markers through various kinds of "noise."

Drawing on a comprehensive model of metareference in videogames that distinguishes different types or dimensions of the latter, Theresa Krampe's chapter "No Longer Safe Before the Screen? Game-Transcending Metareference in Indie

Horror Games" uses the indie games *Imscared: A Pixelated Nightmare* (2016) and *Archimedes* (2016) as case studies to explore what she proposes to call "game-transcending metareference." As a form of metareference that has become common in recent indie horror games, game-transcending metareference is characterized by a "genuine" ontological metalepsis between the videogame and what is outside of it, unsettling the conventional divide between the fictional (game)world and that of the player in the process.

Similarly concerned with the tendency of (especially) horror games to blur distinctions between fictional world, reality, and code, Sarah Thorne's chapter "When Metareference Is the Gameplay: Examining the Multidimensional Layers of Daniel Mullins's *Inscryption*" emphasizes that the indie games designed by Daniel Mullins (which, not coincidentally, are also discussed in various other chapters in the present volume) seem especially keen on exploring the videogame-specific forms and functions of metareference. In particular, Thorne examines how metareference itself becomes the (main point of the) gameplay in Mullins's most recently published title *Inscryption* (2021), as the latter bridges narrative and ludic elements through multilayered *mise-en-abyme* structures, different metaleptic strategies, and a fully-fledged alternate reality game.

Further diversifying the range of theoretical approaches presented in the present volume, Marco Caracciolo's chapter "Metareference and Posthuman Subjectivity in Videogames" analyzes metareference in videogames through the lens of "posthumanism," noting that videogames can question humanist assumptions by integrating posthumanist themes, ideas, and thinking in both their "formal design" and their "subject matter." Connecting this broader theoretical consideration to existing accounts of videogame-specific metareference, Caracciolo then proceeds to analyze in detail what he calls "posthuman subjectivity" in a range of different videogames, again focusing particularly on *Inscryption* (though other relevant videogames such as *Metal Gear Solid* or *Max Payne* are also analyzed).

Likewise foregrounding different kinds of metaleptic transgressions in case studies drawn from the horror genre, but focusing on metaleptic transgressions between different layers within the gameworld (rather than between the videogame and what is outside it), Agata Waszkiewicz's chapter "The Visual Metalepsis as a Palimpsest in *Alan Wake 2* and *Layers of Fear 2*" uses the notions of the cinematic and the palimpsestic to highlight the specific forms of metareferential metalepsis used in these two rather different horror games. Through the concepts of "visual metalepsis," "character metalepsis," and "permeable metalepsis," their analysis examines the complex overlapping of identities and blurring of the lines between the different (ontological) levels of (fictional) reality that ultimately characterizes both *Alan Wake 2* (2023) and *Layers of Fear 2* (2019).

Moving on from metaleptic horror to texts in videogames, Regina Seiwald's chapter "Reading (in) Games: Constructing Meaning through Intradiegetic Metareferences to Text" goes on to analyze a broad variety of (metareferential) text–game relationships in an extensive corpus of (metareferential) videogames, highlighting, comparing, and contrasting occurrences of various forms of intradiegetic texts that range from short one-letter words to whole books, and can be located on a scale from no to full "self-reflexivity." While most chapters collected in the present volume acknowledge that metareference in videogames entails both ludic and narrative aspects, Seiwald arguably goes further than that in stressing, rather uncompromisingly, that "[v]ideogames could not exist without text."

The centrality of text is also echoed in Kübra Aksay, Simone Blessing, Astrid Ensslin, Sebastian R. Richter, and Fiona S. Schönberg's chapter "'The Name of the Reader': Constructing the Bookish Player in *Pentiment.*" In its deliberately multiperspectival approach, the chapter presents a diverse set of theoretical and analytical perspectives on Obsidian Entertainment's 2022 videogame's "bookish" metareferentiality, exploring in detail the complex interrelations between different diegetic books and their aesthetic, ludic, and narrative functions (though it is characteristic of the chapter's multiperspectival approach that the argument presented here also includes an attempt to trace some of *Pentiment*'s literary influences, with a particular focus on Umberto Eco's *The Name of the Rose* [1983 (1980)]).

Moving toward the margins of the set of digital works that are easily recognizable as videogames, Kieron Brown's chapter "Metareference in Comics Games" focuses on manifestations of metareference in so-called comics games, which he conceptualizes as artifacts that are institutionally and paratextually framed as videogames but incorporate comics features into their mechanics and aesthetics. Zooming in on the comics games *Florence* (2018), *Gorogoa* (2017), and *Storyteller* (2023), Brown's analysis highlights how the different approaches of integrating comics characteristics into the frame of videogames that can be observed here entail at least a partial subversion of the conventions of both media forms.

Finally, Jan-Noël Thon's chapter "Postdigital Aesthetics in Recent Indie Games" expands the present volume's theoretical and analytical scope toward what he conceptualizes as the postdigital aesthetics of videogames in general and indie games in particular. Building on a comprehensive account of postdigital aesthetics as entailing the four salient domains of the aesthetic intensification of the digital, the aesthetic transfer from the digital to the nondigital, the aesthetic intensification of the nondigital, and the aesthetic transfer from the nondigital to the digital, Thon offers detailed case studies of the (highly canonical) indie games *Proteus* (2013), *Pony Island* (2016), *Cuphead* (2017), and *What Remains of Edith Finch* (2017).

Taken together, the chapters collected in the present volume offer original theoretical approaches to metareference in videogames, discuss a wide range of case studies of metareferential videogames, and inquire about the cultural work accomplished by such videogames from a range of different disciplinary perspectives. While working on this project, it quickly became clear that meta phenomena are not only ubiquitous in videogames, but that they continue to thrive and evolve there in a manner that exceeds similar developments in other media. Notably, this has also led to the emergence of new forms of metareference that challenge established concepts in transmedial narratology and game studies, while also opening up new creative avenues in videogame design and other areas of digital media design. Horror games, in particular, are currently at the forefront of media forms that experiment with ever-more transgressive metaleptic strategies, harnessing the procedural nature of videogames to blur the boundaries between the storyworld and the actual world, and to reconfigure conventional distributions of agency and control. Other videogames likewise continue to grapple with questions surrounding their semiotic repertoire and their relationship to other media forms, be it as part of a poetics of videogames, alongside a general turn toward hypermediacy, or as an expression of a postdigital sensibility. Looking back on the debates around postmodern metafiction and the so-called metareferential turn while keeping in view videogames' complex representational politics and their often highly problematic entanglements with the exploitation of natural and human resources, one might feel tempted to accuse metareferential media texts in general and metareferential videogames in particular of a certain self-centeredness, engrossed as they are in projects of self-theoretization and canonization. However, aside from the fact that many metareferential videogames, including well-known and oft-cited examples such as *The Stanley Parable* and *Spec Ops: The Line*, are very vocal in their criticism of specific historical, sociocultural, and economic circumstances, processes of metaization also serve as a catalyst for reflections around the aesthetics and philosophy of digital media forms in general and videogames in particular. Demonstrating the ubiquity, formal innovation, and thematic scope of meta phenomena in videogames, the chapters collected in this volume thus make what we hope is a convincing case for metareferential videogames as valuable objects of study. Undoubtedly, much remains to be said about the forms and functions of metareference in and around videogames, but we trust that the rich array of theoretical approaches, philosophical inquiries, and case studies presented throughout the following pages provides an engaging starting point for anyone seeking to gain a better understanding of this pervasive cultural phenomenon, and that it might indeed also entice others to join this ongoing conversation.

Works Cited

Abel, Lionel. 1963. *Metatheatre: A New Vision of Dramatic Form*. New York: Hill and Wang.

Alan Wake 2. 2023. Remedy Entertainment/Epic Games Publishing. PlayStation 5.

Alber, Jan. 2016. *Unnatural Narrative: Impossible Worlds in Fiction and Drama*. Lincoln: University of Nebraska Press.

Alter, Robert. 1975. *Partial Magic: The Novel as a Self-Conscious Genre*. Berkeley: University of California Press.

Archimedes. 2016. Joshua Hughes. Microsoft Windows.

Backe, Hans-Joachim. 2016. "Spiel im Spiel – im (Computer-)Spiel." In *Vergleichen an der Grenze: Beiträge zu Manfred Schmelings komparatistischen Forschungen*, edited by Hans-Joachim Backe, Claudia Schmitt, and Christiane Solte-Gresser, 37–74. Würzburg: Königshausen & Neumann.

Backe, Hans-Joachim. 2018. "Metareferentiality through In-Game Images in Immersive Simulation Games." In *FDG '18: Proceedings of the 13th International Conference on the Foundations of Digital Games*, 25 (1–10).

Backe, Hans-Joachim, and Jan-Noël Thon. 2019. "Playing with Identity: Authors, Narrators, Avatars, and Players in *The Stanley Parable* and *The Beginner's Guide*." *DIEGESIS: Interdisciplinary E-Journal for Narrative Research* 8 (2): 1–25.

Barbie. 2023. Director Greta Gerwig. USA: Warner Bros. Pictures.

Barkman, Christopher. 2021. "'There Is No Point in Saving Anymore': Diegesis and Interactional Metalepsis in *Pony Island* and *Doki Doki Literature Club!*" *Journal of Games Criticism* 5 (1): 1–22.
Bateson, Patrick, and Paul Martin. 2013. *Play, Playfulness, Creativity and Innovation*. Cambridge: Cambridge University Press.
The Beginner's Guide. 2015. Everything Unlimited Ltd. Microsoft Windows.
Bell, Alice. 2016. "Interactional Metalepsis and Unnatural Narratology." *Narrative* 24 (3): 294–310.
Bernhart, Walter, and Werner Wolf, eds. 2010. *Self-Reference in Literature and Music*. Amsterdam: Rodopi.
Bioshock. 2007. 2K Boston/2K Games. Microsoft Windows.
Birdman or (The Unexpected Virtue of Ignorance). 2014. Director Alejandro González Iñárritu. USA: Fox Searchlight Pictures.
Blume, Peter. 2004. *Fiktion und Weltwissen: Der Beitrag nichtfiktionaler Konzepte zur Sinnkonstitution fiktionaler Erzähltexte*. Berlin: Erich Schmidt Verlag.
Bódi, Bettina. 2023. *Videogames and Agency*. New York: Routledge.
Bódi, Bettina, and Jan-Noël Thon. 2020. "Playing Stories? Narrative-Dramatic Agency in *Disco Elysium* (2019) and *Astroneer* (2019)." *Frontiers of Narrative Studies* 6 (2): 157–190.
Butler, Martin, and Arvi Sepp. 2007. "*The Itchy and Scratchy Show*: Beobachtungen zur Metaisierung im amerikanischen Fernsehcartoon *The Simpsons*." In *Metaisierung in Literatur und anderen Medien: Theoretische Grundlagen – Historische Perspektiven – Metagattungen – Funktionen*, edited by Janine Hauthal, Julijana Nadj, Ansgar Nünning, and Henning Peters, 361–376. Berlin: De Gruyter.
Braguinski, Nikita. 2018. "The Resolution of Sound: Understanding Retro Game Audio Beyond the '8-Bit' Horizon." *NECSUS: European Journal of Media Studies* 7 (1): 105–121.
The Cabin in the Woods. 2012. Director Drew Goddard. USA: Lionsgate.
Caruso, Giovanni, Riccardo Fassone, Gabriele Ferri, Stefano Gualeni, and Mauro Salvador. 2013. "*GAME* on Games: The Meta-Panel." In *Proceedings of DiGRA 2013: DeFragging Game Studies*, n.pag.
Caruso, Giovanni, Riccardo Fassone, Gabriele Ferri, Stefano Gualeni, and Mauro Salvador, eds. 2016. Games on Games: Game Design as Critical Reflexive Practice. Special issue *GAME: Games as Art, Media, Entertainment* 5.
Conway, Steven. 2010. "A Circular Wall? Reformulating the Fourth Wall for Videogames." *Journal of Gaming and Virtual Worlds* 2 (2): 145–155.
Cuphead. 2017. StudioMDHR. Microsoft Windows.
Deadpool. 2013. High Moon Studios/Activision. Microsoft Windows.
Doki Doki Literature Club! 2017. Team Salvato. Microsoft Windows.
Eco, Umberto. [1980] 1983. *The Name of the Rose*. San Diego: Harcourt.
Ensslin, Astrid. 2014a. *Literary Gaming*. Cambridge, MA: MIT Press.
Ensslin, Astrid. 2014b. "Playing with Rather Than by the Rules: Metaludicity, Allusive Fallacy, and Illusory Agency in *The Path*." In *Analyzing Digital Fiction*, edited by Alice Bell, Astrid Ensslin, and Hans Kristian Rustad, 75–93. New York: Routledge.
Ensslin, Astrid. 2023. "Video Games as Complex Narratives and Embodied Metalepsis." In *The Routledge Companion to Narrative Theory*, edited by Paul Dawson and Maria Mäkelä, 411–422. New York: Routledge.
Ensslin, Astrid, and Alice Bell. 2021. *Digital Fiction and the Unnatural: Transmedial Narrative Theory, Method, and Analysis*. Columbus: Ohio State University Press.

Far Cry 2. 2008. Ubisoft Montreal/Ubisoft. Microsoft Windows.

Far Cry 3. 2012. Ubisoft Montreal/Ubisoft. Microsoft Windows.

Ferri, Gabriele, Giovanni Caruso, Mauro Salvador, Riccardo Fassone, and Stefano Gualeni. 2016. "Games on Games: Game Design as Critical Reflexive Practice." *GAME: Games as Art, Media, Entertainment* 5: 5–10.

Fest, Bradley J. 2016. "Metaproceduralism: *The Stanley Parable* and the Legacies of Postmodern Metafiction." *Wide Screen* 6 (1): 1–23.

Feyersinger, Erwin. 2011. "The (Meta-)Metareferential Turn in Animation." In *The Metareferential Turn in Contemporary Arts and Media: Forms, Functions, Attempts at Explanation*, edited by Werner Wolf, 445–461. Amsterdam: Rodopi.

Feyersinger, Erwin. 2017. *Metalepsis in Animation: Paradoxical Transgressions of Ontological Levels*. Heidelberg: Winter.

Fleabag. 2016–2019. Creator Phoebe Waller-Bridge. Amazon Prime Video.

Florence. 2018. Mountains/Annapurna Interactive. Android.

Garda, Maria B., and Paweł Grabarczyk. 2016. "Is Every Indie Game Independent? Towards the Concept of Independent Game." *Game Studies: The International Journal of Computer Game Research* 16 (1): n.pag.

Gass, William H. 1970. *Fiction and the Figures of Life*. New York: Knopf.

Gage, Zach. 2009. "Lose/Lose." *STFJ.net: The Digital Portfolio of Zach Gage*. www.stfj.net/art/2009/loselose/.

Genette, Gérard. 1983 [1980]. *Narrative Discourse: An Essay in Method*. Ithaca, NY: Cornell University Press.

Gorogoa. 2017. Jason Roberts/Annapurna Interactive. Microsoft Windows.

Gualeni, Stefano. 2016. "Self-Reflexive Videogames: Observations and Corollaries on Virtual Worlds as Philosophical Artifacts." *GAME: Games as Art, Media, Entertainment* 5: 11–20.

Gualeni, Stefano. 2019. "On the De-Familiarizing and Re-Ontologizing Effects of Glitches and Glitch-Alikes." In *Proceedings of DiGRA 2019: Game, Play and the Emerging Ludo-Mix*, 1–14.

Gymnich, Marion. 2007. "Meta-Film und Meta-TV: Möglichkeiten und Funktionen von Metaisierung in Filmen und Fernsehserien." In *Metaisierung in Literatur und anderen Medien: Theoretische Grundlagen – Historische Perspektiven – Metagattungen – Funktionen*, edited by Janine Hauthal, Julijana Nadj, Ansgar Nünning, and Henning Peters, 127–154. Berlin: De Gruyter.

Harpold, Terry. 2007. "Screw the Grue: Mediality, Metalepsis, Recapture." *Game Studies: The International Journal of Computer Game Research* 7 (1): n.pag.

Hauthal, Janine. 2009. "When Metadrama Is Turned into Metafilm: A Media-Comparative Approach to Metareference." In *Metareference across Media: Theory and Case Studies*, edited by Werner Wolf, 567–589. Amsterdam: Rodopi.

Hauthal, Janine, Julijana Nadj, Ansgar Nünning, and Henning Peters. 2007a. "Metaisierung in Literatur und anderen Medien: Begriffsklärungen, Typologien, Funktionspotenziale und Forschungsdesiderate." In *Metaisierung in Literatur und anderen Medien: Theoretische Grundlagen – Historische Perspektiven – Metagattungen – Funktionen,* edited by Janine Hauthal, Julijana Nadj, Ansgar Nünning, and Henning Peters, 1–21. Berlin: De Gruyter.

Hauthal, Janine, Julijana Nadj, Ansgar Nünning, and Henning Peters, eds. 2007b. *Metaisierung in Literatur und anderen Medien: Theoretische Grundlagen – Historische Perspektiven – Metagattungen – Funktionen.* Berlin: De Gruyter.

Herte, Michelle. 2016. "'Come, Stanley, Let's Find the Story!' On the Ludic and the Narrative Mode of Computer Games in *The Stanley Parable*." *IMAGE: The Interdisciplinary Journal of Image Sciences* 23: 30–42.

The Hex. 2018. Daniel Mullins Games. Microsoft Windows.
House of Cards. 2013–2018. Creator Beau Willimon. Netflix.
Hutcheon, Linda. 1980. *Narcissistic Narrative: The Metafictional Paradox*. Waterloo, Ontario: Wilfrid Laurier University Press.
Imscared: A Pixelated Nightmare. 2016. Ivan Zanotti's MyMadnessWorks. Microsoft Windows.
Inscryption. 2021. Daniel Mullins Games/Devolver Digital. Microsoft Windows.
Jannidis, Fotis. 2009. "Metareference in Computer Games." In *Metareference across Media: Theory and Case Studies*, edited by Werner Wolf, 543–565. Amsterdam: Rodopi.
Juul, Jesper. 2019. *Handmade Pixels: Independent Video Games and the Quest for Authenticity*. Cambridge, MA: MIT Press.
Kindt, Tom, and Hans-Harald Müller. 2006. *The Implied Author: Concept and Controversy*. Berlin: De Gruyter.
Kirkland, Ewan. 2011. "Remediation, Analogue Corruption and the Signification of Evil in Digital Games." In *Promoting and Producing Evil*, edited by Nancy Billias, 227–245. 2nd ed. Amsterdam: Rodopi.
Klimek, Sonja. 2009. "Metalepsis and Its (Anti-)Illusionst Effects in the Arts, Media and Role-Playing Games." In *Metareference across Media: Theory and Case Studies*, edited by Werner Wolf, 169–187. Amsterdam: Rodopi.
Köppe, Tilmann. 2008. *Literatur und Erkenntnis: Studien zur kognitiven Signifikanz fiktionaler literarischer Werke*. Paderborn: mentis.
Krampe, Theresa. 2023. "Rewriting Rules, Changing Worlds: Diegetic and Ludic Forms of Metareference in *The Magic Circle*." *Frontiers of Narrative Studies* 9 (1): 137–157.
Krampe, Theresa. 2025. *Metareference in Videogames*. New York: Routledge.
Krampe, Theresa, Stephanie Lotzow, and Jan-Noël Thon. 2022. "Playful Poetics: Metareferential Interfaces in Recent Indie Games." *Poetics Today* 43 (4): 729–771.
Kukkonen, Karin. 2009. "Textworlds and Metareference in Comics." In *Metareference across Media: Theory and Case Studies*, edited by Werner Wolf, 499–513. Amsterdam: Rodopi.
Kukkonen, Karin. 2011. "Metalepsis in Popular Culture: An Introduction." In *Metalepsis in Popular Culture*, edited by Karin Kukkonen and Sonja Klimek, 1–21. Berlin: De Gruyter.
Layers of Fear 2. 2019. Bloober Team/Gun Media. Microsoft Windows.
Lee, Cindy. 2020. "Best Practices for Pixel Art." In *The Digital Gaming Handbook*, edited by Roberto Dillon, 275–286. Boca Raton: CRC Press.
Lewis, Barry. 2011. "Postmodernism and Fiction." In *The Routledge Companion to Postmodernism*, edited by Stuart Sim, 169–181. 3rd ed. New York: Routledge.
Lieberman, J. Nina. 1977. *Playfulness: Its Relationship to Imagination and Creativity*. New York: Academic Press.
Lose/Lose. 2009. Zach Gage. Mac OS X.
Mader, Ilona. 2017. *Metafiktionalität als Selbst-Dekonstruktion*. Würzburg: Königshausen & Neumann.
The Magic Circle. 2015. Question. Microsoft Windows.
Malina, Debra. 2002. *Breaking the Frame: Metalepsis and the Construction of the Subject*. Columbus: Ohio State University Press.
Max Payne. 2001. Remedy Entertainment/Gathering of Developers, Inc. Microsoft Windows.
Metal Gear Solid. 1998. Konami. Microsoft Windows.
Metal Gear Solid 2: Sons of Liberty. 2001. Konami. PlayStation 2.
Monkey Island 4: Escape from Monkey Island. 2000. LucasArts/Lucasfilm and Disney. Microsoft Windows.

Mukherjee, Souvik. 2015. *Video Games and Storytelling: Reading Games and Playing Books*. Basingstoke: Palgrave Macmillan.
Murray, Janet. 2017. *Hamlet on the Holodeck: The Future of Narrative in Cyberspace.* Updated ed. Cambridge, MA: MIT Press.
My Lady Jane. 2024. Creator Gemma Burgess. Amazon Prime Video.
Neitzel, Britta. 2007. "Metacommunication in Play and in (Computer) Games." In *Self-Reference in the Media*, edited by Winfried Nöth and Nina Bishara, 237–252. Berlin: De Gruyter.
Never Have I Ever. 2020–present. Creators Mindy Kaling and Lang Fisher. Netflix.
Nguyen, C. Thi. 2020. *Games: Agency as Art.* Oxford: Oxford University Press.
Nöth, Winfried. 2007a. "Narrative Self-Reference in a Literary Comic: M.-A. Mathieu's *L'Origine*." *Semiotica* 165: 173–190.
Nöth, Winfried. 2007b. "Self-Reference in the Media: The Semiotic Framework." In *Self-Reference in the Media*, edited by Winfried Nöth and Nina Bishara, 3–30. Berlin: De Gruyter.
Nöth, Winfried, and Nina Bishara, eds. 2007. *Self-Reference in the Media.* Berlin: De Gruyter.
OneShot. 2016. Future Cat LLC/KOMODO. Microsoft Windows.
The Path. 2009. Tale of Tales. Microsoft Windows.
Pentiment. 2022. Obsidian Entertainment/Xbox Game Studios. Microsoft Windows.
Pony Island. 2016. Daniel Mullins Games. Microsoft Windows.
Proteus. 2013. Ed Key and David Kanaga. Microsoft Windows.
Rapp, Bernhard. 2007. "Self-Reflexivity in Computer Games: Analyses of Selected Examples." In *Self-Reference in the Media*, edited by Winfried Nöth and Nina Bishara, 253–265. Berlin: De Gruyter.
Rapp, Bernhard. 2008. *Selbstreflexivität im Computerspiel: Theoretische, analytische und funktionale Zugänge zum Phänomen autothematischer Strategien in Games.* Glücksstadt: Verlag Werner Hülsbusch.
Roche, David. 2022. *Meta in Film and Television Series*. Edinburgh: Edinburgh University Press.
Richardson, Brian. 2015. *Unnatural Narrative: Theory, History, and Practice*. Columbus: Ohio State University Press.
Ryan, Marie-Laure. 1991. *Possible Worlds, Artificial Intelligence, and Narrative Theory.* Bloomington: Indiana University Press.
Ryan, Marie-Laure. 1997. "Postmodernism and the Doctrine of Panfictionality." *Narrative* 5 (2): 165–187.
Ryan, Marie-Laure. 2004. "Metaleptic Machines." *Semiotica* 150 (1): 439–469.
Ryan, Marie-Laure. 2006. *Avatars of Story*. Minneapolis: University of Minnesota Press.
Santaella, Lucia. 2007. "Computer Games: The Epitome of Self-Reference." In *Self-Reference in the Media*, edited by Winfried Nöth and Nina Bishara, 207–218. Berlin: De Gruyter.
Scheffel, Michael. 1997. *Formen selbstreflexiven Erzählens: Eine Typologie und sechs exemplarische Analysen*. Tübingen: Niemeyer.
Schlick, Yaël. 2023. *Metafiction*. New York: Routledge.
Schmeling, Manfred. 1977. *Das Spiel im Spiel: Ein Beitrag zur vergleichenden Literaturkritik*. Rheinfelden: Schäuble.
Scholes, Robert. 1995 [1970]. "Metafiction." In *Metafiction*, edited by Mark Currie, 21–38. London: Longman.
The Secret of Monkey Island. 1990. Lucasfilm Games. Microsoft Windows.

Sicart, Miguel. 2014. *Play Matters*. Cambridge, MA: MIT Press.

Sloan, Robin J.S. 2015. "Videogames as Remediated Memories: Commodified Nostalgia and Hyperreality in *Far Cry 3: Blood Dragon* and *Gone Home*." *Games and Culture* 10 (6): 525–550.

Spec Ops: The Line. 2012. Yager Development/2K Games. Microsoft Windows.

The Stanley Parable. 2013. Galactic Cafe. Microsoft Windows.

Stanton, Richard. 2015. "*Metal Gear Solid 2*: The First Postmodern Video Game." *Eurogamer*, August 16, 2015. www.eurogamer.net/metal-gear-solid-2-the-first-postmodern-video-game.

Stardew Valley. 2016. Chucklefish/Concerned Ape. Microsoft Windows.

Stenros, Jaakko. 2015. "Playfulness, Play, and Games: A Constructionist Ludology Approach." PhD thesis, University of Tampere.

Storyteller. 2023. Daniel Benmergui/Annapurna Interactive. Microsoft Windows.

Sutton-Smith, Brian. 1997. *The Ambiguity of Play*. Cambridge, MA: Harvard University Press.

Terraria. 2011. Re-Logic. Microsoft Windows.

There Is No Game: Wrong Dimension. 2020. Draw Me a Pixel. Microsoft Windows.

Thon, Jan-Noël. 2016. *Transmedial Narratology and Contemporary Media Culture*. Lincoln: University of Nebraska Press.

Thon, Jan-Noël. 2019. "Playing with Fear: The Aesthetics of Horror in Recent Indie Games." *Eludamos: Journal for Computer Game Culture* 10 (1): 197–231.

Thon, Jan-Noël, ed. 2021. *Playfulness across Media*. Special Issue *Eludamos: Journal for Computer Game Culture* 12 (1).

Thorne, Sarah. 2021. "There Is No Immersion: Critical Intervention through Hypermediacy in Metagames." *Eludamos: Journal for Computer Game Culture* 12 (1): 63–85.

Thoss, Jeff. 2011. "'This Strip Doesn't Have a Fourth Wall': Webcomics and the Metareferential Turn." In *The Metareferential Turn in Contemporary Arts and Media: Forms, Functions, Attempts at Explanation*, edited by Werner Wolf, 551–568. Amsterdam: Rodopi.

Thoss, Jeff. 2015. *When Storyworlds Collide: Metalepsis in Popular Fiction, Film and Comics*. Leiden: Brill.

Undertale. 2015. Toby Fox. Microsoft Windows.

Walther, Bo Kampmann. 2007. "Self-Reference in Computer Games: A Formalistic Approach." In *Self-Reference in the Media,* edited by Winfried Nöth and Nina Bishara, 219–236. Berlin: De Gruyter.

Walton, Kendall L. 1990. *Mimesis as Make Believe: On the Foundations of the Representational Arts*. Cambridge, MA: Harvard University Press.

Waszkiewicz, Agata. 2020. "'Together They Are Twofold': Player-Avatar Relationship beyond the Fourth Wall." *Journal of Games Criticism* 4 (1): 1–21.

Waszkiewicz, Agata. 2024. *Metagames: Games about Games*. New York: Routledge.

Waugh, Patricia. 2001 [1984]. *Metafiction: The Theory and Practice of Self-Conscious Fiction*. London: Routledge.

What Remains of Edith Finch. 2017. Giant Sparrow/Annapurna Interactive. PlayStation 4.

What We Do in the Shadows. 2014. Directors Taika Waititi and Jemaine Clement. New Zealand: Madman Entertainment.

Wolf, Werner. 1993. *Ästhetische Illusion und Illusionsdurchbrechung in der Erzählkunst: Theorie und Geschichte mit Schwerpunkt auf englischem illusionsstörenden Erzählen*. Tübingen: Niemeyer.

Wolf, Werner. 2001. "Formen literarischer Selbstreferenz in der Erzählkunst: Versuch einer Typologie und ein Exkurs zur '*mise en cadre*' und '*mise en reflet/série*'." In *Erzählen und*

Erzähltheorie im 20. Jahrhundert: Festschrift für Wilhelm Füger, edited by Jörg Helbig, 49–84. Heidelberg: Winter.

Wolf, Werner. 2005. "Metalepsis as a Transgeneric and Transmedial Phenomenon: A Case Study of the Possibilities of 'Exporting' Narratological Concepts." In *Narratology beyond Literary Criticism: Mediality, Disciplinarity*, edited by Jan Christoph Meister, 83–107. Berlin: De Gruyter.

Wolf, Werner. 2006. "Introduction: Frames, Framings and Framing Borders in Literature and Other Media." In *Framing Borders in Literature and Other Media*, edited by Werner Wolf, 1–40. Amsterdam: Rodopi.

Wolf, Werner. 2009a. "Metareference across Media: The Concept, Its Transmedial Potentials and Problems, Main Forms and Functions." In *Metareference across Media: Theory and Case Studies,* edited by Werner Wolf, 1–85. Amsterdam: Rodopi.

Wolf, Werner, ed. 2009b. *Metareference across Media: Theory and Case Studies.* Amsterdam: Rodopi.

Wolf, Werner. 2011a. "Is There a Metareferential Turn, and If So, How Can It Be Explained?" In *The Metareferential Turn in Contemporary Arts and Media: Forms, Functions, Attempts at Explanation*, edited by Werner Wolf, 1–47. Amsterdam: Rodopi.

Wolf, Werner, ed. 2011b. *The Metareferential Turn in Contemporary Arts and Media: Forms, Functions, Attempts at Explanation*. Amsterdam: Rodopi.

Wolfenstein II: The New Colossus. 2017. Machine Games/Bethesda Softworks. Microsoft Windows.

Wong, Kevin. 2013. "Three Postmodern Games: Self-Reflexive Metacommentary." *The Artifice*, June 20, 2013. https://the-artifice.com/three-postmodern-games-self-reflexive-metacommentary/.

Zipfel, Frank. "Panfictionality/Panfictionalism." In *Narrative Factuality: A Handbook*, edited by Monika Fludernik and Marie-Laure Ryan, 127–132. Berlin: De Gruyter.

Zork. 1977. Infocom/Personal Software and Infocom. PDP-10.

2 Metareferentiality as an Indicator of Procedural Poetics

Hans-Joachim Backe

The concept of poetics has been central to literature since antiquity, and is still widely used today, often with new dimensions and nuances, such as in the German idea of "Kulturpoetik." Other domains have adapted the concept, e.g., Igor Stravinsky's Poetics of Music *(1970), Édouard Glissant's* Poetics of Relation *(1997), Albin Zak's* Poetics of Rock *(2001), or Paul Frosh's* Poetics of Digital Media *(2018). In connection with videogames, though, poetics has never been as widely used as rhetoric (see Bogost 2007) or aesthetics (see Hunicke et al. 2004). Where the term occurs, it is predominantly used to conceptualize poetic games as a category or genre (see Ensslin 2014; Mitchell et al. 2020), or to situate videogames in larger contexts like interactive drama (see Mateas 2001) or interactive narrative (see Ryan 2006). The chapter proposes—before the background of the existing, predominantly prescriptive and theoretical poetics of videogames—a descriptive, analytical poetics that explains relationships between works more nuancedly than established notions like genre. Metareferentiality is crucial for such a poetics, as moments of reflection on a work's own features and on its medium are markers and comments on the immanent poetics of a work.*

Intro: Why Study Metareferential Games

The book this chapter is a part of vividly demonstrates the intensifying interest in the metareferential capacities of videogames. Following Werner Wolf in his re-appraisal of theories of metafiction and self-referentiality (see Wolf 2009), numerous publications have recently engaged with self-reflexive strategies in videogames that are making manifest aspects of the medium—be it by focusing on particular stylistic (see Backe 2018b) or ludic elements (see Krampe 2023), or systematically distinguishing the most prevalent artistic strategies (see Waszkiewicz 2024).

Games are, technically speaking, always highly self-referential, because they can be understood as feedback loops in which playful actions constantly refer back to the rules which partially predicate the following actions. This mechanical, intrinsic self-referentiality has led some researchers to call into question if games can even elicit the kind of meta-reflection that characterizes metafiction, metatheater, meta-cinema, etc. (see, e.g., Walther 2007). Hence, even scholars specializing in the

DOI: 10.4324/9781003538592-2

study of metareferentiality in videogames feel the need to emphasize the use of meta-devices "in a deliberate and purposeful manner as a means of artistic experimentation and/or commentary on the video game industry and rules of specific genres" (Waszkiewicz 2024, 2).

Across media, metareferentiality has been a focal point in investigations of the connection between the materiality of an artifact and its aesthetics, or, more simply put, the medium-specificity of expression: "For critics such as Gass, McCaffery, Waugh, and others, one of the principal features of metafiction is how it draws attention to its own *materiality*, to the language and other materials (novels) out of which it is made, and principally to the fact that it is *written*" (Fest 2016, 7; original emphasis). Work on metareferentiality in videogames has similarly tried "to understand what might be unique about their self-reflexivity" (Fest 2016, 8), and argued for "the need for medium-specific approaches while also challenging us to expand the analytical toolbox for the transmedial study of metareference" (Krampe 2023, 138).

There can be no doubt that the identification, definition, and categorization of metareferentiality in videogames are valuable, and that these questions are far from resolved. Yet while the identification of unique elements, their categorization, and the ambitious search for transmedial constants are necessary, they leave room for other practices. In this chapter, I therefore do not aim to add to the theory of metareferentiality, its typology, or in-depth analyses of individual examples, but instead make the case for one particular application of the existing (as well as future) research in the field.

In this chapter, I propose a descriptive poetics of videogames that is centered around self-reflexive and metareferential strategies. Poetics is, as I will outline in the next section, a term with numerous conflicting definitions and usages, both inside and outside games research. Drawing on David Bordwell's work, I will argue that poetics is a useful, underutilized concept for the study of videogames, and can complement lenses such as procedural rhetoric, genre, and aesthetics.

Procedural rhetoric (see Bogost 2007) has been one of the dominant paradigms in games research for well over a decade, coming out of the identification of procedurality and simulation as defining traits of videogames. Particularly, the work of Janet Murray (1998) and Gonzalo Frasca (2003) articulated quite early the significance of rule-based interaction for the expressive possibilities of videogames. Bogost's procedural rhetoric builds on this work and presents a model for understanding the meaning videogames can express through their processes rather than their representational elements. However, Bogost conceptualizes procedural meaning-making as a rhetoric, with a strong emphasis on persuading and influencing players. Not every videogame aims at persuading its players, which is why the rhetorical approach with its roots in law and politics can be an ill fit for examples without an explicit political or commercial agenda of persuasion. Reframing procedurality as a part of a poetics allows the study of traditions of procedural meaning-making without the often-unproductive insinuation of agendas of persuasion.

A descriptive poetics offers, for similar reasons, a conceptual alternative to genre. When approaching examples from a generic perspective, one inevitably investigates which genre markers are present and how closely the artifact therefore adheres to the formula or prototype of the genre (see Apperley 2006; Arsenault 2009; Gregersen 2014). This makes diversion from traditions and conventions *a priori* an issue when thinking in terms of genre, while poetics can easily be expressed through absence of elements and non-adherence to conventions. This shift of attention to what games do (or do not) include and how they reflect on these creative choices has also been conceptualized as aesthetics (see, e.g., Kirkpatrick 2011; Thon 2022). To me, though, poetics has the advantage that the concept focuses on the artifact rather than the recipient. Not only in literary reader-response approaches, originally termed "Rezeptionsästhetik" (reception aesthetics) (see Warning 1994 [1975]), is this privileging of the recipient apparent, but equally in its Kantian origins and more recent (and widely used) applications like the MDA framework (see Hunicke et al. 2004). Instead of focusing on an "intended user experience," poetics shifts the question to the means that an example employs, and how the presence and absence of elements contextualizes it in a particular tradition. Poetics in the sense I use it here is therefore meant as an approach to videogames that descriptively and analytically foregrounds the elements of an artifact that situate it, sometimes explicitly (e.g., through metareferential means), within an artistic tradition and its conventions.

The Many Meanings of "Poetics"

Poetics is an absolutely ubiquitous term in the humanities, and like most ubiquitous terms, it is exceedingly ill-defined. Anyone who ever studied the practices of storytelling or narrative theory will have learned that Aristotle's *Poetics* marks the starting point and cornerstone of our understanding of theory and practice of narrative. Yet, Aristotle's treatise is famously fragmentary, "among the least finished [of his works], being in parts little more than a series of jottings" (Lucas 1980, x), and neither in the main text nor the extensive commentary of classic editions of the text will readers find a definition of the term itself—at least D.W. Lucas never uses "poetics" as a concept, only ever as Aristotle's title, and makes no reference to poiesis (beyond Antiphanes's text of that title).

That has not stopped critics from lamenting or questioning the state of poetics at various points in history (see Brooks 1994), nor from claiming the concept as the primary and sole domain of their field. One finds definitions of it as "the theoretical and practical study of poetry" (Greene et al. 2012, vii) just as often as "the systematic study of literature as literature" (Rimmon-Kenan 2003, 141). Among scholars of narrative literature, this latter meaning has become so widespread as to make poetics virtually synonymous with approaches like formalism and structuralism (see Chatman 1973) or even literary theory in general (see Culler 1975; Rimmon-Kenan 2003; Todorov 1981). This practice has become widespread among specialized narrative theories that focus on individual genres (see Stockwell 2014), eras (see Hutcheon 2003), abstract phenomena (see Richardson et al. 2013), or that incorporate elements from other disciplines (see Pilkington 2000; Stockwell 2019).

The concept of poetics is frequently applied to even broader phenomena, from transnational artistic influence (see Ramazani 2015) to fundamental issues of culture (see Greenblatt 1989; Stewart 2020) and identity (see Glissant 1997; Sarbin 1997; Showalter 2012). Other disciplines have appropriated the concept, such as ethnography (see Clifford and Marcus 2023 [1986]), while poetics of the image (see Bal 2000; Louvel 2016), of architecture (see Tzonis and Lefaivre 1986), music (see Stravinsky 1970), and cinema (see Bordwell 2012) occupy central positions in the respective disciplines.

While many conceptualizations of poetics from outside of literature build on 20th-century theory, some predate modern narratology. In musicology, for example, poetics was first discussed in

> German music treatises beginning in the late sixteenth century. The designation *musica poetica*, representing written musical works, was added to what had previously been a two-part scheme—*musica theorica* [sic] (abstract theory) and *musica practica* (musical activity). As Edward Lippman has pointed out, the notion of *musica poetica* augmented the conception of musical composition—represented in earlier treatises mostly by the craft of counterpoint—with a concern for rhetoric and aesthetics. The term "poetics," then, came to include both compositional principles and aesthetic beliefs [...].
>
> (Zak 2001, xv; original emphasis)

This holistic understanding of the term in musicology differs vastly from a modern understanding of poetics as the science of the literary, and not only in subject matter: "Whereas interpretations are valuable to readers interested in particular works of literature while criticism and history tell us about particular writers, periods, national literatures, it is primarily poetics which illuminates literature as a peculiar phenomenon of human culture" (Harshav 2007, 238). In other words: While the musicological poetics are an umbrella term, literary poetics is sometimes understood as a particular branch of literary theory.

That does not mean that literary poetics would not be further subdivided. Benjamin Harshav distinguishes between theoretical poetics—"the construction of a system built according to the logic of an aspect, a question or a set of questions" (2007, 230)—and descriptive poetics—"a scholarly activity involving an exhaustive research of the literary aspects of certain specific works of literature" (2007, 230)—and Bakhtin saw his study of the polyphonic novel as "the task of an historical poetics" (2013 [1929], 36). Furthermore, one encounters occasionally attempts at establishing a strict distinction between poetics and poetology, yet this practice is not particularly common in English-language research, and there is no real consensus about the definition of the terms, either (see Robert 2015).

Perhaps unsurprisingly, poetics is used just as heterogeneously within games research. Already in 2001, Michael Mateas proposed a preliminary (and thus ostensibly modest) "Poetics for Interactive Drama and Games," which on closer inspection appears as a set of technocentric—AI is mentioned in the first sentence —prescriptive guidelines for good interactive drama design. Explicitly modeling his approach on Aristotle, Mateas professes to mostly make changes "to address the interactivity added by player agency" (2001, 140). Similarly dealing with videogames as a corollary to a different phenomenon, Lisbeth Klastrup (2003) proposes a poetics of virtual worlds. Fullerton, Morie, and Pearce (2007) use the term in a deferred sense when they draw not on the Aristotelian model, but on Bachelard's (2014 [1957]) appropriation of the concept in his *Poetics of Space*. The original proponents of proceduralism (see Bogost 2007; Wardrip-Fruin 2009) deal with the authoring of processes as a medium-specific property of interactive systems, including games, in a fashion reminiscent of poetics, yet seek their theoretical foundation in rhetoric. In their wake, game designers have repeatedly argued for the commensurability of poetics and (procedural) rhetoric (see Grace 2011; Werning 2021)—a question I will return to further below. Literary-inspired games research has gravitated toward a "prescriptive stance of poetics" (Ryan 2006, 123), often taking a strictly ontological perspective "not interested in meanings and interpretations, but in poetics and possibilities" (Eskelinen 2012, 214). Maybe for that reason, approaches influenced decidedly by literary theory have sometime coined their own equivalent terminology, like Ensslin's "ludostylistics" (2014, 53) and Mitchell and colleagues' "poetic gameplay" (2020), or avoided the concept altogether (see Mukherjee 2015). This is, of course, by no means an exhaustive overview of pertinent games research, and completely leaves out peripherally interesting research into, e.g., literary poetics of representing videogames (see Butterworth-Parr 2024), but it suffices to demonstrate the diversity of engagements with the concept.

Given that poetics is a conceptual as well as terminological quagmire, I will derive my own usage of the term primarily from David Bordwell's *Poetics of Cinema* (2012). This book contains a thorough synthesis of the traditions his (and frequent collaborator Kristin Thompson's) work on film poetics stands in, and in it Bordwell develops his own conceptualization of poetics from a systematic survey of various interpretations of the concept. He identifies three main perspectives. Analytical poetics studies formal elements or devices throughout a corpus of work. Theoretical poetics aims at formulating abstract, universally valid statements about a genre or class of work. Historical poetics seeks to "understand how artworks assume certain forms within a period or across periods" (Bordwell 2012, 13). While these perspectives are in principle distinct, in practice they are usually combined with one of the three being dominant (see Bordwell 2012, 13). These perspectives express the scope and epistemological interest of a given poetics. All of them, in isolation or (the more common) combination, will be pursued descriptively—presenting and organizing findings on their own merits—or prescriptively—articulating value statements about good, proper, or possible artistic expression. Taken together, Bordwell's overview of poetics traditions creates a three-dimensional possibility-space (see Figure 2.1).

Bordwell thus makes it clear that the equation of poetics with prescriptiveness or similar generalizations is untenable. His broad survey of different poetics shows that, e.g., Brian Richardson's program of "descriptive poetics [which] attempts to

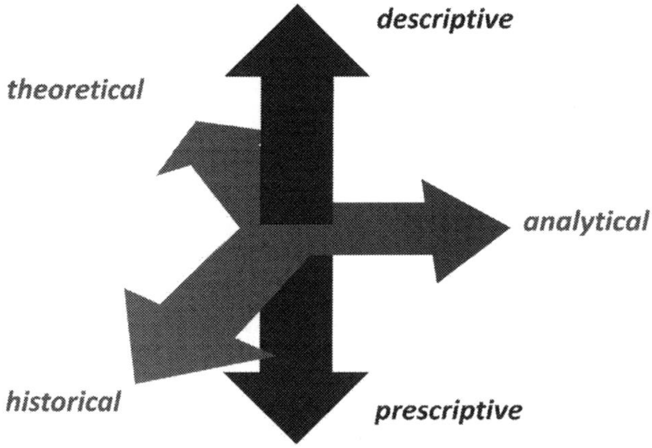

Figure 2.1 Types of poetics according to Bordwell (2012).

identify and model narrative elements, orders, and swerves within works of fiction" (Richardson 2020, 9) is not an outlier, but a valid and regular form of poetics.

Bordwell identifies a common denominator between all different strands: "The poetics of any artistic medium studies the finished work as the result of a process of construction—a process that includes a craft component (such as rules of thumb), the more general principles according to which the work is composed, and its functions, effects, and uses" (2012, 12). Materially, poetics are rooted in "intersubjectively available data that are in principle amenable to alternative explanation" (Bordwell 2012, 15). As a method, it is "best described as a set of assumptions, a heuristic perspective, and a way of asking questions" (Bordwell 2012, 20), "a systematic inquiry into the presuppositions of artistic traditions. It's a practice-based theory of art. We want to know the filmmakers' secrets, especially those they don't know they know" (Bordwell 2012, 22). The idea of the interpreter understanding a work better than its author is one of the cornerstones of hermeneutics, which Dilthey attributed to Schleiermacher (see Dilthey 1990 [1924], 331). Unsurprisingly, Bordwell acknowledges that particularly descriptive-analytical poetics has a kinship with hermeneutics, yet refuses to reduce poetics to mere hermeneutics: "[T]he domination of methods-based thinking has yielded various hermeneutics, but poetics is something else again" (Bordwell 2012, 12).

Characterizing poetics as "something else" might seem overly vague, but it stands in a tradition that goes back to ancient Greece. The closest we get to original definitions of poetics is where ancient texts compare the nature, the function, or the value of behaviors and skills. From them, we can contrastively reconstruct the often-subtle distinctions between poetics and related concepts, and see how poetics occupies a particular meaning that is difficult to articulate if not through distinction from its near-synonyms. *Poesis* means literally "making" or "creating" (Piñeros Glasscock and Tenenbaum 2023, n.pag.), and Aristotle's *Poetics* is therefore a treatise on the principles of (artistic, or, even more specifically, literary) creation. This emphasis of making or creating is unsurprising, because before Aristotle, poetry was rather articulated as a *techné*, a skill (see Lucas 1980, xv, FN2). The skilled doing of *techné* is something based on learning, and thus connected to, yet distinct from, both *praxis*—doing, "acting proper" (Piñeros Glasscock and Tenenbaum 2024, n.pag.)—and *episteme*, i.e., knowing. Even for Aristotle, *techné* remains highly relevant for poetics, because it is the skill used in the bringing-into-existence that characterizes *poesis*. *Poesis* refers to actions that produce something tangible and lasting beyond the activity itself, which is what distinguishes it from *praxis*, where activity is an end in itself: Building a house is *poesis*, while playing the flute is *praxis* (see Parry 2024). That *poesis* includes even architecture, a creative endeavor we today might see as more pragmatic than fiction, stems from another differentiation found in old Greek, namely that from rhetoric. Poetics and rhetoric differ in their relationship to reality and their goal: Rhetoric deals predominantly with truth or reality and aims at persuasion, whereas *poesis* creates something potentially out of imagination for a wide variety of reasons (see Griswold 2024). As the architect and even the builder creates something that needs not have a precedent in reality and is not meant to change people's opinions (although potentially their behavior), these *technés* appear as rather more poetic than rhetoric in nature.

While only very cursory, this look at the original usage of the term illustrates an understanding of poetics as a kind of creative practice that takes origin in imagination rather than reality—which makes it easily applicable to the fanciful artificiality of (creating) videogames. The importance of skill and technology (*techné*) is acknowledged, yet not taken as absolutes, just as the creation of artistic artifacts is not necessarily aimed at the persuasion of others. The perspective shift from procedural rhetoric to procedural poetics I propose here could therefore be characterized as a move from a Platonic to an Aristotelian mindset. While Plato criticizes both rhetoric and poetry, he ideologically gravitates toward the former, because rhetoric is, like philosophy, preoccupied with the truth. Aristotle, on the other hand, focuses on principles of creativity and, while somewhat prescriptive, derives his poetic principles out of the study of aesthetic traditions. That is why I see room for a descriptive, analytical poetics besides the Platonic approaches of the prescriptive game ontologies of, e.g., Eskelinen (2012) and Bogost (2007)—which make broad statements about what is impossible to do in videogames or understand every communicative act in videogames as incomplete syllogisms—or the technologically deterministic poetics of, e.g., Mateas (2001) and Werning (2021)—which see particular software tools like AI or game engines as essential predictors for the expressive potential of videogames.

The Aristotelian stance I propose for the study of games has been explored in some depth regarding other media, e.g., in Albin Zak's poetics of rock music as "not simply recording, but record *making.* Performance is simply the means of inscription through which fully embodied musical essences—musical idea and musical action—are captured by the electrical tracings in particles of iron oxide" (2001, xii; original emphasis). To Zak, understanding the poetics of rock music is only possible when taking into consideration the traditions and technologies of recording performances. Neither recording technologies nor practices fully determine a piece of contemporary music, yet for music produced with recording in mind, they are as crucial to the poetics of rock music as song writing, arrangement, performance, etc. Taking a cue from contemporary poetics research like this, a descriptive, analytical poetics of videogames offers an alternative to procedural rhetoric as well as to what Bordwell calls "doctrinally defined methods" (2012, 12), i.e., approaches based on Marxism, feminism, psychoanalysis, etc.

Metareferential Poetics in Individual Games

Metareferentiality is, if not inherently connected to poetics, then at least a prime locus of poetic self-awareness. Videogames inevitably relate to the traditions and conventions of their medium in a variety of ways. Identifying these traditions is one of the central goals of any poetics, because to "a great extent, an exercise in poetics typically takes as its object a body of conventions" (Bordwell 2012, 15). The identification of conventions is an act of disclosure, an attempt at laying bare deep structures and subtexts, resulting in "the making manifest of layers of representation, signification and existence, their palpable disclosure in the encounter with a particular message, text, artefact or device" (Frosh 2018, 13). The task of "making manifest" lies with the critic and emerges through interpretation, yet is made easier by metareferences, because they comment on and thus foreground traditions in an often-unambiguous manner.

As such, metareferentiality is a strong marker of reflection on a work's own poetics wherever it appears. Even in their weakest form of an offhand, throwaway gesture, an ironic nod, or an ostensibly token acknowledgment of other play artifacts, metareferentiality in videogames always foregrounds that there are traditions and conventions within which videogames are developed and experienced. The more elaborate the metareferentiality, the less ambiguous this dialogue with the precursors and influences, the practices and technologies, the tastes and abilities of developers that shaped a videogame will be. Krampe's (2023) analysis of the explicit metagame *The Magic Circle* (2015), for example, inevitably discusses the poetics of first-person games, even if that is not the goal of the article. The existing research on metareferential games has thus already produced significant findings about various videoludic traditions.

Engagement with poetics is, however, not only found in consistently self-referential games. Individual instances of metareferentiality can signal reflections of poetics that recontextualize the text as a whole. To take one example: *Wolfenstein II: The New Colossus* (2017) can be read throughout as a critique of its genre and the game culture surrounding it (see Backe 2018a), yet explicit metacommentary is limited when compared to, e.g., *The Magic Circle*'s foregrounding of game design and quality assurance in virtually every game element. There is a somewhat out-of-the-way set piece in *Wolfenstein II: The New Colossus* that presents the player with the smallest of arcades, consisting of a pinball machine and a coin-operated videogame (see Figure 2.2).

The pinball machine is non-functional and marked as "out of order" with a handwritten sign. With its wooden trimmings and its US Army recruitment theme—in

Figure 2.2 The arcade in *Wolfenstein II: The New Colossus* (2017).

an alternate history, where Nazi Germany won World War II—it is marked technologically and referentially as a relic of the past. Next to it stands an arcade version of *Wolfenstein 3D* (1992), themed according to the different world order as a pro-Nazi "Wolfstone 3D," and offering a fully playable version of the classic first-person shooter that preserves its level design (see Martin 2019) yet fundamentally changes its meaning by changing the playable character (see Hitchens 2011). With the changes to content and fictional technology, this inclusion of the foundational anthropomorphic first-person shooter (see Pinchbeck 2013, 6–12) goes far beyond mere nostalgia. Portraying it as an arcade machine is anachronistic in several ways that problematize videogame history. In the 1960s of *Wolfenstein II: The New Colossus*, computer technologies from various real-world decades irreverently exist side by side, from punch card-programmed valve computers to miniaturized workstations in the style of C64s, to the 1990s-era 32-bit computing of *Wolfenstein 3D*. The arcade first-person shooter thus induces a complex cognitive dissonance: In real-world terms, it is as outdated and nostalgia-inducing as the pinball machine; in the gameworld, though, it is a piece of boundary-pushing futuristic technology. The arcade is located in the headquarter of the Resistance, and not only are most of the freedom fighters enticed by "Wolfstone 3D's" technological marvel and fun gameplay—a high-score list shows how many crew members have spent time playing it—but none of their countless competent engineers have bothered repairing the patriotic pinball machine.

This installation of games within the context of *Wolfenstein II: The New Colossus* makes it a clear case of Waszkiewicz's "games about games" (2024). The in-game arcade shows how entertainment technologies are inextricably connected to the perception of technological progress. At any point in time, they exist on a spectrum between revolutionary innovation and obsolescence. Nostalgic fascination with historical artifacts and the risk of inaccessibility complicate the players' relationship to them further, as might their theming and narrative. Given that *Wolfenstein II: The New Colossus* was released right after the end of US president Obama's time in office, the defunct pinball machine's name "Yes we can" appears as a political allusion, as it echoes Obama's campaign slogan. Situating this reference to real-world politics of the 2010s next to the propagandistic "Wolfstone 3D" simultaneously emphasizes and downplays the political dimension of videogames. The characters of *Wolfenstein II: The New Colossus* seem to have no problem distancing themselves from the explicit pro-Nazi messaging of the console game. For a contemporary player, this might not be particularly surprising, given how banal and simplistic "Wolfstone 3D" is in this regard. Resistance symbolism and portraits of the resistance leader appear as odd decorations for the world of the game within the game, and will probably appear as having little efficacy as propaganda tools to most players. At the same time, players will either be familiar with *Wolfenstein 3D*'s use of Nazi imagery, or will make that comparison prompted by context.

Just like *Wolfenstein 3D* before it, *Wolfenstein II: The New Colossus* is a mainstream entertainment product, a videogame that will become technically obsolete, that will retain or lose players primarily because of the quality of its gameplay, and that engages with political themes in ways that are prone to misunderstanding, overinterpretation, or disinterest. The inclusion of the arcade is a comment on poetic traditions that signals the developers' reflection of these topics (see Backe 2018a). The legacy of first-person shooters in general and the *Wolfenstein* series in particular comes with conventions that go much deeper than the surface level of fast-paced action gameplay against Nazi villains. Navigating this tradition is precarious for developers, particularly in post-Gamergate game culture (see Braithwaite 2016; Mortensen 2015; Mortensen and Sihvonen 2020). Offering up the reskinned version of the original *Wolfenstein 3D* next to a message about the impermanence of both play technology and political progress is simultaneously a gesture of maturity and defeat: While *Wolfenstein II: The New Colossus* attempts to treat fascism in a responsible fashion, it also stays within the conventions of first-person shooters and tries to not foreground its politics to a degree that would immediately alienate conservative players—a difficult balancing act, yet one that the arcade suggests *Wolfenstein 3D* succeeded in.

Metareferential Poetics of Game Corpora

It lies in the nature of poetics that it looks beyond the individual example, and the discussion of *Wolfenstein II: The New Colossus* already takes a long genre tradition into view. However, poetics becomes an even more meaningful approach when venturing outside of ostensibly well-defined contexts like the first-person shooter genre and a particular franchise.

When we, for example, engage with the traditions of lesser known, smaller corpora of games like the immersive sim, poetics offers a valuable alternative to more established discourses. Centrally associated with *Deus Ex* (2000), immersive sim is a label attached to rather few games that combine aspects of first-person shooters and role-playing games and strongly emphasize player choice.

Even though immersive sim is a concept that originates from a definite source text, Warren Spector's "Postmortem" of *Deus Ex* (see Spector 2000), it has long been hotly contested in several ways. Whether it is a niche phenomenon or not (see Pechalin 2021), whether it should be considered a genre, a design philosophy, or even a paradigm (see Blasonato et al. 2022; Holbeck 2023; rosodude 2020), whether it should be narrowly or loosely defined (see Gaynor 2012; GDC 2022) are questions that have been debated by fans, scholars, and developers alike—all of which does not even touch upon the fundamental critiques of immersion as a concept voiced in academia (see Calleja 2011). All these discussions have merit and have, if nothing else, kept the phenomenon alive in debate and practice for over 20 years. But whether one considers immersive sim a genre or a design philosophy, there is an implication of a finite corpus of examples that can be unequivocally defined by concrete traits—a set-theory approach to corpora that even developers characterize as always running the risk of gatekeeping (see GDC 2022). Both established discourses carry with them significant issues, regardless of this particular discussion: Game genres are widely criticized as unsystematic and untenable (see Apperley 2006; Gregersen 2014), a "history of repeated attempts from academics, critics and institutions to impose order onto a chaotic, messy and fluctuating mass of terms that respects no authority" (Arsenault 2009, 158), whereas "design philosophy" is simultaneously restrictive and vague—are the narrative, art, and technology of games considered part of design, subjugated to design, or irrelevant, and what is meant by "philosophy" in this context? Newer academic terms like the "design ethos" proposed by Bódi—as how game studios "communicate their professional and artistic identity" (2023, 3)—have yet other implications, e.g., in this case are inextricably tied to the corpus of individual development studios.

Shifting the discussion from genre or design philosophy to poetics allows for a different approach that does not strive for the identification of a corpus of examples that adhere to certain principles, but rather follows Bordwell's understanding of poetics in looking for a "body of conventions" (2012, 15) that can be productively adhered to or deviated from. This might sound like a subtle difference, but it resolves some major issues in discussing the immersive sim tradition. As already mentioned, the concept was popularized by Warren Spector in a text that lays out what we might call the poetics of *Deus Ex*. He draws on reflections on player agency developed by his colleague Doug Church, and argues primarily combinatorically when talking about influences from existing genres. The innovation of *Deus Ex* is, to him, the combination of elements from heretofore separate types of games, making *Deus Ex* "part immersive simulation, part role-playing game, part first-person shooter, part adventure game" (Spector 2000, 50). However, it is important to emphasize the provisions Spector makes: First, not all traditions of first-person shooters are adhered to, because "unlike the typical FPS, *Deus Ex* doesn't force you to shoot every virtual thing that moves" (Spector 2000, 50). Second, players have significant freedom to choose whether they want to play the game one way or another, meaning that the different genres are not homogeneously blended, but co-exist in the possibility space of *Deus Ex*. This is why Spector considers *Deus Ex* to be "a genre-busting game" (2000, 50)—not because it combines traits from other genres into a new genre, but because it offers in parallel curated variations of existing game design traditions, thus allowing players to exert agency in ways that are meant to be intuitive, because they draw on those various traditions.

That Spector presents these reflections as a result of his work on a singular game has led many to interpret his postmortem as the recipe for a new genre epitomized by *Deus Ex* (see, e.g., Blasonato et al. 2022). Even those who favor the term design philosophy over genre continue this line of reasoning, only with fewer design elements considered necessary (see rosodude 2020). However, the game design ideal, philosophy, or—as I prefer to think of it—poetics Spector develops in the postmortem is more abstract. His explicitly stated goal is to provide the player with a feeling of agency by drawing selectively on elements from games traditionally considered fundamentally different, and by offering various valid problem-solving approaches. He makes no claim to identifying the perfect combination of elements, but rather more modestly presents *Deus Ex* as his first success at achieving the agency and freedom he wants to afford the player.

The difference between thinking in terms of genre and poetics is maybe most apparent when considering projects that precede *Deus Ex*. Discussions of immersive sim as a genre struggle to categorize examples such as *Thief: The Dark Project* (1998), a project Spector originally spearheaded but eventually left in frustration (see Ars Technica 2021). *Thief: The Dark Project* bears the mark of Spector's experimentation with the conventions of first-person shooters as well as unusual themes and settings. Shooting is done with bow and arrow, which are universal tools rather than weapons and allow to put out torches or attach ropes to out-of-reach ledges and beams. Combat is a rare necessity that takes a backseat to exploration and stealth. The goal is to steal as many valuables as possible and remain undetected as much as possible. This latter restriction is what Spector considered irreconcilable with his vision of free player agency, yet is so deeply rooted in the conceit of *Thief: The Dark Project* that Spector could only leave the project and start over from scratch with *Deus Ex*. Therefore, *Thief: The Dark Project* can only with great difficulty be considered part of a *genre* of immersive sim explicitly defined by Spector through his reflections on the making of *Deus Ex*.

This categorization issue becomes only more complicated when delving deeper into the historical dimension. While there is virtually no disagreement that *Deus Ex* is the first fully fleshed-out immersive sim, there is some debate as to whether *Ultima Underworld* (1992) or *System Shock* (1994) should be considered the beginning of the tradition. Developed by essentially the same team two years apart, both games are clearly precursors of *Deus Ex* as first-person, real-time role-playing games, and from a genre-standpoint, both can equally be construed as the beginning of the tradition. When thinking poetically, though, one might argue that only *Deus Ex* is an expression of the poetics of immersive sim, while these earlier games are still fully rooted in the poetics of role-playing games. One argument for such a view is that developer statements make clear what game *System Shock* should have evolved into. As Doug Church puts it in an interview: "I've been wanting to do a really involved fantasy RPG that uses an indoor/outdoor full 3D engine, has cool conversation stuff, and an interactive story generation engine that can respond quickly and somewhat unexpectedly to player actions" (Yee 1995, 204). Church and his team were envisioning what the *Elder Scrolls* series or, most recently at the time of writing, *Baldur's Gate 3* (2023) have realized: fully fleshed-out, highly systemic, yet strongly narrative role-playing games. When videogames like *Dishonored 2* (2016) adhere to the poetics of immersive sim at a time when Church's vision of the perfectly realized role-playing game has already become reality, it is clear that these games do something different—one might say something less—than a grand role-playing game not out of inability or because of technical limitations, but because it is a conscious aesthetic choice: the expression of a poetics.

The poetics of the immersive sim is generally characterized by subtractive developments, by simplifying or excluding conventions, to an equal or greater degree than by additions to a formula. *Deus Ex* includes significantly stronger role-playing game elements and introduces non-lethal play compared to *System Shock*, but removes cyberspace and the extensive backtracking of the metroidvania tradition. *Bioshock* (2007) does away with role-playing and instead presents the often and controversially discussed ethical choice that leads to multiple endings (which could be said to be a step back compared to earlier games because a stealthy approach is not really viable and the game's enemies have to be killed *en masse*), while also radically simplifying hacking and further linearizing the overarching structure when compared to *Deus Ex*—a strategy not found regularly in the following decade, yet recurring in more recent games such as *Prey* (2017). The study of all these deviations from conventions set by predecessors are as formative and productive as the search for the fulfillment of genre criteria. And they indicate that this poetics is generally characterized by a subtractive component—in the sense that immersive sim as a separate concept only makes sense if it is not identical with a free-form, fully immersive, and agency-driven role-playing game. *Prey*'s game director Raphael Colantonio argued some years ago that the immersive sim concept was becoming obsolete because it had permeated into other genres (see Colantonio 2018), which was generally interpreted in the light of other first-person shooters integrating more varied mechanics and allowing for alternate solutions to problems. His statement might just as well point to the increasing complexity and verisimilitude of role-playing games and the complete realization of Doug Church's vision for immersive games, or to a different creative impasse—namely that the latest subtractions from the poetics of immersive sim were radical and explicit.

Maybe the clearest example of such an explicitly metareferential poetic statement is found in the opening of *"Deathloop"* (2021). While moving down a corridor, player character and player see the words "you know the code" float ephemerally in front of them, leading to the first locked door of the game (see Figure 2.3). To players familiar with the poetics of the immersive sim, this is an allusion to the long-standing tradition, established in *System Shock*, of using the code "451" for the first number lock the player encounters. This convention is, however, subverted. In *"Deathloop"*, the actual code is generated randomly for each new playthrough. Still, when entering "451" as the presumed code, the

Figure 2.3 Knowing the code in *"Deathloop"* (2021).

game acknowledges the convention by letting the player character comment that "old habits die hard" and awarding an achievement to the player. The deviation from immersive sim conventions in *"Deathloop"* is, thus, paradoxical: The game defiantly recalls a tradition it professes not to belong to (see Backe 2022). Traditional views of immersive sim as a genre or a design philosophy that need to be adhered to will struggle with such an *auto-da-fé*, while in terms of poetics, such a metareferential gesture is an explicit statement about the productivity of non-adherence to conventions and the inevitable perpetual change of conventions.

Conclusion

This chapter has explored the applicability of metareferentiality in videogames not as an end in itself, but rather as a creative strategy that highlights reflections of game developers on the poetics of their games embedded in the games themselves. The historical-theoretical section of the chapter has presented an overview of conceptualizations of poetics from literary studies and media studies, including games research, to illustrate the diversity of definitions and applications of the term. It then followed Bordwell's systematization of poetics in five dimensions, which, together with some etymological considerations, allowed the formulation of a need for a descriptive poetics of videogames. The empirical section presented an analysis of *Wolfenstein II: The New Colossus* as an example of foregrounding poetics through metareferential play with traditions and conventions. Going beyond individual examples, it moved to a discussion of immersive sims as a corpus of videogames that benefits particularly from approaching its tradition as a poetics rather than a genre, shifting focus from the identification of constant common denominators to the significance of nonadherence to conventions and the continuous changes this results in.

Metareferentiality is not as foregrounded in this chapter as in many others in this volume. I have taken it somewhat for granted, or, more precisely, treated it as a by-now known quantity. That said, the discussion of examples in the second half of the chapter should have shown that metareference is a crucial marker of reflection on poetics in videogames. Instances of metareference are where videogame poetics become most apparent, through articulation or subversion.

Like any approach that draws primarily on the work instead of its reception, this descriptive poetics runs the risk of appearing detached and apolitical. However, the study of the poetics of any medium could just as much be seen as the precondition for any in-depth engagement with the socio-cultural significance of the artifacts created in it. In the words of Paul Frosh: "Media are poetic infrastructures: they are generators and conduits of *poesis* as an existential power. The commonplace ideas that media create overtly fictional worlds, while at the same time constructing our sense of the real world, society, community and the body politic, are rooted in the poetic capacities of media" (Frosh 2018, xiii).

It is my hope that procedural poetics can become a valid alternative to procedural rhetoric for the study of videogames that do not immediately suggest an intention to persuade their players. Further studies of metareferences in videogames will identify numerous poetics beyond the ones I briefly touched upon here, and a more detailed analysis of the immersive sim poetics will show the importance of many more metareferential elements in examples from the past 30 years. To the extent that I could present it here, procedural poetics is certainly not a fully fleshed-out concept—yet as poetics go, it should have been defined in sufficient detail to at least stimulate some discussion.

Works Cited

"Deathloop". 2021. Arkane Studios Lyon/Bethesda Softworks. Microsoft Windows.

Apperley, Thomas H. 2006. "Genre and Game Studies: Toward a Critical Approach to Video Game Genres." *Simulation & Gaming* 37 (1): 6–23.

Aristotle. 1980. *Poetics*. Edited by Donald William Lucas. Oxford: Clarendon Press.

Ars Technica. 2021. "How *Deus Ex* Blended Genres to Change Shooters Forever | War Stories [Video]." *YouTube*, December 16, 2021. www.youtube.com/watch?v=Bb98qIZfwgc.

Arsenault, Dominic. 2009. "Video Game Genre, Evolution and Innovation." *Eludamos: Journal for Computer Game Culture* 3 (2): 149–176.

Bachelard, Gaston. 2014 [1957]. *The Poetics of Space*. London: Penguin.

Backe, Hans-Joachim. 2018a. "A Redneck Head on a Nazi Body: Subversive Ludo-Narrative Strategies in *Wolfenstein II: The New Colossus*." *Arts* 7 (4): 76.

Backe, Hans-Joachim. 2018b. "Metareferentiality through In-Game Images in Immersive Simulation Game." In *FDG '18: Proceedings of the 13th International Conference on the Foundations of Digital Games*, 25 (1–10).

Backe, Hans-Joachim. 2022. "*"Deathloop"*: The Meta (Modern) Immersive Simulation Game." *Game Studies: The International Journal of Computer Game Research* 22 (2): n.pag.

Bakhtin, Mikhail. 2013 [1929]. *Problems of Dostoevsky's Poetics.* Minneapolis: University of Minnesota Press.

Bal, Mieke. 2000. "Poetics, Today." *Poetics Today* 21 (3): 479–502.

Baldur's Gate 3. 2023. Larian Studios. Microsoft Windows.

Bioshock. 2007. 2K Boston/2K Games. Microsoft Windows.

Blasonato, Myles, Cinzia Cremona, Manolya Kavakli, and Dan Staines. 2022. "Immersive Sims: A New Paradigm or a New Game Genre?" In *Human-Computer Interaction: Theoretical Approaches and Design Methods*, Vol. 13302, edited by Masaaki Kurosu, 18–39. Lecture Notes in Computer Science. Cham: Springer International Publishing.

Bódi, Bettina. 2023. *Videogames and Agency.* New York: Routledge.

Bogost, Ian. 2007. *Persuasive Games: The Expressive Power of Videogames.* Cambridge, MA: MIT Press.

Bordwell, David. 2012. *Poetics of Cinema.* New York: Routledge.

Braithwaite, Andrea. 2016. "It's About Ethics in Games Journalism? Gamergaters and Geek Masculinity." *Social Media + Society* 2 (4): n.pag.

Brooks, Peter. 1994. "Aesthetics and Ideology: What Happened to Poetics?" *Critical Inquiry* 20 (3): 509–523.

Butterworth-Parr, Francis. 2024. "Machphrasis: Towards a Poetics of Video Games in Contemporary Literary Culture." *Games and Culture* 19 (3): 373–390.

Calleja, Gordon. 2011. *In-Game: From Immersion to Incorporation.* Cambridge, MA: MIT Press.

Chatman, Seymour, ed. 1973. *Approaches to Poetics.* New York: Columbia University Press.

Clifford, James, and George E. Marcus. 2023 [1986]. *Writing Culture: The Poetics and Politics of Ethnography.* Berkeley: University of California Press.

Colantonio, Raphael. 2018. "As a Fan of Immersive Sims." *X*, May 5, 2018. https://x.com/rafcolantonio/status/992864422245920768.

Culler, Jonathan D. 1975. *Structuralist Poetics: Structuralism, Linguistics and the Study of Literature.* New York: Routledge.

Deus Ex. 2000. Ion Storm/Eidos Interactive. Microsoft Windows.

Dilthey, Wilhelm. 1990 [1924]. *Die Geistige Welt: Einleitung in die Philosophie des Lebens.* Stuttgart: Teubner/Vandenhoeck & Ruprecht.

Dishonored 2. 2016. Arkane Studios Lyon/Bethesda Softworks. Microsoft Windows.

Ensslin, Astrid. 2014. *Literary Gaming.* Cambridge, MA: MIT Press.

Eskelinen, Markku. 2012. *Cybertext Poetics: The Critical Landscape of New Media Literary Theory.* London: Continuum.

Fest, Bradley J. 2016. "Metaproceduralism: *The Stanley Parable* and the Legacies of Postmodern Metafiction." *Wide Screen* 6 (1): n.pag.

Frasca, Gonzalo. 2003. "Simulation versus Narrative: Introduction to Ludology." In *The Video Game Theory Reader*, edited by Mark J.P. Wolf and Bernard Perron, 221–235. New York: Routledge.

Frosh, Paul. 2018. *The Poetics of Digital Media.* Hoboken: John Wiley & Sons.

Fullerton, Tracy, Jacquelyn Ford Morie, and Celia Pearce. 2007. "A Game of One's Own: Towards a New Gendered Poetics of Digital Space." In *Proceedings of DAC: Digital Experience: Design, Aesthetics, Practice*, 136–146.

Gaynor, Steve. 2012. "A Non-Violent Immersive Sim." *The Fullbright Company*, September 28, 2012. https://fullbright.company/2012/09/28/a-non-violent-immersive-sim/.

GDC. 2022. "Torchbearers: New Generation Immersive Sim Developers." *GDC Vault.* www.gdcvault.com/play/1027692/Level-Design-Summit-Torchbearers-New.

Glissant, Édouard. 1997. *Poetics of Relation.* Chicago: University of Michigan Press.

Grace, Lindsay. 2011. "The Poetics of Game Design, Rhetoric and the Independent Game." In *Proceedings of DiGRA 2011: Think Design Play*, n.pag.

Greenblatt, Stephen. 1989. "Towards a Poetics of Culture." In *The New Historicism*, edited by H. A. Veeser, 1–14. New York: Routledge.

Greene, Roland, Stephen Cushman, Clare Cavanagh, Jahan Ramazani, Paul F. Rouzer, Harris Feinsod, David Marno, and Alexandra Slessarev, eds. 2012. *The Princeton Encyclopedia of Poetry and Poetics*. 4th ed. Princeton: Princeton University Press.

Gregersen, Andreas. 2014. "Generic Structures, Generic Experiences: A Cognitive Experientialist Approach to Video Game Analysis." *Philosophy & Technology* 27 (2): 159–175.

Griswold, Charles L. 2024. "Plato on Rhetoric and Poetry." In *Stanford Encyclopedia of Philosophy*, edited by Edward N. Zalta and Uri Nodelman, n.pag. Spring 2024 Archive Edition. Stanford: The Metaphysics Research Lab, Department of Philosophy, Stanford University.

Harshav, Benjamin. 2007. *Explorations in Poetics.* Stanford: Stanford University Press.

Hitchens, Michael. 2011. "A Survey of First-Person Shooters and Their Avatars." *Game Studies: The International Journal of Computer Game Research* 11 (3): n.pag.

Holbeck, Phillip Casey. 2023. "A Genre of Hybrids: Structured Hybridity Through Communicative Purpose in Immersive Simulation." *Paidia* (Special Issue "Immersive Sims"): n.pag.

Hunicke, Robin, Marc LeBlanc, and Robert Zubek. 2004. "MDA: A Formal Approach to Game Design and Game Research." *Proceedings of the AAAI Workshop on Challenges in Game AI* 4 (1): n.pag.

Hutcheon, Linda. 2003. *A Poetics of Postmodernism: History, Theory, Fiction.* New York: Routledge.

Kirkpatrick, Graeme. 2011. *Aesthetic Theory and the Video Game.* Manchester: Manchester University Press.

Klastrup, Lisbeth. 2003. "A Poetics of Virtual Worlds." In *Proceedings of the Digital Arts and Culture Conference*, 100–109.

Krampe, Theresa. 2023. "Rewriting Rules, Changing Worlds: Diegetic and Ludic Forms of Metareference in *The Magic Circle*." *Frontiers of Narrative Studies* 9 (1): 137–157.

Louvel, Liliane. 2016. *Poetics of the Iconotext.* Edited by Karen Jacobs. New York: Routledge.

Lucas, Donald William. 1980. "Introduction." In *Poetics*, edited by Donald William Lucas. Oxford: Clarendon Press.

The Magic Circle. 2015. Question. Microsoft Windows.

Martin, Paul. 2019. "Morphology and Meaning in 'Castle Wolfenstein 3D'." In *Ludotopia: Spaces, Places and Territories in Computer Games*, edited by Espen Aarseth and Stephan Günzel, 271–294. Bielefeld: transcript.

Mateas, Michael. 2001. "A Preliminary Poetics for Interactive Drama and Games." *Digital Creativity* 12 (3): 140–152.

Mitchell, Alex, Liting Kway, Tiffany Neo, and Yuin Theng Sim. 2020. "A Preliminary Categorization of Techniques for Creating Poetic Gameplay." *Game Studies: The International Journal of Computer Game Research* 20 (2): n.pag.

Mortensen, Torill Elvira. 2015. "Anger, Fear, and Games." *Games and Culture* 13 (8): 787–806.

Mortensen, Torill Elvira, and Tanja Sihvonen. 2020. "Negative Emotions Set in Motion: The Continued Relevance of #GamerGate." In *Palgrave Handbook of International Cybercrime*

and Cyberdeviance, edited by Thomas J. Holt and Adam M. Bossler, 1353–1374. Cham: Palgrave Macmillan.
Mukherjee, Souvik. 2015. *Video Games and Storytelling: Reading Games and Playing Books*. Houndmills: Palgrave Macmillan.
Murray, Janet Horowitz. 1998. *Hamlet on the Holodeck: The Future of Narrative in Cyberspace*. Cambridge, MA: MIT Press.
Parry, Richard. 2024. "Episteme and Techne." In *Stanford Encyclopedia of Philosophy*, edited by Edward N. Zalta and Uri Nodelman, n.pag. Spring 2024 Archive Edition. Stanford: The Metaphysics Research Lab, Department of Philosophy, Stanford University.
Pechalin, Andrei. 2021. "Immersive Sims Are Less Niche Than They Appear." *The Escapist*, April 7, 2021. www.escapistmagazine.com/immersive-sims-are-less-niche-than-they-appear/.
Pilkington, Adrian. 2000. *Poetic Effects: A Relevance Theory Perspective*. Amsterdam: John Benjamins Publishing.
Pinchbeck, Dan. 2013. *Doom: Scarydarkfast*. Ann Arbor: University of Michigan Press.
Piñeros Glasscock, Juan S., and Sergio Tenenbaum. 2023. "Action." In *Stanford Encyclopedia of Philosophy*, edited by Edward N. Zalta and Uri Nodelman, n.pag. Spring 2023 Archive Edition. Stanford: The Metaphysics Research Lab, Department of Philosophy, Stanford University.
Prey. 2017. Arkane Studios/Bethesda Softworks. Microsoft Windows.
Ramazani, Jahan. 2015. "A Transnational Poetics." In *A Transnational Poetics*, edited by Jahan Ramazani, 23–50. Chicago: University of Chicago Press.
Richardson, Brian, Henrik Skov Nielsen, and Jan Alber. 2013. *A Poetics of Unnatural Narrative*. Columbus: Ohio State University Press.
Richardson, Brian. 2020. *A Poetics of Plot for the Twenty-First Century: Theorizing Unruly Narratives*. Columbus: Ohio State University Press.
Rimmon-Kenan, Shlomith. 2003. *Narrative Fiction: Contemporary Poetics*. 2nd ed. New York: Routledge.
Robert, Jörg. 2015. "Poetologie." In *Handbuch literarische Rhetorik,* edited by Rüdiger Zymner, 303–332. Berlin: De Gruyter.
rosodude. 2020. "'Immersive Sim' Is a Design Philosophy, Not a Genre." *RSD's Mods and Tweaks,* December 14, 2020. https://rosodudemods.wordpress.com/2020/12/14/immersive-sim-is-a-design-philosophy-not-a-genre/.
Ryan, Marie-Laure. 2006. *Avatars of Story*. Minneapolis: University of Minnesota Press.
Sarbin, Theodore R. 1997. "The Poetics of Identity." *Theory & Psychology* 7 (1): 67–82.
Showalter, Elaine. 2012. "Towards a Feminist Poetics." In *Women Writing and Writing about Women*, edited by Mary Jacobus, 22–41. New York: Routledge.
Spector, Warren. 2000. "Postmortem: *Deus Ex*." *Game Developer* (November): 50–58.
Stewart, Kathleen. 2020. *A Space on the Side of the Road: Cultural Poetics in an "Other" America*. Princeton: Princeton University Press.
Stockwell, Peter. 2014. *The Poetics of Science Fiction*. New York: Routledge.
Stockwell, Peter. 2019. *Cognitive Poetics: An Introduction*. New York: Routledge.
Stravinsky, Igor. 1970. *Poetics of Music in the Form of Six Lessons*. Cambridge, MA: Harvard University Press.
System Shock. 1994. Looking Glass Technologies/Origin Systems. Microsoft Windows.
Thief: The Dark Project. 1998. Looking Glass Studios/Eidos Interactive. Microsoft Windows.

Thon, Jan-Noël. 2022. "Bildmedium Computerspiel? Zur ästhetischen Komplexität aktueller Indie Games." In *Bildmedien: Materialität – Semiotik – Ästhetik*, edited by Frauke Berndt and Jan-Noël Thon, 441–462. Berlin: De Gruyter.

Todorov, Tzvetan. 1981. *Introduction to Poetics*. Minneapolis: University of Minnesota Press.

Tzonis, Alexander, and Liane Lefaivre. 1986. *Classical Architecture: The Poetics of Order*. Cambridge, MA: MIT Press.

Ultima Underworld. 1992. Blue Sky Productions/Origin Systems. Microsoft Windows.

Walther, Bo Kampmann. 2007. "Self-Reference in Computer Games: A Formalistic Approach." In *Self-Reference in the Media*, edited by Winfried Nöth and Nina Bishara, 219–236. Berlin: De Gruyter.

Wardrip-Fruin, Noah. 2009. *Expressive Processing: Digital Fictions, Computer Games, and Software Studies*. Cambridge, MA: MIT Press.

Warning, Rainer. 1994 [1975]. *Rezeptionsästhetik: Theorie und Praxis*. Munich: Fink.

Waszkiewicz, Agata. 2024. *Metagames: Games about Games*. New York: Routledge.

Werning, Stefan. 2021. *Making Games: The Politics and Poetics of Game Creation Tools*. Cambridge, MA: MIT Press.

Wolf, Werner. 2009. "Metareference across Media: The Concept, Its Transmedial Potentials and Problems, Main Forms and Functions." In *Metareference across Media: Theory and Case Studies*, edited by Werner Wolf, 1–85. Amsterdam: Rodopi.

Wolfenstein 3D. 1992. id Software/Apogee. Microsoft Windows.

Wolfenstein II: The New Colossus. 2017. Machine Games/Bethesda Softworks. Microsoft Windows.

Yee, Bernard. 1995. *System Shock: Strategies and Secrets*. San Francisco: Sybex.

Zak, Albin. 2001. *The Poetics of Rock: Cutting Tracks, Making Records*. Berkeley: University of California Press.

3 Orders of Anti-Illusion

An Analytical Framework for Metareference from a Semiotic Perspective

Martin Hennig

This chapter analyzes metareference in videogames from a semiotic perspective. First, I outline some general theoretical approaches to the semiotics-based study of videogames. In particular, I address the fundamental distinction between object language and metalanguage and discuss the extent to which this distinction can be applied across different media. In a second step, building on this theoretical framework, I propose an analytical framework, distinguishing between individual dimensions of analysis on which metareferences can occur. Finally, I apply these two frameworks in a case study of the independent game The Hex *(2018).* The Hex *contains several metareferential strategies that increase in intensity over the course of the game. I examine and systematize these strategies with regard to the respective markers that suggest a metareferential reading in the sense of metalanguage, focusing on the decoupling of game and narrative that* The Hex *performs as an example of a medium-specific variant of metaization.*

Introduction

Metareference in the media is a promising research topic for several reasons. To name just two: On the one hand, many metareferential techniques (such as metalepsis, unreliable narrators, etc.) can be found across different media, but they often have medium-specific realizations that illustrate the characteristics of the respective media form. On the other hand, metareferences have self-critical potential, which for example points to the integration of a medium into an economic or ideological system or to entrenched conventions and alternative possibilities of staging. From this point of view, the question about the structures of metareference in videogames is also one of the central questions in game studies, if one wants to identify media specifics and if one wants to know what questions and discourses videogames raise about themselves.

Probably the best-known definition of metareference in the media is as follows:

> It is a special, transmedial form of usually non-accidental self-reference produced by signs or sign configurations which are (felt to be) located on a logically higher level, a 'meta-level,' within an artefact or performance; this

DOI: 10.4324/9781003538592-3

> self-reference, which can extend from this artefact to the entire system of the media, forms or implies a statement about an object-level, namely on (aspects of) the medium/system referred to. Where metareference is properly understood, an at least minimal corresponding 'meta-awareness' is elicited in the recipient.
>
> (Wolf 2009, 31; italics omitted)

Basically, the term "signs or sign configurations" refers to a semiotic dimension of metareference. According to the quote, metareference suggests a specific reading of an artistic artifact, more precisely a change in the focus of observation to a logically higher level, which relates to the media artifact itself in its constitution as a media artifact. At the same time, Wolf addresses the side of reception and the necessity of "meta-awareness" if metareference is to be perceived as such. A central question is, of course, how such a meta-reading is stimulated or suggested to the recipient.

This question applies to all media but even more to interactive media such as videogames. Research has asked to what extent the actual interactive gameplay can affect the development of reflexive distance and critical awareness among players (see, e.g., Hennig 2017; Orth 2013, 126; Rapp 2008). Videogames are forced to permanently refer to themselves as games in order to make themselves playable (among other things, they have to refer to their configurability via their interface—for example by displaying instructions on the controls—and permanently break through the diegetic illusion). This is one of the reasons why self-referentiality in games is often perceived to differ from other media (see Gorsolke 2009; Hennig 2017, 267–280; Rapp 2008).

This chapter analyzes metareference in videogames from a semiotic perspective. Modern semiotics began as an inter- and transdisciplinary field with Peirce's philosophy at the end of the 19th century (see Peirce 1992/1998) and de Saussure's *Cours de linguistique générale* (see de Saussure 2011) at the beginning of the 20th century (for an introduction to the history of semiotics, see Nöth 2000). The European and American traditions met after the Second World War with the French school of the 1960s to 1980s (see, e.g., Barthes 1972; Deleuzes 1989; Derrida 1978; Greimas 1987; Metz 1968), which is based on both traditions, as well as the Italian media semiotics (see, e.g., Eco 1979) and Lotman's cultural semiotics (see Lotman 1977). In its three sub-disciplines, semiotics is concerned with (1) the structures and regularities of signs and their meaning (semantics), (2) the possibilities of linking signs in sign systems (syntax), and (3) the communicative use of signs and sign systems (pragmatics). The above-mentioned question addresses all three dimensions: It asks which sign systems (syntax) videogames regularly use for metareferences, which meanings they generate (semantics), and what readings they evoke (pragmatics).

There are several examples of semiotic approaches in game studies, dealing with the medium's various forms of expression and its processes of meaning-making (see Hawreliak 2020; Hennig 2017), the textual qualities of videogames (see Aarseth 1997), the semiotic quality of videogame architecture (see Aroni 2022), or with play and playfulness (see Thibault 2016). We can thus already see that semiotic methods can and have been employed to address a broad thematic range. Insofar as videogames fundamentally operate on the basis of several different sign systems, semiotics provides a coherent analytical inventory. When analyzing metareference, semiotic approaches can be particularly helpful in understanding the interplay of these sign systems.

In the following, I will focus on some general approaches to analyzing metareference from a semiotic perspective, and subsequently present some thoughts on videogame analysis against this background. Finally, I will apply these theoretical considerations in a case study of the independent game *The Hex* (2018). *The Hex* contains several metareferential strategies that increase in intensity over the course of the game (from breaking with genre conventions to a complete disintegration of gameplay). I will examine and systematize these strategies with regard to the respective markers that suggest a metareferential reading.

Metareference from a Semiotic Perspective

From a semiotic perspective, videogames can be described as providing a framework for interaction that is, just as with any media text, constituted through the selection (paradigmatic level) and combination (syntagmatic level) of elements of sign systems in their underlying structure. Consequently, a semiotic analysis has to systematize the different sign systems of the videogame. According to Maren Conrad, following Jurij Lotman (1977), videogames can be described as secondary, performative, and open semiotic systems (see Conrad 2016, 56–60). They are secondary systems because worldmaking in videogames is based on primary sign systems such as image, text, language, etc. At the same time, videogames function as performative or open structures because they (1) model the structures they contain and (2) create new structures in the context of interaction. Although an abstract model of the depicted world may be included as a potential in the game, this structure must be realized by the players.

There are some—in the broader sense—semiotic approaches to metareference in videogames (see Gorsolke 2009; Hennig 2017, 267–280; Rapp 2008; see also the contributions in Nöth and Bishara 2007). In general, these discuss the specific semiotic qualities of metareference in relation to the mediality of videogames. On the one hand, this concerns meta-qualities that characterize the communication of signs in every videogame. Metareferential or, to be more precise, self-referential content is conventionally part of the game structure and cannot be thought of only as part of the diegesis. If a wall in an open-world game is not just a wall but is specifically designed to prevent players from walking past, it always refers to the game itself and its demands (here the necessity of controlling the spatial movement of the players). On the other hand, videogames can also overtly comment on themselves (when, for example, two game characters discuss videogames). While the former thus describe a sort of inherent self-referentiality that always occurs in videogames, the latter more closely corresponds to the notion of metareference as outlined by Wolf (see above) and as it is used in most chapters in this volume.

Explicit meta-strategies can appear in a similar way in different media, but some are also game-specific (when metareferences change through the interaction of the players, for example). To discuss semiotic specifics of explicit metareferences in videogames, I will focus on "Metareference from a Semiotic Perspective" by Winfried Nöth (2009). Nöth's observations are based on a fundamental distinction. In the philosophy of language, a distinction is commonly made between object language and metalanguage (for the related distinction between *suppositio formalis* and *suppositio materialis*, see also Bos 1997). While object language refers to the things of the world, metalanguage reflexively refers to signs and sign usage. So if I say, for example, "There's a dog around the corner," this is part of the object language, because it relates to concrete objects and relations in the world. By contrast, if I say that "The word 'dog' is a noun," then I refer to the sign for dog and the rules of sign usage, so I use metalanguage.

A central aspect of the two language registers is that they can overlap. To understand this, a few remarks on some basic assumptions of sign theory or semiotics are necessary. The conventional model of the sign is the semiotic triangle (see Figure 3.1).

"A *sign*, which this semiotic triangle represents as its lower left corner, is related to an object or *referent* (at the top of the triangle) as well as to a *meaning*, the idea associated with this object (right corner)" (Nöth 2009, 91; original emphases). Let's take the example of the written word "dog." The sign "is the sequence of its letters which we can read, regardless of whether we understand its meaning or not"; its referent is one of the existing dogs to which we may refer by means of this sign, and the meaning of this sign is the "idea, mental image, concept, verbalization, or paraphrase associated with the sign and its object in the mind of those who use the word 'dog'" (Nöth 2009, 91). A possible description of the meaning of the word "dog" is a lexical definition like "A domesticated carnivorous mammal, *Canis familiaris* (or *C. lupus familiaris*), which typically has a long snout, an acute sense of smell, non-retractile claws, and a barking, howling, or whining voice,

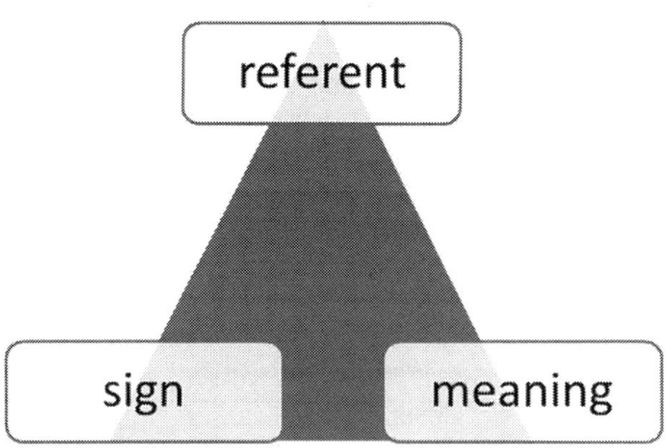

Figure 3.1 Semiotic triangle (object language).

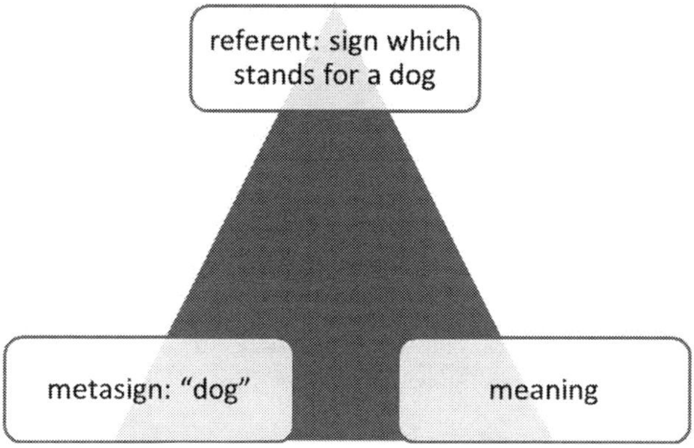

Figure 3.2 Semiotic triangle (metalanguage).

widely kept as a pet or for hunting, herding livestock, guarding, or other utilitarian purposes" ("Dog," *Oxford English Dictionary*).

A similar semiotic triangle can now be established for the language register of metalanguage, which consists of metasigns (see Figure 3.2). According to Nöth, "*Metareference* is the property by which a metasign refers to its referent, which is itself a sign. A *metasign* is evidently also a sign with a referent and a meaning of its own" (Nöth 2009, 92; original emphases). Metalanguage is thus self-reflexive insofar as it refers to the regularities of a sign system to which it itself belongs.

Let's take our exemplary sentence for metalanguage again. In the case of "The word 'dog' is a noun," the referent is the concrete sign to which the metareference refers, which in this case means the word "dog." The fact that this sign is read metalinguistically here is indicated by the two quotation marks in the metasign. The meaning of "dog" in the example of the sentence "the word 'dog' is a noun" then no longer refers to an object in the real world in the sense of an animal (object language), but to the word "dog" as a sign and the rules of sign usage. The meaning, in this case, would be something like a "syntactic construction whose centre consists of a noun and which may serve as a subject or an object of a sentence" (Nöth 2009, 93).

According to Nöth, if we place the two triangles of object language and metalanguage on top of each other, we can see the possible overlap (see 2009, 92). The connection between the two semiotic triangles of the sign and the metasign is the point representing both the referent in the semiotic triangle for metalanguage and the sign in the semiotic triangle for object language.

Indeed, there are signs in our language that belong exclusively to the realm of metalanguage, such as the word "noun," which explicitly refers to the linguistic sphere and uses of language. But the overlap of the two semiotic triangles shows that there are signs that can be used both as signs and as metasigns. The specific way in which the language is used (object or metalanguage) is usually marked, as in the example with the quotation marks.

So what does all this have to do with videogames? Of course, Nöth refers mainly to linguistic examples. However, one question that emerges from his remarks is whether media products other than texts in a narrow sense have structures that function analogously to metalanguage.

Interestingly enough, Nöth denies this. He argues that in non-language-based media, there may be only implicit references to a corresponding reading. Thus, a picture within a picture (which is conventionally called a *mise en abyme*) may suggest a meta-perspective on pictoriality in general because doubling the pictoriality allows the image to stand out as an image, and can, for example, put a focus on the conventions of depiction. At the same time, according to Nöth, this act of reflection would only remain indirect because visual media do not have an explicit repertoire of signs analogous to metalanguage that necessarily refers to a metalevel. Following Nöth, there may exist medium-specific techniques, such as the *mise en abyme* in visual media or breaking the fourth wall at the theater or cinema, that point to the constructedness of a medium, and at least *suggest* a meta-reading. At the same time, a meta-perspective is not necessarily adopted by the recipients.

No matter what one thinks about Nöth's argumentation in relation to other media (a large percentage of research on metareferences would certainly contradict this conclusion), it is clearly necessary to determine which repertoires of signs in videogames function analogously to metalanguage. Some staging strategies that commonly suggest a meta-perspective in visual media seem to transpose a different meaning in the videogame. Self-references, in particular, have other functions here. To give a concrete example: According to Rapp (2008), self-references in videogames—unlike in non-interactive media—are less to be understood as a disturbance or irritation during the game, but rather have an integrating function in the gameplay process and connect the game and its players instead of creating reflexive distance. So, when, for example, at the end of the opening credits of the adventure classic *Day of the Tentacle* (1993), a cow that seems to have accidentally entered the picture breaks the fourth wall by waving to the player, the dimension of interaction is implicitly accentuated. Although the direct address of the players causes an incoherence of the narrated world, it makes them aware of their role in the following gameplay and invites them to become active after the intro as a non-interactive sequence lasting several minutes. In this example, the waving cow crosses the boundary between the intradiegetic position of the characters and objects and the extradiegetic position of the players as part of a narrative metalepsis.[1] But the example also shows media specifics in the sense that reflexive strategies in videogames can have an involving effect. By transcending the intradiegetic level, players are directly invited as active recipients, which is not a situational specificity as in other media but the central media specificity of the videogame (see also Ensslin and Bell 2021). At the same time, the waving cow refers to an outside that is not inherent in the videogame image, so this metalepsis represents the position of the players as potentially autonomous and located outside the logics of medial representation. Players are addressed in a position that is superordinated to the intradiegetic sign processes and which anticipates central characteristics of the gaming situation, insofar as the entire depicted world (for which the waving cow only stands symbolically) is oriented toward the players.

Another medium-specific feature of metareference in videogames is that a metareferential reading can be indicated at the dimension of gameplay or game controls (see also Krampe 2025 on system-centered metareference). Frequently, this process is based on the suspension or re-semanticization of previously established interaction possibilities in the gaming process. An extreme example can be found in *God of War 3* (2010), where the ineffectiveness of the established interaction scheme leads players to a reinterpretation of the interface and previously valid rules for interaction. Here, the vendetta of the demigod Kratos against the ancient world of the gods culminates in the battle against the final opponent Zeus, whereby this epic showdown ironically is the only confrontation in the game that cannot be won through combat. If users continuously push the attack button, which is permanently displayed in the interface, the images of the fight are gradually filled with Zeus's blood until it is no longer possible to recognize anything on the screen. Only when the players do not provide any input for a longer period of time does the game continue. If no input is made, this leads to an ideological self-reflection on the part of the main character regarding the meaningfulness of his campaign of revenge. Hence, the deviation from the usual scheme of interaction in this scene is only indicated at the dimension of game controls, more precisely by the absence of a conventionalized reaction from the program to established inputs.

This provides for a temporary disruption of the gameplay, which is semanticized at the narrative level as a psychological learning process and maturation of the game character Kratos. On the one hand, this sequence can be read as a self-reflexive gesture of the game and a problematization of its own one-sided action schemes (violence leads to the successful fulfilment of the game objectives). On the other hand, however, this reflexivity is merely situational and means nothing beyond itself. Other parts of the game do not suddenly become reinterpretable from a meta-perspective, unless you want to read the sequence in question as a fundamental negation of the entire game, which would be going a bit too far. While the example from the endgame of *God of War 3* can therefore be interpreted as a medium-specific form of metareference, the central question remains whether there are strategies of staging in videogames, similar to the quotation marks in Nöth's example, that suggest a metareferential reading of larger parts of the gameplay.

Analytical Framework

If we are to analyze metareference in videogames, different dimensions of meaning-making must be distinguished from one another. In game studies, the assumption has prevailed that at least three dimensions of the game process must be taken into account when analyzing a game (see Hennig 2017; Thon 2019; on metareference specifically, see Krampe 2023; 2025): (1) the game mechanics, (2) the narrative layer, and (3) the visual representation of both.

First and foremost, the medium-specific dimension of game mechanics should be considered. Games operate in the mode of simulation (see Frasca 2003), in which a dynamic system (e.g., the behavior of the game pieces in *Tetris* [1984]) is represented, which can also mirror systems of the real world (e.g., road traffic regulations, aerodynamics). The reactions of this system are predetermined on a ludic level and can be described using the appropriate ludic terminology (winning conditions, rules of the game, etc.).

One central aim for the analysis of gameplay structures is a reconstruction of the rules of the game. Several types of rules can be distinguished (see Hennig 2017; Juul 2005; Thon 2015): Representation rules (can different visual perspectives be chosen in the game?), narrative rules (to what extent do players have an influence on the narrated story?), interaction rules (which actions are possible within the depicted world and what are their consequences?), and player character rules (can the appearance and characteristics of the player character be changed?). For an analysis of metareference, it seems particularly interesting to examine if and when breaks or deviations from these established rule systems occur. This is the case when unconventional perspectives need to be adopted that, for example, refer to the videogame itself as an instance of surveillance and control; when narratively staged decision-making situations are presented as ineffective (as an example for both, see *The Stanley Parable* [2013]); when established rules of interaction are broken during gameplay (see the example of *God of War 3* above); or when the player character changes unexpectedly or is given unexpected characteristics that do not correspond to the players' decisions (for instance in *Hatoful Boyfriend HD* [2014]).

As soon as a videogame has narrative components beyond its simulative level, it is operating in the mode of worldbuilding. All those components that provide game requirements (character movement, combat, puzzle solving) with a meaning beyond themselves—with meaning in the context of the narrative and the diegesis—can be understood as narratively relevant. The world designs constituted in this way can be described with semiotic and narratological methods of analysis (see Backe 2008; Domsch 2013; Hennig 2017; Juul 2005; Neitzel 2004; Thon 2015). Of particular interest are the central paradigms and the ideology, which are conveyed through the story told, and how these relate to the ludic systems (for example, how is violence, which may be a requirement for action in the system of rules of a game, framed in the narrated story). This relationship is also relevant for the analysis of metareference. For instance, a deviation from an established system of rules can be explained narratively—if, for example, a restriction of interaction possibilities results from the imprisonment of the game character. With metareference, it is to be expected that transgressions in the ludic rule system cannot be explained on the narrative dimension or the diegesis, but refer to the game system "outside."

The dimension of visual representation can be seen as a mediator between interactive and narrative game elements. In this respect, the digital image consists of two image layers: a machine-readable depth structure and a visible surface (see Manovich 2002, 46). This means on the one hand that methods of semiotic image analysis (see Nöth 2005) can be applied here with relation to the visible surface.

But on the other, the results must be consistently related to the depth structure of the videogame. Thus, image objects are usually determined by both a ludic and a narrative meaning. Videogame images can be viewed as forms of action, in the sense of Austin's speech act theory (see Austin 1962); as performative image acts that invite players to perform certain actions and enable them to play by acting in and on the basis of images (see Hensel 2018, 57–58). This begs the question of whether there are also certain image forms that guide players to a metareferential reading. Classically, one would think of *mise en abyme* structures here, although, according to Nöth and others (see, e.g., Wolf 2009), these do not necessarily lead to a metareferential reading. However, this thesis would have to be specified depending on the media context. In the context of games, *mise en abyme* structures would for the most part be equated with games-within-games (see also the analysis below) or gameworlds within a gameworld (see Backe 2016; Seiwald 2019).

In the following, ludic, narrative, and visual aspects of metareferences are discussed. Semiotics provides analytical tools for all these dimensions (of course, not all of them will be relevant in this case study; for a broader overview, see Hennig 2017) and regards their interaction as the interaction of sign systems.

Case Study: Metareference in *The Hex*

The following is a more detailed examination of the independent game *The Hex* (see also Hennig 2023) by developer Daniel Mullins, which is widely regarded as a metareferential game. Why is that? Following the above-mentioned analytical scheme, the first thing to look at would be the dimension of game mechanics. *The Hex* is difficult to reduce to a simple denominator in terms of game mechanics or game genres. In principle, the game follows the interaction rules of a point-and-click adventure. Various characters, all of whom are player characters from different fictional videogames, meet in a hostel. Players embody a different character in each section of the game that takes place within the hostel, where they engage in conversation with the other characters and solve a number of comparatively simple puzzles in order to unlock memories of the current player character. These memories include the characters' previous appearances in their own fictional videogame series, which form playable levels in *The Hex*. Each of these levels follows a different genre or different interaction rules. These genres and rules are very diverse and include a platformer, a fighting game, a strategy game, a role-playing game, and so on (for a discussion of videogame genre theory, see Apperley 2006; Arsenault 2009; Hennig and Krah 2023).

Within these games-within-the-game, there are constant breaks with genre conventions. These breaks foreground the theme(s) of play/games and make gaming conventions visible. This happens in every dimension mentioned above (ludic, narrative, and visual). Of course, the ludic and narrative dimension are only accessible through the (audio)visual dimension in the reception (which may also encompass haptic aspects). The following analysis of both dimensions therefore always includes a description of the corresponding visual components.

Ludic and Visual Dimension

Typical for *The Hex* are frequent deviations from conventional rules of interaction in the respective genre sequences. In the fighting game, the players must compete against the opponent "three hats." True to the motto of the hat game, a rubber duck changes its position among the hats and the players can only land a hit (according to the rules of a fighting game) if the correct hat with the duck is attacked. At this moment, the game *The Hex* is characterized by two sets of interaction rules: first, the rules and maxims of the digital fighting game, and second, the rules and maxims of the game of hats. Players, that is, can only win the fighting game if they follow the rules of another game at the same time.

However, even considering this non-conventionality in relation to the videogame context, *The Hex* is not very strongly metareferential at this point. In this case, two systems are simulated on the ludic level that have their significance in the context of games and gaming. By mirroring itself within the framework of the *mise en abyme* structure of a game-within-the-game, *The Hex* invokes the thematic field of play and playing as a meta-theme. Analogous to Nöth's metalanguage, this opens up a space of possibility for statements about games per se. But although a meta-reading is suggested in the example sequence, no media-reflexive statements can be deduced from the situation. This begs the question: Which parts of *The Hex* are clearly metareferential? Of course, not every game element can be read as a meta-element in this way. The individual sections of the game *The Hex* are still subject to specific genre rules and maxims that must be followed by the players if they want to progress. In the fighting game, you fight, in the jump 'n' run, you jump and run. Does this mean that the meta-elements are specified in the narrative dimension?

Narrative and Visual Dimension

In addition to the gameplay dimension, there are breaks regarding narrative conventions that can be described as metalepses. Metaleptic breaks in *The Hex* occur for example when, in the aforementioned fighting game, the life bar attributable to the interface suddenly falls down from the upper edge of the screen and injures the played character (on metareferential interfaces, see also Krampe et al. 2022). In the conventional videogame image, the interface can be understood as all those components of the game process that serve the direct communication between program and user, in the form of the configuration of program variables (level of difficulty, display, controls, etc.) or information about the game's states. Configurative elements are usually outsourced from the actual game process in the form of menu structures. Informative elements such as diagrams, which provide the players with information that is not represented diegetically (ammunition, life indicators, score, etc.), are conventionally part of the videogame image and lie "above" the representation of the depicted world on an image layer that is to be understood as extradiegetic and represents diegetic states through a symbolic sign relationship (e.g., when an opponent's shot reduces the player character's health score from 100 points to 80 points). In the case described, the symbolic sign relationship changes to an indexical one: The battle in the depicted world causally leads to damage of the life bar. Here, the interface transforms from a part of the videogame image that merely represents diegetic actions symbolically into a performative image act, which directly influences the course of the game. At the same time, the ludic meaning of the life bar expands to a meaning in the depicted world: It becomes an intradiegetic object that falls on the main character's head. This integrates the interface into the usual double structure of the videogame image with a ludic and narrative significance (see above). This structure now also extends to the visual components of the interface that are conventionally interpretable as standing "outside" the narrative representation of the gameworld. At this point, the boundaries between ludic and narrative elements on the visual dimension become blurred.

Some other metaleptic border crossings go one step further, namely, game-based conventions and aspects of the integration of games into media and economic systems of the real world are referenced (and partly broken) during the game. For example, the jump 'n' run sections recur several times throughout *The Hex*, in each case depicting a different instalment of a fictional videogame series. Implicitly, the specific sequence of the jump 'n' run levels in *The Hex* tells the story of the economic and creative decline of this fictional series. In the later jump 'n' run sections, players must jump back and forth between text boxes that refer to the aesthetics of comments on the game distribution platform Steam[2] and contain critical valuations on the development of the game series from fictional users. This is a motivic transgression of the boundary between game and game reception or between a game and its (in this case, of course, fictional) paratexts (see Genette 1997) and a metaleptic break between the fictional gameworld and *The Hex* as a commercial product, which is also distributed via Steam.

Corresponding to this critical thematization of the problematic effects of serialization and commercialization on product quality, the visual appearance of the player character in the jump 'n' run sections suffers in the course of the individual levels, respectively parts of the fictional series, and shows clear signs of the degeneration of the former jump 'n' run star in the last level (sunglasses and signs of aging). This also represents a clear break with the conventions of platformers. The change in appearance of the played character represents temporality, which is conventionally not thematic in the more child-oriented jump 'n' run genre (Mario does not age). In general, a visible aging process of the player character is rather unusual in many game genres; even when looking at the dimension of player character rules it is not common that the age of the character can be changed by the users (except for role-playing games, of course).

These observations are still insufficient to suggest a purely metareferential reading of *The Hex*, however (in the sense that the game *The Hex* itself is reflected here). It is true that these examples break with conventions of representation and storytelling in platformers and blur the boundary between the real world and the game. Yet, the game mechanics remain genre-compliant. In the example of the jump 'n' run levels, the Steam text boxes primarily fulfill a narrative function. They tell the story of the decline of the fictional game series and provide an explanation of the main character's changed appearance. In terms of game mechanics, however, these blocks still represent conventional jumping objects.

In addition, there are a number of examples of metalepses in games that do not necessarily serve the purpose of self-reflection but should rather be seen as a situational gag. There are some examples in which a narrator continuously addresses the players directly and thus breaks the fourth wall, but the degree to which this also conveys statements about the game in a media-reflexive sense varies. Only consider the differences between the more extensively media-reflexive narrator(s) of *The Stanley Parable*, and the narrator of *Bastion* (2011) who, while still conveying statements about the game, does so to a lesser extent. The central question remains what the constituents of this "more or less" are.[3] Two central aspects to answering the question on a paradigmatic (interaction of ludic and narrative [meta-]elements) and a syntagmatic level (development over the course of the game) appear to be the following.

Interaction of Ludic and Narrative (Meta-)Elements

As we have already seen above in our discussion of the aged jump 'n' run star, the narrative dimension of *The Hex* does not remain unbroken either (this concerns the paradigmatic dimension, i.e., the question of which game elements are included in the metaization). There are narrative developments in *The Hex* that are quite unusual in and of themselves and force players to also reinterpret the ludic dimension. For example, the role-playing sections produce a break with typical norms and values of the genre: Toward the end of the role-playing game embedded within *The Hex*, it becomes apparent that the actions of the players have unintentionally furthered the plans of the antagonist of the hypodiegetic gameworld Legendaria, resulting in an apocalypse. This development links the familiar game structure of a role-playing game to a narrative that is unusual in the genre context and breaks with the general convention, at least in the "AAA" mass-market, of combining a successful playthrough with a narrative happy ending[4] (respectively, the narrative rules usually ensure that a negative ending to the story can be prevented by the players). More than that, the original game objectives are now recognizable as "false" game objectives in retrospect via the narrative. Here one can clearly see how the individual parts of the game contribute to the overall meaning and how they can also take on new meanings in their interaction.

Development over the Course of the Game

For an interpretation of *The Hex* as a metareferential game, it is also crucial that the metaization increases over the course of the game quantitatively and qualitatively (this affects the syntagmatic dimension, i.e., the question of how the meta-elements are combined with each other over the course of the game). While the first few games-within-the game are characterized by only situational genre breaks, the game segments in the last quarter of the game can hardly be assigned to any one specific genre. As an absolute escalation of the continuous breaks with the conventions of specific game genres, *The Hex* is ultimately heading toward a complete genre collapse. The characters and settings of the individual levels become increasingly intermingled as the game progresses, so that the fantasy world of the role-playing game is suddenly occupied by the science fiction motifs of an isometric shooter, or that the player must brutally eliminate the cute enemies from the jump 'n' run sections with heavy weaponry. In the narrative framework, all the games depicted in *The Hex* are the work of a single developer (a fictionalized version of the real developer of *The Hex*, Daniel Mullins), but the characters gradually take on a life of their own and the ensuing genre collapse is a commentary on the developer's failed attempt to meet market-shaped genre expectations. At the end of the game, familiar game structures are continuously paired with unusual motifs or (depending on the perspective) familiar narrative motifs are mixed with interaction rules that are highly unconventional in the respective genre context.

Conclusion

What, then, are the main strategies *The Hex* employs to create metareference? In principle, the game invokes familiar genre structures in the games-within-the-game. These ludic, narrative, and visual structures are foregrounded as strictly genre-bound elements due to the reduced form of the in-game sequences that condense a genre into an essence. The later mixing of genre contexts then accentuates the boundaries of the genres. What is common in the context of a jump 'n' run game seems out of context against the background of a shooter, and so forth.

All in all, *The Hex* combines different strategies of metaization. (1) It uses different game mechanics at the same time and interlinks them and (2) it binds familiar interaction rules to unconventional narrative frameworks or motifs. This creates moments of irritation. In their unconventional connection, game and narration become visible as such and can be experienced as independent sign systems. The generic conventions of the games market (which are, of course, linked to economic considerations in the videogame industry) become visible and it becomes clear how natural and unquestioned certain connections between game and narrative usually seem but are actually not. For example, certain forms of action presuppose very specific narrative settings—the shooter's specific maxim of violence does not work in a platformer, which in turn relies on a very specific type of player character that is disconnected from the temporal progression of the world, as in a fairy tale.

Analogous to this critical view of the implicit rules of game culture, *The Hex* contains a number of metaleptic breaks that identify and reflect on videogame conventions and boundaries and the game as a commercial product of a specific developer in the real world. Visual elements that are conventionally outside the diegetic representation, such as the interface, are incorporated into the—at the same time ludic and narrative—logic of the videogame image (which makes the visual conventions as such visible in the first place) and usual elements of game paratexts (like Steam comments) can also be found in *The Hex*, but in fictionalized forms.

In summary, the analogy to the quotation marks mentioned by Nöth (respectively the question of how/when metareference is sufficiently marked to be recognizable as such[5]), at least in the case of the videogame *The Hex*, seems to lie precisely in a combination of these different strategies. First and foremost, there is the unusual combination of game and narrative that *The Hex* performs in many ways, which makes both dimensions in conflict with each other (or in the transgression of conventional visual boundaries between the two dimensions) recognizable as individual dimensions. This seems to be a media-specific variant of metaization. At the same time, the metaization extends paradigmatically to all dimensions of the game (images, ludic gameplay, narrative framework) and their relationship to each other and, in the syntagmatic progression, encompasses all components of the game. Precisely because of the level-bound gameplay, which is typical for videogames and provides for a more situation-bound experience of reception, it is central to the metaization effect (and it also seems to me to be more central than in other media) that the metaization not only occurs in isolated instances but recurs throughout the entire game.

The case study showed that a potential of semiotic approaches to the study of metareferences in videogames lies in asking about their equivalents to metalinguistic markers. The central question here is not *if* the videogame communicates in a metalanguage, but rather how it expresses metareferences in a medium-specific way, especially through the interrelation of its individual (ludic, narrative, and visual) parts—and not just through traditional narrative techniques.

However, since games are played and not passively received, it seems to me that another central question is how long a metareferential game remains playable. At the end of *The Hex*, the fictional characters team up to kill the (fictional version of the) game developer Daniel Mullins. A completely metaized game ultimately threatens to become unplayable (game rules are broken, the narrative can no longer guide the gameplay, etc.). At the climax of metaization, *The Hex* consequently depicts the death of the game developer and thus, in a figurative sense, wipes out the condition of the possibility of play(ing).

Notes

1 The metalepsis is a narrative strategy which crosses the boundaries between separate diegetic worlds or between intra- and extradiegesis, e.g., in a classical literary context between narrator and characters (see Genette 1980, 152–154; for a discussion of metalepsis in videogames, see, e.g., Bell 2016; Conrad 2016; Ensslin and Bell 2021; Krampe et al. 2022; Ryan 2006; Thon 2016; Waszkiewicz 2020; Wolf 2005; as well as the chapters by Caracciolo, Krampe, Thorne, and Waszkiewicz in this volume).

2 Steam is an internet distribution platform for computer games, software, films, series, and computer devices developed and operated by Valve.

3 The structural distribution of meta-elements (and its effect on how "meta" the entire artifact is considered to be) is also discussed in, e.g., Nünning 2004; Rapp 2008.

4 For example, when *Mass Effect 3* (2012) did not offer a happy ending, this led to such massive fan protests that the developer BioWare was ultimately forced to deliver an extended version via download. However, the new ending only provides additional

information; the outcome of the story has basically been preserved. For different forms of endings in videogames, see Herte 2022.

5 See also the chapters by Hübschmann and Seiwald in this volume.

Works Cited

Aarseth, Espen. 1997. *Cybertext: Perspectives on Ergodic Literature.* Baltimore: Johns Hopkins University Press.

Apperley, Thomas H. 2006. "Genre and Game Studies: Toward a Critical Approach to Video Game Genres." *Simulation and Gaming* 37 (1): 6–23.

Aroni, Gabriele. 2022. *The Semiotics of Architecture in Video Games*. London: Bloomsbury.

Arsenault, Dominic. 2009. "Video Game Genre, Evolution and Innovation". *Eludamos: Journal for Computer Game Culture* 3 (2): 149–176.

Austin, John Langshaw. 1962. *How to Do Things with Words*. Oxford, UK: Clarendon Press.

Backe, Hans-Joachim. 2008. *Strukturen und Funktionen des Erzählens im Computerspiel: Eine typologische Einführung*. Würzburg: Königshausen & Neumann.

Backe, Hans-Joachim. 2016. "Das Spiel im Spiel – im (Computer-)Spiel." In *Vergleichen an der Grenze: Beiträge zu Manfred Schmelings komparatistischen Forschungen*, edited by Hans-Joachim Backe, Claudia Schmitt, and Christiane Solte-Gresser, 37–74. Würzburg: Königshausen & Neumann.

Barthes, Roland. 1972. *Mythologies*. London: Paladin.

Bastion. 2011. Supergiant Games/Warner Bros. Interactive. Microsoft Windows.

Bell, Alice. 2016. "Interactional Metalepsis and Unnatural Narratology." *Narrative* 24 (3): 294–310.

Bos, Egbert P. 1997. "Speaking about Signs: Fourteenth-Century Views on *Suppositio Materialis*." In *Der muoz mir süezer worte jehen: Liber amicorum für Norbert Voorwinden*, edited by Ludo Jongen and Sjaak Onderdelinden, 71–86. Amsterdam: Rodopi.

Conrad, Maren. 2016. "Das Computerspiel als performatives sekundäres semiotisches System: Skizze und Theorie eines Modellvorschlags." In *Spielzeichen: Theorien, Analysen und Kontexte des zeitgenössischen Computerspiels*, edited by Martin Hennig and Hans Krah, 43–67. Glückstadt: Verlag Werner Hülsbusch.

Day of the Tentacle. 1993. LucasArts. Microsoft Windows.

Deleuze, Gilles. 1989. *Cinema 1: The Movement Image*. London: The Athlone Press.

Derrida, Jacques. 1978. *Writing and Difference*. Chicago: University of Chicago Press.

de Saussure, Ferdinand. 2011. *Course in General Linguistics*. New York: Columbia University Press.

"Dog." 2024. In *Oxford English Dictionary*, September 2024. https://doi.org/10.1093/OED/6646229330.

Domsch, Sebastian. 2013. *Storyplaying: Agency and Narrative in Video Games*. Berlin: De Gruyter.

Eco, Umberto. 1979. *A Theory of Semiotics*. Bloomington: Indiana University Press.

Ensslin, Astrid, and Alice Bell. 2021. *Digital Fiction and the Unnatural: Transmedial Narrative Theory, Method, and Analysis*. Columbus: Ohio State University Press.

Frasca, Gonzalo. 2003. "Simulation versus Narrative: Introduction to Ludology." In *The Video Game Theory Reader*, edited by Mark J.P. Wolf and Bernard Perron, 221–236. New York: Routledge.

Genette, Gérard. 1980. *Narrative Discourse: An Essay in Method.* Ithaca, NY: Cornell University Press.

Genette, Gérard. 1997. *Paratexts: Thresholds of Interpretation*. Cambridge, UK: Cambridge University Press.

God of War 3. 2010. SCE Studios Santa Monica/Sony Computer Entertainment. PlayStation 3.

Gorsolke, Stefan. 2009. *Interaktivität in narrativen Medien: Das Spiel von Selbst- und Fremdreferenz*. Marburg: Tectum.

Greimas, Algirdas Julien. 1987. *On Meaning: Selected Writings in Semiotic Theory*. Minneapolis: University of Minnesota Press.

Hatoful Boyfriend HD. 2014. Mediatonic/Devolver Digital. Microsoft Windows.

Hawreliak, Jason. 2020. *Multimodal Semiotics and Rhetoric in Videogames*. New York: Routledge.

Hennig, Martin. 2017. *Spielräume als Weltentwürfe: Kultursemiotik des Videospiels*. Marburg: Schüren.

Hennig, Martin. 2023. "Palimpseste: Spielgenres und Hypertextualität." In *Spielzeichen IV: Genres – Systematiken, Kontexte, Entwicklungen*, edited by Martin Hennig and Hans Krah, 117–134. Glückstadt: Verlag Werner Hülsbusch.

Hennig, Martin and Hans Krah. 2023. "Spielzeichen IV: Genres – Einführung in den Band." In *Spielzeichen IV: Genres – Systematiken, Kontexte, Entwicklungen*, edited by Martin Hennig and Hans Krah, 7–24. Glückstadt: Verlag Werner Hülsbusch.

Hensel, Thomas. 2018. "Bild." In *Game Studies*, edited by Benjamin Beil, Thomas Hensel, and Andreas Rauscher, 47–62. Wiesbaden: Springer.

Herte, Michelle. 2022. *Forms and Functions of Endings in Narrative Digital Games*. New York: Routledge.

The Hex. 2018. Daniel Mullins Games. Microsoft Windows.

Juul, Jesper. 2005. *Half-Real: Video Games between Real Rules and Fictional Worlds*. Cambridge, MA: MIT Press.

Krampe, Theresa. 2023. "Rewriting Rules, Changing Worlds: Diegetic and Ludic Forms of Metareference in *The Magic Circle*." *Frontiers of Narrative Studies* 9 (1): 137–157.

Krampe, Theresa. 2025. *Metareference in Videogames*. London: Routledge.

Krampe, Theresa, Stephanie Lotzow, and Jan-Noël Thon. 2022. "Playful Poetics: Metareferential Interfaces in Recent Indie Games." *Poetics Today* 43 (4): 729–771.

Lotman, Jurij. 1977. *The Structure of the Artistic Text*. Ann Arbor: University of Michigan.

Manovich, Lev. 2002. *The Language of New Media*. Cambridge, MA: MIT Press.

Mass Effect 3. 2012. BioWare/Electronic Arts. Microsoft Windows.

Metz, Christian. 1968. *Film Language: A Semiotics of the Cinema*. Chicago: University of Chicago Press.

Neitzel, Britta. 2004. "Gespielte Geschichten: Struktur- und prozessanalytische Untersuchungen der Narrativität von Videospielen." PhD thesis, University of Weimar. https://doi.org/10.25643/bauhaus-universitaet.69.

Nöth, Winfried. 2000. "Geschichte der Semiotik." In *Handbuch der Semiotik*, edited by Winfried Nöth, 1–57. Stuttgart: Metzler.

Nöth, Winfried. 2005. "Zeichentheoretische Grundlagen der Bildwissenschaft." In *Bildwissenschaft zwischen Reflexion und Anwendung*, edited by Klaus Sachs-Hombach, 33–44. Cologne: Halem.

Nöth, Winfried. 2009. "Metareference from a Semiotic Perspective." In *Metareference across Media: Theory and Case Studies*, edited by Werner Wolf, 87–120. Amsterdam: Rodopi.

Nöth, Winfried, and Nina Bishara, eds. 2007. *Self-Reference in the Media*. Berlin: De Gruyter.

Nünning, Angar. 2004. "On Metanarrative: Towards a Definition, a Typology and an Outline of the Functions of Metanarrative Commentary." In *The Dynamics of Narrative Form: Studies in Anglo-American Narratology*, edited by John Pier, 11–57. Berlin: De Gruyter.

Orth, Dominik. 2013. "'Game over' für den Fortschritt? Überlegungen zur Rolle der Technik in dystopischen Computerspielen." In *Technik in Dystopien*, edited by Viviana Chilese and Heinz-Peter Preußer, 121–126. Heidelberg: Winter.

Peirce, Charles Sanders. 1992/1998. *The Essential Peirce: Selected Philosophical Writings: Vol. 1 (1867–1893), Vol. 2 (1893–1913)*, edited by Nathan Houser and Christian Kloesel, Peirce Edition Project. Bloomington: Indiana University Press.

Rapp, Bernhard. 2008. *Selbstreflexivität im Computerspiel: Theoretische, analytische und funktionale Zugänge zum Phänomen autothematischer Strategien in Games.* Boizenburg: Verlag Werner Hülsbusch.

Ryan, Marie-Laure. 2006. *Avatars of Story*. Minneapolis: University of Minnesota Press.

Seiwald, Regina. 2019. "Games within Games: The Two (or More) Fictional Levels of Video Games." In *Videogame Sciences and Arts*, edited by Nelson Zagalo, Anna Isabel Veloso, Liliana Costa, and Óscar Mealha, 18–31. Cham: Springer.

The Stanley Parable. 2013. Galactic Cafe. Microsoft Windows.

Tetris. 1984. Alexei Paschitnow. Game Boy.

Thibault, Mattia. 2016. "Lotman and Play: For a Theory of Playfulness Based on Semiotics of Culture." *Sign Systems Studies* 44 (3): 295–325.

Thon, Jan-Noël. 2015. "Game Studies und Narratologie." In *Game Studies: Aktuelle Ansätze der Computerspielforschung*, edited by Klaus Sachs-Hombach and Jan-Noël Thon, 104–164. Cologne: Halem.

Thon, Jan-Noël. 2016. *Transmedial Narratology and Contemporary Media Culture*. Lincoln: University of Nebraska Press.

Thon, Jan-Noël. 2019. "Playing with Fear: The Aesthetics of Horror in Recent Indie Games." *Eludamos: Journal for Computer Game Culture* 10 (1): 197–231.

Waszkiewicz, Agata. 2020. "'Together They Are Twofold': Player-Avatar Relationship beyond the Fourth Wall." *Journal of Games Criticism* 4 (1): 1–21.

Wolf, Werner. 2005. "Metalepsis as a Transgeneric and Transmedial Phenomenon: A Case Study of the Possibilities of 'Exporting' Narratological Concepts." In *Narratology beyond Literary Criticism: Mediality, Disciplinarity*, edited by Jan Christoph Meister, 83–107. Berlin: De Gruyter.

Wolf, Werner. 2009. "Metareference across Media: The Concept, Its Transmedial Potentials and Problems, Main Forms and Functions." In *Metareference across Media: Theory and Case Studies*, edited by Werner Wolf, 1–85. Amsterdam: Rodopi.

4 Not Salient Enough?

Videogame-Specific Marker Failure of Implicit Metareference in *Far Cry 2* and *Far Cry 3*

Dominik Hübschmann

This chapter argues that the additional medium-specific possibilities of implicit metareference in videogames are accompanied by the requirement of more or clearer markers to indicate the presence of a metalevel. Since an implicit metareferential comment is not conveyed by the surface meaning of the sign configuration, markers are necessary to prompt the recipient to read beyond the conventional meaning. Using Far Cry 2 *(2008) and* Far Cry 3 *(2012) as case studies, three categories of potential marker failure due to noise, player perception, and decoding issues are illustrated. By considering the system-theoretical concepts of interpenetration and structural coupling to describe the player–videogame relationship, the analysis of these categories identifies the increased complexity and consequent necessity of complexity reduction as the principal causes of an increased probability of marker failure in videogames.*

Introduction

An implicit metareferential comment can be an effective method for reflecting on the mediality of a work of art or a media genre. By deviating from convention, elements of a semiotic system can draw attention to themselves as part of a semiotic system. In this manner, each sign can function as its own metasign in the sense of a sign that refers to a sign (see Nöth 2009, 100; see also the chapter by Hennig in this volume). Instead of a metareferential "telling," it can be thought of as a metareferential "showing" (Wolf 2009, 47).[1] Accordingly, a metareferential statement can be more persuasive if it is implicit rather than explicit, because it involves the recipient more directly and therefore requires less abstraction to comprehend (see Hill 2004, 33). However, the deviation must be salient enough to draw attention to the sign itself in the first place. As Ian Bogost has noted, videogames also have the potential to be highly persuasive due to their capacity to represent processes through processes and to make statements about them, a technique he termed "procedural rhetoric" (2007, 1–64). This suggests that implicit metareferences in videogames have the potential to be extremely persuasive. However, it also raises the question of how this potential is activated, and whether the specific mediality of videogames makes activation more difficult.

DOI: 10.4324/9781003538592-4

Narrative and ludic conventions, as well as the relationship between the narrative and ludic modes, can significantly complicate this question, as can be seen in the following example. In 2007, Clint Hocking coined the term "ludonarrative dissonance" in a blog post about *Bioshock* (2007): "*Bioshock* seems to suffer from a powerful dissonance between what it is about as a game, and what it is about as a story" (Hocking 2007, n.pag.). He goes on to advise that one should learn from the mistakes of *Bioshock* to "create a new generation of games that do manage to successfully marry their ludic and narrative themes into a consistent and fully realized whole" (Hocking 2007, n.pag.; see also the chapter by Backe in this volume). A year after that post, *Far Cry 2* (2008), the videogame Hocking worked on as game director, was released. And indeed, gameplay and narration in *Far Cry 2* are not opposed, as Hocking criticized in *Bioshock*. Instead, the gameplay is consistent with the narrative spiral of violence and is repeatedly interrupted by unpredictable and genre-untypical incidents. Gun jams, malaria seizures, opponents dying in agony or being revived by their comrades after being hit, and respawning enemies interrupt the player's intended actions and draw attention to the manner of ludic representation. By creating ludonarrative harmony—the ludic representation of violence is adapted to what it represents, namely, violence as messy and destructive—*Far Cry 2* departs from and exposes the ludonarrative dissonance typically found in shooters or action-adventure games, many of which present ludic virtual violence as harmless fun.[2] Werner Wolf describes this procedure of creating implicit metareference as "foregrounding through salient deviation" (2009, 47). This strategy is also possible in reverse, as shown in *Far Cry 3* (2012). Like its predecessor, *Far Cry 3* addresses the issue of ludonarrative dissonance and the legitimation of ludic virtual violence. Killing in *Far Cry 3* is part of an overall enjoyable gameplay process. This is paralleled by a storyworld in which killing is portrayed as a fun game for those who master it. Crucially, however, the videogame also clearly shows the cost as those who play the "killing game" become either insane or monsters. The represented process of killing is adjusted to the ludic process of the representation.

Using the examples of *Far Cry 2* and *Far Cry 3*, this chapter examines the criteria for determining the salience of metareference in videogames and shows the medium-specific obstacles for markers of implicit metareference. The simultaneity of two modes of representation (sign-based representation and process-based representation, which I will refer to as narrative and ludic representation) seems to require more, or more salient, deviations to mark metareference (see Backe 2016, 54–56). First, one mode of representation may draw attention to itself in such a way that deviations within the other mode are not noticed.[3] Second, there is usually a difference in the reliability of the representation of the two modes, which can lead to inconsistencies between ludic and narrative representation (see Thon 2015, 130–131). As this divergence is a common characteristic of many games, to varying degrees, it leads to the assumption that a high threshold must be exceeded before deviations or inconsistencies are perceived as markers of metareference.

The metacomment in both videogames is considered to be implicit, defined *ex negativo*, when it is not "made by the conventional, denotational meaning of a sign (configuration)" (Wolf 2009, 39). To identify an implicit metacomment, recipients must be made aware of the presence of a metalevel. An implicit metareferential statement must be recognizable and verifiable as a meaning-constituting device of the work, as Irina O. Rajewsky (2002, 61–65) states for the closely related phenomenon of intermediality. The marker is therefore an instruction or signal to read the sign configuration differently than usual, metareferentially:

> [M]arkers are requisite in order to ensure a metareferential reception. Such markers can vary in their obviousness and can range from devices that enhance the salience of foregrounded medial devices to the supplementary employment of explicit metareference in framing paratexts or in the vicinity of implicit elements.
>
> (Wolf 2009, 40–41)

The existence of metareference does not solely depend on the interpretive performance of the recipient, even where there are multiple plausible meanings of the metacomment. Wolf proposes to distinguish implicit metareference from non-metareferential elements on the grounds that the former is "essential" (2009, 48) to the understanding of a text. However, as Hans-Joachim Backe points out, this is problematic insofar as it seems to presuppose the existence of one "correct" (2016, 53) interpretation of a text. To nevertheless be able to take into account the obviousness of markers of implicit metareference, it seems useful to consider the extent to which they enable or hinder understanding. In his investigation of markers of intertextuality, Jörg Helbig states:

> The reader gets "stuck" on a marked text element, on a string of signs of higher complexity that forces increased, conscious attention during reception, so that the subconscious process of rearranging an individual horizon of knowledge that permanently accompanies reception is brought to consciousness by "disrupting" signals.
>
> (Helbig 1996, 65; my translation)

Following Helbig, I refer to a marker as a deictic sign whose signifier is an element that differs from most other elements it relates to in a syntagmatic or paradigmatic way, as it bears a feature that the unmarked elements do not bear. These features include, for example, positioning within the work, audiovisual emphasis, intermediality, or explicit metareferentiality. A marker of metareference points directly or indirectly to the chain of signs from which a metacomment is made. The marker itself may or may not be part of the metacomment. The dominant function of the marker is indexical, i.e., it directs the player's attention to the metalevel, even if the signifier and the signified each have different semiotic functions in addition (see Nöth 2009, 107; 2000, 186).

Since it is an instrument of communication control, the obviousness of markers can be related to the probability of communication failure (see Helbig 1996, 64–82). Jurij Lotman's (1977) concept of the artistic text is suitable for categorizing the basic types of failure of artistic communication along an axis of increasing activation of attention. Since videogames are not texts according to Lotman's definition of the artistic text (see Lotman 1977, 51–53; as well as Erdbeer 2015, 16), there is a danger of overlooking medium-specific aspects if Lotman's concept is used without reflection. This will be addressed in the following section through the use of systems theory, which is more appropriate for describing the relationship between the player and the videogame. Thus, the relationship between the player and the videogame itself can be examined as a possible cause of marker failure.[4]

Artistic Communication

With Lotman, an implicit metacomment can be described as a message encoded in an artistic language. In contrast to a natural language like English (a primary language), artistic language is characterized by deviations from the rules of the underlying primary language. By relating the deviations of the primary language to each other, a new overlapping structure is formed. This again, in relation to the natural language, results in the secondary, artistic language (see Lotman 1977, 20–49). In an English poem, the underlying primary language is English, but additional meaning is constituted by deviating from standard language syntax. This deviation in the selection and arrangement of words, such as in end rhymes, conveys artistic information, whereas the principle of end rhymes is part of artistic language. In this respect, the device of artistic language corresponds to the implicit metareference described above. Lotman distinguishes between the language of the sender (synthetic code) and that of the receiver (analytic code), both of which, in the case of natural language, are based on conventions. In the case of artistic communication, analytic and synthetic code always differ to a certain degree (see Lotman 1977, 295): "[T]he receiver must not only decipher a message with the help of a particular code, but must determine the 'language' in which the text is encoded" (Lotman 1977, 24). A misunderstanding of an artistically coded message occurs when (a) the recipient perceives the present work as non-artistic, i.e., deciphers the synthetically artistically coded message in an analytical conventional way, for example, when a satirical format is taken seriously; (b) when "[t]he receiver attempts to perceive the text according to familiar canons, but through trial and error is convinced of the necessity of creating a new code, one as yet unknown to him"[5] (Lotman 1977, 25), as in the example of Kharms's redheaded man (see note 1); or (c) when information is consumed by noise (see Lotman 1977, 75).[6] Noise can be caused by censorship, physical destruction, the lack of knowledge of the primary language, static noise in radio transmissions, physical limitations, technical malfunctions and limitations, etc. These misunderstandings result in the categories *marker perception failure*, *marker decoding failure*, and *noise-related marker failure*, to which phenomena of the videogames examined are assigned in the following section.

First, however, to take the procedural character of the videogame into account and to dissolve the metaphor of the transmission channel,[7] it is useful to refer to Niklas Luhmann's (1995, 2021) systems theory. Central to Luhmann's systems theory is the operational closure of systems. According to this, a system is created through a sequence of connectable operations. In a social system, communication can always be connected with communication. Everything that is not part of the system is the environment of the system and cannot be connected to its operations (see Luhmann 2021, 52). But operational closure does not exclude causal relationships (see Luhmann 2021, 65–66). Philipp Bojahr (2012), for instance, uses Luhmann's term "interpenetration" to describe the relation between videogame and player in his study of gaming disruptions in videogames. "[I]nterpenetration exists [. . .] when both systems enable each other by introducing their own already-constituted complexity into each other" (Luhmann 1995, 213). An example of interpenetration is the relation between psychic systems and social systems, neither of which could exist without the other. Whereby Luhmann emphasizes that "the interpenetrating systems remain environments for each other" (1995, 214). Interpenetration refers to the more general relation of player system and videogame system: There would be no videogames without players and vice versa. It is the precondition for the procedural utilization of both systems in the concrete act of gameplay, which can be described as "structural coupling" (see Jahraus 2012, 121; Luhmann 2021, 83–101; Maturana and Varela 1992, 95–99): Since systems are operationally closed, other systems can only causally affect the system through irritation, stimulation, disturbance, or "perturbation," to use the term coined by Humberto Maturana and Francisco Varela (1992, 97–99). This is made possible by excluding the majority of events in the environment. Only by reducing the complexity of the environment can an internal change of state be induced by some events in the environment (see Luhmann 2021, 86). This is due to the limited capacity of any system to respond to the entirety of its environment. Structural coupling occurs as long as two systems "act as mutual sources of perturbation, triggering changes of state" (Maturana and Varela 1992, 99).

Interpenetration is a special case of complexity reduction, as the complexity of a certain system within the environment is internalized (see Luhmann 1981, 157). Nightlife, for example, is conditioned by the constant availability of artificial light. The complexity of energy generation, the power grid, the production of light sources, etc. is internalized in nightlife and, to put it simply, reduced to the assumption that if you press the switch, the light comes on. The respective system forms expectations regarding the perturbations of the other system and has certain patterns according to which subsequent actions are possible (see Luhmann 2021, 86). Jürgen Fritz (2011) has described how these patterns are applied and adapted during gameplay, which I will discuss in more detail in the upcoming sections on marker perception failure and marker decoding failure. In contrast to Fritz and Bojahr, according to whom perturbations are those changes of state that interrupt the flow of gameplay, I will stick more closely to Maturana's and Varela's concept of perturbation and use it to describe any change of state in the videogame system that triggers a change of state in the player system and vice versa.

A marker of implicit metareference would therefore be a change of state within the videogame system to which the player cannot react "locally" or "quickly" via the highly selective patterns formed by interpenetration and structural coupling. Rather, such a perturbation requires the application of a broader pattern, the lower complexity reduction of which results in slower processing (see Luhmann 2021,

89–90). By applying this broader pattern, it is possible to react to changes of state in the videogame that have no counterparts within the specified patterns that are usually applied. The player takes a step back, so to speak, and observes themselves selecting events that they process as information during gameplay. This "zooming out" is equivalent to evoking medium awareness as a precondition for understanding a metacomment.

Noise-Related Marker Failure

Failure due to noise occurs when there is no perturbation in the player system. From the player's perspective, the marked element remains absent and therefore cannot direct their attention to the more complex chain of signs of the implicit metacomment.

Markers of implicit metareference can be found in *Far Cry 2*'s quest series regarding war correspondent Reuben Oluwagembi. Early in the videogame, Reuben asks the player to collect tape recordings of an interview between himself and the antagonist, the "Jackal." This side quest is in many ways a marker of the videogame's metareferential examination of the representation of violence in media, specifically in videogames. The constellation of characters creates an intermedial reference to *Apocalypse Now* (1979)—and by implication its source material, *Heart of Darkness* (Conrad 1902)—as the relationship between Reuben and the Jackal parallels that of the journalist (played by Dennis Hopper) and Colonel Kurtz (Marlon Brando) in the film. Even more striking is the content of these tapes, especially the first one, which records the Jackal as saying:

> You can't break a man the way you break a dog or a horse. The harder you beat a man, the taller he stands. To break a man's will, to break his spirit, you have to break his mind. Men have this idea that we can fight with dignity, that there is a proper way to kill someone. It's absurd. It's anaesthetic. We need it to endure the bloody horror of murder. You must destroy that idea. Show them what a messy, terrible thing it is to kill a man, and then show them that you relish in it. Shoot to wound, then execute the wounded. Burn them. Take them in close combat. Destroy their preconceptions of what a man is, and you become their personal monster. When they fear you, you become stronger, you become better. But let's never forget: It's a display. It's a posture, like a lion's roar or a gorilla thumping at his chest. If you lose yourself in the display, if you succumb to the horror, then you become the monster. You become reduced. Not more than a man, but less, and it can be fatal.

What seems like the half-mad ravings of a videogame villain is double coded, i.e., this passage can be read as a metareferential comment on *Far Cry 2*'s own game mechanics. This becomes particularly evident when considering the Jackal's comments in conjunction with the gameplay, which involves shooting, wounding, and executing enemies as well as burning them with flamethrowers or Molotov cocktails. Unlike other action videogames, *Far Cry 2* makes the player experience the messiness of combat by repeatedly interrupting the planned course of action through the mechanics of jamming and exploding weapons and malaria seizures. What is more, the videogame "represents through its mechanic of respawning enemies at guard posts that the civil war raging in the gameworld cannot be won by the player character" (Backe 2022, n.pag.). Killing is neither glorified on the narrative nor the ludic level; there is no noble way to kill and violence remains ultimately futile.

As evocative as this implicit metareference may be, it is also easily overlooked, which would result in a noise-related marker failure: During the scripted sequence while meeting Reuben, only the first two sentences of the tape are played before the recording stops. To hear the entire message, the player must switch to the menu and select the individual tapes (see Figure 4.1). The other tapes are hidden within the gameworld where they function as collectibles and can often only be found using a diegetic GPS device that starts beeping when the player is in the nearby area.

In *Far Cry 3*, there is a similar possibility of noise-related marker failure. Next to a gun shop in Badtown, which is the location for several story missions, sits a female NPC I will refer to as "Badtown woman." If the player moves close to the woman, two different monologues can be triggered. The first monologue consists of four phrases that refer to characters from *Far Cry* (2004) and *Far Cry 2*. The second monologue is only triggered when the player is pursuing special missions:

> Oh little puppet they painted you red, you're all red … they dipped you in a bucket and you drank all the paint… oh you don't drink the paint you naughty boy… you're a puppet, a puppet hollow inside… wood, glue… I can see your strings… white boy, dance […] little puppet dance for me, kill for me eh, show me your paint inside… I turn you inside out […] they don't want you to know it's a game to them… run, jump, kill, die, I kill them I eat them, I drink their blood […] we'll see who wins the fucking game.[8]

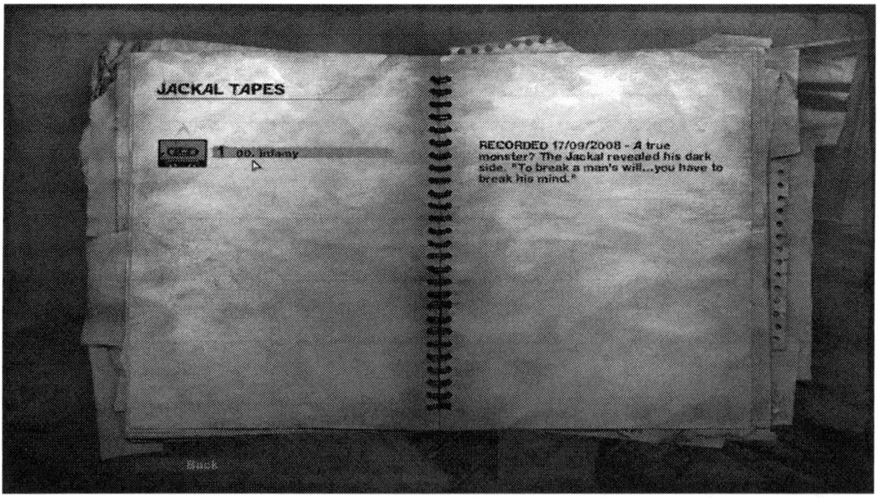

Figure 4.1 Access to the collected tapes via the menu in *Far Cry 2*.

This epistemological metalepsis (see Wolf 2007, 42; 2009, 52–53) contains the semantic metareferential lexemes "game" and "win" and refers to the ontological difference between avatar and player by designating Jason as a hollow, externally controlled puppet that runs, jumps, kills, and dies for the player's pleasure. The strategic positioning in a frequently visited part of the gameworld reduces, but does not rule out, the probability of noise-related marker failure, especially since the monologue is interrupted as soon as the player interacts with the NPC in the adjacent gun shop.

In these cases, a noise-related failure may occur due to a lower complexity reduction in the videogame, which makes the triggering of a marker contingent. "Complexity [...] means being forced to select; being forced to select means contingency; and contingency means risk" (Luhmann 1995, 25). Complexity requires countermeasures to reduce complexity, either by (partially) restricting the player through generalization—the player's inputs are treated indifferently during cutscenes or scripted events—or by creating redundancies: "A better solution is to simply accept that players will miss important signals. Then, instead of forcing them to absorb the one signal we have, we send that signal several times. Redundancy means that even if the player misses half of the content in the game [...], he still gets enough to understand the critical parts" (Sylvester 2013, 230; see also Lotman 1977, 23–24).

The increased complexity of the videogame at the level of technical requirements and production can also lead to noise-related marker failures in the form of bugs, glitches, or incompatibilities with the hardware (see also Bojahr 2012, 152–153). Due to a bug in *Far Cry 2*, it can happen that after collecting the tape about a boy stealing a corpse's boots, only this recording is played when further tapes are found. In the sense that art can transform noise into information, this might fulfill the function of a marker, since technical disturbances of the videogame refer to its nature as a technical artifact (see Lotman 1977, 75–77, as well as the chapter by Thon in this volume). Because a metacomment is marked several times, the bug that destroys the intended marker can itself be associated with further markers and generate medium awareness. Nonetheless, the medium-specific probability of actual bugs serving as markers is very low—as will be shown in the following sections—so the technical complexity of the videogame generally increases the probability of noise-related marker failure.

Marker Perception Failure

A marker perception failure occurs when an intended change of state by the videogame does not result in an adjustment of the player's pattern. The marker is not consumed by noise but falls victim to the player's complexity reduction. This happens automatically and is not perceived, just as the blind spot in the eye is not perceived (see Foerster 1985, 26–27). The impact of marker perception failure in the context of implicit metareference can be illustrated by another example:

During the search for the player character Jason's friends in *Far Cry 3*, the player receives information that one of them is with the NPC Dr. Earnhardt. To trigger the cutscene that introduces the mission, the player must enter Earnhardt's greenhouse. The following sequence begins with Jason's gaze being drawn to three bowls of

Figure 4.2 Dr. Earnhardt in *Far Cry 3.*

differently colored pills—introducing drugs as the main plausibility strategy in *Far Cry 3*. As he is about to reach for them, Dr. Earnhardt enters the scene, asking, "[s]ee anything you fancy? I like the red ones myself. The purples will give you a lift on a grey day. Everything is excellent, really," and adds after a brief reflection, "[o]h not the yellows, don't take them, they're liable to kill you. The mix is not quite right yet. Well, that said, Dr. Earnhardt here. Or, in and out, as the case may be." His appearance (see Figure 4.2) and behavior portray him as something in-between a mad doctor and a junkie.[9] When Jason asks for his friend, Earnhardt answers, "[h]a… I'm distilling a batch later today," assuming Jason to be "speaking in code." Once this misunderstanding is cleared up, Earnhardt instructs Jason to gather cave mushrooms for his friend's medical treatment. As an instruction on where to find them, he says, "[p]eruse the cliffs to the west." Once the cutscene has been completed, the mission "Mushrooms in the Deep" and its description "Find an entrance to the cave" are displayed on the HUD. Two flashing icons, one on the minimap and one in the three-dimensional gameworld, point to the corresponding location. Contrary to Earnhardt's instructions, the icons mark a location north of the Doctor's house (see A in Figure 4.3). Approaching the marked spot, Jason acknowledges this: "These cliffs aren't west." And before even seeing the entrance he resignedly states, "[g]reat. He didn't mention the cave was underwater." A few climbing passages follow, which turn into a drug-induced hallucination.[10] Finally, Jason reaches the cave mushrooms he is looking for and returns to Earnhardt. Due to the level design, the only way the player can leave the cave is through a different opening than the one they entered. This second cave opening is indeed located near the western cliffs, as Earnhardt described: Had the player followed the narratorial quest description, or so the videogame suggests,[11] they would have had an easier time since a short path from the western cliffs (see B in Figure 4.3) would have led them to the cave and the location of the mushrooms.

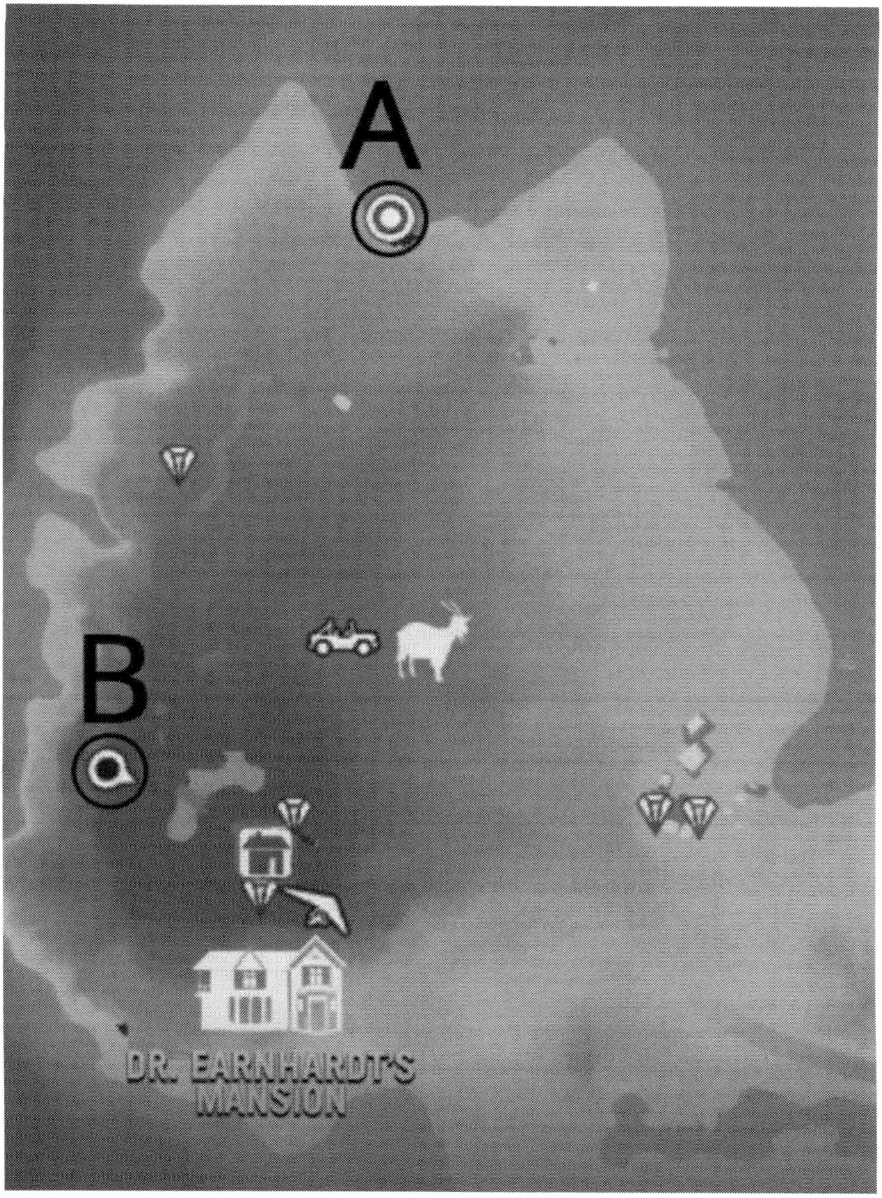

Figure 4.3 Location of the "Mushrooms in the Deep" mission according to the HUD (A) and the narrative mission description (B) on the map in *Far Cry 3*.

In this mission, the videogame demonstrates how the player's knowledge and goals "overwrite" the avatar's knowledge and goals. This emphasizes the avatar's function as a tool; a means for the player to achieve the ludic goals (see Nöth et al. 2008,

154–160). In particular, it draws attention to the consequences for the avatar as part of the storyworld: Appropriate behavior within the storyworld would seemingly have spared Jason cave dives, risky jumps, and hallucinations, all of which are potentially life-threatening. This passage can in itself be read as an implicit metacomment. In addition, it also reinforces the metacomment that weaves through the entire videogame.

Critical to the perception of this small-scale metacomment, and thus its perception as a marker of the large-scale metacomment, are both the perception of the contradiction of the extradiegetic (ludic) element of the mission marker and the diegetic element of the narratorial mission description, and the perception that the ludic overlay has misled the player. Players must recognize that Dr. Earnhardt's description was correct and the mission marker was unreliable; that there was no plausible reason within the storyworld for Jason to suspect the underwater entrance to the cave in the north. Although the focus on the game goals to the neglect of the storyworld is criticized here, this can easily be overlooked for the same reason.[12] The probability that this marker is not noticed by the player may be due to the principle of charity (see Walton 1990, 183; Thon 2016, 61), as inconsistencies between the ludic and narrative presentation are the rule rather than the exception. The convention that not all ludic elements reliably represent the storyworld allows the player to ignore such inconsistencies (see Thon 2015, 126–138). Unlike inconsistencies in other media, inconsistencies in videogames cannot be assumed to be intentional unnatural phenomena (see Alber 2016, 46). Such inconsistencies are thus incorporated into the experienced player's pattern and are automatically and unconsciously filtered out as unimportant (see Fritz 2011, 128).

Yet, the possibility of failure for this type of marker is not only due to the player's knowledge of the medium but also due to the affordances of the medium. The videogame must be played to continue. When the player is in a "ludic mode of reception" (Fahlenbrach and Schröter 2015, 177), their attention is limited to those elements that are relevant to continue the videogame. "The forms of structural coupling thus limit the perception of the stimuli offered by the videogame and at the same time make it easier for the player to receive the specific influences and to 'adjust' to them" (Fritz 2011, 26; my translation). In cognitive science, the failure to detect something unexpected when attention is focused on something else is known as inattentional blindness (see Levin and Baker 2015; Mack and Rock 1998; as well as Baumbach 2019). The type of the task being attended to and the context in which it occurs are critical. While it is easy to be distracted by non-task-related stimuli when the task has low perceptual load, they are more effectively filtered out when the perceptual load is high (see Lavie et al. 2004; Lavie 2010). This is due to a limited attentional capacity (see Eriksen and Eriksen 1974). "[W]hen the target task is easy, spare attentional resources 'spill over' to the distractor [...]. As the target task becomes more difficult, fewer attentional resources remain to process the extraneous distractor" (Green and Bavelier 2003, 534).[13] The other major influence on perception is the situation in which the perceiver finds themselves, as it determines how much divided attention is paid to potential threats or obstacles to the task. Task-irrelevant stimuli, even if salient, are more likely to be faded out when the situation requires divided attention (see Foulsham 2015).[14] Action videogames put

> a load on divided attention, requiring the player at all times to monitor different parts of the screen as well as shifting their attention between different features of the scene such as when looking for a sniper versus searching for an active killer bot. Combined with such a load on divided attention, is the need to switch attentional mode on demand as the game requires to shift from visual search mode to engaging in a highly focused, aiming mode during fighting. [...] Last but not least, action video games put a heavy load on pacing or the need to execute actions or take decisions under tight time constraints.
>
> (Nguyen and Bavelier 2023, 12)

This explains the necessity and convention of encouraging a narrative mode of reception by restricting the player's freedom of movement and action through cutscenes or scripted events (see Fahlenbrach and Schröter 2015, 181–183). Reducing the complexity of the videogame reduces contingency by excluding perturbations of the player and thereby simplifies the player's selection process: The player has more attentional capacity available to process the narrative stimuli, since no primary ludic task requires their selective attention and they do not have to keep an eye on potentially ludically relevant stimuli, such as threats or advantages of the game goals, with their divided attention.[15] The structural coupling is therefore loosened by the videogame.

In the case of the "Mushroom in the Deep" mission, the selection of relevant stimuli, i.e., complexity management, is up to the player. Back in the ludic mode of perception, most players will not consciously choose between the narrative information and the information provided by the HUD, and then select the latter, easier one. Instead, they automatically ignore the former.[16] The player is then likely to take Jason's remarks not as an indication of this inconsistency, but as a further indication of Dr. Earnhardt's unreliability as a source of information, which is entirely consistent with the storyworld. This interpretation is further supported by Jason's remark inside the cave: "This crazy doctor better know what he's doing." On the surface, the construction of Earnhardt's mental illness is used to make Jason's risky mushroom hunt plausible (see Görgen and Simond 2020, 410). Jason's irritation is limited to the storyworld and does not extend to the player. Both the videogame's affordances, which require player selection, and the knowledge of the limitations of the videogame, which automates this selection as a pattern, result in an increased medium-specific potential for marker perception failure. This potential increases as the marker's features become less relevant to the task.

Marker Decoding Failure

Once the player has noticed a marker, they must match it to the corresponding code. Unlike in the case of a marker perception failure, the marker has caught the player's attention and caused them to "stumble." A marker decoding failure occurs when the player cannot react to the perturbation by the marker by automatically applying a pattern and instead shifts to an alternative pattern that does not account for metareferentiality. In a conscious process "through trial and error [the player] is convinced of the necessity of creating a new code" (Lotman 1977, 25).

Let's take another look at the Badtown woman in *Far Cry 3*. Her more often-used phrases, which refer to characters from the first two titles in the *Far Cry* series, are unlikely to fail due to noise and have the potential to catch the player's attention. Her contradictory statements in the surface meaning of signs are very likely to be recognized by the player.

> What about me, a war journist [sic], looking for a story to redeem me after I ... I exaggerated the truth …
>
> No! I was a smuggler and a ship captain trapped here after the Jackal sold me out!
>
> My name is Jackie, I am a weapons dealer … Nobody believes me, but they blow up my boat. But I survived!
>
> Shut up! They killed my husband, I was a doctor before they threw me in a stinking cell!

These contradictions can easily be attributed to intradiegetic phenomena. Without knowledge about the alluded characters in *Far Cry* and *Far Cry 2*, it is very likely that the Badtown woman's statements will be explained by her mental health. Unlike Dr. Earnhardt, however, she is not already framed as "crazy," which is why in this case a marker decoding failure is more likely than a marker perception failure.[17] Even if the references are recognized, they have little potential for irritation if the individual parts of the *Far Cry* series are located in a coherent storyworld.[18] In this case, a media consciousness is awakened for a brief moment, which is naturalized again with the knowledge that a unified world is represented beyond the scope of one part of the series, i.e., the irritation is read heteroreferentially. Remaining discrepancies can be explained by diegetic mental illness as above.[19]

The intuitively more obvious marker—the metalepsis in the puppet monologue of the Badtown woman—can also fall victim to marker decoding failure since the semantic metareferential lexemes "game" and "win" are already naturalized in advance. In my experience, this second monologue is only triggered when the mission from CIA spy Willis, whose hut is in close proximity to the Badtown woman, is active. At the first opportunity to hear this monologue, the player has already witnessed several instances of metaphorical use of said semantic metareferential lexemes. In order to observe Willis unnoticed before he talks to him, Jason plays poker in the Badtown pub. During the poker game, Jason's fellow players talk about the events of the first mission, in which Jason was able to escape the villain, Vaas. When the conversation turns to the appearance of the fugitive, Jason interrupts and goes all in. Noticing this, Willis, who was standing at the bar, walks over and comments: "Nice play." In the following conversation with Willis, which leads to the first mission given by him, the exchange of favors is described as a "game": "I can help you, but you gotta play the game. There's something I'm looking for. We'll trade favors." Leaving Willis's hut, Jason echoes this view of his dealings with Willis: "I'll play ball as long as it gets me closer to finding my friends." This metaphor is further developed when Jason subsequently makes a phone call to get information about Hoyt, who was mentioned by Willis: "Hoyt Volker. Stay away from him, Jason. You think Vaas is crazy. All the evil on the island, it comes from Hoyt. He took Vaas's mind away from him, it is he who pulls the strings." While the extensive use of game metaphors throughout the videogame is itself a marker of metareference, in this case, it provides a heteroreferential explanation for the epistemological metalepsis, which increases the probability of marker decoding failure. If the previously established code has been internalized, the monologue of the Badtown woman can be deciphered heteroreferentially as follows: Jason is the puppet in a game Willis is playing against Hoyt.

A central metareferential device of *Far Cry 3* is to set player and avatar in relation to each other; Jason's intradiegetic motivation mirrors the player's extradiegetic motivation. Thus, the intradiegetic negotiation of the legitimization and the joy of killing can be metareferentially related to videogames. This device is narrowed down in the monologue of the Badtown woman and marks the existence of a metalevel. But without reference to the concrete gaming situation, the hardware or software of the videogame,[20] markings through *mise en abyme* and metareferential lexemes are likely to be decoded heteroreferentially (see Backe 2016, 65).

As with the puppet monologue and the unreliable mission marker, *Far Cry 3* seems to make repeated offers to naturalize markers. This even applies to the most prominent markers in the videogame. Vaas's famous monologue about the "definition of insanity," while certainly readable as a (meta)reference to repetition as a basic aspect of the videogame, can also be interpreted as a (hetero) reference to Vaas's repeated efforts to kill Jason. The same goes for the tutorial, in which Jason's brother Grant is introduced in the tradition of the stereotypical action hero but is then shot so that the inexperienced Jason must take his role. This marker is supported by the previous break with the player's expectations when the supposed intro video turns out to be a diegetic vacation video on Jason's smartphone. However, the tutorial does not break with ludic expectations: The player, who takes the role of Jason, is unlikely to expect to remain a passive sidekick watching Grant's heroics for long. These kinds of marker decoding failures due to naturalization are not a medium-specific phenomenon.

> Most readers will do whatever they can to salvage a world in which they can achieve some degree of immersion, because make-believe, the mental game responsible for this experience, corresponds to a fundamental need of the human mind and is simply more pleasurable than the game of pure self-reflexivity.
>
> (Ryan 2022, 161)

The marker decoding failures due to the principle of charity, and hence the increased potential for these kinds of failures to occur in the first place, are more clearly medium-specific. What happens automatically in the case of marker perception failures happens consciously in the case of marker decoding failures. The player "stumbles" over inconsistencies but explains them in terms of production conditions or attributes them to the fact that videogames do not always integrate ludic elements in the diegesis. The frustrating gameplay in *Far Cry 2* is hard to ignore. At the very least, when the first jamming weapon or malaria seizure in a firefight leads to a game over, the player has to consciously deal with these limitations. They can do this, at least in part, by adjusting their pattern, i.e., not using weapons dropped by enemies, replacing weapons as soon as they get dirty, and improving their durability as soon as possible. The necessity of a problem-oriented adaptation of the player's pattern is a characteristic of playful challenge. Unexpected challenges are therefore always self-referential, since the previous approach must be reflected upon (see Fritz 2011, 79–85). A marker of implicit metareference via a disruption or variation of the gameplay must therefore be very pronounced in order not to be read self-referentially as an increasing level of difficulty.

In the vast majority of (video)games, gameplay is not purely self-referential, but refers heteroreferentially to other processes, establishing a second level of signification (see Backe 2016, 54–56; Bogost 2007, 14). In this sense, the difficulty itself, i.e., the need to adjust the player's pattern, can be a "rhetorical tool" (Frasca 2003, 228) that makes the difficulties of the represented process experienceable.[21] A sufficient adaptation of the pattern in *Far Cry 2* with regard to the gameplay is hardly possible, as although the probability of disruptions can be reduced, they still remain unpredictable. From a purely ludic perspective, they must be considered unfair, or at least unpredictable. Rather than consider this unpredictability as part of the representation of combat, it can also be externally explained by poor game design.

This leads back to the difficulties Wolf mentioned in deciding when a salient deviation is salient enough to qualify as implicitly metareferential (see 2009, 47). The unpredictability of the gameplay in *Far Cry 2* is part of the comment formulated on a metalevel, but it can also be read heteroreferentially (as particularly realistic) and self-referentially (as particularly challenging). It is worth noting that in *Far Cry 2*, gameplay is both an element of the metareferential second-order statement and a marker of metareference. By interrupting the flow of the gameplay, "the salience of foregrounded medial devices" (Wolf 2009, 40–41) is enhanced. But, as already discussed, once this marker has attracted the player's attention, it can be explained internally or externally. A higher medium-specific probability of marker decoding failure is less due to the fact that disruptions or deviations in the ludic process (as well as the narrative contradictions mentioned above) can be read heteroreferentially, as this is a transmedial phenomenon, but rather that they are understood self-referentially, as a playful challenge.

Even markers via inter- and intramedial references or metalepsis can be understood as Easter eggs, i.e., a playful challenge that has already been overcome by recognizing them. Regarding the popularity of *Apocalypse Now* and *Star Wars* (1977), it is very unlikely that the player will not recognize the references in *Far Cry 3* when Jason advises his younger brother to "use the force" when flying a helicopter under heavy fire while Wagner's *Ride of the Valkyries* is playing. But rather than take these references as an instruction to reconstruct a (metareferential) meaning of the videogame against the foil of these films (see Helbig 1996, 149), these markers can easily be understood as a mere "tongue-in-cheek play with the knowing-recognizing" (Helbig 1996, 219; my translation) player.[22] The same applies to other markers of metareferentiality. The references can be recognized but remain "below the threshold of (intended) triggering of reflections centered on the medium itself" (Wolf 2007, 33; my translation). That this potential for marker decoding failure in videogames is conventionally high can also be deduced from the fact that previous game studies approaches consider metareference in videogames to have a primarily entertaining function without "a claim to 'deep meaning'" (Jannidis 2009, 557; see also Rapp 2008).

Conclusion

The possibilities of referring to specific player input and of representing processes through processes expand the repertoire of metareferential devices in videogames compared to other media. In particular, implicit metareferences benefit from direct player involvement, as this allows conscious decisions and the resulting actions to become part of the metareference, in addition to passive reception. *Far Cry 2* and *Far Cry 3* do not explicitly tell us about the problems that arise from a ludonarrative dissonant representation of violence, but they do make it possible to experience these problems through play. However, the technical and semiotic complexity of videogames, which enables this medium-specific metareferential potential in the first place, also makes it more difficult to activate. This was shown by the examples taken from both games, which indicate an increased medium-specific potential for marker failure of implicit metareference. Noise-related failures can be caused by a low level of complexity reduction on the part of the videogame, if redundancy is not used to ensure that the player does not unconsciously skip markers. Furthermore, the intricate production of videogames and specific hardware and software requirements are a significant source of bugs that can cause markers to fall victim. Marker perception failures and marker decoding failures are usually caused by an overly high reduction in complexity on the part of the player and emerge from the causes of noise-related marker failures, both through interpenetration (in the sense of a medium-specific principle of charity) and through structural coupling, i.e., the process of gameplay, in the sense of attentional control.

Based on the examples, no increased probability of heteroreferential reading of markers could be derived. In contrast to *Far Cry 2*, it became apparent that the markers in *Far Cry 3* were mainly realized via the narrative representation, while at the same time the videogame offered ample cues with the help of which these markers can be naturalized. The examined markers in *Far Cry 3* are less salient in the sense that they can easily be overlooked, as they do not occur via the ludic representation, i.e., they do not interrupt the gameplay, and even if they are perceived, they can be read heteroreferentially. Since action videogames require a strong reduction of complexity from the player during the ludic representation, they are particularly suitable for illustrating the decrease in marker salience through an additional level of signification. However, for a further investigation of medium-specific markers of metareference and mechanisms to avoid marker failures, it seems reasonable to also examine metareferential walking simulators and adventure games, since their reduction of ludic representation is already a genre-specific countermeasure.

Notes

1 For example, a short text by Daniil Kharms implicitly refers to the way storyworlds are constructed in the reader's mind by specifying a redheaded man through deviations until there is nothing left of him. Evidence of the effectiveness of this implicit metareference can be seen in the use of Kharms's text to emphasize the theoretical explanations of this topic (see Martínez and Scheffel 2012, 133). "There was a redheaded man who had no eyes or ears. He didn't have hair either, so he was called a redhead arbitrarily. He couldn't talk because he had no mouth. He didn't have a nose either. He didn't even have arms or legs. He had no stomach, he had no back, no spine, and he didn't have any insides at all. There was nothing! So, we don't even know who we're talking about. We'd better not talk about him any more" (Kharms 2009, 45).

2 For an examination of the pleasure of ludic virtual violence see also Bareither 2016; Hartmann 2017.

3 In general, the significance that Helbig ascribes to markers through code changes seems to be weakened in multimodal media if it only affects one information channel (see Hübschmann 2022, note 17; Helbig 1996, 117).

4 Metareferential statements are usually marked in several ways, as is the case with *Far Cry 2* and *Far Cry 3*. The aim of this chapter is not to examine all markers, but to explore the ways in which some fail in order to draw conclusions about the medium-specific causes of these failures.

5 A certain overlap of the codes, e.g. the underlying natural language, is a basic condition for understanding (see Lotman 1977, 25).

6 Although Lotman ascribes to art the ability to transform noise in the transmission channel into information, an artistic message is not immune to noise.

7 The transmission model assumes that a piece of knowledge is being transmitted from the sender to the receiver. The sender receives what was not there before. However, this implies that an observer would have to know what was in the mind of the receiver before and after receiving this piece of knowledge (see Luhmann 2021, 214).

8 There are no subtitles available for the Badtown woman monologues.

9 Arno Görgen and Stefan Simond have called this type of construction of mental illness "somatic externalization" (2020, 420–422), which mainly refers to pop-cultural interpretations of mental illness.

10 The ontological status of this passage is clearly marked by a priori contextual content markers (mushrooms releasing spores, Jason's cough) and simultaneous representational and content markers (blurred image, physical impossibilities); on the representation of subjectivity, see also Thon 2016, 265–326.

11 In fact, the quest cannot be completed this way. While the location can be reached by going west and using the second entrance, the mushrooms are missing as an interactable object unless the player takes the more complicated route. The videogame thus in fact forces the player to take the route that runs counter to Earnhardt's description to complete the mission.

12 Like hidden clues in detective stories, but without the final denouement that draws "attention to attention and its limitations" (Baumbach 2019, 43; see also Emmott et al. 2013).

13 The term high perceptual load should not be confused with a high cognitive load. In contrast, attention can easily be diverted by extraneous distractors in tasks that require in-depth thinking (high cognitive load).

14 This phenomenon can be observed in Let's Play videos, where viewers may notice something that the player does not.
15 This is also the basic principle of walking simulators, which enable a narrative mode of reception by permanently restricting the player's actions.
16 Players who regularly play action videogames have enhanced attentional control, which makes it easier to perform simple cognitive tasks with a high perceptual load and to automatically fade out task-irrelevant distractions (see Bavelier and Föcker 2015; Föcker et al. 2018; Green and Bavelier 2003; Nguyen and Bavelier 2023).
17 The use of stereotypical representations of mental illness emphasizes the NPC's deviance from the player as a rational observer. This results in highly problematic strategies of othering and instrumentalizing mental illness to make hostile or disruptive encounters with these NPCs plausible (see Görgen and Simond 2020, 418–420; see also Görgen 2018).
18 The reappearance of characters such as Willis and Hurk reinforces this assumption in the subsequent parts.
19 An example of this is the Reddit post "Crazy Woman in Badtown Big Theory," written by an anonymous user (see Anonymous 2021).
20 For examples of this type of explicit marker, see Erdbeer 2018, 89–90; Krampe 2021, 194–197.
21 On a small scale, *Stray* (2022) does this when the inverted controls refer to the difficulties the animal avatar has navigating with a cardboard box on its head. On a larger scale, both *Star Wars Jedi Knight: Mysteries of the Sith* (1998) and *Hellblade: Senua's Sacrifice* (2017) meaningfully vary their mechanics in the final battle to allow the player to experience the protagonists' process of realization: Both videogames can only be completed when the player stops fighting (see also the discussion of *God of War 3* in the chapter by Hennig in this volume).
22 *Far Cry 3* contains a multitude of intermedial references, realized in quite diverse ways. The *Star Wars* quote refers to the success of the sci-fi classic in providing an entertaining cinematic representation of war after the Vietnam War (see Holert and Terkessidis 2002, 103).

Works Cited

Alber, Jan. 2016. *Unnatural Narrative: Impossible Worlds in Fiction and Drama.* Lincoln: University of Nebraska Press.

Anonymous. 2021. "Crazy Woman in Badtown Big Theory." *Reddit*, June 16, 2021. www.reddit.com/r/farcry/comments/o19ye5/crazy_woman_in_badtown_big_theory/.

Apocalypse Now. 1979. Director Francis Ford Coppola. USA: Omni Zoetrope.

Backe, Hans-Joachim. 2016. "Spiel im Spiel – im (Computer-)Spiel." In *Vergleichen an der Grenze: Beiträge zu Manfred Schmelings komparatistischen Forschungen*, edited by Hans-Joachim Backe, Claudia Schmitt, and Christiane Solte-Gresser, 37–74. Würzburg: Königshausen & Neumann.

Backe, Hans-Joachim. 2022. "*"Deathloop"*: The Meta(modern) Immersive Simulation Game." *Game Studies: The International Journal of Computer Game Research* 22 (2): n.pag.

Bareither, Christoph. 2016. *Gewalt im Computerspiel: Facetten eines Vergnügens.* Bielefeld: transcript.

Baumbach, Sibylle. 2019. "Mind the Narratives: Toward a Cultural Narratology of Attention." In *Narrative in Culture*, edited by Astrid Erll and Roy Sommer, 37–56. Berlin: De Gruyter.

Bavelier, Daphne, and Julia Föcker. 2015. "Action Video Games in the Spotlight: The Case of Attentional Control." In *The Handbook of Attention*, edited by Jonathan Fawcett, Evan Risko, and Alan Kingstone, 525–546. Cambridge, MA: MIT Press.

BioShock. 2007. 2K Boston/2K Games. Microsoft Windows.

Bogost, Ian. 2007. *Persuasive Games: The Expressive Power of Videogames*. Cambridge, MA: MIT Press.

Bojahr, Philipp. 2012. "Störungen des Computerspielens." In *Theorien des Computerspiels zur Einführung*, edited by Gamescoop, 147–178. Hamburg: Junius.

Conrad, Joseph. 1902. *Heart of Darkness*. Edinburgh: William Blackwood.

Emmott, Catherine, Anthony J. Sanford, and Marc Alexander. 2013. "Rhetorical Control of Readers' Attention: Psychological and Stylistic Perspectives on Foreground and Background in Narrative." In *Stories and Minds: Cognitive Approaches to Literary Narrative*, edited by Lars Bernaerts, Dirk de Geest, Luc Herman, and Bart Vervaeck, 39–57. Lincoln: University of Nebraska Press.

Erdbeer, Robert Matthias. 2015. "Poetik der Modelle." *Textpraxis* 11 (2): n.pag.

Erdbeer, Robert Matthias. 2018. "On the Verge of the Game: Shared Narrative and Playability." In *The Parahuman: Grace and Gravity*, edited by Kamelia Spasova, Darin Tenev, and Maria Kalinova, 79–115. Sofia: St. Kliment Ohridski University Press.

Eriksen, Barbara, and Charles W. Eriksen. 1974. "Effects of Noise Letters upon the Identification of a Target Letter in a Nonsearch Task." *Perception & Psychophysics* 16 (1): 143–149.

Fahlenbrach, Kathrin, and Felix Schröter. 2015. "Game Studies und Rezeptionsästhetik." In *Game Studies: Aktuelle Ansätze der Computerspielforschung*, edited by Klaus Sachs-Hombach and Jan-Noël Thon, 165–208. Cologne: Halem.

Far Cry. 2004. Crytek Studios/Ubisoft. Microsoft Windows.

Far Cry 2. 2008. Ubisoft Montreal/Ubisoft. Microsoft Windows.

Far Cry 3. 2012. Ubisoft Montreal/Ubisoft. Microsoft Windows.

Föcker, Julia, Daniel Cole, Anton L. Beer, and Daphne Bavelier. 2018. "Neural Bases of Enhanced Attentional Control: Lessons from Action Video Game Players." *Brain and Behavior* 8 (7): 1–18.

Foerster, Heinz von. 1985. "Über das Konstruieren von Wirklichkeiten." In *Sicht und Einsicht: Versuche zu einer operativen Erkenntnistheorie*, edited and translated by Wolfram K. Köck, 25–42. Wiesbaden: Springer.

Foulsham, Tom. 2015. "Scene Perception." In *The Handbook of Attention*, edited by Jonathan Fawcett, Evan Risko, and Alan Kingstone, 257–280. Cambridge, MA: MIT Press.

Frasca, Gonzalo. 2003. "Simulation versus Narrative: Introduction to Ludology." In *The Video Game Theory Reader*, edited by Mark J.P. Wolf and Bernard Perron, 221–236. New York: Routledge.

Fritz, Jürgen. 2011. *Wie Computerspieler ins Spiel kommen: Theorien und Modelle zur Nutzung und Wirkung virtueller Spielwelten*. Berlin: Vistas.

Görgen, Arno. 2018. "Die Vulnerabilität des Anderen: Marginalisierungen des Non-Playable Characters in digitalen Spielen." In *Digitale Spiele: Interdisziplinäre Perspektiven zu Diskursfeldern, Inszenierung und Musik*, edited by Borchert Hust, 73–88. Bielefeld: transcript.

Görgen, Arno, and Stefan Simond. 2020. "Mental Health als Authentizitätsfiktion im digitalen Spiel." In *Spielzeichen III: Kulturen im Computerspiel/Kulturen des* Computerspiels, edited by Martin Hennig and Hans Krah, 406–434. Glückstadt: Verlag Werner Hülsbusch.

Green, C. Shawn, and Daphne Bavelier. 2003. "Action Video Game Modifies Visual Selective Attention." *Nature* 423: 534–537.

Hartmann, Tilo. 2017. "The 'Moral Disengagement in Violent Videogames' Model." *Game Studies: The International Journal of Computer Game Research* 17 (2): n.pag.

Helbig, Jörg. 1996. *Intertextualität und Markierung: Untersuchungen zur Systematik und Funktion der Signalisierung von Intertextualität.* Heidelberg: Winter.

Hellblade: Senua's Sacrifice. 2017. Ninja Theory. Microsoft Windows.

Hill, Charles A. 2004. "The Psychology of Rhetoric Images." In *Defining Visual Rhetorics*, edited by Charles A. Hill, 25–40. Mahwah, NJ: Lawrence Erlbaum Associates.

Hocking, Clint. 2007. "Ludonarrative Dissonance in Bioshock." *Click Nothing*, October 7, 2007. https://clicknothing.typepad.com/click_nothing/2007/10/ludonarrative-d.html.

Holert, Tom, and Mark Terkessidis. 2002. *Entsichert: Krieg als Massenkultur im 21. Jahrhundert*. Cologne: Kiepenheuer & Witsch.

Hübschmann, Dominik. 2022. "'My Imagination Is as Real as My Body:' Realitätssystemische Unsicherheit in *What Remains of Edith Finch*." *Paidia* (Special Issue "Phantastik im/und Computerspiel"): n.pag.

Jahraus, Oliver. 2012. "Strukturelle Kopplung." In *Luhmann-Handbuch*, edited by Oliver Jahraus, Armin Nassehi, Mario Grizelj, Irmhild Saake, Christian Kirchmeier, and Julian Müller, 121–122. Stuttgart: Metzler.

Jannidis, Fotis. 2009. "Metareference in Computer Games." In *Metareference across Media: Theory and Case Studies*, edited by Werner Wolf, 543–565. Amsterdam: Rodopi.

Kharms, Daniil. 2009. "Blue Notebook #10." In *Today I Wrote Nothing: The Selected Writings of Daniil Kharms*, edited and translated by Matvei Yankelevich, 45. New York: Overlook Duckworth.

Krampe, Theresa. 2021. "The World Machine: Self-Reflexive Worldbuilding in *OneShot*." In *Game | World | Architectonics: Transdisciplinary Approaches on Structures and Mechanics, Levels and Spaces, Aesthetics and Perception*, edited by Marc Bonner, 187–200. Heidelberg: Heidelberg University Publishing.

Lavie, Nilli. 2010. "Attention, Distraction, and Cognitive Control Under Load." *Curr Dir Psychol Sci* 19 (3): 143–148.

Lavie, Nilli, Aleksandra Hirst, Jan W. de Fockert, and Essi Viding. 2004. "Load Theory of Selective Attention and Cognitive Control." *Journal of Experimental Psychology. General* 133 (3): 339–354.

Levin, Daniel, and Lewis Baker. 2015. "Change Blindness and Inattentional Blindness." In *The Handbook of Attention*, edited by Jonathan Fawcett, Evan Risko, and Alan Kingstone, 199–231. Cambridge, MA: MIT Press.

Lotman, Jurij. 1977. *The Structure of the Artistic Text.* Ann Arbor: University of Michigan Press.

Luhmann, Niklas. 1981. "Interpenetration: Zum Verhältnis personaler und sozialer Systeme." In *Soziologische Aufklärung 3: Soziales System, Gesellschaft, Organisation*, edited by Niklas Luhmann, 151–170. Wiesbaden: VS Verlag für Sozialwissenschaften.

Luhmann, Niklas. 1995. *Social Systems.* Stanford: Stanford University Press.

Luhmann, Niklas. 2021. *Introduction to Systems Theory*, edited by Dirk Baecker. Cambridge, UK: Polity.

Mack, Arien, and Irvin Rock. 1998. *Inattentional Blindness.* Cambridge, MA: MIT Press.

Martínez, Matías, and Michael Scheffel. 2012. *Einführung in die Erzähltheorie.* Munich: C. H. Beck.

Maturana, Humberto, and Francisco Varela. 1992. *The Tree of Knowledge: The Biological Roots of Human Understanding.* Boston: Shambhala.

Nguyen, Arthur, and Daphne Bavelier. 2023. "Play in Video Games." *Neuroscience and Biobehavioral Reviews* 153: n.pag.

Nöth, Winfried, Nina Bishara, and Britta Neitzel. 2008. *Mediale Selbstreferenz: Grundlagen und Fallstudien zu Werbung, Computerspiel und den Comics.* Cologne: Halem.

Nöth, Winfried. 2000. *Handbuch der Semiotik*. Stuttgart: Metzler.

Nöth, Winfried. 2009. "Metareference from a Semiotic Perspective." In *Metareference across Media: Theory and Case Studies*, edited by Werner Wolf, 89–120. Amsterdam: Rodopi.

Rajewsky, Irina O. 2002. *Intermedialität.* Tübingen: Francke.

Rapp, Bernhard. 2008. *Selbstreflexivität im Computerspiel*. Boizenburg: Verlag Werner Hülsbusch.

Ryan, Marie-Laure. 2022. *A New Anatomy of Storyworlds: What Is, What If, As If.* Columbus: Ohio State University Press.

Star Wars. 1977. Director George Lucas. USA: Lucasfilm Ltd.

Star Wars Jedi Knight: Mysteries of the Sith. 1998. LucasArts. Microsoft Windows.

Stray. 2022. BlueTwelve Studio/Annapurna Interactive. Microsoft Windows.

Sylvester, Tynan. 2013. *Designing Games: A Guide to Engineering Experiences.* Beijing: O'Reilly.

Thon, Jan-Noël. 2015. "Game Studies und Narratologie." In *Game Studies: Aktuelle Ansätze der Computerspielforschung*, edited by Klaus Sachs-Hombach and Jan-Noël Thon, 104–164. Cologne: Halem.

Thon, Jan-Noël. 2016. *Transmedial Narratology and Contemporary Media Culture.* Lincoln: University of Nebraska Press.

Walton, Kendall L. 1990. *Mimesis as Make-Believe: On the Foundations of the Representational Arts*. Cambridge, MA: Harvard University Press.

Wolf, Werner. 2007. "Metaisierung als transgenerisches und transmediales Phänomen: Ein Systematisierungsversuch metareferentieller Formen und Begriffe in Literatur und anderen Medien." In *Metaisierung in Literatur und anderen Medien: Theoretische Grundlagen, Historische Perspektiven, Metagattungen, Funktionen*, edited by Janine Hauthal, 25–64. Berlin: De Gruyter.

Wolf, Werner. 2009. "Metareference across Media: The Concept, Its Transmedial Potentials and Problems, Main Forms and Functions." In *Metareference across Media: Theory and Case Studies*, edited by Werner Wolf, 1–85. Amsterdam: Rodopi.

5 No Longer Safe Before the Screen?

Game-Transcending Metareference in Indie Horror Games

Theresa Krampe

Currently, a new and medium-specific form of metareference is taking shape in videogames. This form, which I propose to call "game-transcending metareference," is characterized by a genuine ontological metalepsis between the videogame and what is outside it. Indie horror games, in particular, can be observed to manipulate the real computer's operating system or involve the player in a kind of alternate reality game that takes them well beyond the game's own program window. Thereby, these games not only blur the boundaries between fiction and reality but also undermine the assumption that the player is invulnerable; protected from real-life consequences by the magic circle of play. In this chapter, I analyze the use of game-transcending metareference in contemporary indie horror games with a particular focus on their impact on the player's emotional experience. Using Imscared: A Pixelated Nightmare *(2016) and* Archimedes *(2016) as my main case studies, I argue that game-transcending metareference is an effective means of creating a player-centered kind of horror that relies not so much on the fear elicited by the narrative or gameplay, but rather on videogames' uncanny ability to transgress the supposedly inviolable boundary to "real life."*

When *Imscared: A Pixelated Nightmare* (hereafter: *Imscared*) first appeared on the platform Game Jolt in 2012, it quickly became something of a viral phenomenon. Part of the hype was certainly due to the immense reach of YouTubers such as Markiplier and PewDiePie, both of whom published "Let's Play" videos of *Imscared* shortly after its first release.[1] What appears to have attracted streamers and players to this small indie game is the way it "messes with" the actual player and their computer. Among other things, *Imscared* creates a new file on the player's desktop, shuts down of its own accord, and opens webpages via the computer's browser. When sifting through the comments section of Markiplier's (2012) Let's Play video, one encounters several discussions of whether the game is a virus or even safe to play, as well as many players remarking they found the game "scary" or "creepy." User @user-tf9xy9bh6i, for instance, writes: "Wow... went to play it [...] and it wasn't overly scary, however my GOD was it creepy! What a great

DOI: 10.4324/9781003538592-5

concept. Frightening and similar to what you would expect from a CreepyPasta" (2013, n.pag.). Two aspects seem immediately interesting about this comment. First, the user attempts to articulate an emotional experience that is similar to, yet differs qualitatively from, conventional "scary games," a notion that I will explore in more detail throughout this chapter. Second, the comparison to creepypasta, i.e., to horror stories and urban legends related to digital media and culture that spread via the internet, is instructive.[2] It associates *Imscared*, as well as other videogames like it, with the "supernatural media virus," a term introduced by Rahel Schmitz to describe a common trope that "gives narrative shape to fears that are specific to the era of the internet" (2021, 13). The game's virus-like behavior—as well as the themes of isolation, cyberstalking, and data security it invokes—demonstrate its attunement to the anxieties around new media, including digital surveillance technologies, and of course computer viruses.

What sets videogames such as *Imscared* apart from other creepypasta-style narratives as well as from most other self-reflexive media is the use of game-transcending metareference: a form of metareference characterized by an ontological transgression between the videogame in which it occurs, and the outside world. Indeed, recent years have seen the appearance of several titles that make this particular metaleptic jump by interfering with the player's computer, or by requiring the player to add, delete, or otherwise manipulate the data stored there. Some also involve the player in a kind of alternate reality game (ARG)[3] that takes them well beyond the videogame's own program window. With a few exceptions such as the puzzle adventure *OneShot* (2016), these strategies seem particularly popular within the genre of indie horror games. Notable examples include *Imscared*, *Archimedes* (2016), *Mirror Layers* (2016), and *Doki Doki Literature Club!* (2017). This correlation is perhaps unsurprising, considering that the functions of game-transcending metareference align rather well with those of horror. Demonstrating videogames' uncanny ability to "really" transgress the supposedly inviolable boundary between the world of the game and the world of the player, game-transcending metareference creates a horror experience that feels up close and personal and instils a very real sense of vulnerability in the player.

In this chapter, I offer a deep-dive into the forms and functions of game-transcending metareference in contemporary indie horror games. To do so, I first analyze the different game-transcending strategies these games employ and discuss their affinity with horror, with particular emphasis on the cultural functions of contemporary meta-horror to negotiate anxieties around digital media. Second, I argue that game-transcending metareference occasions a shift in the player's experience of horror insofar as the convergence of ontologically distinct worlds evokes a sense of unease that likewise extends beyond the game, to the player's self before the screen. I supplement my theoretical argument with detailed analyses of two case studies, Ivan Zanotti's *Imscared* (the 2016 Steam version)[4] and Joshua Hughes's *Archimedes*, both of which employ a plethora of noteworthy metareferential strategies that cross the supposedly inviolable boundary to "real life."

Game-Transcending Metareference

Following the conceptualization proposed in the introduction to this volume, metareference is here understood as a form of medial self-reflexivity through which various media texts comment on themselves from a higher metalevel and draw the recipient's attention to their medial identity (see also Wolf 2009). As I have argued more extensively elsewhere (see Krampe 2023, 2025), it is useful to systematically analyze the *form* of a metareferential element in a videogame by inquiring after the layer of communication on which it occurs.[5] This allows us to distinguish between gameworld-centered forms of metareference and system-centered ones. Gameworld-centered forms are situated within the gameworld, i.e., within the same layer of communication as the events and characters. Typical examples include videogame characters that become aware of their fictionality or speak to the player in so-called fourth-wall breaks (e.g., in *Max Payne* [2001]; see also Conway 2010; Van de Mosselaer 2022; Waszkiewicz 2020). System-centered forms, by contrast, arise from the game's underlying system of rules and software operations. The use of unconventional game mechanics that subvert player expectations or draw attention to design conventions are examples of system-centered metareference (e.g., in *The Hex* [2018]; see also the chapter by Hennig in this volume). Another common strategy is to use metalepses that cut across the layers of gameworld and game system, such as when extradiegetic interfaces suddenly intrude upon the gameworld or vice versa (e.g., in *There Is No Game: Wrong Dimension* [2020]; see also Thorne 2021).

There is, however, a growing cluster of videogames that employ the as-of-yet unusual form of game-transcending metareference. This involves layers of communication that are strictly speaking located outside the videogame proper, such as the operating system and the hardware of the computer or console, in a metaleptic transgression. Importantly, the metalepses in question are not limited to a "quick glance across levels" (Ryan 2006, 207) in the sense of a rhetorical metalepsis. Neither does the transgression remain a mere suggestion. Instead, for an element to qualify as game-transcending metareference, it must genuinely cross the boundary between the game and what is outside it. The game, in other words, "really" (materially, ontologically) accesses the actual world, typically via the user's system (Ryan 2006, 226; see also Ensslin and Bell 2021, 71; Krampe et al. 2022). An instructive example can be found in *Doki Doki Literature Club!*, a visual novel-style indie game that juxtaposes the conventions of dating simulators with elements of psychological horror. Toward the end of the game, the player must defeat the antagonist Monika by going to the game folder on the actual computer and deleting the file monika.chr., which causes her visual representation to dissolve into pixels and disappear from the gameworld. The game thus crosses, or rather requires the player to cross, the boundary between the gameworld, as represented in the game window, and the data stored on the actual computer, as represented by the desktop interface. Since the player is not only asked to imagine their interaction with Monika to extend across the boundary between the gameworld and the actual world but must in fact interact with elements outside the game to influence the fictional events, the example clearly goes beyond fourth-wall breaks and other forms of rhetorical metalepsis.[6] The defamiliarizing nature of game-transcending metareference also sets it apart from conventional interactional metalepses, i.e., the routine crossings between hardware and gameworld that occur during the player's interaction with a videogame (see Bell 2016; Ensslin and Bell 2021).[7]

The potential of videogames as well as other forms of digital-born interactive fiction to affect the player's computer was recognized by Marie-Laure Ryan nearly two decades ago. In "Metaleptic Machines," she writes:

> [I]n contrast to the inability of verbal narratives to stage metaleptic events that literally affect the ground level of the stack [what I broadly refer to as the actual world; TK], it would be fairly easy to write a computer game that destroys the user's system. Such a feature would, of course, be self-defeating from a commercial point of view.
>
> (Ryan 2004, 461)

With the exception of a few precursors,[8] videogames have only recently begun to make use of this potential, notably in the context of indie horror games. Arguably, the affinity between game-transcending metareference and indie horror is due to two interrelated factors. First, they share a concern with the anxieties around new media technologies, and second, game-transcending strategies are very effective at dissolving the boundaries between fiction and reality, which is conducive to horror as it makes the experience feel more real to the player. In the following, I will explore each of these hypotheses in turn, drawing on examples and analyses from my two case studies *Imscared* and *Archimedes*.

Meta-Horror Games Reflect Anxieties around Digital Media

Considering the sheer diversity of narrative elements, styles, and game mechanics that can be considered under the label "indie horror games," it would go beyond the scope of this chapter to provide an exhaustive description of the genre (but see, e.g., Marak 2021; Thon 2019).[9] Instead, let me home in on an emerging subgenre that we might refer to as game-transcending meta-horror. Using the transgressive impetus of game-transcending metareference, these games reinvigorate familiar tropes of viruses, hostile takeovers, and self-aware software and thereby stimulate a critical engagement with contemporary digital media and online cultures. Their main concerns connect to the well-established function of metareferential horror titles as commentators on contemporaneous developments in the media landscape. This function is apparent in the many novels, films, and more recently videogames that represent cursed or haunted media (see Sconce 2000), from Bram Stoker's *Dracula* (1897) and the Lovecraftian short stories of the 1920s and 1930s via films such as *The Ring* (2002) to *Alan Wake* (2010). Representing horrors that literally arise from books, video tapes, paintings, mobile phones, or videogame cartridges, these narratives address the mixture of fascination and anxiety that seems to surface whenever a new medium establishes itself. It is therefore hardly surprising that the rise of so-called "new media"—and, on an even grander scale, sociocultural developments in the context of globalization and digitalization—are also accompanied by the manifestation of new discourses and imaginaries in horror. Examining contemporary gothic fiction, Rahel Schmitz (2021) argues that the virus, specifically what she refers to as the "supernatural media virus," has become a recurring trope in horror fiction, and one that is particularly responsive to concerns around digitalization. As "a paranormal entity that follows the logic of contagion and that exploits modern media as well as society's interconnectedness in order to spread its malevolent influence," the supernatural media virus "conjoins two cultural key metaphors—the virus and the network—and pairs them with diverse media" (Schmitz 2021, 13–14).

The supernatural media virus trope is central to *Imscared* and *Archimedes*. Both games feature monsters that combine traditional horror imagery and mechanics (distorted bodies, death masks, chase sequences, and jumpscares) with an aesthetic that is specific to the digital and reminiscent of the computer virus and the glitch. In *Imscared*, the player is dropped into a gameworld of narrow, fleshy corridors, fog-filled hedge mazes, underground car parks, and other dark places that they must navigate while steering clear of the elusive entity Whiteface and its alter ego, HER. As the subtitle *A Pixelated Nightmare* suggests, the game uses a pixelated art style, which creates the impression of an amateurish, low-tech production. On the one hand, this choice of audiovisual aesthetics aligns with Juul's (2019) observations regarding the rise of "independent style" in that *Imscared* harkens back to an earlier, and supposedly more authentic, age of videogame creation. On the other hand, the visuals also add to the game's uncanny atmosphere—uncanny in the sense of something eerily familiar, yet strange[10]—as they defamiliarize the shapes of bodies, walls, and furniture (see Marak 2021, 177).

Archimedes, a short horror game developed by part-time indie developer Joshua Hughes and published via Steam in 2016, likewise employs an overall low-tech, retro style, though it hinges less on the use of pixel art than on the *mise en abyme*-like representation of an old desktop interface within the game. When first started, *Archimedes* pretends to install an operating system called "intra" on the player's computer. Henceforth, the player spends most of the game interacting with what looks like a somewhat glitchy Windows 95 desktop interface (see Figure 5.1). At the beginning of the game, the fictional desktop's chat window opens, and the player receives a message from a character named User2409. User2409 introduces themselves as an employee of the fictional biomedical corporation ARC and asks the player to investigate a series of strange events that have been happening at the office. Using the functions available on the fictional computer, including the chat, a browser, and a search directory, the player gradually uncovers that ARC accidentally set free an alien supervirus that had lain dormant under permafrost for several decades until it was rediscovered. Since the virus can travel between humans and computers, it spreads very quickly until, at the end of the game, it manages to infect the player's computer.

Archimedes's metareferential strategies create strong parallels between the virus and the theme of ghostly, haunted media. The *mise en abyme*-style reduplication of the desktop not only acts as a metareferential interface (see Krampe et al. 2022) that draws attention to the mediality of the game as a software application

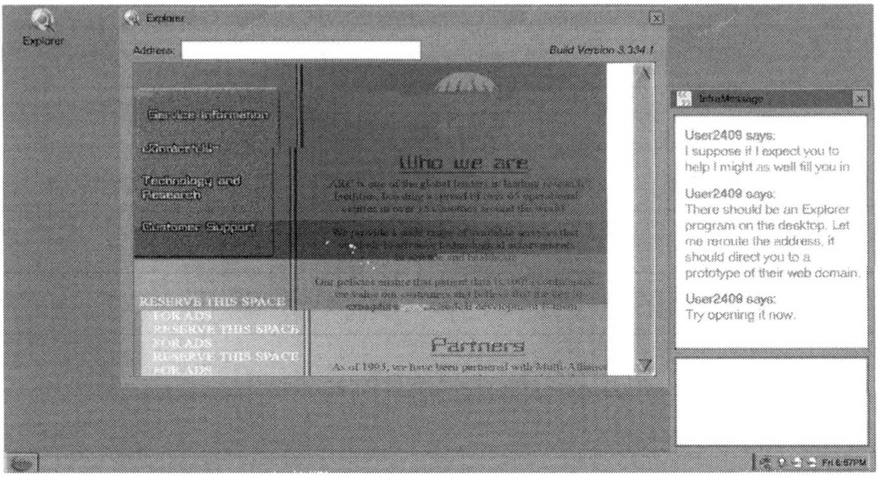

Figure 5.1 Interacting with the Windows 95-style desktop interface in *Archimedes.*

Figure 5.2 Use of glitch aesthetics in *Archimedes.*

installed on the player's computer. It also refers to an earlier era of computer programming and internet culture that haunts the present via the game's Windows 95-style desktop. The deliberate use of "glitch-alikes" (see Gualeni 2019; as well as Menkman 2011; and the chapter by Thon in this volume) further develops the idea of a transgressive, digital media virus. Strong colors, visual and sonic distortions as well as the hypermediated display of a frozen screen with multiple, overlapping windows cite the familiar phenomenon of audiovisual glitches (see Figure 5.2). As the perceptible manifestations of errors in the system, glitches "distort the mimetic […] aspects of the game" (Csönge 2023, 198) and focus the player's attention on the software operations within the game system. Yet, *Archimedes* draws on the destabilizing, and vertigo-inducing effects of glitches not only to increase the player's medium awareness but also to, metaphorically speaking, breathe life into software. As Eben Holmes writes, "[t]he animus, which seems to make its presence felt in such situations, is nothing less than the spirit of the machine itself, the trace of the quasi-animate registers and loops" (2010, 262).

The monster itself remains invisible and without substance for the most part of the game, as seems appropriate for a supervirus. Yet, at the very end, when attempting to take control of the player's computer, it does materialize on screen in the form of a skull-shaped face, accompanied by a proliferation of (simulated) glitches. Invisible, yet present on screen, at once alien and familiar, organic and inorganic, *Archimedes*'s virus is a paradigm case of the "uncanny in-between or neither" (Schmitz 2021, 29) that Schmitz identifies as typical of the supernatural media virus. As an alien supervirus frozen in ice, it is out of time and space and yet, it is very much of the time in that it speaks to present-day concerns about global pandemics and computer viruses. It thus puts a spin on the conventional characteristics of the monster as a signifier of threat and impurity (see Carrol 1990, 28). Like many other contemporary horror texts, *Archimedes* intertwines the idea of impurity as disease with a second meaning; as something that is categorically interstitial, even contradictory (see Carrol 1990, 32). Quoting Schmitz, the supernatural media virus not only "transgress[es] national, social, geographical, and bodily boundaries, but it also evades such dichotomous categories as dead/living" (2021, 25)—and, one might feel tempted to add, software and mind, or indeed fact and fiction.[11]

Crucially, neither *Archimedes* nor *Imscared* stop at destabilizing ontological boundaries on a thematic level, but both games enact the ideas of liminality and transgression through their very form. In this context, game-transcending metareference acts as a powerful support of the supernatural media virus trope because it showcases very real possibilities of contamination between the game software and the user's system. *Imscared* strongly associates its game-transcending mechanics with the appearance of the monster-as-virus from the very start. The game begins with a disclaimer message, cautioning the player that "the game will try to deceive You as many times as it can," thus positioning the player as the protagonist and the game itself as the monster/antagonist. *Imscared* also creates a new folder on the player's desktop within which new files appear at certain points in the game. Soon after the player has entered the gameworld, a jump scare encounter with Whiteface—an entity that looks like a floating white face—occurs, upon which the game freezes to a "blue screen of death" (see Figure 5.3). Reading the small print on the blue screen reveals that it is not the result of an actual error but part of the game. Among other things, it advises the player again to "make sure the game is not trying to deceive you" and also directs them to the newly created game folder on the desktop "for further instructions." Checking the folder, the player will find that a new document, "Attention.txt," has appeared. In addition to some hints concerning gameplay, the document contains the following message:

Figure 5.3 The fake blue screen in *Imscared.*

> There is a way to turn an entity into data. They have a life of their own, and it is difficult to distinguish them from normal computer files. In our actions of everyday, while we sit at the computer, this byte entity observes us, and studies our every move and fear.

The message suggests that Whiteface is made of data, is possibly also a personification of the game's software, and that it can freely move between the game and the player's computer. What sounds like the somewhat hackneyed narrative premise of a machine achieving consciousness, however, is given credibility by the use of game-transcending metareference. The appearance of the new folder and .txt file not merely narrates but demonstrates the game's ability to metaleptically interfere with the user's system.

Imscared further reinforces the idea of software having "a life of its own" and studying the player's "every move and fear" by means of additional metareferential elements situated within and across all layers of communication. For example, the game repeatedly closes on its own or presents the player with fake endings, upon which it must be restarted, to the point where restarting becomes one of the main means of progressing the game. In other instances, the game opens a tab in the computer's default browser and then redirects the player to a *YouTube* video (e.g., the unlisted video "Hidden Passage" [Bury Her 2015]), creating a direct, metaleptic link between text and paratext (see Figure 5.4).[12] The visual aesthetics of this sequence—a succession of windows opening and closing of their own accord—is no less interesting since these kinds of images are frequently used in film and TV to represent digital devices being hacked or infected by computer viruses. All of this adds to the player's sense of losing control as Whiteface

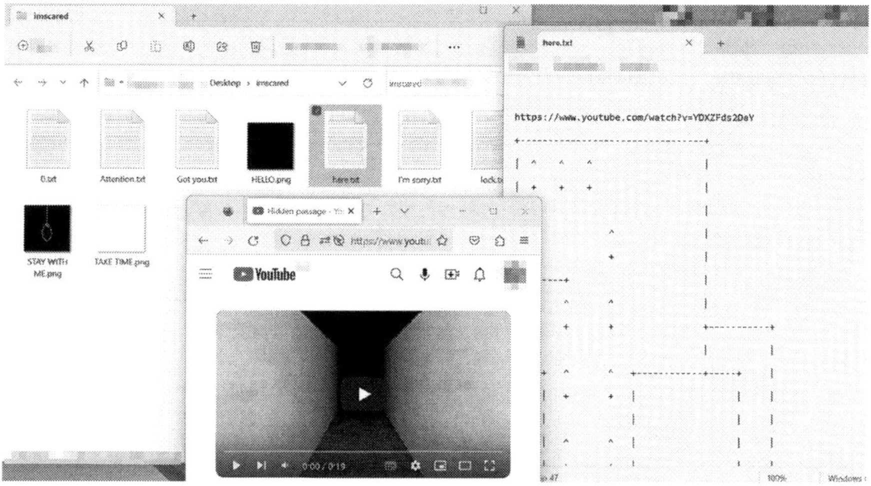

Figure 5.4 Solving an in-game puzzle across multiple program windows in *Imscared.*

takes over and becomes a poltergeist in the player's machine. Taken together, the audiovisual aesthetics, the narrative cues provided by the .txt documents, and the game's unruly behavior connect the metareferential exhibition of the game's specific procedural mediality to a broader, heteroreferential comment on threats of surveillance, cyberstalking, or hacking that have long ceased to be merely science fictional.

Archimedes, too, underscores the idea of transgressing the boundary to real life by means of game-transcending metareference. In partial contrast to *Imscared*, it relies less on the metaleptic crossing between the game and the actual computer's operating system and instead takes the use of ARG-style game mechanics to extremes, repeatedly referring the player to software applications and websites outside the game. The chat messages the player receives from the fictional character User2409, as well as the documents they can discover on the fictional desktop, often contain links and QR-codes that lead the player to MediaFire and Google Drive. From there, they must retrieve real files and a .zip folder with images, audio recordings, or story snippets that are needed to progress in the game. In another instance, the game refers them to Google Maps or an equivalent application, where they must search for a specific real-world location in Nepal whose coordinates form a password that unlocks new information within the fictional world of the game.[13]

A game-transcending metareferential element that is particularly invasive with regard to the player's sense of security occurs during the endgame of *Archimedes* when the (fictional representation of the) player realizes that the virus has spread to their system. Simultaneously, tensions come to a head at ARC and User2409—whose name, he now reveals, is Isaac—is disconnected from the chat, but not before offering to help the player and asking them to send a message to a Gmail address. Sending the message via the in-game "IntraMail" email application is impossible, so at this point, it is in fact necessary to use an actual email service to contact the fictional Isaac. The use of actual emails is highly effective in addressing the player as their real-world self, especially if the player was indeed using their personal email rather than creating a dummy account. Once the player has sent a message to the address provided by Isaac, the reply arrives promptly and advises the player to defeat the alien supervirus with the help of another computer virus, which Isaac has helpfully included in the email text, for the player to copy and paste. As the player copies the lines of code from the email and pastes them to the in-game console on the fictional desktop, the text becomes part of the gameworld by way of descending metalepsis.[14] The email also refers the player to a *YouTube* tutorial video from which they can learn how to open the (fictional) terminal in the (fictional) intraOS, into which they will need to insert the virus. Completing these steps leads to a cutscene showing the alien supervirus being purged from the player's computer. Thereafter, the game window only shows the message "Cannot locate files. [sic] please insert disc to install an Operating System."

To make this perfectly clear, *Archimedes* neither deletes the player's actual Windows operating system, nor does it infect their computer with malware that affects it beyond the time/space of playing the game. Nevertheless, its strategies can be described as game-transcending due to the player's real interaction with software applications outside the game. When the player downloads and sifts through the .zip files, this effectively extends the "magic circle" of play (see Salen and Zimmerman 2004) beyond the game proper and onto the browser, the MediaFire and Google drive servers, as well as the download folder on the player's computer. The mechanics of the ARG-style gameplay mirror interactions with digital media that, for many people, have become part and parcel of their everyday lives. In addition, the *Archimedes* ARG closely resembles certain aspects of phishing attacks (spam emails, fake links, malware downloads, etc.) and their aftermath, and hence remind the player of the risks involved in their casual interactions with digital media (see also Bell 2021; Ensslin and Bell 2021, 75). In a cultural climate in which virus anxiety is not only widespread but also justified, this may well cause players to take the game as an actual threat and worry about their privacy and the safety of the data on their computer. This gradual slippage of the in-game threat into real life also brings me to my second argument, namely, that game-transcending metareference influences the player's emotional response to videoludic horror by undermining the assumption that the player is invulnerable, or at least protected from real-life consequences (as well as from the monsters within the gameworld) by the magic circle of play.

Game-Transcending Metareference Impacts Player Emotions

Most writers, critics, and audiences agree that the main emotional response horror wants to elicit is fear, though often mixed with a plethora of related feelings such as disgust, dread, unease, or awe (see, e.g., Carrol 1990, 14; Perron 2018, 4). Fear can be conceived of in terms of a stimulus, and a physical response: Believing oneself to be threatened by a monster (cognitive dimension) typically leads to physical responses such as trembling, screaming, or fleeing (see Carrol 1990, 24–28; Tan 2011 [1996], 45). This poses a challenge for the study of fiction. As a rule, videogame players or film viewers know full well that the monster is not real, and neither is the threat to their physical bodies before the screen, and yet they may experience strong emotional reactions toward the fictional characters and events. This so-called paradox of fiction (see Radford 1975) has been discussed, solved, or dismissed in different ways. Kendall Walton, for instance, argues that audiences participate in a game of make believe in which there is a monster, and in which they feel threatened and afraid (see Walton 1978, 13–14; as well as Carrol 1990, 71). This may cause them to experience a state of "quasi-fear" (Walton 1978, 8) that can be very intense, to the point of causing involuntary physical reactions such as elevated heart rates or even screaming. However, in contradistinction to real fear, audiences do not believe themselves in any actual danger and do not take any deliberate actions to remedy the situation (see Walton 1978, 8).

Walton's account has been criticized by Carrol, who points out that the recipient's emotional response is genuine in the sense that they do not merely pretend to be afraid (see Carrol 1990, 74–75; as well as Tavinor 2009, 140–141). Videogames, due to their interactivity, raise even further objections. For one thing, players are active participants in the gameworld and usually hold some degree of interactive agency over the events taking place within it. Consequently, and in contradistinction to, e.g., film audiences (see Tan 2011, 75–76), they have an action repertoire at their disposal and may also experience self-reflexive emotions such as guilt, shame, and a sense of responsibility toward characters (see Tavinor 2009, 130–149; Van de Mosselaer 2018, 287). Hence, emotions elicited by videogames may very well motivate deliberate actions (see Van de Mosselaer 2018, 281–287). It is, for instance, not unusual for players to try and save videogame characters they have grown fond of, even if that means expending additional ergodic effort. Whether or not fictional propositions provoke actions thus appears to be a matter of context and medial affordances, rather than a matter of real vs. quasi-emotions. Nevertheless, the point still stands that players normally choose actions that are appropriate to the designed experience, such as using the game controls to fight or flee the in-game monster, instead of running from the room or calling the police as they would when confronted with a threat in the actual world.

For our present purpose, the most helpful approach to dealing with these observations is to conceive of the emotional response elicited by horror games as art horror, i.e., as a genuine emotion that arises from mental models and images provoked by a text or artifact (see, e.g., Carrol 1990, 8; Perron 2018, 86; Tan 2011, 65). The fact that we are willingly and knowingly engaging with an aesthetic illusion is the relevant context that influences our response such that we can experience fear as cathartic or even pleasurable, rather than utterly unpleasant and traumatic. That same context also influences our action tendencies, leading us to respond in a manner that is appropriate to the situation of playing a game. Drawing on Ed Tan's study of emotion in film viewers, Bernard Perron (2005;

2018) has proposed to divide the player's response to horror games into three general types of emotions: Fiction emotions, gameplay emotions, and artifact emotions. Fiction emotions are directed toward the events and characters in the gameworld; gameplay emotions arise "from our actions in the game [...] and the consequent reactions of the game(-world)" (Perron 2005, 3), and artifact emotions are directed toward the videogame as an artifact, and comprise enjoyment, appreciation, and astonishment—or, conversely, displeasure and frustration—with its formal features and craftsmanship (see Perron 2005, 2; as well as Kuijpers et al. 2017, 37–39; Tan 2011, 64–66; Thon 2019).

When trying to understand the subtle shifts in the emotional design of game-transcending meta-horror, it is thus helpful to keep in mind that different dimensions of videogames may also evoke different, yet mutually intertwined, types of emotions. Artifact emotions, in particular, can be expected to play a strong role in metareferential videogames, which are after all concerned with exhibiting their artifice. This intuition is confirmed by the player testimonies in reviews and comment sections about *Imscared* and *Archimedes*, many of which indicate that players' enjoyment stems at least partially from their appreciation of the innovative concepts and craftsmanship found in these games (see Steam 2024a; 2024b). Still, the multiple crossings between gameworld and actual world in game-transcending meta-horror not only intensify artifact emotions, but also affect fiction and gameplay emotions. While both case studies do employ conventional horror elements such as jump scares, horrible places, and of course monsters, I would argue that neither of them is overly concerned with creating art horror in the traditional sense. The atmosphere in both gameworlds is arguably better described as creepy and unsettling rather than genuinely scary, and so is the emotional response they evoke. There are few rounded characters to fear for, and hardly any cues that would encourage the player to imagine any of them as possible people with motivations and emotions. Gameplay is generally not difficult and, with a few exceptions such as *Imscared*'s car park and graveyard chase sequences, there is no fail state and consequently little reason to fear for the physical integrity of the player character. Admittedly, the limited resources with which the games were created might have featured into the comparatively tame narrative and gameplay. The much more interesting observation, however, is that both games shift the emphasis from sympathetic emotions and a kind of fear experienced within the gameworld and in the shoes of a player character to a sense of unease and concern for the player's own self before the screen—or, at any rate, for the integrity of their computer system and data. In that sense, game-transcending metareference can help create an emotional experience that is, almost paradoxically, at once more detached and more personal than what we usually expect from horror games.

For starters, *Archimedes* and *Imscared* (as well as similar games such as *Doki Doki Literature Club!* or *Mirror Layers*) make a point of addressing the actual player in a very immediate sense. Not only do the player characters remain nondescript, but both games make it very clear that the player is not supposed to imagine themselves in the shoes of a fictional proxy, but rather as a direct participant in the events represented on screen. When interacting with the graphical user interfaces of the (non-fictional) Windows operating system as part of the gameplay of either *Archimedes* or *Imscared*, the player essentially acts and thinks as a user of a computer. They recenter to their actual body before the screen; a body that physically interacts with the hardware and software of the computer. Such metaleptic jumps between the gameworld and the player's self before the screen further unsettle the already precarious sense of "double-situatedness" (Ensslin 2009, 158) that is often ascribed to videogame players. As they alternate from actual world to gameworld and back again, they become conscious of being at once perched before a computer screen and re-embodied as an agent in the gameworld.

As I have mentioned earlier, game-transcending metareference can furthermore demonstrate the game's ability to "really" affect the player's system. *Imscared* does so primarily by creating several files on the players' actual desktop and by opening the browser, i.e., by means of ascending ontological metalepses from the gameworld to the Windows operating system. Within the gameworld, these uncanny events are then attributed to the agency of the fictional monster, Whiteface. Katarzyna Marak and colleagues describe the effect as follows:

> [*Imscared*] tricks the player into believing that the game software is gaining some sort of control over the player's computer, thus escaping the confinement of the software interface. […] [T]he direct consequence […] is the arousal of a new kind of uneasiness in the players, the kind that other horror games, not to mention the texts of other media, cannot.
>
> (Marak et al. 2019, 235)

Player testimonies such as this recent Steam review confirm the authors' argument:

> [sic] Many moments of me feeling uncomfortable that my computer was ACTUALLY corrupted, my privacy breached. That "uh-oh" when a random browser opens out of complete nowhere […]. Not to mention the many bone-chilling moments where I feel that I've done something I REALLY should not have done.
>
> (Mr. Awesome 2024, n.pag.)

These quotes indicate that *Imscared* can evoke real, player-centered unease because it convincingly suggests a metaleptic jump into the player's real life. I would even go as far as saying that the game does not just trick the player into thinking that it can control the computer, but that at least some of the transgressions it performs are quite real. The game presents itself as a software program that is, in essence, identical to a computer virus and thus poses, at least potentially, a real threat.

Archimedes, too, elicits a "new kind of uneasiness" (Marak et al. 2019, 235) in the player that likewise stems from the realization that the ontological boundary between the gameworld and "real life" is no longer impenetrable. To continue playing the game, the player must, among other things, click several links leading to websites, open an email signed by someone that does not exist, and even download files from external servers. These ARG-typical mechanics are conducive to extending the fictional world and blending it with the player's reality. On top of that, from a cybersecurity perspective, the player just performed several high-risk actions so that the idea of a virus overtaking their actual computer becomes quite plausible.[15] The subsequent appearance of the virus/monster can thus be genuinely unsettling and makes good use of videogames' medium-specific capacity to appeal to the player's sense of responsibility. The virus only materializes after the player has engaged in precisely the kinds of irresponsible behaviors that are likely to incur computer viruses in real life, suggesting a causal relation between their real actions and the (fictional) spread of the supervirus. *Archimedes* reinforces the notion of complicity and the accompanying feelings of guilt, shame, and anxiety by tying them to the player's "actually" risky actions and the overall porosity of the boundary between game and outside world (see also Schmitz 2021, 25).

Both *Archimedes* and *Imscared*, then, use metareferential strategies to directly address the player as well as to demonstrate the system's vulnerability to threats such as computer viruses. Their game-transcending elements underscore the cross-contamination between the gameworld and what is outside it, allowing two distinct ontological planes to bleed into one another in a material sense. As I have argued in the previous section, this contemporizes the supernatural media virus trope, creating ambiguity between "data and spirit, save files and human identity" and thereby negotiating anxieties regarding "the primacy of incorporeal information within contemporary network society" (Sanders 2018, 139). Game-transcending metareference furthermore alters the player's emotional engagement with the game. Where horror games conventionally elicit fear as a result of scare tactics, ludic challenges, sympathy for the characters, or the precarious position of the player character, the effect of *Imscared* and *Archimedes* is better described as uncanny: a kind of creepy horror that builds on the liminal and the strangely familiar. Like the game-transcending mechanics, the feeling of unease also extends beyond the game and onto the player's real-world self, causing them to experience a real sense of vulnerability.

This qualitative change in emotional response can be explained with reference to the game's "ontological resonance," a term proposed by Alice Bell to capture the "prolonged response and aura of significance" recipients may experience during and after reading/playing, and "which is generated by perceived bidirectional ontological transfers between the actual world and a storyworld" (2021, 445).[16] In plainer words, readers or players are made to feel as though the storyworld and the actual world converge, or mix (see also Ensslin and Bell 2021, 78). Similar effects, which Bell describes as "passive ontological resonance" (2021, 448), can also occur in noninteractive fiction since readers/viewers generally project real-world knowledge into the storyworld and are also believed to transfer certain aspects of their mediated experience back to the actual world. However, due to the player's active role and their already ambiguous positioning vis-à-vis the gameworld, videogames and interactive fictions can create particularly effective blends of fiction and reality and provoke particularly strong ontological resonances.

In *Archimedes* and *Imscared*, strategies and devices such as the fourth-wall breaking direct address ("the game will try to deceive You"), the foregrounding of the desktop interface, or the use of fake glitches already advances the convergence between the fictional and actual world. The real game-changer, however, is once again the use of game-transcending metareference. Rather than a "*perceived* bidirectional ontological transfer" (Bell 2021, 445; my emphasis), these games present the player with an actual transfer (of data) that thoroughly destabilizes the boundary between the game and what is outside it. The "aura of significance" (Bell 2021, 446) generated by the idea of malevolent digital entities taking over the player's computer, data, and eventually personal life is consequently much more profound. The player's own interaction with the game files and game-external applications such as *YouTube* or Google Maps even intensifies ontological resonance in a twofold manner, first due to the genuine ontological transgression taking place, and second because most players habitually use these applications in real life and for nonfictional purposes. All of this increases the likelihood for the fictional world to intertwine with the player's reality and daily life, creates ambiguity about the ontological status of the events that occur while playing the games, and consequently upends the player's immunity to real-life consequences. This, then, is the source of the real art horror that game-transcending metareference is in a unique position to create.

Conclusion

In this chapter, I have been concerned with a small but growing subset of indie horror games that use game-transcending forms of metareference, i.e., forms that make a genuine metaleptic jump between the game and the outside world. Their main strategies revolve around the manipulation of files on the actual computer's operating system as well as the arrangement of a kind of ARG in the course of which the player must go back and forth between the gameworld and game-external webpages and software applications. Using *Imscared* and *Archimedes* as case studies, I have shown how these metareferential elements tie in with the cultural function of horror to give expression to and negotiate anxieties around technological progress, digitalization, and new media. At the center of both games, we find an uncanny type of monster that connects horror-typical themes of threat, impurity, and infection with contemporary concerns around data, privacy, and cybersecurity. Whiteface and the alien supervirus are both elusive entities that appear to be many things at once: monster, computer virus, sentient software, ghost in the machine. The perpetual transgression of ontological boundaries on both the thematic and formal levels underscores an increasing insecurity when it comes to distinguishing fictional and virtual worlds from real life. In the trope of the supernatural media virus as realized in games like *Imscared* and *Archimedes*, we thus find a monster that is highly appropriate for the (post)digital age.

I have then argued that the innovative and highly disruptive formal strategies employed in both case studies also profoundly affect the player's emotional experience. By way of their own interaction with game data, the player is (re)positioned as the user of a computer: returned to their own body before the screen, as it were. Involving the player in a very direct sense, without a fictional player character as an intermediary, game-transcending meta-horror games encroach upon our personal space and real-world selves. Needless to say, most players will not actually believe that there is a sentient being lurking among the files on their computer, or an alien supervirus out to kill them. Still, game-transcending metareference does introduce shifts in the conventional emotional makeup of horror games and creates a particularly strong, active, and player-centered ontological resonance. What game-transcending metareference can bring about, more than any other form of metareference and arguably more than any other scare tactic, is a real sense of vulnerability that stems from the acute awareness that the boundary between the fictional, the virtual, and the real are no longer inviolable. So, in the end, it is in this sense, by way of our data and our online selves, that we are, indeed, no longer safe before the screen.

Notes

1 As of September 2024, the Let's Play by Markiplier (2012) stands at roughly 2.3 million views; the video by PewDiePie (2012) was viewed just over 3.5 million times. For a book-length scholarly discussion of videogame streaming, see Taylor 2018; on the influence of streaming on indie game production and promotion, see Parker and Perks 2021.

2 It is not unusual for creepypasta-style narratives to break the fourth wall and to involve their audiences in a kind of ARG (see note 3 below) that takes place across various platforms and media (see e.g., Sanders 2018; Zawacki 2024). On the level of content, creepypasta also tends to signal its close ties to digital technology and the internet: Recurring motifs include cursed chain emails, haunted hardware, or lost TV episodes (see Sanders 2018, 137). The well-known "Slender Man" myth, for instance, originated from a 2009 Photoshop challenge and quickly spread across the internet as people created and circulated more images, short stories, and even videos (see Schmitz 2021, 11–12). Incidentally, the tall, faceless figure of Slender Man bears some resemblance to *Imscared*'s main antagonists, Whiteface and HER, as well as other, similarly elusive entitites in "cult" indie horror games such as *Yume Nikki* (2004) or *Undertale* (2015). *Imscared* and *Archimedes* furthermore share key motifs—sentient videogames, strange data, disturbing glitches, mutating viruses that spread to the player's computer—with "Ben Drowned" (see Hall 2010; as well as Sanders 2018 for an analysis), a videogame-themed creepypasta about a haunted cartridge, which in turn seems to have inspired games like Daniel Mullins's *Inscryption* (2021) (see also the chapters by Caracciolo as well as Thorne in this volume). Parallels such as these hint at the web of intertextual and intermedial references in which these kinds of texts are embedded.

3 ARGs are decentralized and transmedial experiences that invite active audience participation. Typically, they take place across both real and virtual spaces, including various webpages, social media platforms, and the player's actual-world surroundings. Their status as fiction is not necessarily explicit, which further contributes to the blurring of fiction and reality (see Jagoda 2024; see also, e.g., Garcia and Niemeyer 2017; McGonigal 2011 [in particular Part II: Reinventing Reality]). While ARGs are normally considered separate from videogames, some indie games incorporate ARG-like elements. The game designer Daniel Mullins, for example, is well-known for linking his games to ARGs (see also the chapter by Thorne in this volume for an analysis of the *Inscryption* ARG).

4 In 2016, four years after its original release, an expanded version of *Imscared* was published via Steam and received a major update in 2022. All screenshots and close readings are based on the updated Steam version.

5 More specifically, I am proposing an analytical model for the study of metareference in videogames that describes individual elements according to their form and content, where form refers to the layer of communication on which an element is situated, and content to the layer of communication to which it refers. In this chapter, I am only using those parts of the model that are immediately relevant to my present interest in the formal dimension of metareference and its relation to the experience of videoludic horror (but see Krampe 2025 for a detailed discussion).

6 By referring to moments in which characters speak across world boundaries as rhetorical metalepsis, I am following Ryan's (2004; 2006) terminology and her proposed distinction between rhetorical and ontological metalepsis. Thon instead uses the term "epistemic metalepses" to describe characters' " 'impossible knowledge' of 'higher-order' subworlds" (2016, 66). Similarly, Werner Wolf (2009) distinguishes between rhetorical, epistemological, and ontological metalepsis (see also, on metalepsis in digital fiction, Ensslin and Bell 2021; Krampe et al. 2022; Waszkiewicz 2024; and on fourth-wall breaks in videogames, Conway 2010; Van de Mosselaer 2022; Waszkiewicz 2020; 2024).

7 Alice Bell and Astrid Ensslin use the term "interactional metalepsis" to emphasize that ontological crossings routinely occur in videogames (see, e.g., Bell 2016; Ensslin and Bell 2021). The player interacts with the (fictional) gameworld via (real) hardware interfaces such as the keyboard or controller. The pointer or avatar then functions as the player's "trace" or "double" (Ensslin and Bell 2021, 52) in the gameworld. Since interactional metalepses are highly conventionalized, they are unlikely to qualify as metareferential unless otherwise marked (see Ensslin and Bell 2021, 49–58).

8 *X-Men* (1993), for instance, requires the player to reset their actual console, the Sega Genesis, to eliminate a fictional virus within the gameworld (see also Conway 2010, 149).

9 The label "indie," for one, is notoriously difficult to define as it can refer to the relative financial and creative independence of the developers, to games created by small teams on a low budget, to a countermovement to the AAA industry, to a particular "low-tech" style, or any combination of the above (see Garda and Grabarczyk 2016; Juul 2019; Krampe et al. 2022). Horror, meanwhile, encompasses subgenres as diverse as slasher horror, psychological horror, survival horror, and many more (see Perron 2018).

10 The uncanny, especially in its more modern application to (media) aesthetics (see, e.g., Royle 2003), seems an apt term to describe the experience of playing game-transcending meta-horror. Concerned with "the strange, weird and mysterious," the uncanny provokes "feelings of uncertainty, in particular regarding the reality of who one is and what is being experienced" (Royle 2003, 1). Originally, the concept was explicated by Freud (1971 [1919]) who, in a play on the meanings of the German term *unheimlich*, describes the uncanny as "nothing new or foreign, but something familiar and old" (1971, 241). Something that is repressed but recurs or comes to light to arouse "dread and creeping horror" (1971, 219). Uncanny themes—the appearance of doubles, the return of the strangely familiar, and the blurring of boundaries especially between living and dead, animate and inanimate (see Freud 1971; Royle 2003)—are part of videogames almost by definition. They can be found in the relationship between player and player character, in the mirroring of gameworld and game system, in genre-typical loops and repetitions, or in the (re)turn to retro and pixel styles. While the inherent uncanniness of videogames is diminished with the player's increasing familiarity with their medium-specific

characteristics, meta-horror and creepypasta unmask their uncanny operations once again (see Sanders 2018, 141–143).

11 On the liminality of the uncanny, see also Royle 2003; Sanders 2018.

12 For the purposes of this chapter, a broad understanding of paratexts as the productions around the text itself is sufficient. In the case of videogames, paratexts may thus encompass a vast variety of forms, from the title and packaging via trailers and blurbs to Let's Plays, reaction videos, or discussions in online communities. Note, however, that there are different (often more specific and/or narrower) approaches to paratextuality in game studies. For detailed discussions, see Švelch 2020, as well as the contributions in the recent edited volumes by Beil et al. 2021 and Seiwald and Vollans 2023. See also the chapter by Seiwald in this volume.

13 Incidentally, Kangtega mountain used to be a blank spot on Google Maps that quickly gave rise to real-world conspiracy theories (see cvr 2016).

14 The distinction between ascending and descending metalepsis is an established way of taxonomizing different forms of metalepsis in transmedial narratology. Ascending metalepsis denotes movements from a lower-level to a higher-level subworld, for instance from an embedded, second-order storyworld to a first-order storyworld, or from a first-order storyworld to the extradiegetic level. Descending metareference denotes the reverse movement from a higher to a lower level of embedding (see Ensslin and Bell 2021, 51–58; Kukkonen 2011, 3–9; Ryan 2006, 204).

15 Once again, a look at the Steam reviews is revealing. Though the majority of players conclude from the fact that the software is advertised as a game that it must be safe to download and play, others recommend additional safety measures ("just open it in your sandbox if you are cautious" [batfinx 2018, n.pag.]; "I was a little wary of [the download files] but I scanned them and they're safe" [gtrspctr 2016, n.pag.]); or even stopped playing altogether (see Devil、神鬼莫測 2017). This chimes with Patrick Jagoda's argument that ARGs can "take on a world making and building power that can *make (a participant) believe* in an alternate reality" (2024, 204; original emphasis). Players, that is, can temporarily mistake the designed experience for reality.

16 Ensslin and Bell also introduce the term "emotional metalepsis" (2021, 79) to describe the transfer of feelings from storyworld to actual world, as when players fall in love with fictional characters. However, this is not quite what happens in *Imscared* and *Archimedes*, since players do not necessarily share the feelings of a fictional character or project their feelings onto them but are rather made to experience self-reflexive emotions that are brought about because they consciously engage with the game as an artifact and simulation system, i.e., with its hardware and software, and with the multipurpose platform of the computer on which it runs.

Works Cited

Alan Wake. 2010. Remedy Entertainment/Microsoft Game Studios. Xbox 360.

Archimedes. 2016. Joshua Hughes. Microsoft Windows.

Batfinx. 2018. Review of *Archimedes*. *Steam*, March 5, 2018. https://steamcommunity.com/profiles/76561198310540345/recommended/530920/.

Beil, Benjamin, Gundolf S. Freyermuth, and Hanns Christian Schmidt, eds. 2021. *Paratextualizing Games: Investigations on the Paraphernalia and Peripheries of Play*. Bielefeld: transcript.

Bell, Alice. 2016. "Interactional Metalepsis and Unnatural Narratology." *Narrative* 24 (3): 294–310.

Bell, Alice. 2021. "'It All Feels Too Real': Digital Storyworlds and Ontological Resonance." *Style* 55 (3): 430–452.

Bury Her. 2016. "Hidden Passage." *YouTube*, January 3, 2016. www.youtube.com/watch?v=YDXZFds2DaY.

Carrol, Noël. 1990. *The Philosophy of Horror: Or, Paradoxes of the Heart*. New York: Routledge.

Conway, Steven. 2010. "A Circular Wall? Reformulating the Fourth Wall for Video Games." *Journal of Gaming and Virtual Worlds* 2 (2): 145–155.

Csönge, Tamás. 2023. "Medium Specific Uncanny in Contemporary Video Games." *Acta Universitatis Sapientiae, Film and Media Studies* 24: 185–202.

cvr. 2016. "Is Part of Himalayan Mountain Kangtega a Secret Base?" *skeptics*, June 12, 2016. https://skeptics.stackexchange.com/questions/34267/is-part-of-himalayan-mountain-kangtega-a-secret-base.

Devil、神鬼莫測. 2017. Review of *Archimedes*. *Steam*, September 13, 2017. https://steamcommunity.com/id/Devil_NaT/recommended/530920/.

Doki Doki Literature Club! 2017. Team Salvato. Microsoft Windows.

Ensslin, Astrid. 2009. "Respiratory Narrative: Multimodality and Cybernetic Corporeality in 'Physio-Cybertext'." In *New Perspectives on Narrative and Multimodality*, edited by Ruth Page, 155–165. Abingdon: Routledge.

Ensslin, Astrid, and Alice Bell. 2021. *Digital Fiction and the Unnatural: Transmedial Narrative Theory, Method, and Analysis*. Columbus: Ohio State University Press.

Freud, Sigmund. 1971 [1919]. "The 'Uncanny'." In *The Standard Edition of the Complete Psychological Works of Sigmund Freud*, Vol. 17, edited and translated by James Strachey, 217–256. London: Hogarth Press.

Garcia, Antero, and Greg Niemeyer, eds. 2017. *Alternate Reality Games and the Cusp of Digital Gameplay*. New York: Bloomsbury.

Garda, Maria B., and Paweł Grabarczyk. 2016. "Is Every Indie Game Independent? Towards the Concept of Independent Game." *Game Studies: The International Journal of Computer Game Research* 16 (1): n.pag.

gtrspctr. 2016. Review of *Archimedes*. *Steam*, October 10, 2016. https://steamcommunity.com/id/gtrspctr/recommended/530920/.

Gualeni, Stefano. 2019. "On the De-Familiarizing and Re-Ontologizing Effects of Glitches and Glitch-Alikes." In *Proceedings of the 2019 Conference: Game, Play and the Emerging Ludo-Mix*, n.pag.

Hall, Alexander (@Jadusable). 2010. "Ben Drowned." *4chan*, September 07–15, 2010. Archived at *Jadusable Wiki*. https://jadusable.withinhubris.com/The_Haunted_Cartridge_(arc)#Original_.2Fx.2F_version.

The Hex. 2018. Daniel Mullins Games. Microsoft Windows.

Holmes, Eben. 2010. "Strange Reality: On Glitches and Uncanny Play." *Eludamos: Journal for Computer Game Culture* 4 (2): 255–276.

Imscared: A Pixelated Nightmare. 2016. Ivan Zanotti's MyMadnessWorks. Microsoft Windows.

Inscryption. 2021. Daniel Mullins Games/Devolver Digital. Microsoft Windows.

Jagoda, Patrick. 2024. "From Suspension of Disbelief to Production of Belief: The Case of Alternate Reality Games." In *The Routledge Handbook of Fiction and Belief*, edited by Alison James, Akihiro Kubo, and Françoise Lavocat, 196–208. New York: Routledge.

Juul, Jesper. 2019. *Handmade Pixels: Independent Video Games and the Quest for Authenticity*. Cambridge, MA: MIT Press.

Krampe, Theresa. 2023. "Rewriting Rules, Changing Worlds: Diegetic and Ludic Forms of Metareference in *The Magic Circle*." *Frontiers of Narrative Studies* 9 (1): 137–157.
Krampe, Theresa. 2025. *Metareference in Videogames*. New York: Routledge.
Krampe, Theresa, Stephanie Lotzow, and Jan-Noël Thon. 2022. "Playful Poetics: Metareferential Interfaces in Recent Indie Games." *Poetics Today* 43 (4): 729–771.
Kuijpers, Moniek M., Frank Hakemulder, Katalin Balint, Miruna M. Doicaru, and Ed S. Tan. 2017. "Towards a New Understanding of Absorbing Reading Experiences." In *Narrative Absorption*, edited by Frank Hakemulder, Moniek M. Kuijpers, Ed S. Tan, Katalin Bálint, and Miruna M. Doicaru, 29–48. Amsterdam: John Benjamins.
Kukkonen, Karin. 2011. "Metalepsis in Popular Culture: An Introduction." In *Metalepsis in Popular Culture*, edited by Karin Kukkonen and Sonja Klimek, 1–20. Berlin: De Gruyter.
Marak, Katarzyna. 2021. "Independent Horror Games between 2010 and 2020: Selected Characteristic Features and Discernible Trends." *Images: The International Journal of European Film, Performing Arts and Audiovisual Communication* 29 (38): 175–190.
Marak, Katarzyna, Miłosz Markocki, and Dariusz Brzostek. 2019. *Gameplay, Emotions, and Narrative: Independent Games Experienced.* Pittsburgh, PA: ETC Press.
Markiplier. 2012. "*Imscared*." *YouTube*, November 28, 2012. www.youtube.com/watch?v=rcZPSkkfLEc.
Max Payne. 2001. Remedy Entertainment/Gathering of Developers, Inc. Microsoft Windows.
McGonigal, Jane. 2011. *Reality Is Broken: Why Games Make Us Better and How They Can Change the World.* New York: Penguin Press.
Menkman, Rosa. 2011. *The Glitch Momentum.* Amsterdam: Institute of Network Cultures.
Mirror Layers. 2016. Revolab. Microsoft Windows.
Mr. Awesome. 2024. Review of *Imscared. Steam*, February 17, 2024. https://steamcommunity.com/profiles/76561199088748237/recommended/429720/.
OneShot. 2016. Future Cat LLC/KOMODO. Microsoft Windows.
Parker, Felan, and Matthew Perks. 2021. "Streaming Ambivalence: Livestreaming and Indie Game Development." *Convergence* 27 (6): 1735–1752.
Perron, Bernard. 2005. "A Cognitive Psychological Approach to Gameplay Emotions." *Proceedings of DiGRA 2005: Changing Views—Worlds in Play*, n.pag.
Perron, Bernard. 2018. *The World of Scary Video Games: A Study in Videoludic Horror.* London: Bloomsbury.
PewDiePie. 2012. "WHITE FACE HAUNTS MY COMPUTER! – *Imscared: A Pixelated Nightmare* – Part 1." *YouTube*, December 4, 2012. www.youtube.com/watch?v=eDjuT37iycM.
Radford, Colin. 1975. "How Can We Be Moved by the Fate of Anna Karenina?" *Proceedings of the Aristotelian Society*, 49: 67–80.
The Ring. 2002. Director Gore Verbinski. Dreamworks Pictures.
Royle, Nicholas. 2003. *The Uncanny.* Manchester: Manchester University Press.
Ryan, Marie-Laure. 2004. "Metaleptic Machines." *Semiotica* 150 (1): 439–469.
Ryan, Marie-Laure. 2006. *Avatars of Story.* Minneapolis: University of Minnesota Press.
Salen, Katie Tekinbaş, and Eric Zimmerman. 2004. *Rules of Play: Game Design Fundamentals*. Cambridge, MA: MIT Press.
Sanders, John. 2018. "'You Shouldn't Have Done That': 'Ben Drowned' and the Uncanny Horror of the Haunted Cartridge." *Gamevironments* 9: 135–169.
Schmitz, Rahel Sixta. 2021. *The Supernatural Media Virus: Virus Anxiety in Gothic Fiction since 1990.* Bielefeld: transcript.

Sconce, Jeffrey. 2000. *Haunted Media: Electronic Presence from Telegraphy to Television.* Durham: Duke University Press.

Seiwald, Regina, and Edwin Vollans, eds. 2023. *(Not) In the Game: History, Paratexts, and Games.* Berlin: De Gruyter.

Steam. 2024a. "*Archimedes.*" *Steam.* https://store.steampowered.com/app/530920/Archimedes/.

Steam 2024b. "*Imscared.*" *Steam.* https://store.steampowered.com/app/429720/IMSCARED/.

Stoker, Bram. 2009 [1807]. *Dracula.* Ware: Wordsworth.

Švelch, Jan. 2020. "Paratextuality in Game Studies: A Theoretical Review and Citation Analysis." *Game Studies: The International Journal of Computer Game Research* 20 (2): n.pag.

Tan, Ed S., ed. 2011 [1996]. *Emotion and the Structure of Narrative Film: Film as an Emotion Machine.* New York: Routledge.

Tavinor, Grant. 2009. *The Art of Videogames.* Chichester: Wiley-Blackwell.

Taylor, T.L. 2018. *Watch Me Play: Twitch and the Rise of Game Live Streaming.* Princeton: Princeton University Press.

There Is No Game: Wrong Dimension. 2020. Draw Me a Pixel. Microsoft Windows.

Thon, Jan-Noël. 2016. *Transmedial Narratology and Contemporary Media Culture.* Lincoln: University of Nebraska Press.

Thon, Jan-Noël. 2019. "Playing with Fear: The Aesthetics of Horror in Recent Indie Games." *Eludamos: Journal for Computer Game Culture* 10 (1): 197–231.

Thorne, Sarah. 2021. "There Is No Immersion: Critical Intervention through Hypermediacy in Metagames." *Eludamos: Journal for Computer Game Culture* 12 (1): 63–85.

Undertale. 2015. Toby Fox. Microsoft Windows.

user-tf9xy9bh6i. 2013. "Wow... Went to Play It (and One of the Few I Bothered Doing That With) and It Wasn't Overly Scary, However My GOD Was It Creepy!" *YouTube* 2013 (comment posted to "Imscared" by Markiplier). www.youtube.com/watch?v=rcZPSkkfLEc&lc=Ugh0K3Lya_7Vi3gCoAEC.

Van de Mosselaer, Nele. 2018. "How Can We Be Moved to Shoot Zombies? A Paradox of Fictional Emotions *and* Actions in Interactive Fiction." *Journal of Literary Theory* 12 (2): 279–299.

Van de Mosselaer, Nele. 2022. "Breaking the Fourth Wall in Videogames." In *Being and Value in Technology*, edited by Enrico Terrone and Vera Tripodi, 163–186. Cham: Palgrave Macmillan.

Walton, Kendall L. 1978. "Fearing Fictions." *The Journal of Philosophy* 75 (1): 5–27.

Waszkiewicz, Agata. 2020. "'Together They Are Twofold': Player-Avatar Relationship beyond the Fourth Wall." *Journal of Games Criticism* 4 (1): n.pag.

Waszkiewicz, Agata. 2024. *Metagames: Games about Games.* New York: Routledge.

Wolf, Werner. 2009. "Metareference across Media: The Concept, Its Transmedial Potentials and Problems, Main Forms and Functions." In *Metareference across Media: Theory and Case Studies*, edited by Werner Wolf, 1–85. Amsterdam: Rodopi.

X-Men. 1993. Western Technologies Inc./Sega. Sega Genesis.

Yume Nikki. 2004. Kikiyama/Playism. Microsoft Windows.

Zawacki, Alexander J. 2024. "Glitches and Ghosts: The Digital Uncanny in Video Games and Creepypasta. *Horror Studies* 15 (1): 83–98.

6 When Metareference Is the Gameplay

Examining the Multidimensional Layers of Daniel Mullins's *Inscryption*

Sarah Thorne

This chapter examines the use of metareference as a central game mechanic in Daniel Mullins's Inscryption *(2021), a deck building roguelike that reveals itself to be so much more. While Mullins is well-known for creating works that challenge videogame conventions,* Inscryption *is particularly notable for its playful blending of game genres to create an experience that extends beyond the screen. Through its use of mise en abyme, the game creates a metaleptic narrative with layers that are not only deep but also reach back into the real world.* Inscryption *serves as a critical case study for examining the primacy of immediacy in contemporary culture and the use of metareference to disrupt immersion and facilitate reflection about both the game and the tenuous boundaries between games and reality.*

Introduction

While videogames and metareference are certainly not strangers, indie games arguably offer a special place for more fully exploring and experimenting with the possibilities for metareferentiality in videogames. The past decade has seen the release of a number of high-profile indie games that fall under the category of metagames, a loosely characterized subgenre of games that explore the idea of games as games, games within games, and games about games. One of the foremost creators releasing games in this category is Daniel Mullins, whose works include *Pony Island* (2016) (now scheduled to receive a sequel), *The Hex* (2018), and *Inscryption* (2021). Any of these games would be an apt study for this collection on metareference (see also, respectively, the chapters by Thon, Hennig, and Caracciolo in this volume); however, this chapter focuses on Mullins's more recent work, *Inscryption*, and examines it as an in-depth case study on the complexity and layers of metareferentiality used in indie games. In *Inscryption*, metareference is central to both the narrative and mechanics of the game; indeed, in many ways, metareference is the gameplay. Examining Mullins's *Pony Island*, Damien Schlarb argues that "frame-breaking here functions not as a story-telling device but becomes the whole point of the game. Players are constantly confronting the fact that they are playing a video game" (2019, 207). Likewise, in *Inscryption*, Mullins continues to explore the depth and utility of metareference in games through a multilayered *mise en abyme*

DOI: 10.4324/9781003538592-6

and other metaleptic strategies to weave a complex narrative that extends beyond the game itself.

Mediation and Metareference

Metareference is often used in games as a source of entertainment for players (see Jannidis 2009). Creating fourth-wall breaking intrusions and Easter Eggs earned through player effort or specialized game knowledge are valuable rewards for players and keep them engaged and eager to explore gameworlds. Yet, metareference is also a useful tool for social commentary and critique; by breaking boundaries, metareference defamiliarizes its object of analysis and invites new perspectives. As Werner Wolf explains, metareference "establishes a secondary reference to texts and media (and related issues) as such by, as it were, viewing them 'from the outside' of a meta-level from whose perspective they are consequently seen as different from unmediated reality and the content of represented worlds" (2009, 22–23). This metalevel enables the audience to see the subject from a new, and sometimes even impossible, point of view. Ian Bogost has made an analogous argument about games, writing that they excel at "taking the tidy, ordinary world apart and putting it back together again in surprising, ghastly new ways" (2017, n.pag.). Likewise, metareferentiality in games is an effective tool for examining the relationship of games to the world by drawing attention to the ways that this world is mediated through popular culture (see Backe 2018).

In *Immediacy, or The Style of Too Late Capitalism*, Anna Kornbluh argues that contemporary society is characterized by a sense of immediacy; as she writes, immediacy is "a master category for making sense of twenty-first-century cultural production" (2023, 6). In *Remediation*, Jay Bolter and Richard Grusin (1999) provide important groundwork on the theorization of this term, which they employ to describe the perception of an experience as "unmediated," such as the promise of virtual reality to offer the feeling of being fully present in a virtual world. In reflecting on our contemporary moment, Kornbluh argues that "[i]mmediacy crushes mediation" (2023, 6) and in so doing, it removes the space for critical distance: "A painting isn't an efficient way to send a message or achieve a goal, but beholding its inefficient indirection can stimulate thought" (Kornbluh 2023, 5). Richard Grusin (2004, 21) makes a similar claim in his work on premediation, arguing that such encounters with immediacy are traumatic. As a result, he explains, news media now premediate future events so that audiences will never again experience the shock of an event like 9/11. Through premediation, "the future emerges into the present, that is, the moment when the future has already become the past, by extending our media networks into the future" (Grusin 2004, 37). For both Kornbluh and Grusin, the result of a relentless exposure to immediacy is a constant low level of anxiety. Paradoxically, our immersive devices are also precisely the tools that we reach for to shield us from the overwhelm caused by immediacy.

Videogames are fundamentally linked to the logic of immediacy. Not only because of emerging spatial computing technologies like virtual, augmented, mixed, and extended reality, but also through the rhetoric and the sometimes false promises that the medium will transport players to immersive virtual worlds. While immersion is hardly a quality exclusive to games (see also the chapter by Brown in this volume), what underlies their promises for greater immersion is immediacy. The premise of Johan Huizinga's "magic circle" makes a similar investment in the immersive qualities of games, as he argues that the space of gameplay is sequestered from reality: "Inside the circle of the game the laws and customs of ordinary life no longer count. We are different and do things differently" (Huizinga 1949, 12). The concept of the magic circle, however, has been thoroughly criticized in game studies (see Boluk and LeMieux 2017; Consalvo 2009). The delineation between games, play, and the "real" world is not so clear. While there are many reasons that reality permeates the boundaries of games, metareference is also a source of intrusion on the immersion and immediacy experienced by players. Not unlike Huizinga's "spoil-sport," who "shatters the play-world itself" (1949, 11), metareference also disrupts the play experience by drawing players' attention to the superficiality of these boundaries and the constructed nature of the game.

Examining the emergence of the metareferential turn in both media and scholarship, Wolf theorizes that "the noticeable prominence [...] of metareferential devices [...] renders another explanatory facet a likely candidate for illuminating the metareferential turn, namely metareference as a reaction to a binary opposition which seems to have become particularly unstable in our culture and which can best be explored by, or become the object of play in, metareference: the opposition of reality vs fiction" (2011, 36). Surveying the growth of the metagame subgenre, it is clear that many of these games reflect on the binary between reality and fiction (see Backe 2018). Games like *The Magic Circle* (2015) and *There Is No Game: Wrong Dimension* (2020), for instance, employ metareference to comment on games as a medium and the conditions in which they are made: that is, in a politically and economically conservative industry that prefers to revive existing intellectual properties, rather than engage in experimentation (see Thorne 2021, 63). Immediacy is a central quality of mainstream blockbuster games. Bolter and Grusin also note similar trends across other media industries: "To fulfill our apparently insatiable desire for immediacy, 'live' point-of-view television programs show viewers what it is like to accompany a police officer on a dangerous raid or to be a skydiver or a race car driver hurtling through space. Filmmakers routinely spend tens of millions of dollars to film on location or to recreate period costumes and places in order to make their viewers feel as if they were 'really' there" (Bolter and Grusin 1999, 5). With the release of XR (or spatial computing) headsets like PS VR, Meta Quest 3, and Apple Vision Pro, it is clear that there is a significant investment in these immersive technologies, but they are nevertheless technologies that lend themselves to simulation rather than experimentation. The increasing cost to develop games also encourages a more risk-averse industry. Recent rumors around *Grand Theft Auto VI* have speculated that this new release will cost $2 billion USD to develop, which would set a record for the most expensive game made (see Alt 2023). Publicly traded game companies, however, are usually quiet about the costs of development to avoid raising concern among investors. Nevertheless, it is apparent that Take-Two Interactive is making a significant investment in its existing intellectual properties. Such conservatism, Kornbluh argues, is characteristic of immediacy: "Prequel, quel, sequel, quel surprise, a universe-sprawl of story bleed that is homogenous and low risk, each content vehicle functioning less as narrative representation and more as commercial for its own distension" (Kornbluh 2023, 138).

While indie developers are not immune to the pressures faced by the AAA industry, they are also not a homogenous category, and indie games have historically been a site for experimentation (see Jagoda 2018). For this reason, I identify indie games as crucial to critique and disruption. In particular, they are uniquely positioned to comment and reflect on the relationship of games and game creation to the world that they inhabit. The mechanism through which many of these games have done so is through metareference (see Krampe et al. 2022). Kornbluh likewise argues that "the meta" is in opposition to immediacy: "[w]here postmodernism revels in mediation—intertextuality, irony, the meta—immediacy negates mediation to effect flow and indistinction [...]. Immediacy precipitates blur, a demediated meld that lacks the contours to array heterogeneity" (Kornbluh 2023, 13). Although Kornbluh's definition of immediacy is rather abstract and not tied to any particular medium, it is clear that it is an experience that is characterized by immersion, instant gratification, and superficiality. Metareference undermines these qualities by subverting expectations and demanding more of audiences to understand the work. In *Inscryption*, Mullins cleverly plays with the opposition between reality and fiction through a complex *mise en abyme* that layers the game's narrative and gameplay to blur the distinction between the game and reality until it comes full circle as an ouroboros.

A Card Game

Inscryption is a difficult game to describe. Inevitably, those intimately familiar with the game will identify gaps or additional connections that could have been made in this analysis; however, the purpose of this chapter is not to produce an exhaustive list of its metareferences, but to survey the structure and strategic use of *mise en abyme* and other metaleptic devices to understand how metareference is employed to support both the game's narrative and gameplay.

Among other things, *Inscryption* is a first-person, 3D, deckbuilding, roguelike card game. Its most novel feature, however, is its use of *mise en abyme* to layer both its narrative and gameplay. In *Avatars of Story* (2006), Marie-Laure Ryan explains such nesting structures and metalepsis by using the analogy of "the stack," which she borrows from computer programming. This comparison is also useful here, as *Inscryption* offers a similar structure where its narrative is intimately tied to its own digital existence. As Ryan explains, "[e]very language-based fictional narrative involves at least two levels: a real-world level, on which an author communicates with a reader, and a primary fictional level, on which a narrator communicates with a narratee within an imaginary world. Whenever a narrative

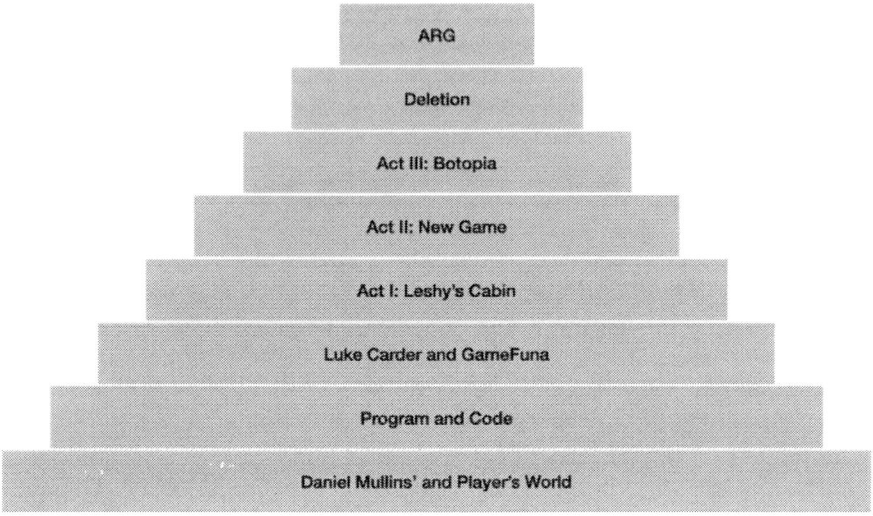

Figure 6.1 The layered structure of *Inscryption.*

generates another narrative it adds another level to the narrative stack" (2006, 204). Games are similarly divided between the real-world level of the developer and the fictional world of the game, though these divisions might look quite different in non-narrative media. Peter McDonald theorizes an analogous claim regarding games in *Run and Jump* (2024): Focusing on the platformer genre, McDonald argues that "[e]very game contains two—or more—games hidden within it. Together they create a meta-language that any platforming game can use to reflect on its position within the genre. Collectibles, power-ups, and secrets are tools for the designer to anticipate and suggest variations in the style of play and reincorporate those variations into the fabric of the game" (2024, 110). These features exceed the fictional world of the game and reveal the intervention of the developer by implying alternate and competing approaches to play. In addition to these same three features, *Inscryption* incorporates a number of such layers of games within games (see Figure 6.1).

"Okay. Time to figure out what's on this thing," a disembodied voice says expectantly as the player launches *Inscryption.* The whirr of a computer is heard in the background. Although its significance is likely to be missed, this audio clip marks the player's first encounter with a rhetorical metalepsis, a brief interruption breaking through from another layer of the narrative.

ACT I: Leshy's Cabin

Once the game is loaded, it begins in medias res: From the menu screen, players are not able to access the option to start a "new game," but instead must choose "continue." Continue what, they are not sure, but this opening sequence is likely to raise suspicion about what is to follow. Those familiar with Mullins's work will know that he has employed similar interface tricks in his previous games (see Krampe et al. 2022). A floppy disk—an apparent skeuomorph—appears briefly on the screen, signaling, perhaps, that the game is being saved. A mysterious figure, who we will later learn is named Leshy, sits opposite the player with an arrangement of cards between them. While most of the cards depict "beasts," a number of cards are also able to speak to the player (the stoat, stinkbug, and stunted wolf). Between rounds of card battles, players interact with a board game map that depicts a forest. The map offers different paths to travel and opportunities to build the player's deck by gaining new cards and powering up existing cards. The game will proceed through numerous matches against Leshy, before players realize that they can stand up and move away from the table, revealing a new layer to the game. *Inscryption* is not only a card game, but players are also trapped in a cabin that is equipped with puzzles in a way that resembles an escape room. This creates a kind of ludic *mise en abyme*, rather than a new narrative level, where players play a game within a game within the same narrative frame. Players will alternate between playing the card game with Leshy and attempting to solve the mysteries of the cabin.

After defeating Leshy at his card game, the disembodied voice returns and exclaims, "Did I just—I think I just beat him! … Oop." Our view suddenly shifts from a first-person perspective to that of a recording camera in a free fall—presumably caused by an accidental bump—revealing the living room of an unassuming modern home. This moment introduces a new narrative level of the *mise en abyme*. Players next see the loading screen for the camera's software, "Kam Werks." Within this software, players gain access to the content of its memory card, which includes eight video clips. Players learn that they have been playing as Luke Carder, a YouTuber, whose channel, "The Lucky Carder," specializes in opening collectable card packs. In one video, we discover that his voice was the one heard upon launching the game and the whirr of the computer was the sound of a loading floppy disk. Yet, although players play as Luke, they seemingly simultaneously occupy the impossible and contradictory perspective of his camera, which he uses to record content for his channel.

Drawing on the film techniques of found footage horror films, Luke's videos reveal that he had initially purchased a number of vintage card packs of the physical card game of "Inscryption" at a garage sale.[1] Through the clips Luke had recorded to upload to his channel, we learn that he obtained a digital copy of "Inscryption" after discovering a set of coordinates written on one of the cards in the card pack that appeared to have been tampered with. Additional footage shows Luke following the coordinates to a remote location in the woods where he digs up a floppy disk containing the game players had been playing moments ago. The next video shows Luke purchasing a floppy disk drive to read the disk which contains the game that we are presently playing. After watching each of the clips, the player reappears in Leshy's cabin and locates the "new game" button that had been missing from the game's menu screen.

ACT II: New Game

Returning to the menu now allows players to start a new game which begins Act II. Rather than a continuation of Leshy's cabin, the gameworld is changed. Instead of a first-person perspective in a 3D world, the player is now embodied as a pixelated avatar in an isometric view of a role-playing-game-styled game. Through a narrative montage, they learn that Leshy was one of four "Scrybes," Leshy, Grimora, Magnificus, and P03—three of which were represented by the talking cards in Leshy's game. Now in Act II, the other Scrybes are free and each has their own card deck created through "their own method of [...] Inscryption to create cards." Each deck has a unique game mechanic that alters how cards are played (including sacrifice, bones, gems, or energy). Ultimately, the player will have to defeat each of the Scrybes in order to complete the "New Game" version of "Inscryption," and, at the end, the player is told that they must take the place of one of the Scrybes.

While Act II appears as a ludic *mise en abyme*, we learn at the end of Act II that it is not simply a game within a game, as the escape room cabin was to Leshy's card game, but rather that this version of "Inscryption" was the "Original Inscryption" game,[2] and Leshy's cabin was created as a trap for the other Scrybes. He had used his method of inscryption, a camera, to turn the other Scrybes into cards. By defeating Leshy, the player has undone the trap; however, it is unclear at this point in the game why this trap has been set.

Midway through Act II, the text "Battery Low" flashes on the screen and the player is once again taken to the interface for the memory card of Luke's recording camera where players gain access to eight new videos. In the first clip, Luke reads aloud an email he has written to the collectable card game company, GameFuna, to ask about the digital version of "Inscryption." A subsequent clip offers the company's response which denies any knowledge of its existence and requests that Luke send them the hardware that he claims to possess. A later video shows a woman at Luke's door who appears to be from GameFuna. Luke denies knowledge of the floppy disk and digital version of "Inscryption." Many of these videos are glitchy, not only distorting the visuals, but they also occasionally reveal binary code that can be decoded by players to reveal additional clues about the circumstances of the game (see Figure 6.2).

After the player defeats each of the Scrybes in Act II, P03, the Scrybe of Technology, emerges to revel in Leshy's defeat. He criticizes Leshy and states, "[i]t's no wonder we're back here again. And we would've been sooner if the disk wasn't lost…" This moment represents yet another metalepsis whereby P03 reveals that the Scrybes are not only conscious, but aware they are contained on the floppy disk that had been buried in the woods. This recognition introduces an ontological metalepsis that collapses what should be a clear distinction between the (fictional) real world and the gameworlds of "Inscryption." Outlining the distinction between rhetorical and ontological metalepsis, Ryan writes:

> Whereas rhetorical metalepsis maintains the levels of the stack distinct from each other, ontological metalepsis opens a passage between levels that results in their interpenetration, or mutual contamination. These levels, needless to say, must be

Figure 6.2 Glitches alter Luke's unedited *YouTube* video. The binary code spells out "KARNOFFEL CODE."

> separated by the type of boundary that I call ontological: a switch between two radically distinct worlds, such as "the real" versus "the imaginary," or the world of "normal" (or lucid) mental activity versus the world of dream or hallucination.
> (Ryan 2006, 207)

When P03 confronts Leshy, it enacts precisely what Ryan describes as the players' understanding of the relationship between the layers of the stack and reveals that this disk carries not only significance, but perhaps danger. It was clearly buried with intention and not meant to be found by Luke.

At the end of Act II, regardless of which Scrybe players choose to replace, the player will battle P03. However, P03 will ultimately disrupt the game by playing a glitching card that will quickly cause the screen to become overwhelmed with glitches and code that indicate that the code of the "New Game" version of "Inscryption" is becoming corrupt and replaced with P03's own: "P03.Factory." These screen glitches act as rhetorical metalepses, becoming "diegetically and semiotically productive" (Schlarb 2019, 196), by revealing the underlying stack of the (fictional) code that supports the representational level of the game. These layers of code, however, are later revealed to be critical to the game's narrative rather than merely aesthetic glitches (see also the chapter by Thon in this volume).

ACT III: Botopia

When the glitches clear, players find themselves in the familiar first-person point of view from the opening of the game, but they now sit opposite P03 as the game master with a board game map of Botopia. This world establishes yet another layer to the *mise en abyme*. Like Leshy's cabin, players are also able to stand and explore P03's factory. P03 explains that Botopia is "ruled over by four… uh… Uberbots… And you've got to get out there and beat them. Why? To perform *The Great Transcendence* of course. Doesn't matter what that means. You want it, Ok?" It is clear from the tone that it is likely that "The Great Transcendence" is something that players do not want; but, nevertheless, the only way to continue the game is to play.

While much of the gameplay is the same as before, it introduces new card mechanics and strategies for optimizing one's deck. Act III also reveals critical new information about the context of "Inscryption" and the relationship between the Scrybes. Midway through the player's exploration of Botopia, the text "Memory Card Is Full" appears across the screen and interrupts gameplay. As in Act II, this rhetorical metalepsis signals a shift to a different narrative level and players again gain access to the memory card of Luke's camera and eight new videos.

Through these clips, we learn that Luke contacts the woman that had sold him the "Inscryption" card packs at a garage sale. Mrs. Hobbes tells Luke that the cards had belonged to her daughter, Kaycee, who had been employed by GameFuna; however, she had died at work some time ago under somewhat suspicious circumstances. It becomes clear that Kaycee was responsible for burying the "Inscryption" disk in the woods. Attentive players will also recall that Kaycee's name is referenced throughout each act of *Inscryption*. This knowledge exposes yet another ontological metalepsis whereby a character from the "real" fictional world breaks ontological boundaries by also appearing within the game. While a number of the remaining videos are corrupt, in others, Luke expresses fear that there are people outside of his home in the night and he begins to behave strangely.

Returning to P03's factory, players will have to engage in a number of boss battles that introduce new moments of metalepsis. In the final boss battle of the game, players encounter the Archivist, who expresses keen interest in the player's files: "I eagerly await the opportunity to explore your hard drive. Files and directories are my specialty you see. […] You will need to grant me access to your hard drive. […] I assure you, no harm will come of it. Here comes your actual files. I hope no one is watching! Now. Do recommend an exemplary file to me and do take into account its *size*." An interface appears on the screen revealing the player's complete file directory. Noteworthy is that the Archivist shows an awareness of the real world and that players may be live streaming their gameplay and first warns players that their files will be shown. Players will be asked to select large files that will deal damage to their opponent a number of times throughout the card battle.

In the next segment, the player will be asked to choose a file that "is very special […] a file that is dearest to your heart. And one that shows *age*." After making a selection, the Archivist will comment on its age and adds: "Now, let us place that file in a card. You didn't choose a file that was *too* dear, did you? For, if this card dies, I will *delete the file from your disk*. Please, do not tempt me. I am completely serious." The age of the file chosen will determine the health and power stats of the card. While the game does not quite delete the file if the card is lost, it does create a .txt file using an identical name with a message that requests that players "play by the rules" and delete the file as they had previously agreed. In examining the potential for metalepsis in computer games to intrude on reality, Ryan asks, "[w]hat would it take for metalepsis to *really* spill into the real world and affect it *physically*? It would be fairly easy to write a computer game that destroys the user's system. Such a feature would of course be self-defeating from a commercial point of view, since once the word got out, nobody would buy the product" (2006, 226). Mullins clearly also arrived at the same conclusion, as the game only encourages the player to enforce this outcome, rather than actually deleting the file. *Inscryption*, however, also inverts this view of metalepsis to consider how the real world might come to bear upon the game (see also the chapter by Krampe in this volume). He does this by, in part, allowing the player's actual files to alter the player's battle with the Archivist (the file size and age affect the power of attacks and cards); however, in an earlier battle, against Golly (a boss connected to the internet), the game draws on the player's Steam friends list to populate one round of their battle. In this moment, Golly exclaims that she is getting a signal: "W-what are these? Are these… your friends?" The player's Steam friends appear as cards on the board and must be defeated. During this battle, Golly will also attempt to receive information from the web: "Woah! A new signal! Someone is trying to send you a *card*! Let's see if we can receive it… It worked! Let's see what it looks like." If no one else is playing this section of the game at this precise moment, it will deliver a card "from the web," which is a predetermined default card ("Mummy Lord"). Players will have the opportunity shortly thereafter to create a card that will be sent to other players (if there are any players currently at this stage of the game, they will receive your card).

Defeating the boss battles of Act III leads to "The Great Transcendence" and the conclusion of both "Inscryption" and *Inscryption*. P03 returns and derides Luke (and also the player) for assisting with his plan: "You prepared The Great Transcendence for me. Without even knowing what it was. But… You understand it now, right? Right Luke? I mean… *you finished making the game*… You gave me access to your hard drive… You took screenshots for the store page. And you connected me to the internet to upload it all! I mean… If you didn't realize what you were doing… You'd have to be pretty stupid. But what did I expect? You're a stupid, stupid, idiot gamer like the rest." P03's speech exemplifies a kind of metaleptic awareness (see Macrae 2019; Thon 2016; Waszkiewicz 2024) that acknowledges his cognizance of the world outside and his own presence in a videogame. Yet, as players now learn, "The Great Transcendence" is precisely P03's plan to resolve that metaleptic conflict by uploading "Inscryption" to the internet. Moments before the upload is complete, P03 is stopped by the Scrybes. Grimora quickly accesses the files on the floppy disk, revealing a mysterious file called OLD_DATA, and chooses to delete the contents of the disk, consequently also deleting the Scrybes in the process. The deletion process marks the end of the game and the player will have the opportunity to play friendly rounds of "Inscryption" with each of the Scrybes before they are deleted. During the player's game with Grimora, she explains that she chose to delete the disk not only for selfish reasons (to end her existence trapped on the disk), but because hidden "deep beneath the data of Inscryption… at the very bottom of the well… there is something truly evil."

Figure 6.3 The redacted files in OLD_DATA.

As "Inscryption" is deleted and the Scrybes disappear along with it, the final files to remain are the mysterious OLD_DATA files. When the player opens this zip file, the screen begins filling with redacted images, text, and the identification card for a member of the United States of America Department of Defense (see Figure 6.3). What is displayed on the screen devolves into television static and Luke is heard yelling in the background. Our perspective pulls back and we now see Luke destroying the disk with a hammer. Luke attempts to contact a journalist about these strange events but is murdered by a GameFuna employee before he has a chance to explain what he has seen.

For many players, this moment appears to be the end of the game, but there remain many questions about the seemingly sentient Scrybes, GameFuna, and the OLD_DATA and its redacted files. These questions prompted some keen players to look for additional clues in the game that uncovered an alternate reality game (ARG) that extends far beyond *Inscryption* and into the real world.

ARG

While some parts of the ARG are no longer accessible, its events have been thoroughly documented online (see, e.g., Flemmonade 2021; DaBigKahuna n.d.). The ARG, ultimately, brings the stack full circle (see Figure 6.1), extending *Inscryption*'s multitiered, metaleptic *mise en abyme* back into the real world. The ARG involves players seeking out clues that may appear in the game, its code, or be located outside of *Inscryption* entirely. Clues may require players to edit the game's code, alter video settings, translate Polish text, or venture outside. These clues must be further decoded and combined in order to form ciphers that the player must enter in a secret terminal window that is accessible at the start of Act II. These ciphers unlock a chat dialogue between three people that provide partial answers to the game's mysteries by revealing that the OLD_DATA is tied to German encryption codes from World War II. The so-called Karnöffel Code was derived from a deck of playing cards that would later be acquired by the Soviets and would play a role in the Cold War. The Karnöffel Code has something to do with the sentience of the Scrybes, but this remains somewhat of a mystery. These clues are uncovered not only by examining *Inscryption* in detail (e.g., looking for binary code hidden in its glitched videos, see Figure 6.2), but also by playing Mullins's other games that are available on his itch.io page. One clue, for instance, leads players to a game called *Beneath the Ice*, which was created for a game jam in 2014 (seven years before the release of *Inscryption*). In this fishing game, if players send their fishing line to the correct depth, they will retrieve a "strange disk" with a code that can be used to solve one of three parts of a cipher in *Inscryption*. Many of these clues also require modifying the code or adding files to the directories of these games in order for them to work. The depth and complexity of steps that are involved in the ARG cannot be overstated. And as revealed through the *Beneath the Ice* example, the ARG extends not only beyond the boundaries of *Inscryption* but also reaches impossibly back through time to provide answers to mysteries in *Inscryption*. Here, this form of metalepsis is used to amplify the difficulty of piecing together the clues.

Continuing the stacked structure of *Inscryption*, the ARG also makes use of *mise en abyme* as it restages the events that set *Inscryption* in motion. This event occurs when two players investigate the geographical coordinates referenced in the game (the same coordinates that Luke had found written on a card in the "Inscryption" card pack purchased from the garage sale). The coordinates lead them to Stanley Park in Vancouver, Canada. As relayed in the community ARG documentation, "[a]fter visiting the location for the first time with a phone whose battery was almost depleted, they looked for a power bank in the city and returned. In the meantime, Daniel Mullins and Kevin Saxby (the actor playing Luke Carder) went to a nearby pub, and there the four of them met up" (DaBigKahuna n.d., n.pag.). The group returned to the site and filmed the ARG players digging up a muddied "Inscryption" floppy disk (though Mullins had also provided the players with a second clean and functional disk). In the video, the pair are shown to be attacked (and presumably murdered) by Mullins after retrieving the disk (see Firefox529 2021). While meant to be a humorous moment, for the audience and ARG participants, it acts as a kind of ontological metalepsis. The boundaries between the game and the real world, between reality and fiction, between immediacy and mediation fully collapse and the structure of the game takes the form of an ouroboros. Ryan also addresses such cyclical structures, writing that:

> Another way to represent ontological metalepsis is through the image of the snake that bites its own tail, a literal rendering of the concept of the strange loop. A strange loop phenomenon, according to Hofstadter, "occurs whenever, by moving upwards (or downwards) through the levels of some hierarchical system, we unexpectedly find ourselves right back where we started" (1980, 10).
> (Ryan 2006, 208–209)

When the ARG meets with reality, the structure of the game, its stack, comes full circle, feeding into itself: The players now find themselves acting out the very events experienced by Luke, which were also previously experienced by Kaycee. The intentionality behind this cyclical structure is also reinforced by the presence of ouroboros cards in *Inscryption* across each of its three acts (although in Act III, the card is referred to as Ourobot). For players of the ARG not able to visit Stanley Park, a series of clues lead players to a webpage (www.kaminskimfg.com/orderform) that allowed them to enter their mailing address. This page soon became inactive, but players who were able to submit their address were each mailed a floppy disk from Mullins that contained additional clues. Like Luke, players that received a floppy disk also had to purchase a disk drive to read its contents.

The contents of these disks deliver the final three clues of the ARG. One disk offers the message: "THANKYOUFOR#|PLAYING##|NSCRYPTIONFRIEND" (DaBigKahuna n.d., n.pag.). While clearly a message from Mullins, this text is also used to solve the final cipher and unlock the final pieces of the chat dialogue that elaborate on the Karnöffel Code's history and how it ended up on a floppy disk at GameFuna. A second floppy disk received during the ARG contains a partial link to a *YouTube* video, that links to an unlisted video that shows Luke's computer completing P03's upload of "Inscryption" to the internet (see Kaminski Mfg 2021). The video file is aptly named 10.19.mp4, mirroring the real launch date of *Inscryption*, which reveals that P03 was successful and that it is that version of "Inscryption" that the player is presently playing. The final floppy disk text file reads "The End," marking the conclusion of the ARG.

While *Inscryption*, on its own, already challenges the logic of immediacy by denying players a respite from its ever-changing gameplay mechanics and multilayered, metaleptic narrative, its ARG adds a critical dimension that calls into question the boundaries between reality and fiction in two ways. First, it invites players to reflect on the developer and their role in crafting the game experience. While most players would agree that games are art, there is a simultaneous, and somewhat contradictory, belief held by some players that games are purely entertainment made for their audiences. They might, for instance, consider ways the game could be improved and made more fun, rather than examine the game on its own terms. This minor but vocal group of gamers have complained that games are becoming political (as though games were not always already political) (see Miller 2020), but such views are at odds with the idea that games, like other media, are also made as a form of expression outside of commercial interest. The signature metareferential style of Mullins's work highlights his status as an auteur and the authorial intention in his work. Having players examine his corpus of work to solve puzzles in *Inscryption* and also his, perhaps inadvertent, emergence in the ARG (see Firefox529 2021), makes him inseparable from his work.

The second way that *Inscryption*'s ARG disrupts the binary between reality and fiction is by inviting players to apply the logical thinking and puzzle-solving skills utilized throughout the game to the real world. While initially this work might be localized in *Inscryption*, the investigation quickly spills outside of the game. While games are often thought of as a place for escaping reality, the ARG elements of *Inscryption* reveal that the skills learned by playing games are transferable to the real world. In *Reality Is Broken* (2011), Jane McGonigal makes an analogous claim and argues that if we approached real life with the same confidence and enthusiasm that we approach videogames, we might be able to collaborate to transform the world for the better. ARGs, she asserts, are particularly adept at making this claim visible; as she writes, "[t]he best ARGs are the ones that, like the best traditional computer and video games, help us create more satisfying work for ourselves, cultivate better hopes of success, strengthen our social bonds and activate our social networks, and give us the chance to contribute to something bigger than ourselves" (McGonigal 2011, 127). While McGonigal's claims about the power of games to bring about real-world change can feel overly optimistic, when surveying the challenging puzzles presented to players in *Inscryption*'s ARG, it is hard to deny that what people can achieve when they collaborate in a game context is impressive.

Games within Games

Inscryption makes use of many forms of metareference and does so following a particular logic. Rhetorical metalepses, like the interruptions from Luke's camera (tipping over, low battery, and memory card is full), are used as a transition to another layer of the narrative stack. These moments lead to opportunities to learn about Luke's world and the origin of "Inscryption."

Glitches are used throughout the game as rhetorical metalepses; however, they are commonly associated with nefarious figures (such as P03 or GameFuna's attempts to conceal important information). These glitches often work metaludically (see Ensslin 2014) to simultaneously reveal and conceal clues for the ARG as they draw players' attention to the material layer of code which becomes critical to understanding the game.

While *Inscryption* is already an example of a ludic *mise en abyme* (containing games within games), it is also an example of a game that is simultaneously "two games" in McDonald's sense in that it makes use of collectibles, power-ups, and secrets to deepen its gameplay. McDonald approaches these three game elements as stripped of their utility (outside of their objective use value to players) to consider their discursive purpose. Collectibles, power-ups, and secrets act metaludically in the game, not only inviting players to reflect on gameplay and strategies, but they also act metaleptically as a kind of intrusion from the game developer on the gameworld by, for instance, serving as suggestions (from a metalevel) about how the game should be played and thereby extending the game beyond its most superficial level. McDonald provides the example of collecting coins that have been carefully distributed throughout a level. Collectibles, he argues, "are a powerful tool for the designer to communicate about the nascent possibilities for play that a level provides. Platforms offer an architecture or a playground, but collectibles show the player how to inhabit that world with rhythms, pacing, atmosphere, and drama" (McDonald 2024, 112). Similarly, power-ups encourage novel approaches to play: "platforming levels are designed to work regardless of the special abilities a player might have, because she may just as well avoid a power-up as choose it" (McDonald 2024, 114). Finally, secrets engage players in pursuits outside of the game's explicit goals: "[H]idden goals require sleuthing and painstaking trial and error. Such elusive ends point beyond themselves to the player's creativity and ability to generate new metagames. Secrets offer a discourse of devious intelligences, but as a metadiscourse they speak to the reasons we play and the pleasures that draw us repeatedly into video games" (McDonald 2024, 123). Although McDonald is referring specifically to the platformer genre, *Inscryption* enacts each of these features in its own way: There are cards (and achievements) to collect; one's cards can be powered up in a number of ways that create different styles of play, and, as discussed at length already, the game is full of secrets (some of which act as rabbit holes leading to the ARG). Once players have completed *Inscryption*, they will also be able to access Mullins's "Kaycee's mod," which further extends the gameplay of Ļeshy's cabin, allowing the player to continue playing, experiment with cards, and new card combinations. Although the mod appears to be external to "Inscryption," it is clear from its use of Kaycee's name that it is still intertwined with the events of the game. Skilled players will be able to unlock additional background information about the context of how "Inscryption" came to be by completing the mod's challenges.

Although McDonald is speaking specifically about platformers, through these complex and intersecting elements, *Inscryption* illustrates the kind of depth that McDonald describes as possible in games using these mechanics. As he outlines,

> If it has collectibles, power-ups, or secrets, there is at least a second game hiding within the first. These virtual others do not necessarily align, so there might well be three other games hinted at in the margins. Why stop there? The possibilities mix and match in combinatorial formations. If I am right that these three elements, stripped of their primarily utilitarian function, are paradigmatic of the genre, then things get even weirder. In that case, when we imagine a new, virtual game brought into existence by searching for secrets or following the path of collectibles, that second game would have its own secrets, power-ups, and collectibles. These virtual secrets would suggest a third level of imaginary game, and so on. In that *mise en abyme* or infinite regress is a web that unites all platforming games. Through the slight changes to the level, the mechanics, and the goals suggested by collectibles, power-ups, and secrets, one game subtly changes into another.
>
> (McDonald 2024, 123)

As shown in Figure 6.1, *Inscryption* offers a complex metareferential narrative *mise en abyme*, but this stack is also doubled by its ludic metagame layers relating both to the explicit games within its game (the varied versions of "Inscryption"), its ARG, and its unseen games of collectibles, power-ups, and secrets.

Conclusion

Metareference is a critical tool for developers to employ in games. While metareference can be used to reward players for their intimate knowledge of games or game conventions, it can also be employed to support and enhance either (or both) the narrative and gameplay. Across his games, Mullins has leveraged metareference as a critical element of his signature style, making his games recognizable as his own. Metareference in *Inscryption* is used to implode the distinctions between players, reality, games, and the code used to create them; *Inscryption*'s ARG, in particular, reflects on the relationship between games and reality. *Inscryption* employs *mise en abyme* as a strategy to continually unseat the player's expectations and encourage them to be adaptive. It uses rhetorical metalepsis to interrupt gameplay and signal shifts between narrative layers, which often lead to moments of ontological metalepsis that contaminate the once clean separations between each level of the stack. Metareference is effective because we live in a world dominated by immediacy. Its intrusions disrupt our immersion and create hypermediated moments that, through their strangeness, draw attention and encourage reflection about the experience. Although with overuse, it is possible that its power to defamiliarize will wane; for instance, it is likely that players today no longer react with panic when a game uses glitches or crashes, but instead quickly recognize such moments as rhetorical uses of these malfunctions. *Inscryption*, however, makes the case that the impactfulness of metareference has not yet been exhausted when employed with purpose, rather than for entertainment.

Notes

1 *Inscryption* contains references to a number of fictional versions of games with the same name. Italics will be used for *Inscryption*, the game purchased and downloaded by players, while references to the fictional physical card game or videogame versions of "Inscryption" played by Luke will appear in quotation marks.
2 In the Steam achievements for *Inscryption*, the achievements associated with Act II refer to the game as "Original Inscryption."

Works Cited

Alt, Eric. 2023. "*GTA 6: Grand Theft Auto VI* Could Smash Revenue Records." *BBC*, December 15, 2023. www.bbc.com/worklife/article/20231214-gta-6-grand-theft-auto-vi-could-smash-revenue-records#.

Backe, Hans-Joachim. 2018. "Metareferentiality through In-Game Images in Immersive Simulation Game." In *FDG '18: Proceedings of the 13th International Conference on the Foundations of Digital Games*, 25 (1–10).

Beneath the Ice. 2014. Daniel Mullins Games/Daniel Mullins Games. Microsoft Windows.

Bogost, Ian. 2017. "Video Games Are Better Without Stories." *The Atlantic*, April 25, 2017. www.theatlantic.com/technology/archive/2017/04/video-games-stories/524148/.

Bolter, J. David, and Richard A. Grusin. 1999. *Remediation: Understanding New Media*. Cambridge, MA: MIT Press.

Boluk, Stephanie, and Patrick LeMieux. 2017. *Metagaming: Playing, Competing, Spectating, Cheating, Trading, Making, and Breaking Videogames*. Minneapolis: University of Minnesota Press.

Consalvo, Mia. 2009. "There Is No Magic Circle." *Games and Culture* 4 (4): 408–417.

DaBigKahuna. n.d. "DaBigKahuna's Big Ol' Catch-Me-Up Inscryption Guide(Secret Ending Hunt)." https://docs.google.com/document/u/2/d/e/2PACX-1vTXY6k5k-6p_kjjI_scaBtAjn495e9HqOz8vl95YSBdycjcfU1TUjjT6uWv5b-1R0xvC1SZxGV99Qt7/pub.

Ensslin, Astrid. 2014. *Literary Gaming*. Cambridge, MA: MIT Press.

Firefox529. 2021. "Secret Ending." *Twitch*, October 22, 2021. https://clips.twitch.tv/ArbitraryHotCockroachPicoMause-w4I4hGivhsCmFXUM.

Flemmonade. 2021. "The Inscryption ARG: What Is the Karnoffel Code?." *YouTube*, December 21, 2021. www.youtube.com/watch?v=1DkK5ZML2G0.

Grand Theft Auto VI. Forthcoming. Rockstar Games/Take-Two Interactive.

Grusin, Richard. 2004. "Premediation." *Criticism* 46 (1): 17–39.

The Hex. 2018. Daniel Mullins Games. Microsoft Windows.

Hofstadter, Douglas. 1980. *Gödel, Escher, Bach: An Eternal Golden Braid*. New York: Vintage Books.

Huizinga, Johan. 1949. *Homo Ludens: A Study of the Play-Element in Culture*. London: Routledge and Kegan Paul.

Inscryption. 2021. Daniel Mullins Games/Devolver Digital. Microsoft Windows.

Jagoda, Patrick. 2018. "On Difficulty in Video Games: Mechanics, Interpretation, Affect." *Critical Inquiry* 45 (1): 199–233.

Jannidis, Fotis. 2009. "Metareference in Computer Games." In *Metareference across Media: Theory and Case Studies*, edited by Werner Wolf, 543–565. Amsterdam: Rodopi.

Kaminski Mfg. 2021. "10-19.mp4." *YouTube*, October 24, 2021. www.youtube.com/watch?v=e-FuQZ6hTS0.

Kornbluh, Anna. 2023. *Immediacy, or The Style of Too-Late Capitalism*. London: Verso.

Krampe, Theresa, Stephanie Lotzow, and Jan-Noël Thon. 2022. "Playful Poetics: Metareferential Interfaces in Recent Indie Games." *Poetics Today* 43 (4): 729–771.

Macrae, Andrea. 2019. *Discourse Deixis in Metafiction: The Language of Metanarration, Metalepsis and Disnarration*. New York: Routledge.

The Magic Circle. 2015. Question. Microsoft Windows.

McDonald, Peter. 2024. *Run and Jump: The Meaning of the 2D Platformer*. Cambridge, MA: MIT Press.

McGonigal, Jane. 2011. *Reality Is Broken: Why Games Make Us Better and How They Can Change the World*. New York: Penguin Press.

Miller, Lucy. 2020. "*Wolfenstein II* and MAGA as Fandom." *Transformative Works and Cultures* 32: n.pag.

Pony Island. 2016. Daniel Mullins Games. Microsoft Windows.

Ryan, Marie-Laure. 2006. *Avatars of Story*. Minneapolis: University of Minnesota Press.

Schlarb, Damien. 2019. "Narrative Glitches: Action Adventure Games and Metaleptic Convergence." In *Playing the Field: Video Games and American Studies*, edited by Sascha Pöhlmann, 195–210. Berlin: De Gruyter.

There Is No Game: Wrong Dimension. 2020. Draw Me A Pixel. Microsoft Windows.

Thon, Jan-Noël. 2016. *Transmedial Narratology and Contemporary Media Culture*. Lincoln: University of Nebraska Press.

Thorne, Sarah. 2021. "There Is No Immersion: Critical Intervention through Hypermediacy in Metagames." *Eludamos: Journal for Computer Game Culture* 12 (1): 63–85.

Waszkiewicz, Agata. 2024. *Metagames: Games about Games*. New York: Routledge.

Wolf, Werner. 2009. "Metareference across Media: The Concept, Its Transmedial Potentials and Problems, Main Forms and Functions." In *Metareference across Media: Theory and Case Studies*, edited by Werner Wolf, 1–85. Amsterdam: Rodopi.

Wolf, Werner. 2011. "Is There a Metareferential Turn, and If So, How Can It Be Explained?" In *The Metareferential Turn in Contemporary Arts and Media: Forms, Functions, Attempts at Explanation*, edited by Werner Wolf, 1–47. Amsterdam: Rodopi.

7 Metareference and Posthuman Subjectivity in Videogames

Marco Caracciolo

This chapter argues that metareferential techniques in videogames can disrupt the ontological boundaries that surround the concept and experience of the subject in Western modernity. Metareference in games thus resonates with, and stages, key ideas emerging from posthumanist philosophy, particularly the critique of rigid distinctions between the human mind and nonhuman materiality. After surveying existing work on metareference in games, the chapter turns to posthumanist debates on subjectivity and samples the philosophical frameworks introduced by thinkers including Karen Barad and Rosi Braidotti. Finally, I offer an extended analysis of Inscryption *(2021) as an indie game performing a posthumanist understanding of the subject through metareferences to the player and the foregrounding of material mediation.*

"Video games are beginning to tap their potential as a platform on which the specific nature of the interactivity they propose [...] is conducive to the affective exploration of various posthumanist agendas" (Milesi 2022, 580), writes Laurent Milesi. Posthumanism is a loose term for a set of theories that challenge a long history of humanist thinking in the Western world. Rooted in a reappraisal of classical philosophy, humanism emerged in Italy during the Renaissance and underwent considerable expansion in the Enlightenment period (see Law 2011, chap. 1). It places human beings at the center of the universe, intellectually or morally, suggesting that our cognitive apparatus can serve as a yardstick for philosophy. In practice, however, that lofty ideal has often led to the privileging of a certain understanding of the human (Western, male, able-bodied, and so on). Posthumanism attempts to disrupt that anthropocentric view and the ideological assumptions that go with it. To quote from one of its main theorists, Cary Wolfe, posthumanism emphasizes the way in which " 'the human' is achieved by escaping or repressing not just its animal origins in nature, the biological, and the evolutionary, but more generally by transcending the bonds of materiality and embodiment altogether" (2010, xv).

Of course, both "humanism" and "posthumanism" are large words: There are undoubtedly many philosophical complications and nuances to the former, and even the latter is less a coordinated movement than an umbrella concept for approaches

DOI: 10.4324/9781003538592-7

that understand the "post" in posthumanism in profoundly different ways. Wolfe himself, for example, is careful to uncouple his version of posthumanism from a seemingly related philosophy, that of "transhumanism." If posthumanism aims to reclaim the "biological" and "evolutionary" origins of the human, as well as its embodied "materiality" (Wolfe 2010, xv), transhumanism posits that these dimensions can be transcended through technology.[1] Also distancing themselves from transhumanism, Ivan Callus, Stefan Herbrechter, and Manuela Rossini develop a "critical posthumanism" (2014) that, in dialogue with thinkers such as Donna Haraway (e.g., Haraway 1991) and Katherine Hayles (e.g., Hayles 1999), interrogates the deep link between humanity and "non-human others (animals, plants, the inorganic, machines, gods, systems and various figures of liminality—from ghosts to angels, from cyborgs to zombies)" (Callus et al. 2014, 111–112). In other words, Milesi is right to use the plural form "agendas" when discussing videogames' exploration of posthumanism, because as this list of "non-human others" indicates, posthumanist thinkers are often engaging in considerably different projects. Nevertheless, Milesi's point still stands that videogames are becoming an increasingly important springboard for posthumanist ideas.

That is my starting point in this chapter: Videogames can question humanist assumptions, not merely by integrating posthumanism as a theme but also by deploying mechanics that translate or perform posthumanist thinking through digital narrative and gameplay.[2] I am certainly not the first game scholar to investigate the posthumanist potential of the medium: Ian Bogost's (2012) work played an important role in bringing together posthumanist theory (particularly Object-Oriented Ontology or OOO) and videogame studies. More recent scholarship by Darshana Jayemanne (2017), Sonia Fizek (2022), and Cody Mejeur (2023) has picked up where Bogost left off, bringing a number of posthumanist insights to bear on game analysis. Research on ecogames, or games that stage environmental issues and questions, is also clearly influenced by posthumanist philosophy (see, e.g., Chang 2019; Op de Beke et al. 2024).

There is still much work to do, particularly in terms of understanding how posthumanist ideas may be implicated in the formal design of games as well as in their subject matter. My specific focus here is on how games may use metareference to undermine a humanist conception of the (human) subject—a conception critiqued by posthumanist thinkers including the already-mentioned Wolfe (2010), Karen Barad (2007), and Rosi Braidotti (2013). The human subject is no longer seen as unitary and separate from the nonhuman world—a Cartesian "res cogitans" dualistically uncoupled from the world of things and bodies. Instead, for these posthumanist theorists human subjectivity is deeply rooted in the body, as well as in the evolutionary history we share with nonhuman animals. Moreover, the subject is multiple and divided—often because of how it is shaped by the environment in which living beings are embedded. As I argue in this chapter, this posthumanist understanding of subjectivity can become bound up, in contemporary videogames, with metareferential devices.[3] Following Werner Wolf, I see metareference as any form of self-reference in a semiotic medium that "establishes a secondary reference to texts and media (and related issues) [...] by, as it were, viewing them 'from the outside'" (2009, 22). In other words, metareference occurs when a text (verbal or otherwise) refers to itself in a way that invites the audience to take an external perspective on the medium, considering its semiotic constructedness.

Typically, in the case of fictional texts, this means that the (perceived) ontological separation between the real world and the fictional world is disrupted, although the extent of that disruption can vary significantly. For instance, in a famous scene of *Max Payne* (2001), the titular protagonist hallucinates that he is a character in a videogame: "The paranoid feeling of someone controlling my every step. I was in a computer game. […] [I]t was the most horrible thing I could think of." This is an instance of what Wolf (building on earlier work by Nelles [1992]) calls "epistemological metalepsis," which involves "'impossible' knowledge fictional characters appear to have of their being mere characters" (Wolf 2009, 53): Max seems to sense the player's controlling presence, even if this remark is explicitly framed by the game as the result of a drug-induced hallucination. This type of metalepsis is clearly a metareferential device in that it blurs the assumed ontological distinction between real world and gameworld, player and fictional character. To use James Phelan's terminology, the game collapses a "mimetic" (2007, 5) way of understanding the protagonist—as existing in an autonomous, lifelike world—and a "synthetic" (2007, 6) one, whereby Max Payne is a digital construct. This operation produces a moment of ontological blurring that is a result of metareferentiality: Real and fictional worlds appear to converge, if only fleetingly, in the character's awareness of his being "in a computer game." Other devices (including stronger forms of metareference, through metalepsis or alternative means) are able to prolong and deepen that blurring, as I will show below.[4]

Metareferentiality (understood as the sustained use of metareference in a text) tends to disrupt the (perceived) ontological separation between reality and the gameworld. While this idea is more or less widely accepted in literary and game studies, I argue in this chapter that metareferential techniques can also disrupt the ontological boundaries that surround the human subject in Western modernity. These boundaries have been carefully policed by humanist thinking, which has cast the human as the site of agency, intentionality, and morality, opposing it to a nonhuman world seen as inert, passive, and amoral. Metareferentiality thus performs double ontological work: on the level of the game vs. reality distinction, and on the level of the ontology of the subject in post-Enlightenment Western culture. In the next section, I survey existing work on metareference in games. I then turn to posthumanist debates on subjectivity and sample the philosophical framework introduced by two poststructuralist thinkers in particular, Barad (2007) and Braidotti (2013). Finally, I offer an extended analysis of *Inscryption* (2021) as a game performing a posthumanist understanding of the subject through metareferentiality.

Metareference in Games

Broadly speaking, scholarship on metareference in games falls into two categories: work that discusses, usually in a taxonomic vein, how metareference operates on the level of game design, and work that interrogates its functions. My primary interest in this chapter lies in the latter approach, and particularly in how game metareference can pursue a critique of humanist conceptions of subjectivity. Nevertheless, it will be useful to keep a taxonomy in mind: To that end, I will build on the accounts of metareference formulated by Agata Waszkiewicz (2020) and Theresa Krampe (2023).[5]

Waszkiewicz positions instances of metareference and self-reflexivity in games on a scale that goes from localized devices to more radical strategies that are far harder for the player to ignore. Waszkiewicz's first type of metareference involves fiction-aware characters, like Max Payne in the example mentioned above (see Waszkiewicz 2020, 5). This is the weakest instance of metareference in that the player is not directly involved in the character's realization: We are mere witnesses to the protagonist's coming close to what we know is an extratextual truth. However, at least in *Max Payne*, the game still frames the protagonist's comment as a hallucination. As a result, the ontological divide between the game and reality is only *implicitly* questioned. Waszkiewicz's second and third types create a higher degree of player involvement, since the game's audience is directly addressed by the game (or by one of its characters). In the second type, the address to the player is "one-directional," in that we cannot respond to it: "the player is acknowledged (often through a direct verbal comment directed at them with the use of the second person pronouns) but is not given means of reciprocating the contact" (Waszkiewicz 2020, 6). The game *The Stanley Parable* (2013) exemplifies this type of metareference, for instance when the voiceover narrator comments on the player's choice *not* to follow the narrator's instructions. Waszkiewicz highlights the potential of this metareferential device for defamiliarizing game conventions and producing something akin to Brechtian "Verfremdung."[6] For instance, *The Stanley Parable* can be read as a satirical reflection on the mind-numbing predictability of mainstream gaming, with the metareferential dimension of the game contributing considerably to that critique.[7]

Finally, for Waszkiewicz, some games allow the player to respond directly to a metareferential address: The main example here is a famous sequence in Hideo Kojima's *Metal Gear Solid* (1998) in which one of the game's bosses, Psycho Mantis, has access to the save files on the console—including save files created by other games—and can comment on the player's taste for certain genres. The metareference here is two-directional since the player can "speak back" (Waszkiewicz 2020, 7): Defeating this boss requires changing controls (switching from gamepad to keyboard, in the PC version, or plugging the controller into a different port in the PlayStation version). Because these manipulations are typically seen as external to the game world, Kojima's choice to weave them into a boss fight strongly disrupts the ontological separation between reality and the game. Thus, as we move along Waszkiewicz's taxonomy, metareferentiality deepens its "counterontological" dimension—that is, its potential to challenge ontological distinctions that players will tend to assume based on prior interactions with the game medium (and fictional practices in other media).[8]

Krampe's (2023) work enriches this approach by locating metareference on the level of both the gameworld and the ludic systems that give rise to the player's experience of gameplay. The former (which Krampe labels diegetic metareference) points to the game's narrativity, including phenomena such as metalepsis found across a wide range of media. This is the level of analysis on which Waszkiewicz's (2020) discussion tends to operate. However, as Krampe suggests, games are also capable of "ludic metareference," which highlights the conventions underlying the game's interface and mechanics. Through ludic metareference, games encourage "the player's reflexive and subversive engagement with [their] rules" (Krampe 2023, 143). Of course, as Krampe argues, diegetic and ludic metareference rarely appear in isolation: The narrative dimension of metareference typically helps frame or explain the foregrounding of game rules and conventions, as in most of the examples I discussed above. For instance, the narrator's comments in *The Stanley Parable* integrate on the diegetic level the player's ludic decision to disregard an implicit instruction.

Even this brief overview should show that metareference in games fulfills a variety of functions. In many instances, metareferential devices deepen engagement with a game's narrative and its characters without affecting gameplay in any significant way.[9] Think again about Max Payne realizing that he might be "in a computer game," which does nothing in terms of advancing the player's interaction with *Max Payne*'s ludic mechanics. In fact, most Remedy Entertainment games, including *Alan Wake* (2010), *Alan Wake 2* (2023), and *Control* (2019), work in this way (see also the chapter by Waskziewicz in this volume): In terms of what Krampe (2023) calls diegetic metareference, these games push metareferentiality to a degree that is perhaps unprecedented in videogame history. By contrast, on the level of ludic metareference they appear far less experimental; in fact, they do not feel very different from most other survival or action games. Similarly, many games feature Easter Eggs that are metareferential but also completely inconsequential from a gameplay perspective: They serve as in-jokes, reinforcing the player's sense of belonging to a particular fan community. By contrast, Kojima's experimental boss fight in *Metal Gear Solid* suggests that metareferentiality can also be aligned with unconventional gameplay mechanics.

In one of the earliest discussions of metareference in games, Fotis Jannidis sees metareference as primarily "enhancing a game's entertainment effect" (2009, 562). Of course, "entertainment" is not an easy concept to pin down, but it seems clear that it should not be understood too narrowly—as a function of "mere" enjoyment. In fact, Waszkiewicz's commentary on *The Stanley Parable* shows that metareferentiality can also function ideologically, as part of games' procedural rhetoric in Bogost's (2007) terminology: It can be used as a means of critiquing the conventions of gameplay and as a springboard for constructing a wide range of meanings.[10] Alice Bell and Jan Alber's (2012) overview of the functions of metalepsis can be useful to unpack these meanings, if we extend it from metalepsis to metareference more generally. In addition to "escapism" (which probably overlaps with Jannidis's "entertainment effect"), Bell and Alber see metalepsis as performing a number of functions: It can flaunt authorial control over the narrative, but also possibly signal the erosion of such control; it can highlight "the power and potential danger of fiction" (2012, 180); and, lastly, it can hint at opportunities for mutual understanding between the author and the fictional characters they created. In addition to this foregrounding or questioning of authorial agency, I will show that metareferential techniques can help games pursue a posthumanist project of interrogating the limits and blind spots of human subjectivity as Western modernity has conceptualized it. Disrupting the perceived ontology of videogames (through the gameworld vs. reality separation) thus becomes a conduit for a broader exploration of the ontology of the subject. Before turning to my example in the final section, I will offer a thumbnail sketch of posthumanist work on subjectivity.

Posthumanist Subjectivities

Posthumanist thinking, as I mentioned in the introduction, is not a coherent philosophy but rather a loosely related set of ideas. One of the commonalities between these approaches is the interest in unsettling dualistic binaries that have become entrenched in Western modernity in the wake of the Enlightenment—with subject vs. object being perhaps the most significant of these binaries. Thus, many writers aligned with posthumanism question this separation as simplistic and, ultimately, biased toward anthropocentrism (since the subject is invariably understood as human or at least human-like in Western thinking).

For example, in *Meeting the Universe Halfway* (2007), Karen Barad starts by surveying how subjectivity has been discussed by poststructuralist theorists including Michel Foucault (1975) and Judith Butler (1993). Both theorists, as Barad underlines, focus on how (a certain understanding of) the human subject is produced through the regulation of the body. In poststructuralist work, this regulation is primarily social and cultural—a matter of discourse rather than biological and physical reality. By contrast, posthumanist thinkers like Barad invoke the idea of materiality to unsettle the (human) subject vs. (nonhuman) object divide. Subjectivity is closely bound up with the body's agency: This potential for action is the body's materiality, as opposed to matter understood (dualistically) as passive and inert.[11] However, from a posthumanist perspective (which in this respect differs fundamentally from its poststructuralist antecedents), materiality is not confined to the human domain: It is a property of living bodies (human and nonhuman) as well as of the environmental and physical processes that shape life on Earth. The subject vs. object distinction is problematized by suggesting that the (human) subject is fundamentally entangled with material (nonhuman) entities, from the animals we share a long evolutionary history with to the climate patterns that influence cultural evolution. The subject is no longer exclusively human, and the object—seen as active materiality instead of inert matter—directly informs the subject. Barad captures this reciprocity by introducing the neologism "intra-action," which unlike the more standard "interaction" "signifies the mutual constitution of entangled agencies" (2007, 33).[12]

An important consequence of this opening up of subjectivity to nonhuman agencies is that the subject is no longer viewed as monolithic or self-contained. The most influential critique of this unitary conception of subjectivity can be found in Rosi Braidotti's (2013) posthumanist work. The subject becomes relational—that is, in dialogue with realities that are conventionally seen as external to it. A good illustration of this dialogue can be found in the everyday concept of "atmosphere."[13] Atmosphere is, etymologically at least, something that surrounds the subject: It can be physical (temperature, humidity, etc.) or emotional (e.g., the atmosphere of a job interview or tense work meeting). Atmosphere is not merely an "external" property of the world, but something that weighs on and informs the subject through the unique relation that is established between individual experience and environment, whether the environment is understood physically, socially, or emotionally. The concept of atmosphere thus begins to describe the way in which, from a posthumanist perspective, the boundaries of the subject are constantly blurred or permeable.

Moreover, as Braidotti argues, the posthumanist subject is also dynamic and multiple: not a single, invariable "nugget" of subjectivity but rather an evolving process that reflects an "enlarged sense of inter-connection between self and others, including the non-human or 'earth' others" (2013, 49). The subject, in other words, changes as it encounters other subjects (human and animal) and forms of materiality (including those environmental processes that are conceptualized as passive and inert in Western modernity). The effects of this philosophy of intra-action and inter-connection are also felt in ethical terms, since ethical responsibility in Braidotti's work is extended to nonhuman life forms and the physical environment. This ethics thus marks a radical departure from a humanist ethics founded on the agency and autonomy of the liberal subject.[14]

Theorists of the posthuman are, of course, aware of how speculative and counterintuitive this understanding of subjectivity is. As Braidotti argues, the "postanthropocentric shift away from the hierarchical relations that had privileged 'Man' requires a form of estrangement and a radical repositioning on the part of the subject. The best method to accomplish this is through the strategy of defamiliarization or critical distance from the dominant vision of the subject" (Braidotti 2013, 88). It is no coincidence that Braidotti writes about "defamiliarization" here, an operation associated with the effects of art since Viktor Shklovsky's (1965) early formalist work and more recently discussed in the context of game studies by Mitchell and colleagues (2020). If the picture of subjectivity painted by poststructuralist thinking is far from our everyday understanding of the human subject in the West, the arts can help close that gap: They can disrupt the ontology of the subject in a way that performs—in the sense of illustrating and putting into practice—posthumanist ideas. That is the way in which I read metareferentiality in *Inscryption* in the next section: Through numerous metareferential strategies, the game stages a breakdown of the conventionally understood human subject and instead points to its environmental openness, its entanglement with a range of material realities.

Before developing this reading of *Inscryption*, two qualifications are in order. First, I am not claiming that the game's developers read posthumanist theory, or that they intended to capture posthumanist ideas in their work. Likewise, I am not suggesting that posthumanism is the only framework for interpreting the game's obsession with metareferentiality (see, e.g., the chapter by Thorne in this volume for an alternative reading). It is, however, a helpful way of articulating the game's unconventional approach to genre, style, and what Markku Eskelinen (2001) influentially called the "gaming situation." Second, *Inscryption* is far from being the only metareferential game that resonates with posthumanist ideas. Metareferential strategies tend to recur in works that explore the relationship between human societies and the nonhuman world in times of climate crisis, as I have argued in collaboration with Gry Ulstein (see Caracciolo and Ulstein 2022). In literary fiction, the immersive techniques of realism are increasingly unable to encapsulate the strange reality of living in times of climate change.[15] By contrast, the puzzling ontology of metareference is, at least in principle, well positioned to describe how the climate crisis is muddling the ontological separation of human beings and nonhuman realities. In games, too, titles like *OneShot* (2016) and *Immortality* (2022) can be productively read in that context, as digital texts that employ metareference to unsettle a culturally entrenched (but reductive and outdated) understanding of the human. Ecogaming is a significant frame for reading these games, including arguably *Inscryption*.[16] However, it is also important to stress that this reappraisal of the humanist subject goes far beyond a narrow understanding of games with an ecological "message." Instead of pushing a specific agenda, these games create opportunities for rethinking human subjectivity at a more fundamental level—but it is up to individual players to take advantage of these opportunities in interpretation.

Talking Animals and OLD_DATA in *Inscryption*

Saying that *Inscryption* is a deck-building videogame wouldn't be inaccurate, but it would be a gross simplification of the game's experimental blend of styles and genres. As I will argue, metareferential techniques spanning Waszkiewicz's typology make a central contribution to the player's experience of the game on both a diegetic and a ludic level (see, again, Krampe 2023). The game opens with an offscreen voice stating "Okay. Time to figure out what's on this thing," followed by the sounds of a disk being inserted into a computer, and the computer itself booting up. This opening, through its foregrounding of physical media (and therefore of materiality), evokes a particular kind of 1990s nostalgia, which is of course a recurrent element in indie games (see Thibault 2016; as well as the chapter by Thon in this volume).[17] The offscreen voice will not return until the end of Act I. For now, players find themselves in a dark room, seated at a table and facing a mysterious figure, his eyes the only visible feature of his body. The environment is presented from a first-person perspective. The figure across the table acts as a game master of sorts, first introducing the player (referred to as "the Challenger") to the rules of the card game, then opposing them in a series of card battles.

In essence, the player starts with a few cards and can draw more from the deck. The game takes place on a 3-by-4 grid; both the player and the opponent play cards in the row that is closest to them, then the opponent's cards advance one row to challenge the player's cards (see Figure 7.1). The cards themselves depict various

Figure 7.1 The main screen in *Inscryption* (Act I), with the opponent's eyes visible across the table.

animals (the wolf, the hedgehog, etc.) and have both an attack power and a certain number of health points. Each card deals damage corresponding to its attack power: If the game master has a card directly in front of one of the player's cards, the damage will affect that card (and possibly "kill" the creature, with the card leaving the grid); if not, the game master himself takes damage: When either the game master or the player are down to zero health points, they lose the game. Complications are added as we play, of course: Playing certain high-value cards requires "sacrificing" other cards, some cards have special abilities that allow them to ignore the opposing card in their attacks or attack in multiple directions, and so on. Between battles, the player uses a map to navigate a forest (presented from a top-down perspective), with several branching paths leading to encounters that enable players to expand their deck or upgrade their cards. The player's journey is punctuated by increasingly difficult card battles: If the player is defeated, they are returned to the beginning of each level and lose their progression (including all the cards they acquired in the course of a playthrough). At the end of each level, the player faces a boss impersonated by the game master, who puts on a mask for these encounters.

The game has a sinister atmosphere, emphasized by the fairytale flavor of the cards and the mysteriousness of the situation in which we find ourselves (including the identity of our opponent). In essence, though, what I have described so far consists in the videogame simulation of a tabletop card game, with some "roguelike" elements blended in (because of how the player's progression is reset after each defeat). A first complication is that, as the player soon realizes, they can stand up from the table and move around a wood-paneled cabin. Here, we encounter a number of puzzles similar to those typically found in adventure games: Solving these puzzles advances the narrative of Act I, as I will explain below. Ostensibly, our goal is to escape from the cabin, where we seem to be captive. Thus, we have three game genres fused together: deck-building, roguelike, and escape-the-room-style adventure. However, much more striking than the game's generic hybridity (at least for the purposes of my argument) is a further twist on the game's basic formula: Some of the cards we collect and play in our encounters come to life and speak to us.

The Stoat, one of the starting cards, seems rather unremarkable in terms of attack power, until dialogue lines start appearing under the animal's image: The Stoat, we are surprised to find out, addresses the player character directly. "There's a way out for both of us," signals the Stoat early on in the game, hinting at both the player character's captivity in the room and at the animal's being trapped inside the card. Later, the Stoat starts advising the player on what card to play next; he also shows us how to rescue their companion, the Stunted Wolf, who has been locked away by the game master. Retrieving the Stunted Wolf card requires standing up from the table and turning the hands of a clock in a certain way, as instructed by the Stoat, to open a secret compartment underneath. Together with a third talking card, the Stinkbug, the animals help the player defeat the game master. As often in this type of second-person address, the "you" form in the Stoat's statements is ambiguous.[18] For instance, when the Stoat declares "You sacrificed me. *While I was sleeping*. It was the right play. I get it," the "you" could refer to the player's avatar but also to the flesh-and-blood player of *Inscryption*, since both are playing a card game: the former (within the fictional world of the game) in its tabletop form, the latter as a computer simulation. This device is a metareferential comment on the game's ludic system, since it explicitly foregrounds the player's strategic choice to "sacrifice" the card. The result aligns with Waszkiewicz's third type of metareference, a direct address to the player with the possibility of responding to the game—although, as I mentioned, the address is shrouded in the ambiguity of the second-person form.

The address also gives rise to ontological ambiguity, in that the gameworld (where the player character is located) seems to blend with the real world (in which the actual player decides what card to play next).[19] However, another set of ontological boundaries is blurred at the same time: The playing card becomes animate, in that the Stoat acts in a way that shows consciousness and intentionality. This twist evokes the materiality of the nonhuman, inanimate world as a site of intra-action, to use Barad's terminology. Further, the Stoat speaks in a way that suggests subjectivity of a kind we normally associate with human beings. The metareferential technique thus overlaps with anthropomorphism, which is employed strategically by the game to unsettle the link between subjectivity and the human form.[20] Far from being a human prerogative, the subject is extended to the nonhuman world (including both the seemingly inert card and the animal it represents): The anthropocentric subject of Western modernity is thus challenged by the game's metareferential play with ontological boundaries.

As the game progresses, the challenge becomes even more radical, since the game's story weaves computer simulation itself into a posthumanist understanding of subjectivity. This operation involves insistent metareferentiality of Waszkiewicz's first type at the level of the game's frame narrative. At the end of Act I, the player defeats the game master. However, rather than ending the game, this takes us back to the offscreen voice we heard at the beginning of *Inscryption*: It belongs to a character named Luke Carder, who reveals in a series of video clips that he has located a mysterious floppy disk containing a game titled *Inscryption*. The metareferential *mise en abyme* is hard to miss, but the story that revolves around it is far more convoluted and can only be reconstructed through multiple playthroughs, requiring specific choices for the full picture to emerge (see also the chapter by Thorne in this volume).[21]

Throughout Acts II and III, the game's metareferential plot amplifies the ontological blurring introduced by the second-person address in Act I. The floppy disk retrieved by Carder appears to be controlled by a deranged AI known as OLD_DATA, which is capable of lending sentience to fictional characters.[22] This suggests that the Stoat and the other talking cards of Act I are a product of this entity's manipulations. OLD_DATA is even capable of reading real files on the player's computer: In Act III, the player is periodically asked to "sacrifice" one of these files in the same way as cards were sacrificed to play more powerful cards in Act I (see Figure 7.2 for the permissions request). Nothing is actually deleted, but the metareferential twist (Waszkiewicz's third type, since the player must respond directly) remains unsettling precisely because of how it disrupts the normally rigid distinction between material reality and the gameworld. This is a version of the horror fiction trope of the dangerous narrative overstepping its boundaries, as in *The Ring*'s (2002) cursed video tape, but here it becomes bound up with computer simulation and a particularly radical form of metareferentiality.[23]

The details of this metareferential plot are less important for my purposes than the conceptual stakes of OLD_DATA's attempt to take over *Inscryption*. If

Figure 7.2 Inscryption asking players for permission to access real files on their computer.

the anthropomorphized animal cards of Act I stretched subjectivity to the animal domain, the rest of the game goes much further: It ascribes intentionality and subjectivity to computer simulation by imagining that the very game we are playing is the product of an evil AI. The subject becomes multiple and emerges relationally from interactions with the representation of animal life and computer intelligence. The equation of subjectivity and the human form is destabilized on several fronts and extended to both the animal and the technological domain, echoing—and performing in videogame form—contemporary discussions on the posthuman subject.

Conclusion

This chapter has discussed how metareferential techniques in games may perform double ontological work. As discussed by theorists such as Wolf (2009), metareference disrupts the presumed ontological segregation of fictional practices like videogames (and other narrative media): that is, the assumption of a fundamental disconnect between the real world and the worlds of fiction. Through their explicit self-awareness, metareferential devices can evoke and at the same time blur ontological boundaries. While this blurring serves multiple functions, I have focused here on how metareference in games can stage a breakdown of the default ontology of the Western subject. This ontology implies a unitary human "I" endowed with unique forms of agency and consciousness, which differentiate it categorically from the domain of material things or processes as well as animal life. This conception of the subject has come under scrutiny in posthumanist philosophies (see, e.g., Braidotti 2013; Wolfe 2010) that highlight the multiplicity and relationality of subjectivity—how subjects, human and nonhuman, are always entangled with the world of material phenomena. If contemporary theory can speculate about this entangled subject, narrative media—including videogames—can stage it through story and interactive gameplay. This is what my reading of *Inscryption* has exemplified by discussing how the game's insistent metareferentiality addresses the player directly and turns a version of the game itself into a central element of the plot.

This engagement with posthumanist ideas is not uncommon in contemporary games, and particularly in the independent gaming landscape. Games that embrace metareferential forms similar to those found in *Inscryption* include the already mentioned *OneShot* and *Immortality*, as well as more mainstream titles like *Alan Wake 2*. Metareferential strategies in these "philosophical games" (Gualeni 2022) serve as a tool for querying and questioning the unitary humanist subject: They unsettle distinctions between human consciousness, animal sentience, and artificial intelligence in ways that draw both the real player and the game's characters into sophisticated ontological play.

Notes

1 For more on the distinction between posthumanism and transhumanism, see also Miah 2009.

2 Sicart 2008 offers a comprehensive discussion of the concept of "mechanic" in videogames.
3 See also my discussion in Caracciolo 2021, which focuses on contemporary literature and its negotiations of subjectivity but converges with my argument in this chapter on a conceptual level.
4 My premise here is that metalepsis often serves as a strong form of metareference, but I am not implying that the function of metalepsis is always metareferential (see Bell and Alber 2012 for further discussion). Conversely, there are numerous metareferential strategies that do not involve metalepsis, including for example covert references to genre-based conventions and expectations.
5 See also Krampe et al. 2022 for a broader discussion of metareference in indie games, including many of the games I discuss in this section.
6 The Shklovskian concept of defamiliarization is also central to Mitchell et al.'s (2020) approach to what they call "poetic gameplay."
7 For more on the metareferentiality of *The Stanley Parable* and its effects, see Sarian 2020.
8 These violations of ontological assumptions play a central role in Pascal Boyer's (1994) cognitive account of religion; see also Lisa Zunshine's (2008) discussion of "strange concepts" in fictional narrative, which builds on Boyer's work. It is important to stress that, when I use words like "ontology" and "(counter)ontological" in this chapter, I am referring to a perceived ontological separation between fiction and reality (from the perspective of contemporary audiences) and not making a stronger, philosophical claim on the ontology of fiction.
9 I am assuming here and throughout that videogames are, in Marie-Laure Ryan's words, an "art of compromise between narrative and gameplay" (2006, 198), and that engaging with games involves juggling narrative and ludic values (see Caracciolo 2015).
10 See also Backe and Thon's (2019) reading of *The Stanley Parable*, which also touches on the question of authorial agency (see below).
11 See also Latour, who notes that, "[b]etween materiality and matter, it seems that we are going to have to choose" (2017, 70).
12 Agency has been studied in relation to videogames, too, in ways that converge with Barad's posthumanist account (see Taylor 2009). Bódi and Thon (2020) offer a helpful distinction between four dimensions of player agency.
13 See also Gernot Böhme's (2016) work on atmosphere as environmental aesthetics.
14 On posthumanist ethics, see MacCormack's (2017) comprehensive discussion.
15 See Ghosh 2016 for a seminal formulation of this argument.
16 See, e.g., Chang 2019; Op de Beke et al. 2024. The latter includes several contributions that tie in with the posthumanist framework adopted here.
17 For further discussion of the aesthetics of indie games, see Juul 2019; Thon 2022.
18 David Herman calls this ambiguous type of second-person address "doubly deictic" (2002, 353).
19 Relevant here is Alice Bell's (2021) concept of "ontological resonance," which describes a similar kind of overlap between digital fiction and reality.
20 For more on this strategic use of anthropomorphic representation, see Iovino 2015.
21 My comments here build on extensive discussions on platforms such as the *Inscryption* Wiki (https://inscryption.fandom.com/) and the *Inscryption* subreddit.
22 Not all players agree with this reading, though. See Drecon1984's (2022) alternative theory, which links the characters' sentience to a human actor operating within the complex backstory of *Inscryption*, the (fictional) software company GameWorks.

23 See Ryan 2004; Krampe et al. 2022, 737–739; as well as the chapter by Krampe in this volume for more on this type of metareference that toys with the possibility of destroying the system it runs on.

Works Cited

Alan Wake. 2010. Remedy Entertainment/Microsoft Game Studios. Microsoft Windows.

Alan Wake 2. 2023. Remedy Entertainment/Epic Games. Microsoft Windows.

Backe, Hans-Joachim, and Jan-Noël Thon. 2019. "Playing with Identity: Authors, Narrators, Avatars, and Players in *The Stanley Parable* and *The Beginner's Guide*." *DIEGESIS: Interdisciplinary E-Journal for Narrative Research* 8 (2): 1–25.

Barad, Karen. 2007. *Meeting the Universe Halfway: Quantum Physics and the Entanglement of Matter and Meaning*. Durham: Duke University Press.

Bell, Alice. 2021. "'It All Feels Too Real': Digital Storyworlds and 'Ontological Resonance.'" *Style* 55 (3): 430–452.

Bell, Alice, and Jan Alber. 2012. "Ontological Metalepsis and Unnatural Narratology." *Journal of Narrative Theory* 42 (2): 166–192.

Bódi, Bettina, and Jan-Noël Thon. 2020. "Playing Stories? Narrative-Dramatic Agency in *Disco Elysium* (2019) and *Astroneer* (2019)." *Frontiers of Narrative Studies* 6 (2): 157–190.

Bogost, Ian. 2007. *Persuasive Games: The Expressive Power of Videogames*. Cambridge, MA: MIT Press.

Bogost, Ian. 2012. *Alien Phenomenology, or What It's Like to Be a Thing*. Minneapolis: University of Minnesota Press.

Böhme, Gernot. 2016. *The Aesthetics of Atmospheres*, edited by Jean-Paul Thibaud. New York: Routledge.

Boyer, Pascal. 1994. "Cognitive Constraints on Cultural Representations: Natural Ontologies and Religious Ideas." In *Mapping the Mind: Domain Specificity in Cognition and Culture*, edited by Lawrence A. Hirschfeld and Susan A. Gelman, 391–411. Cambridge: Cambridge University Press.

Braidotti, Rosi. 2013. *The Posthuman*. Cambridge: Polity Press.

Butler, Judith. 1993. *Bodies That Matter: On the Discursive Limits of "Sex"*. New York: Routledge.

Callus, Ivan, Stefan Herbrechter, and Manuela Rossini. 2014. "Introduction: Dis/Locating Posthumanism in European Literary and Critical Traditions." *European Journal of English Studies* 18 (2): 103–120.

Caracciolo, Marco. 2015. "Playing *Home*: Video Game Experiences Between Narrative and Ludic Interests." *Narrative* 23 (3): 231–251.

Caracciolo, Marco. 2021. "Ontological Instability and the Place of the Subject in Contemporary Fiction." *Style* 55 (3): 367–384.

Caracciolo, Marco, and Gry Ulstein. 2022. "The Weird and the Meta in Jeff VanderMeer's *Dead Astronauts*." *Configurations* 30 (1): 1–23.

Chang, Alenda Y. 2019. *Playing Nature: Ecology in Video Games*. Minneapolis: University of Minnesota Press.

Control. 2019. Remedy Entertainment/505 Games. Microsoft Windows.

Drecon1984. 2022. "I Think People Misunderstand the OLD_DATA." *Reddit,* January 30, 2022. www.reddit.com/r/inscryption/comments/sgfd8q/i_think_people_misunderstand_the_old_data/.

Eskelinen, Markku. 2001. "The Gaming Situation." *Game Studies: The International Journal of Computer Game Research* 1 (1): n.pag.

Fizek, Sonia. 2022. *Playing at a Distance: Borderlands of Video Game Aesthetic*. Cambridge, MA: MIT Press.

Foucault, Michel. 1975. *Discipline and Punish: The Birth of the Prison*. New York: Random House.

Ghosh, Amitav. 2016. *The Great Derangement: Climate Change and the Unthinkable*. Chicago: University of Chicago Press.

Gualeni, Stefano. 2022. "Philosophical Games." In *Encyclopedia of Ludic Terms*, edited by Paweł Grabarczyk, n.pag. https://eolt.org/articles/philosophical-games.

Haraway, Donna. 1991. "A Cyborg Manifesto: Science, Technology, and Socialist-Feminism in the Late Twentieth Century." In *Simians, Cyborgs and Women: The Reinvention of Nature*, 149–181. New York: Routledge.

Hayles, N. Katherine. 1999. *How We Became Posthuman: Virtual Bodies in Cybernetics, Literature, and Informatics*. Chicago: University of Chicago Press.

Herman, David. 2002. *Story Logic: Problems and Possibilities of Narrative*. Lincoln: University of Nebraska Press.

Immortality. 2022. Sam Barlow/Half Mermaid Productions. Microsoft Windows.

Inscryption. 2021. Daniel Mullins Games/Devolver Digital. Microsoft Windows.

Iovino, Serenella. 2015. "The Living Diffractions of Matter and Text: Narrative Agency, Strategic Anthropomorphism, and How Interpretation Works." *Anglia* 133: 69–86.

Jannidis, Fotis. 2009. "Metareference in Computer Games." In *Metareference across Media: Theory and Case Studies*, edited by Werner Wolf, 543–565. Amsterdam: Rodopi.

Jayemanne, Darshana. 2017. *Performativity in Art, Literature, and Videogames*. Cham: Palgrave Macmillan.

Juul, Jesper. 2019. *Handmade Pixels: Independent Video Games and the Quest for Authenticity*. Cambridge, MA: MIT Press.

Krampe, Theresa. 2023. "Rewriting Rules, Changing Worlds: Diegetic and Ludic Forms of Metareference in *The Magic Circle*." *Frontiers of Narrative Studies* 9 (1): 137–157.

Krampe, Theresa, Stephanie Lotzow, and Jan-Noël Thon. 2022. "Playful Poetics: Metareferential Interfaces in Recent Indie Games." *Poetics Today* 43 (4): 729–771.

Latour, Bruno. 2017. *Facing Gaia: Eight Lectures on the New Climatic Regime*. Cambridge: Polity Press.

Law, Stephen. 2011. *Humanism: A Very Short Introduction*. Oxford: Oxford University Press.

MacCormack, Patricia. 2017. *Posthuman Ethics: Embodiment and Cultural Theory*. New York: Routledge.

Max Payne. 2001. Remedy Entertainment/Rockstar Games. Microsoft Windows.

Mejeur, Cody. 2023. "Games as Critical Literature: Playing with Transhumanism, Embodied Cognition, and Narrative Difference in *SOMA*." In *Global Perspectives on Digital Literature*, edited by Torsa Ghosal, 67–80. New York: Routledge.

Metal Gear Solid. 1998. Konami Computer Entertainment Japan/Konami. PlayStation.

Miah, Andy. 2009. "A Critical History of Posthumanism." In *Medical Enhancement and Posthumanity*, edited by Bert Gordijn and Ruth Chadwick, 71–94. Dordrecht: Springer.

Milesi, Laurent. 2022. "Posthumanism and Digital Gaming." In *Palgrave Handbook of Critical Posthumanism*, edited by Stefan Herbrechter, Ivan Callus, Manuela Rossini, Marija Grech, Megen de Bruin-Molé, and Christopher John Müller, 575–606. Cham: Springer International Publishing.

Mitchell, Alex, Liting Kway, Tiffany Neo, and Yuin Theng Sim. 2020. "A Preliminary Categorization of Techniques for Creating Poetic Gameplay." *Game Studies: The International Journal of Computer Game Research* 20 (2): n.pag.

Nelles, William. 1992. "Stories within Stories: Narrative Levels and Embedded Narrative." *Studies in the Literary Imagination* 25 (1): 79–96.

OneShot. 2016. Future Cat/Komodo. Microsoft Windows.

Op de Beke, Laura, Joost Raessens, Stefan Werning, and Gerald Farca, eds. 2024. *Ecogames: Playful Perspectives on the Climate Crisis*. Amsterdam: Amsterdam University Press.

Phelan, James. 2007. *Experiencing Fiction: Judgments, Progressions, and the Rhetorical Theory of Narrative*. Columbus: Ohio State University Press.

The Ring. 2002. Director Gore Verbinski. USA: DreamWorks Pictures.

Ryan, Marie-Laure. 2004. "Metaleptic Machines." *Semiotica* 2004 (150): 439–469.

Ryan, Marie-Laure. 2006. *Avatars of Story*. Minneapolis: University of Minnesota Press.

Sarian, Antranig Arek. 2020. "Paradox and Pedagogy in *The Stanley Parable*." *Games and Culture* 15 (2): 179–197.

Shklovsky, Viktor. 1965. "Art as Technique." In *Russian Formalist Criticism: Four Essays*, edited by Lee T. Lemon and Marion J. Reis, 3–24. Lincoln: University of Nebraska Press.

Sicart, Miguel. 2008. "Defining Game Mechanics." *Game Studies: The International Journal of Computer Game Research* 8 (2): n.pag.

The Stanley Parable. 2013. Galactic Cafe/Galactic Cafe. Microsoft Windows.

Taylor, T. L. 2009. "The Assemblage of Play." *Games and Culture* 4 (4): 331–339.

Thibault, Mattia. 2016. "Post-Digital Games: The Influence of Nostalgia in Indie Games' Graphic Regimes." *Gamevironments* 4: 1–23.

Thon, Jan-Noël. 2022. "Bildmedium Computerspiel? Zur ästhetischen Komplexität aktueller Indie Games." In *Bildmedien: Festschrift für Klaus Sachs-Hombach zum 65. Geburtstag*, edited by Frauke Berndt and Jan-Noël Thon, 441–462. Berlin: De Gruyter.

Waszkiewicz, Agata. 2020. "'Together They Are Twofold': Player-Avatar Relationship beyond the Fourth Wall." *Journal of Games Criticism* 4 (1): 1–21.

Wolf, Werner. 2009. "Metareference across Media: The Concept, Its Transmedial Potential and Problems, Main Forms and Functions." In *Metareference across Media: Theory and Case Studies*, edited by Werner Wolf, 1–85. Amsterdam: Rodopi.

Wolfe, Cary. 2010. *What Is Posthumanism?* Minneapolis: University of Minnesota Press.

Zunshine, Lisa. 2008. *Strange Concepts and the Stories They Make Possible: Cognition, Culture, Narrative*. Baltimore: Johns Hopkins University Press.

8 The Visual Metalepsis as a Palimpsest in *Alan Wake 2* and *Layers of Fear 2*

Agata Waszkiewicz

The chapter discusses visual and sonic representations of metaleptic transgressions in two horror games that, due to their clear and rich references to cinema and television, can be described as cinematic in more than one meaning of the word. First, the critically acclaimed Alan Wake 2 *(2023) is discussed in terms of its superimpositions of one image on another to showcase the moments in which both characters and locations attempt an ontological metalepsis. Second, the complex, continuous, and fluid overlaps of identities in* Layers of Fear 2 *(2019) are discussed as an example of visual and sonic metalepsis that blurs the lines between the fictional realities up to the point where they are no longer distinguishable from one another. The name of palimpsestic metalepsis is proposed for these transgressions, signaling both the ontological equality of two locations or realities and the paradoxical character of the transgression.*

Introduction

First defined by Gérard Genette as "any intrusion by the extradiegetic narrator or narratee into the diegetic universe […] or the inverse" (1980, 234–235), metalepsis tends to be described as an act of impossible, paradoxical transition between two ontologically different worlds (see Macrae 2019; McHale 1977; Ryan 2006). Genette further characterizes it as the movement across the boundary between two worlds: the world of narration and the world being narrated. The first world involves the narrative's communicative situation, while the second is the fictional storyworld. Metalepsis, therefore, involves three main elements: narrative worlds (diegetic universes), narrative boundaries, and the direction of their transgression (see also the chapter by Krampe in this volume on "genuine" ontological metalepsis).

The most common examples used to illustrate such an occurrence revolve around the authors, narrators, and characters of the fictional works. And so, an author entering the world of their creation, a narrator turning their attention to the reader, or characters escaping the story of their origin all would be examples of metaleptic transgression, even though differing in the direction (ascending or descending; horizontal or vertical) (see Bell and Alber 2012; Limoges 2011) and

DOI: 10.4324/9781003538592-8

the quality of said move (rhetorical or ontological) (see Kukkonen and Klimek 2011; Macrae 2019; Thon 2016).

For the explanation of how metalepsis can occur between these different worlds, I draw from a version of frame analysis, a conceptual framework initially adapted for the study of tabletop games by Gary Alan Fine (1983) before making its way into the videogame context (see Linderoth 2012; Mackay 2001; Waskul and Lust 2004; see also the chapter by Brown in this volume). In my research, I resonate with the division between a fictional world (see Jørgensen 2013); a non-diegetic level comprising the user interface and other elements of the interface invisible to the characters inhabiting the fictional worlds; and an extra-fictional level, which corresponds to Fine's "primary framework" (1983, 186)—a "real world" populated by the players.

Even though the definitions might vary between the scholars and remain ill-defined at times, the biggest body of work on metalepsis within videogames has been focused on the elusive threshold between the fictional and extrafictional (the "fiction/real boundary"), i.e., the fourth-wall break (see Krampe et al. 2022; Van de Mosselaer 2022; Waszkiewicz 2020b; 2024). This is not surprising. The unique mode of engagement between the player and the game already problematizes the fourth wall to the degree that its existence has been questioned by some scholars (see Jørgensen 2013), while others argued that the closeness of the player to the characters is what makes the subversiveness of the fourth-wall breaking act pleasurable to witness (see Waszkiewicz 2024).

At the same time, less attention has been paid to game studies research on the metaleptic transgressions occurring within the constraints of the fictional gameworld, so that is what I look at in this chapter. I especially consider horizontal or vertical metalepsis in two horror games focused on the theme of art and artists: Remedy Entertainment's *Alan Wake 2* (2023) and Bloober Team's *Layers of Fear 2* (2019). With both games paying homage to cinema and television, and playing with the obsessiveness of the act of creation undertaken by artists (the writer and the actor, respectively), they both use audiovisual techniques to signal the instability of the in-game realities and to challenge the borders between what is real, what is imagined, and what is remembered. Drawing on Matthew Campora's (2009) concept of "sonic metalepsis" and Piotr Kubiński's (2014) "palimpsestic attempt," I look at how the metalepsis is visualized on the screen and what it means for the player's interpretation of the characters. First, I focus on how *Alan Wake 2* incorporates mostly visual metalepses to play with the impossibility of space, before examining how *Layers of Fear 2* uses similar techniques to explore the interconnected, continuously overlapping possible identities of its protagonist.

Cinematic Metagames

As Ivan Girina explains, videogames "share both content (storylines, tropes, iconography) and aesthetic (framing, camera, movements, editing, genres) elements with cinema" (2015, 16–17); causing them often to be described—in their entirety or parts, e.g., cutscenes—as "cinematic." Bettina Bódi notes that " 'cinematic'-ness" in games "suggests that gameplay experience might trigger an emotional reaction akin to those triggered by film viewing" (2023, 76), showing a rather positive use of the word. At the same time, Girina points out that, often the comparison with film is evoked to devalue the artistic impact of videogames in the spirit of the notion that "more cinematic equals 'better'" since cinema stands "higher in our dominant cultural hierarchies" (2015, 9–10). He further notes that "the word cinematic carries a stigma," for example, when it is used to refer to "the non-interactive videos—otherwise called cutscenes—used to convey narrative information in games" (Girina 2015, 9). However, the close relationship between them might suggest that videogames, rather than taking inspiration only from real life, heavily "*remediate* cinema" (Rehak 2003, 104; original emphasis).

Both *Alan Wake 2* and *Layers of Fear 2* are, at their core, not just games about games but games about art: film and television in particular. *Alan Wake 2*, like the first game of the same title (*Alan Wake* [2010]), follows the eponymous bestselling thriller writer Alan Wake, whose writing has been taken over by an evil entity called the Dark Presence. Having trapped Alan in the nightmare Dark Place, an alternate dimension following the twisted logic of dreams and imagination, the Dark Presence proceeds to use his writing to influence both realities. In *Layers of Fear 2*, the player controls the Actor, whose identity is only revealed at the end of the game, depending on the player's choices. Here, the real mixes with memories and the fiction evoked within the theatrical performance and play, as the Actor explores a ship, both the current one, turned into an experimental, immersive stage, and the one from the past, carrying traumatic memories of the voyage across the Atlantic in the Actor's childhood.

Both games interact with cinema in at least two main ways: by including film footage into the gameplay and through quotations of or references to existing, classic, and famous films. The former differs in the degree of interactivity. Still, while the games do not necessarily allow the players to influence the events of the recordings (so they not fall under the broad spectrum of "interactive films"),[1] they do offer some way of interacting with the film footage. *Alan Wake 2* makes extensive use of entirely full-motion movie footage with the actors portraying characters and thereby plays with the characters' feeling of losing a grip on reality. There are several moments in which the animated Alan Wake interacts with a television screen, only to be transported into a fictional talk show where he and other characters, now portrayed by the actors and recorded on film, play out non-interactive sequences. Notably, these occur only when Wake is trapped in the Dark Place. By contrast, *Layers of Fear 2* does not show its characters until a very short moment toward the end of the game, but it features interactive moments in which, by manipulating the footage from a film projector in a specific way, the environment can be altered. For example, when the film is stopped at the right moment, the elements of the (formerly projected) doors materialize on the wall, subsequently allowing the character to leave the room.

In terms of the reference or quotation, the indebtedness of both *Alan Wake* games to literary horror and thriller genres is obvious: Stephen King is referenced in the very first scene of the first game; the sleepy, small town of Bright Falls is unmistakably based on the town of Twin Peaks from the eponymous television show, and the investigation of the cult's killing in *Alan Wake 2* and even the visual metalepsis described below seem to reference the *True Detective* (2014–) television show. Additionally, *Control* (2019), a previous game released by Remedy featuring the Federal Bureau of Control tasked with collecting and securing various objects of power, is clearly based on the *The X-Files* (1993–2018) series and the SCP Foundation website's project.

While these references might be obvious, they are not as overt as the direct quotations used in *Layers of Fear 2*, featuring recognizable locations, settings, and imagery from such films as *The Wizard of Oz* (1939), *Repulsion* (1965), *The Shining* (1980), or *Se7en* (1995). These quotations differ in the level of detail from single objects, for example, the famous carpet from the Overlook Hotel in *The Shining*, to more extensive scenes, such as an elaborate recreation of *Se7en*'s sin-based crime scenes in the final section of the game. Since I have already looked into the direct referentiality of *Layers of Fear 2* by applying Matteo Bittanti's (2003) model of film-game references elsewhere (see Waszkiewicz 2020a), this is not a subject of the analysis in this chapter. Instead, I will analyze how the two games use audio-visual techniques known from film through which the lines are blurred between various levels of meaning.

Visual Metalepsis as a Palimpsest in *Alan Wake 2*

Despite its innovative narrative, the original *Alan Wake*'s story is quite straightforward. When the eponymous bestselling author of thrillers finds himself burnt out, his wife, Alice, convinces him to take a short break in a charming, picturesque cabin in the middle of Cauldron Lake near the small, sleepy city of Bright Falls, Washington. Despite her assurance, and to no surprise to the players, Alice had an ulterior motive, hoping that the holiday would help break Alan's writer's block. Quickly, things go awry as the lake house is engulfed by the Dark Presence, which takes Alice. Realizing that the Dark Presence is using his writing to gain power and change the real world and, eventually, enter and dominate it, Alan has to fight monsters seemingly coming from his books in a world consumed by darkness. Bound by the rules of the genre he is writing, the hero cannot have a happy ending but can only save Alice by entering the Dark Place in her stead.

Alan Wake 2, which picks up 13 years after the events of the first one (both in terms of the in-game and in the real-world timelines), divides the story between two playable protagonists: the writer, who is still trapped in the Dark Place, and a new character, FBI agent Saga Anderson, who investigates murders in Bright Falls that are linked to Alan's disappearance. Although the characters are separated for most of the game, remaining within their respective realities, their paths cross several times; most notably, they have brief moments of contact in the spaces where the lines between the two worlds are the thinnest. Unsurprisingly, the separation of the worlds is only illusory, and the reality becomes gradually infected by Alan's writing and the Darkness, leaking shadows into it and changing the past events of those in the area, turning their lives into stories. The points where the two worlds become very close to each other are referred to as Overlaps and they allow either a short transgression to the place in-between, or provide an entry point to the Darkness. Entering the Overlaps, Saga usually needs to travel through space that loops on itself several times before encountering the chapter's boss.

Space and time loops are inherent to videogame design. Considering the importance of the imagery of a loop as symbolizing Alan Wake's journey through the Dark Place, it seems clear that the game offers both a metacommentary on how space and time are present in videogames in general, and on the recent trend of using time loops as a mechanic and as a narrative device in titles such as *"Deathloop"* (2021) or *Returnal* (2021) (see also the chapter by Backe in this volume). Christopher Barkman, discussing the latter, argues that "time loops narrativize something that is already implicit across most videogames—repetition" (2022, 1). Drawing on Brendan Keogh's statement that "time travel is a banal feature of videogame play" (2018, 145), he further emphasized that "[e]very game with a save/load feature already contains time loops. Acknowledging them within the gameworld essentially narrativizes elements like repetition and failure that are frequently part of play but outside of a game's storyworld" (Barkman 2022, 1). Alan Wake, trapped in the never-ending nightmare, is bound to travel through it repeatedly before discovering at the end of the first playthrough that, in his own words, "it is not a loop, it is a spiral." This discovery allows him to, seemingly, break the hold the Dark Place has on him in the alternative ending of the New Game + (which is framed as another loop in itself). On a smaller scale, Saga experiences similar loops in the aforementioned Overlaps, the imagery of which can certainly be linked to the impossible architecture of Escher's paintings and other impossible shapes favored by surrealists on the one hand and to the concept of a palimpsest on the other. Whereas the comparison to Escher's impossible, infinite architectures that wrap on themselves might be more fitting of different games by the discussed developers, such as *Layers of Fear* (2016) and *Control*, there is no doubt about the dream-like nature of the Dark Place and the Overlaps.

To this discussion, however, a more useful idea is the concept of a palimpsest, that is a medieval manuscript written on a material from which the previous text was scraped more or less completely (see also the chapter by Aksay et al. in this volume). As Sarah Dillon stresses, "the process that creates palimpsests is one of layering" (2005, 243) while palimpsest by itself is a phenomenon "where otherwise unrelated texts are involved and entangled, intricately interwoven, interrupting and inhabiting each other" (2005, 245). After Thomas De Quincey's 1845 essay "The Palimpsest," the metaphor became commonly used in various disciplines until it made its way to literature thanks to Genette (1997). In game studies, the concept of the palimpsest has been used to describe how AR games such as *Pokémon GO* (2016) rely on the meaning inscribed upon existing spaces (see Clowater 2021), how transmedial characters migrate from various adaptations of the source text, maintaining their character and identity (see Albersten 2019), or to describe the paradox of a character's seeming knowledge of certain events that, in fact, stem from the player repeating the playthrough, e.g., due to previous failure (see Kubiński 2014).

It is not without significance that the metaphor of palimpsest is often evoked in urban studies (see Engbersen 2001; Huyssen, 2003). While, as the following section will detail, the palimpsestic metalepsis occurs with or sometimes to the characters, the uniqueness of the metalepsis in *Alan Wake 2*, I argue, comes from precisely how locations behave. Several times in the game, both around said Overlaps (in Saga's chapters) and toward the end of the game (in Alan's), the two locations become so close to each other that they attempt to occupy the same space. The metaleptic transgressions are brief and the images are flickering on the screen, making it difficult to focus on the details. One such moment takes place when Saga completes a ritual involving a dead man's heart, which in turn opens the first Overlap in a forest. What has thus far been a tree now becomes a passage that, as Saga makes her way through it, suddenly starts to resemble an abandoned subway tunnel. The image is seamlessly superimposed on the screen, and the shape of the crossing perfectly matches that of the circular, concrete walls of the underground passage that the player later visits in Alan's chapters. True to their name, the Overlaps, the places where the two worlds come dangerously close to each other, bring two locations into one space. As Alan traverses the Dark Place, he witnesses similar effects at times when he comes close to the other side: As he leaves said subway station, he seemingly sees the forest and a murder scene investigated before by Saga, or the surroundings resemble that of the flooded basement she has investigated in the "real" world.

Sam Lake, the lead writer of *Alan Wake 2* and creative director at Remedy Entertainment, often admits his fascination with the television shows *Twin Peaks* and *True Detective*, and the influences of both on his games are quite obvious. Whereas some locations, characters, and themes of *Alan Wake* clearly reference *Twin Peaks*, I want to draw a parallel between the palimpsestic metalepsis in the games and a similar visual device used in the opening sequences of *True Detective*. Although in the show, the overlays combine landscapes and people, merging them into inhuman creatures (see Figure 8.1) and thus is perhaps more reminiscent of the character metalepsis I discuss in the next section, Julia Bee's consideration of the fluidity of the images of the show's opening is worth noting here:

> Dissolving frames alter and intensify the show's images in the process of constant variation. With the intro of *True Detective* the thinking about experience becomes thinking with experience. The stream of images opens up an immanent way of researching media with media. In the intro, images experience images, they fold into each other and thereby create an ecological experience as well as an experience of the milieu.
>
> (Bee 2019, 263)

The fluidity of the images blurring into each other is crucial, because it changes the ontological interpretation of the images from static and flat to "three-dimensional," as the "process is not simply experienced from the outside, it is experienced *as* process: A process full of micro shifts that intensify the emerging continuity of fading and becoming of images at the very same time" (Bee 2019, 263; original emphasis).

In *Alan Wake 2,* the same fluidity is crucial in the visualization of how the secondary location (i.e., the subway station) is pulled into the primary (i.e., the forest): The images never stay still and, in fact, vanish as soon as the player character stops to

Figure 8.1 The double-exposure image from the opening of *True Detective*, season 1.

admire them. This seems to emphasize the fluidity and temporality of a metaleptic transgression, putting the "move" in "movement." Although the characters do cross over from one world to another, for example when Alan makes his way into the real world (at least seemingly, as he is later revealed to still be trapped in the Dark Place) or when Saga enters the Dark Place, but the fluidity of the superimposition continuously reminds us of the instability of the borders between the realities.

Character Metalepsis in *Alan Wake 2*

The second most important type of visual metalepsis in *Alan Wake 2* features the superimposition of another character's close-up (from the front or featuring a very Hitchcockian profile) or silhouette on the primary character. In these cases, instead of another location appearing on top of the primary one, it is a character who briefly appears on the screen. It is perhaps important to note here that both cases include some interaction either between two objects or (at least) two characters. In other words, the location or character that is crossing over does not appear in an empty space but arrives in a space that is already occupied. This, in turn could explain the temporality and incompleteness of the transgression, which never results in a full transference: The paradoxical character of the movement between the worlds is strengthened by the inability of the two to coexist.

In *Alan Wake 2*, character palimpsests can be seen in three main contexts. Firstly, through the collectible Echoes, snippets of memories or ideas from Alan's previous books, showing his fictional detective Alex Casey discussing the crime scenes and events that Alan finds himself at. Once triggered (by looking at them from a correct angle), they show a silhouette of Alex Casey, often with the additional shadowy

Figure 8.2 The visual of the scene triggered by interacting with an Echo, showing playable Alan Wake and the shadow-like silhouette of Alex Casey mid-transition into the enlarged close-up of his profile.

close-up superimposed over the surroundings (see Figure 8.2). The Echo ends after Alex's narration is done.

The second context in which such palimpsests are regularly occurring is Saga's Mind Palace, a both narrative and a ludic space within her mind where she can examine clues, upgrade her weapons, revisit videos and music collected throughout the game, and, when encountering a dead end, profile other characters. Because of its dual character as both fictional and non-diegetic space (in which the player has access to collected recordings, songs, clues, but also weapon upgrades, etc.), the Mind Palace already emphasizes this duality. One of the available mechanics there is profiling, during which Saga connects with the victims or suspects to obtain additional information (see Figure 8.3). Finally, in a handful of narratively important moments, predominantly in Saga's chapters, there are overlaps of Saga's and Alan's figures.

Thus, when writing about visual metalepsis in the context of the superimposition of one image over another that signifies the moments of impossibility when two different places try to occupy the same space, I draw a parallel to Matthew Campora's (2009) "sonic metalepsis," created through the overlapping of the sound over imagery that does not fit it. While describing their specific use in *Eternal Sunshine of the Spotless Mind*, Campora notes that

> [s]ound bridges, as they are normally used, provide continuity across shots separated by time and/or space. [...] [They] are used not only to link scenes with distinct spatio-temporal frames, but also those with distinct ontologies. More importantly, these sound bridges are often used in a manner that disrupts

Figure 8.3 Saga profiling Cynthia, who shows up behind her both as a full-body silhouette and as an additional shadow overlay.

> the boundaries between the narrative strands, and in some cases, actually brings about their erasure altogether.
>
> (2009, 124)

In the abovementioned film, the sonic metalepsis signifies the shift in narration that shows the character's growing realization that something is not quite right: that "he is somehow both awake and not-awake at the same time" (Campora 2009, 126). Importantly, "this awareness is brought about, in part, by sonic metalepsis: The conversation [between the characters] crosses the boundary between the waking […] and the internal-subjective … levels" (Campora 2009, 126). Campora stresses there the difference between sonic bridges providing a temporal continuity across the shots and those that represent "the direct subjective aural experience" (2009, 126–127) of the character, allowing both the character and the viewers to understand the shift. In this case, it is a "rhetorical-metaleptic sound bridge, in which a voice originating in a lower level—in this case, a dialogue on the intradiegetic level—crosses the boundary to address a higher level, the metadiegetic" (Campora 2009, 127).

The first of the aforementioned moments in which other characters are visible on the screen while not physically present are the Echoes, i.e., collectible remnants of Alan's ideas. When seen from a correct angle, they reveal parts of one of the stories starring Alan's famous book protagonist, detective Alex Casey. As fascinating as this character's ontological status is, untangling it would require a much more detailed discussion. The first complication stems from the fact that the game features two characters named Alex Casey: Alan Wake's fictional protagonist and Saga's FBI partner who resents the comparison. However, the similarities do not end here as both characters are portrayed by the same actors: voiced by the late James McCaffrey, and played by Sam Lake.[2] In the Dark Place, Casey appears in several iterations: as a book/film character (as an Echo); as a flesh-and-blood character who can physically interact and confront Alan Wake, without, however, awareness of his own fictionality; and in the full-motion cinematics during the talk show interviews as Sam Lake, the actor who portrays the character in the films based on Alan's novels. Thus, the three versions show the character on three different levels of meaning, realizing the three types of metalepsis as identified by Jan Alber and Alice Bell (2012): ascending, descending, and hierarchical. Ascending, which describes the situation in which, usually, a character climbs up to a higher level of meaning, is realized when Alex Casey, a fictional character from Alan Wake's books, enters the world in which his author resides. It can be argued that the descending metalepsis, which describes the transgression occurring in the other direction, usually with an author or creator stepping down into the text of their creation, takes place when Sam Lake (as the actor Sam Lake) meets with Alan Wake in the dream-like talk show. Finally, hierarchical metalepsis, describing movements between different worlds of the same ontological status, takes place when Alan crosses between the Dark Place and the in-game real world.

The character palimpsests that occur around Saga take place in what constitutes the game's reality, during the section when the player controls Saga. The first becomes significant during the investigations she conducts within her Mind Palace. Saga's ability allows her to connect with another person—usually without their knowledge—and read their thoughts or feelings, thus gaining access to information she would not be able to obtain otherwise. During profiling, she sits at a table while focusing on the specific person and a question, which triggers another superimposed set of images and a voiceover. While Saga remains transfixed and almost frozen in time during these sessions, the images appear around her, changing size and angle, but showing little movement of the characters within any one picture.

The next situation of character metalepsis with Saga being the primary character features Alan Wake. While the game lets players collect the pages of Alan's world-altering manuscript, the majority of them are to be stored in Saga's Mind Palace and while they offer additional information on the characters and events, they are not crucial for the narrative. However, the few times the pages are narratively prominent, Saga picks them up and reads. Then, Wake becomes visible on the screen, seen in two or three different poses as he is reading out the page while writing the manuscript. This, then, adds a temporal element to the impossibility of this connection, reminiscent more closely of Campora's sonic metalepsis. In the Dark Place, time is non-linear and fragmented, forcing those trapped in it to travel in the locations that are encompassed within the loop, repeating their actions, thus allowing impossible interactions between characters separated by time. Here, what is paradoxical is not only the simultaneous on-screen presence and physical absence of Alan, but also the fact that he is narrating the pages that have already been completed.

The impossibility of these transgressions is emphasized by Bell and Alber as not only a defining characteristic of ontological metalepsis, but also one that differentiates it from other types of metalepsis, such as rhetorical. They note that "only ontological metalepses involve disorienting transgressions of boundaries that are physically or logically impossible, and hence properly unnatural" (Bell and

Alber 2012, 167). Furthermore, they stress that "[s]ome ontological metalepses are also logically impossible because they violate the principle of non-contradiction whereby two contradictory states of affairs cannot be true at the same time, which means, for example, that the same character cannot exist in two ontologically distinct domains simultaneously" (Bell and Alber 2012, 167). The rule of non-contradiction is violated when the characters break the time boundaries and speak to each other from different moments in time or space.

When considering the difference between ontological and rhetorical metalepsis, Marie-Laure Ryan notes that the latter "opens a small window that allows a quick glance across levels, but the window closes after a few sentences, and the operation ends up reasserting the existence of the boundaries," while the former "opens a passage between levels that result in their interpenetration, or mutual contamination" (2006, 207). Because such time constraints are rare for metalepsis, maybe with the exclusion of fourth-wall breaking that often offers just a short glimpse through the usually unacknowledged fourth wall, these visual metalepses are quite unique. The characters (and locations) have managed to partially cross over to the other world, which is a quality of an ontological metalepsis, while, however, maintaining the transiency of the event which, instead, for Ryan is a quality of rhetorical metalepsis.

Another element that makes these occurrences unusual relates to the fact that the movement does not only occur between worlds, but also between the diegetic/non-diegetic boundary. Jørgensen traces the meaning of the concept of diegesis to film theory in which the distinction allows one "to separate elements that can be said to be part of the depicted fictional world from elements that the fictional characters cannot see or hear and which should be considered non-existent in the fictional world" (2011, 78). She further shows how this applies to film sound, stating that "dialogue between two characters is seen as diegetic, while background score music is seen as non-diegetic" (Jørgensen 2011, 78). Such complication of the levels on which the metalepsis occurs further emphasize that *Alan Wake 2*, at its core, is about blending fiction with reality—regardless of whether this means blending different subworlds within the gameworld, or whether it also includes the player's reality.

Permeable Metalepsis in *Layers of Fear 2*

Even though the title suggests narrative continuity with the first game in the series, *Layers of Fear 2* offers a completely new story. It bears similarities to the 2016 game mostly in terms of its gameplay, which can be classified as a walking simulator,[3] and the highly abstract visual narration. The game follows an actor exploring a ship that has been transformed into a stage for an experimental, immersive play. The Actor's identity is only confirmed at the end of the game and contingent on the player's choices, but the player becomes gradually aware that it is one of the pair of siblings, Lily or James. The game is divided into five acts differing in terms of gameplay, main themes, and even visual techniques: "The Unmooring," "The Hunt," "Bloody Roots," "Breathe," and "Forever." Between the acts, the player is returned to the Actor's room and the deck around it, which additionally serves as a nondiegetic space reflecting the player's progress: Each section showcases collected objects, including film posters, photographic slides, phonograph interviews, and other items. The narrative is paused in those semi-diegetic spaces so the player can piece together the elements of the story and attempt to guess the identity of the Actor. Perhaps the most curious things are the posters alluding more or less clearly to real famous films: They show a leading actress and/or actor, both sporting an identical birthmark. Each chapter begins with a short black-and-white film narrated by the Director.

The game's narrative is delivered through scattered notes and the pieces of dialogue triggered by a collection of in-game items. The polyphonic, unreliable voices and the memories that blur the present and past create a sense of confusion, deceiving both the character and the player as to what is real and what is fiction. At the beginning of the game, the Director seems to be a real person—or at least as real as the Actor—and a note can be found explaining that he is known for making "the actors jump through hoops before he even lets them on the set. Supposed to be some new method of building the character." However, as the story progresses, he seems to be embodying the Actor's inner darkness—not unlike the presence of Alan's evil doppelgänger Mr. Scratch—and can even be interpreted as an internalized figure of the Actor's abusive father.

As the Actor explores the ship, memories trigger of the time they sneaked aboard a ship to the United States to escape their abusive parent and the traumatic journey that followed. The story is presented to the player through voiceover that blurs real and false memories of the harsh journey and the make-believe plays Lily designed to keep her younger brother James occupied while the children struggled to remain undetected while scavenging for food. The game in which the siblings pretended to be a pirate captain and her quartermaster establishes an additional layer of a play-within-the-play which runs parallel to the play set up by the Director in the game's present time. Especially in the first parts of the game, the exploration of the ship reveals theater sets and unfinished stage decorations, some of which clearly link to the events of Lily/James's past and further facilitate the blurring of the realities.

As the game includes multiple interlaced narrative layers reflecting many types of play, it evokes a *mise-en-abyme* structure that repeats the image within itself. One level showcases the confrontation between the Actor and the Director in the stage play while on another, there is a children's play of imagination. Through the unreliable narration and the symbolism, the player is also subjected to a play with identity. Finally, the Director's cinematics and the omnipresent allusions to, on the one hand, cinema in general and, on the other, to very specific, real film titles, create a closer association with the player's world. Despite the heavy indebtedness to theatrical tradition, the game pays constant homage to classic cinema, creating a collaboration between the game's interactivity and the cinematic aesthetic and symbolism. However, it could be argued that this synergy is already evoked by the choice of the first-person exploration-based gameplay, which heavily draws from the walking simulator genre.

Although the metalepsis is not visualized in the same way as in *Alan Wake 2*, the overlap of the identities is polyphonic—if not permeable—and ontological in nature, making it an even more complex case. Whereas in *Alan Wake 2*, the agents transgressing between the worlds were most of the time distinctively different at the beginning—with the notable exception of Alex Casey, whose closeness to all his alternative versions positions him uniquely on the borders between the worlds, rather than within them—in *Layers of Fear 2*, the metalepsis is caused by two interconnected identities trying to occupy one space. Through almost the entire game, it is not clear which of the siblings is the Actor as their memories of each other merge and collapse into one another, changing the speaker they point to, and becoming indistinguishable from the play and the fiction. Where in *Alan Wake 2*, the moments of overlap are clearly signified by visual techniques, here the realities are ontologically so close to each other that one cannot be sure how many there actually are between the past and the present, the Director's play and the childhood games, and so on. However, there are visible aesthetic changes that indicate that the transition has occurred. For example, in the first chapter, the Actor finds themselves among stage decorations that include a ship (which adds another layer of *mise en abyme*), which then almost comes to life when the wood-and-paper decorations begin to move, the paper sun starts to shine, and the image becomes blurry and shaky, bringing back the memories (in the form of voices) of the journey the Actor took with their sibling in the past. When the sequence is completed, the ship calms down and once again become a soulless, inanimate object—and the Actor moves on to the backstage areas.

The obvious impossibility of these shifts between realities is additionally ensured by the fact that, as we learn further into the game, only one of the siblings survived the journey to America in their youth. Thus, what occurs is some form of an observer's effect, which in physics describes the disturbance of the outcome by the sole act of observation. The moment at the end of the game when the Actor looks into the mirror and reveals feminine- or masculine-coded features, establishing themselves as James *or* Lily, not only fixes one actual reality (one in which Lily is alive, but James dead, or vice versa), but also suggests that this was the case throughout the entire game. And so, at that moment, because of the player's choices, it becomes so that this reality was *always* true.

The metaleptic transgressions differ from those discussed earlier: Not only do the different realities take over the physical space at the same time, like in the case of fiction and past taking over the ship decorations in what we understand as the reality, but the characters also slip into each other's place. If in *Alan Wake 2* the characters are fighting against the Dark Presence/Place, and the space is, in a truly Gothic fashion, its own force and has its own personality, in *Layers of Fear 2*, the space seems to be more dependent on the character who brings it to life. In other words, the world changes when one personality shifts into another.

Although when Brian Richardson (2006) wrote about a permeable narrator, he referred to narratorial voices specifically rather than more generally understood narration, his concept can be of use here. Describing a situation in which different narratorial voices collapse into one another, he explained it as "the uncanny and inexplicable intrusion of the voice of another within the narrator's consciousness" which "threatens to violate the principle of an autonomous, individual consciousness that is presupposed by all current theories of the narrator" (Richardson 2006, 95). He additionally notes that the permeable narrator "slips (or is collapsed) into other minds and discourses and speaks what should be impossible for it to know" (Richardson 2006, xi), also perhaps positioning the Director as indistinguishable from the twofold Actor, considering that the play he sets up seems to be too closely tailored to the Actor's particular experiences.

Although the siblings and the Director, who are the three main voices heard throughout the game in response to the discovery of new objects and locations, are not strictly narrators, they seem to have specific realities attached to them, and they pull them into existence every time they resurface. For this reason, Brian McHale's concepts of a "strange loop" (1977, 119)[4] in the structure of narrative levels or a "short circuit" between the "fictional world and the ontological level occupied by the author" (1977, 213) is a useful reconceptualization of Genette's "transgressions." The loop metaphor is particularly enticing here: In both games, the imagery of a loop is important both narratively (in *Alan Wake 2*) and in terms of the design of the games' spaces. Both games repeat the imagery of a looping hallway[5] which, by evoking the sense of the uncanny, "is the primary source of psychological discomfort" (Kalinowski 2019, 58).

Four times in a game the player is presented with a choice and, depending on whether they have mostly obeyed or disobeyed the Director's orders (or remained indecisive for the third, much darker ending),[6] the Actor will be revealed as Lily or James. The Director's narration and the messages found around the ship do point toward one of these two endings (and, thus, a necessity for making a decision) as its main goal, framing the game's story as both the Actor's psychological journey of dealing with their traumatic past and as an actor's task to find the character they play. One of these notes reads: "Inside every actor is the one part they were born to play. The one character they were meant to build. Chip away the bloody marble. Give form to formless. Until all that remains… is the truth." The moment in which we finally see the character is significant for several reasons as it finally restores order and disentangles the worlds that have been collapsing into each other. By showing a face of a character who, until this point, had no discernible features, the game establishes a firm fourth wall between itself and the extra-fictional level of meaning, highlighting the ontological difference between the player and the character. This shows another difference between the two games discussed here: Where *Layers of Fear 2*'s positive endings ensure the restoration of balance and safely secure the fiction behind the fourth wall, *Alan Wake 2* seems to never bring attention to the fourth wall, suggesting that perhaps there is none, leaving the player in a state of existential insecurity after they turn off the game.

Conclusions

Both discussed games share clear similarities in terms of their evident fascination with film and the use of visual palimpsests as a unique method of blending the lines between various fictional worlds. Drawing from the existing theory on metalepsis in videogames, which most often is interested in the movements of the characters,

I additionally focused on what happens when locations commit such transgressions discussed and, most importantly, on what metalepsis *looks like* in the moment of its occurrence.

The transgressions shown in the two games are not exactly the same: Whereas in *Alan Wake 2* they are more literal, showing the exact moment where two worlds or characters collide, in *Layers of Fear 2*, the whole world temporarily changes to reflect whether for that moment the world is real, imagined, or a part of the play, having Lily or James pull their entire surrounding reality into short, temporal actuality. Regardless of whether it is the locations or the characters that are transgressing into the space they do not—and usually cannot—belong to, the metaleptic movement in these games was characterized by fluidity, as emphasized either by the way images appear on the screen and can be seen only as the player character moves (*Alan Wake 2*) or as the continuous act of shifting realities (*Layers of Fear 2*).

Acknowledgments

This chapter is part of a project titled "Meta-Games and the Player-Character Relationship," funded in part or whole by the National Science Centre, Poland (grant no. 2021/41/N/HS2/02029).

Notes

1 The term "interactive film," otherwise known as "audience participation film" or "decision cinema" (Hales 2015, 36) describes a "moving image content in the form of prerecorded sequences" (Hales 2015, 37), usually in the form of live-action footage, that can be interacted with by the audience members. Neither Bloober Team's nor Remedy Entertainment's games can be considered fully such interactive films, but they both heavily engage with the format.

2 An additional layer of overt metareference is worth pointing out here: McCaffrey has previously voiced Max Payne, the detective protagonist of Remedy's first series *Max Payne* (2001), portrayed again by Sam Lake. Due to copyright issues, Remedy currently does not hold the rights to the titles and, thus, cannot bring Max Payne to the Remedy Connected Universe. However, the link between Max Payne and Alex Casey was heavily hinted on when, for example, Lake-as-Casey makes the characteristic Max Payne expression in one of the cutscenes.

3 "Walking simulator" is the name coined for the exploratory, first-person games that offer no combat or otherwise high-pressure mechanics, giving the players time to discover the story (see Grabarczyk 2016; Kagen 2022; Consalvo and Paul 2019; and the chapter by Thon in this volume).

4 Which works here particularly well considering *Alan Wake 2*'s symbolism of a Dark Place as an endless loop.

5 The looping hallway became a popular setting for independent horror games after it was popularized by Hideo Kojima and Guillermo del Toro's *P.T.* (2014), which is an acronym for a "playable teaser," suggesting it was a demo of a full, never released game.

6 The third ending sees the still anonymous Actor cowering in the dark, scolded for their indecisiveness by the Rat Queen, an antagonist of both the first and the second game.

Works Cited

Alan Wake. 2010. Remedy Entertainment/Microsoft Game Studios. Xbox S.

Alan Wake 2. 2023. Remedy Entertainment/Epic Games Publishing. PlayStation 5.

Albertsen, Anita N.B. 2019. "Palimpsest Characters in Transfictional Storytelling: On Migrating *Penny Dreadful* Characters from Television to Comic Books." *Continuum* 33 (2): 242–257.

Barkman, Christopher. 2022. "Videogame Time Loops." In *Proceedings of DiGRA Australia 2022*, 1–3.

Bee, Julia. 2019. "Pure Experience and *True Detective*: Immediation, Diagrams, Milieu." In *Immediation I*, edited by Erin Manning, Anna Munster, and Bodil Marie Stavning Thomsen, 256–271. London: Open Humanities Press.

Bell, Alice, and Jan Alber. 2012. "Ontological Metalepsis and Unnatural Narratology." *Journal of Narrative Theory* 42 (2): 166–192.

Bódi, Bettina. 2023. *Videogames and Agency*. New York: Routledge.

Bittanti, Matteo, 2003. "The Technoludic Film: Images of Video Games in Movies (1973–2001)." In *Entertainment Computing: Technologies and Application,* edited by Ryohei Nakatsu and Junichi Hoshino, 307–312. New York: Springer.

Campora, Matthew. 2009. "Art Cinema and New Hollywood: Multiform Narrative and Sonic Metalepsis in *Eternal Sunshine of the Spotless Mind*: Research Article." *New Review of Film and Television Studies* 7 (2): 119–131.

Clowater, Victoria. 2021. "*Pokémon Go* as Palimpsest: Creating Layers of Meaning through Augmented Reality." *Loading…: The Journal of the Canadian Game Studies Association* 14 (24): 104–121.

Consalvo, Mia, and Christopher A. Paul. 2019. *Real Games: What's Legitimate and What's Not in Contemporary Videogames*. Cambridge, MA: MIT Press.

Control. 2019. Remedy Entertainment/505 Games. PlayStation 5.

"Deathloop". 2021. Arkane Studios/Bethesda Softworks. Microsoft Windows.

De Quincey, Thomas. 2013. *Confessions of an English Opium-Eater and Other Writings*. Oxford: Oxford University Press.

Dillon, Sarah. 2005. "Reinscribing De Quincey's Palimpsest: The Significance of the Palimpsest in Contemporary Literary and Cultural Studies." *Textual Practice* 19 (3): 243–263.

Engbersen, Godfried. 2001. "The Urban Palimpsest." *Focaal: European Journal of Anthropology* 38: 125–138.

Eternal Sunshine of the Spotless Mind. 2004. Director Michel Gondry. USA: Focus Features.

Fine, Gary Alan. 1983. *Shared Fantasy: Role Playing Games as Social Worlds*. Chicago: University of Chicago Press.

Genette, Gérard. 1980. *Narrative Discourse: An Essay in Method*. Ithaca, NY: Cornell University Press.

Genette, Gerard. 1997. *Palimpsests: Literature in the Second Degree*. Lincoln: University of Nebraska Press.

Girina, Ivan. 2015. "Cinematic Games: The Aesthetic Influence of Cinema on Video Games." PhD thesis, University of Warwick.

Grabarczyk, Paweł, 2016. "It's Like a Walk in The Park: On Why Are Walking Simulators So Controversial." *Transformacje* 1 (3–4): 241–263.

Hales, Chris. 2015. "Interactive Cinema in the Digital Age." In *Interactive Digital Narrative*, edited by Hartmut Koenitz, Gabriele Ferri, Mads Haahr, Diğdem Sezen, and Tonguç İbrahim Sezen, 36–50. New York: Routledge.

Huyssen, Andreas. 2003. *Present Pasts: Urban Palimpsests and the Politics of Memory*. Stanford: Stanford University Press.

Jørgensen, Kristine. 2011. "Time for New Terminology? Diegetic and Non-Diegetic Sounds in Computer Games Revisited." In *Game Sound Technology and Player Interaction: Concepts and Developments*, edited by Mark Grimshaw, 78–97. New York: IGI Global.

Jørgensen, Kristine. 2013. *Gameworld Interfaces*. Cambridge, MA: MIT Press.

Kagen, Melissa. 2022. *Wandering Games*. Cambridge, MA: MIT Press.

Kalinowski, Anna Maria. 2019. "Silent Halls: PT, Freud, and Psychological Horror." *Press Start* 5 (1): 57–66.

Keogh, Brendan. 2018. *A Play of Bodies: How We Perceive Videogames*. Cambridge, MA: MIT Press.

Krampe, Theresa, Stephanie Lotzow, and Jan-Noël Thon. 2022. "Playful Poetics: Metareferential Interfaces in Recent Indie Games." *Poetics Today* 43 (4): 729–771.

Kubiński, Piotr. 2014. "Immersion vs. Emersive Effects in Videogames." In *Engaging with Videogames: Play, Theory and Practice*, edited by Dawn Stobbart and Monica Evans, 133–141. Oxford: Brill.

Kukkonen, Karin, and Sonja Klimek, eds. 2011. *Metalepsis in Popular Culture*. Berlin: De Gruyter.

Layers of Fear. 2016. Bloober Team/Aspyr. Microsoft Windows.

Layers of Fear. 2023. Bloober Team. Microsoft Windows.

Layers of Fear 2. 2019. Bloober Team/Gun Media. Microsoft Windows.

Linderoth, Jonas. 2012. "Why Gamers Don't Learn More: An Ecological Approach to Games as Learning Environments." *Journal of Gaming & Virtual Worlds* 4 (1): 45–62.

Limoges, Jean-Marc. 2011. "Metalepsis in the Cartoons of Tex Avery: Expanding the Boundaries of Transgression." In *Metalepsis in Popular Culture*, edited by Karin Kukkonen Karin and Sonja Klimek, 196–212. Berlin: De Gruyter.

Mackay, Daniel. 2001. *The Fantasy Role-Playing Game: A New Performing Art*. Jefferson: McFarland.

Macrae, Andrea. 2019. *Discourse Deixis in Metafiction: The Language of Metanarration, Metalepsis and Disnarration*. New York: Routledge.

Max Payne. 2001. Remedy Entertainment. Microsoft Windows.

McHale, Brian. 1977. *Postmodernist Fiction*. London: Routledge.

Pokémon GO. 2016. Niantic/Niantic. Android.

P.T. 2014. Kojima Productions/Konami. Microsoft Windows.

Rehak, Bob. 2003. "Playing at Being: Psychoanalysis and the Avatar." In *The Video Game Theory Reader*, edited by Mark J.P. Wolf and Bernard Perron, 103–127. New York: Routledge.

Repulsion. 1965. Director Roman Polański. UK: Compton Films.

Returnal. 2021. Housemarque/Sony Interactive Entertainment. Microsoft Windows.

Richardson, Brian. 2006. *Unnatural Voices: Extreme Narration in Modern and Contemporary Fiction*. Columbus: Ohio State University Press.

Ryan, Marie-Laure. 2006. *Avatars of Story*. Minneapolis: University of Minnesota Press.

Se7en. 1995. Director David Fincher. USA: Arnold Kopelson Productions.

The Shining. 1980. Director Stanley Kubrick. UK: The Producer Circle Company.

Thon, Jan-Noël. 2016. *Transmedial Narratology and Contemporary Media Culture*. Lincoln: University of Nebraska Press.

True Detective. 2014–. Creator Nic Pizzolatto. HBO.

Twin Peaks. 1993–2018. Creator David Lynch. ABC.

Van de Mosselaer, Nele. 2022. "Breaking the Fourth Wall in Videogames." In *Being and Value in Technology*, edited by Enrico Terrone and Vera Tripodi, 163–186. London: Palgrave Macmillan.

Waskul, Dennis, and Matt Lust. 2004. "Role-Playing and Playing Roles: The Person, Player, and Persona in Fantasy Role-Playing." *Symbolic Interaction* 27 (3): 333–356.

Waszkiewicz, Agata. 2020a. "Audiovisual Media Convergence and the Metareferential Strategies in *Layers of Fear 2*." *Panoptikum* 24 (31): 68–79.

Waszkiewicz, Agata. 2020b. "'Together They Are Twofold': Player-Avatar Relationship beyond the Fourth Wall." *Journal of Games Criticism* 4 (1): n.pag.

Waszkiewicz, Agata. 2024. *Metagames: Games about Games*. New York: Routledge.

The Wizard of Oz. 1939. Director Victor Felming. USA: MGM.

The X-Files. 1993–2018. Creator Chris Carter. 20th Century Fox Television.

9 Reading (in) Games

Constructing Meaning through Intradiegetic Metareferences to Text

Regina Seiwald

This chapter explores the intrinsic relationship between text and videogames, focusing on how both paratextual and intradiegetic texts shape the gaming experience. Paratexts, such as game menus and system interfaces, serve as bridges between the player and the gameworld, often unnoticed unless emphasized. Intradiegetic texts, embedded within the gameworld, on the other hand, can form part of the narrative, influencing player decisions. Both forms of text can occur as metareferences, where texts reflect on their own construction. This chapter examines various games to map out the spectrum of self-reflexive and non-self-reflexive texts, highlighting the role of genre and pacing in shaping player interaction with in-game text. By focusing on the interplay between text, game structure, and player engagement, this analysis also emphasizes the various effects of self-reflexivity of these metareferences, showing that they can break the fourth wall, enhance narrative depth, or guide gameplay.

Introduction: The Relationship between Text and Videogames

Videogames could not exist without text. Forming the skeleton around which digital experiences come to life, the typed word, in the form of code, constitutes an intrinsic part of the very nature of games. While this form of writing often hides behind visual representations and haptic explorations, players may also encounter text in games themselves. On the one hand, games contain extradiegetic written elements relating to the game system, i.e., "the game's ludic system as well as the software, most of which is hidden from the player's conscious perception" (Krampe 2023, 141), such as the source code, copyright information, game descriptions in online stores, menu navigation, or avatar naming. If these forms of text occur outside of the game's fictional world, they are akin to what Gérard Genette termed "paratexts"—"accompanying productions" (1997, 1) that "*present* [the text], in the usual sense of the verb, but also in its strongest meaning: to *make it present*, to assure its presence in the world, its *reception* and its consumption" (1991, 261; original emphases). These elements are mostly necessary parts without which a game could not be released. Paratexts are located between the player's reality and the fictional world of the game, serving a bridging function by which

DOI: 10.4324/9781003538592-9

we can access the game. Usually, they are not ludic but factual, and players do not attribute any special importance to them because they are, according to Jonathan Gray, "as organic and naturally occurring a part of our mediated environment as are movies and television [and videogames] themselves" (2010, 23). Despite their "quiet" presence, the importance of paratexts should not be underestimated as they "shape our understanding of their connected text, give us clues as to how we might engage with it, what it is, and how we should make sense of it" (Seiwald and Vollans 2023, 3). Paratextual elements thus provide the contextual framework in which we engage with a text and guide the relationship we have with it.

In most cases, paratexts are so conventional that we often only see them if their representation departs from the norm. In that form, they are akin to what Theresa Krampe, Stephanie Lotzow, and Jan-Noël Thon have referred to as *metareferential interfaces*, "interfaces that foreground and draw attention to their own mediality" (Krampe et al. 2022, 729). Elements of metareferential interfaces include "WIMP [windows, icons, mouse, pointer] interface devices, menus, and extradiegetic overlays that audiovisually communicate important information about the videogame's ludic system and game state, but are usually not perceived as part of either its storyworld *or* its game spaces" (Krampe et al. 2022, 730; original emphasis). In this sense, metareferential interfaces are paratexts with a playful twist: they ludically point toward themselves by highlighting that they are constructed artifacts. In that regard, the concept of metareferential interfaces differs from that of paratexts because paratexts are not always self-referential. As a recent study by Jan Švelch (2020) shows, game studies often uses the term "paratext" in a very broad sense to denote any element somehow related to a game, such as merchandise products, trailers, or Let's Plays. In other words, while metareferential interfaces are paratexts, the term "paratexts" also refers to elements that are not metareferential.

On the other hand, we also find intradiegetic text occurring *in* and forming a part *of* the gameworld, i.e., "the (fictional) storyworld of a videogame" (Krampe 2023, 141): a character reads a short note, a poster on the wall provides additional information, or a letter frames the game's narrative. In some games, text even becomes integral to the story, for example when the player's decision-making process is influenced by a note, such as when Henry, the playable character in *Firewatch* (2016), gains additional insights into an abandoned campsite based on a handwritten note attached to a tent, or when players need to decipher the meaning of a sentence fragment by translating hieroglyph-like characters in *Heaven's Vault* (2019). In these two examples and similar cases, text implicitly or explicitly emphasizes its own status as text by being mediated in its reception process through a world that differs from the player's reality because it is fictional (see also the chapter by Aksay et al. in this volume). *Implicit* here means that the textual status is only suggested, for example by the genre (a letter, a note, a poster, etc.) or by an in-game character reading it. *Explicit* refers to actual comments on the textual status, e.g., when text fragments are referred to as such, collected and arranged in a manner to create a story in *Alan Wake 2* (2023). In the secondary narrative level of this game, detective Saga Anderson can organize clues she collected in the form of photos, files, and short written notes in a way that makes most sense to her in a given moment. And Alan himself can even experience a scene, go to his desk, physically rewrite it based on the insights he got when he first experienced it (e.g., through a clue on a note), and relive the scene under new circumstances (see also the chapter by Waszkiewicz in this volume). In all these instances, players do not encounter this kind of text first-hand and in their own reality but in a fictional world while assuming the role of an avatar and/or behaving as if they were in this world.

Based on this preliminary discussion, this chapter aims at defining the circumstances under which in-game texts constitute metareferences and discusses their effects on the textual status of the game. Metareferences are defined by Werner Wolf as "self-reflection with a metadimension" (Wolf 2009, 22), which, according to Krampe, can "comment on themselves from a logically higher level of reflection" (Krampe 2023, 139). In reference to Wolf (see Wolf 2009, 22), Krampe further argues that this kind of metadimension does not only concern a game's story and fictionality, but can relate to the games system itself, such as rules, computing technology, or mechanics of engagement. While the discussion that follows also takes the stance that metareferences can relate to all aspects of a game, it wants to challenge Wolf's statement by probing if a text always *has* to be self-referential to constitute a metareference.

As a key focus, this chapter studies the impact of metareferentiality—a game's characteristic of incorporating metareferences in its fictional world—on the game. This is done by raising questions regarding medium-related issues, the textuality of videogames, and the unique reception process of games, which demands active engagement from players in the meaning-making process. The first part of this chapter addresses the theoretical framework of the text–game relationship by determining the conditions under which in-game text constitutes a metareference. To do so, it looks at the relationship between self-reflexivity and metareferentiality, explicitness of references, and player engagement with texts. For the latter, the concepts of game genres and sequence pacing will be considered because they influence a player's reaction to in-game text.

The second part of this chapter engages with varieties of text–game relationships in a defined corpus of case study games. It addresses various forms of intradiegetic text occurring in gameworlds, ranging from short one-letter words to whole books. Each form of text will be placed on a scale between fully self-reflexive and not self-reflexive to explain what makes a text a metareference. And for each form of text, several case study games were chosen that vary in genre, mode of engagement, and narrative style to ensure that a broad spectrum of text–game relationships is covered. The section begins by looking at short non-narrative notes in *Control* (2019), *Resident Evil 4* (2005), *The Stanley Parable* (2013) and its *Ultra Deluxe* (2022) re-issue. Next, longer text in the form of diaries, notebooks, and files is studied in *Uncharted 4: A Thief's End* (2016), *Silent Hill 4: The Room* (2004), and *Alan Wake 2*. This is followed by an analysis of two-way communication in the form of letters, e-mails, and text messages in *Fears to Fathom: Home Alone* (2021), *Gone Home* (2013), and *Dear Esther* (2012). The fourth part of this section focuses on books in games, in particular games of the *The Last of Us* (2013–2020) series, *Minecraft* (2011), and *Alan Wake* (2010). This section concludes with games that use text as an integral part of their composition, namely *Bury Me, My Love* (2017), *Heaven's Vault*, and *Stories Untold* (2017). Text-based games, such as *Zork: The Great Underground Empire* (1980), are not considered in the context of this chapter because for those games, text *is* the game, and hence they do not establish a metareference via text, but they *are* text.

This progression from small to large amounts of text helps to map the potential for self-reflexive metareferences in contrast to in-game text that is solely a reference but lacking the "meta" component. Although other forms of text may appear in games, the number and variation of games and textual forms analyzed in this chapter allows readers to gain a better understanding of the text–game relationship as a whole, which can be adapted to fit their individual games research. At the end of this chapter, the reader will hopefully have a better understanding of (1) the unique characteristics of metareferences generated by incorporating text in games, (2) the various forms of how intradiegetic text can occur in games, and (3) how we can distinguish between text that constitutes metareferences and text that does not do so.

Part I: In-Game Texts as Metareferences

When we look at the history of videogames, we notice that the relationship between games and text has always been an intrinsic one. The medium possesses the ability to incorporate a sheer endless number of texts, often with the aim of making the gameworld more authentic, more approachable, and richer. As suggested in the introduction to this chapter, in-game texts can take on various forms, and their manifold functions and meanings are now addressed from a theoretical perspective. To do so, various characteristics of in-game texts are discussed to map out a framework that allows researchers to determine the metareferentiality of text in games on a case-by-case basis.

In general, texts incorporated in games can either be non-self-reflexive, i.e., they are *not* explicit about their textual status, or self-reflexive, i.e., they highlight that they *are* text and a constructed artifact. The first feature applies to the majority of in-game texts as this kind of text forms an "organic" part of the gameworld that does not emphasize its textuality. If the latter feature applies, however, these texts always constitute a metareference. In the context of the text–game relationship, this reflection on the artifactuality of the text is located in the (metaphorical and literal) space of gameworld-building and gameworld-reception, meaning that text may contribute to a sense of artifactuality of the game as a whole. While these elements are intradiegetic, i.e., they share the same fictional world of the in-game characters, their function may well be extradiegetic, pointing outwards to the act of creation or the creator(s).

If these texts occurring in games are well embedded within the gameworld, they can break the "fourth wall" without endangering the player's "willing suspension of disbelief" (Coleridge 2014 [1817], 208) because these in-game texts can function as metareferences from within and toward the medium itself. They point inwards to the core of what defines a (video)game: playing with the manifold possibilities of ludic and narratological construction and representation. However, it is important that these texts occurring in games are incorporated in such a way that they form part of the gameworld or its mechanics. If this is not the case, they pose the risk of players becoming detached from what Johan Huizinga has termed the "magic circle": When we play, games are "marked off" as "temporary worlds within the ordinary world, dedicated to the performance of an act apart" (Huizinga 1955, 10). We experience them as different from our world, but also related to it. Therefore, while previous studies have already thoroughly researched the self-reflexive nature of metareferential practices (see, e.g., Ensslin 2014; Ferri et al. 2016; Fest 2016; Gualeni 2016; Seiwald 2019), the discussion that follows does not understand the metareferential links established by embedding texts in videogames as solely self-reflexive. Instead, it presents this characteristic as one side of the spectrum. The other side is populated by metareferences that show the many transmedial possibilities games afford us without necessarily urging players to be critical of the game itself, while equally emphasizing the textuality of the in-game text through intertextuality (see Seiwald 2022). Self-reflexivity is a spectrum, and in-game texts can occur in any place on it. The difference between self-reflexive and non-self-reflexive metareferences is therefore one concerning a core characteristic of the embedded text.

Besides the degree of explicitness regarding the textual status of elements incorporated in games, genre expectations influence the player's actual engagement with a text. Although genres are traditionally defined as a "codification of discursive properties" (Todorov 1976, 162), they are also "systems of expectations and hypothesis" (Neale 2000, 158). This means that while it is possible to create a game that corresponds to the practices associated with a given genre, the player engages with it from the perspective of their personal experience. The links made between the structures and rules employed in the game and the way players receive and react to them define if a game is perceived as approachable, playable, and enjoyable by the individual player. If players are familiar with certain structures of the game, such as navigation, degree of action, or engagement with NPCs, it becomes easier for them to generate predictions and react to the game in a manner expected and presupposed by the game maker(s). An example is that first-person shooters allow players to experience the action from a first-person perspective and the knowledge that this is the case encourages players to act in and react to the game in a certain way. Deviations from this horizon of expectations are welcome as they are considered an innovation, but the degree of novelty is important here. If the number of familiar elements is too low, players might find their experience of a game alienating. Nonetheless, videogame genres are not neatly defined categories of standardization; instead, they are sets of criteria, shifting over time, and associated with a specific kind of games. One such set of criteria is the incorporation of text in games. Players who decide to play a slow-paced narrative game, such as *What Remains of Edith Finch* (2017), approach it with the expectation that they will be reading a lot of text (see also the chapter by Thon in this volume). Players who play *Call of Duty: Black Ops Cold War* (2020), however, expect a game with fast-paced action. They are subsequently less inclined to pause and read a long letter or a diary, which goes against some of the key components of first-person shooters, namely agility and commotion. This means that while all game genres can incorporate text, questions of textual quality and quantity need to be considered.

Besides genre expectations, pacing—as the speed of sequences—is crucial for the incorporation of intradiegetic text because text slows down a game. Pacing in videogames is split into pacing controlled by the game and its characters, especially NPCs, and player-controlled pacing (see Wolf 2010, 86). If the game-controlled pacing is well-mapped onto the kind of text included in a certain sequence, it is possible to go beyond the expectations traditionally associated with a certain game or genre. *Final Fantasy VI* (1994), for example, managed to create a truly immersive story for its players, despite—or because of—its reliance on extensive text. Upon its release, the game has not only pushed the boundaries of game mechanics, but also laid the foundation for new advancements in narrative games.

Player-controlled pacing also needs to match player expectations. For example, in *Call of Duty: Black Ops Cold War*, players can sometimes access computers by choosing from a set of pre-defined access codes. As a reward, they receive information, such as a printout of communication records that potentially influences the game. These sequences are slow-paced and rely on writing, but they are nonetheless well-embedded in this gameworld, which focuses on spying, infiltration, and knowledge. If, however, the text unsettles the gameworld because it does not sit well within the pace of the game sequence, players are likely to skip it or, if the cutscene cannot be skipped, disengage from the game. For instance, *Always Sometimes Monsters* (2014) is a text-based game, and hence one would assume that players approach it with a degree of willingness to read. However, besides the written dialogues, the game also includes other text, such as letters and notes, which cannot be skipped. These artifacts take away a lot of the (already fairly pre-defined) player engagement. Player reviews frequently address this issue with in-game text, such as this review on Steam Community:

> i was somewhat under the impression that it would be more of a visual novel than [a] game, but here i am dealing with slow as ♥♥♥♥ transitions, movement and interface. every time i want to do anything, i'm waiting just a bit too long and it adds up quickly.
>
> i'm only like 1hr in and i sort of wish… expectations (?) were better set, so i would have an idea on how i might want to proceed.
>
> and the prologue-- the trailer sets the game up as being more true-to-life or mature (i was ready for that good pretentious ♥♥♥♥) and then it opens up with the hitman. the dialogue wasn't very believable. i get it, it just didn't come off right. odd way to set the pace maybe.
>
> (wayne 2014)

As this review shows, this player considers the incorporation and kind of text in *Always Sometimes Monsters* as alienating even though they approached it with expectations that it was a visual novel and not a "traditional" walking simulator game. Indeed, the line between visual novels and walking simulators is a fine one, and Melissa Kagen attributes the following characteristics to the latter: "Walking simulators are exploratory, nonviolent video games without points, goals, or tasks, in which the undying, third-person player character (PC) wanders around a narratively rich space" (Kagen 2022, 1). Part of the criticism *Always Sometimes Monsters* received is that it blends the worst of games, i.e., long, unimportant, and unskippable narrative sequences, with the worst of visual novels, i.e., a story that is just not convincing. The imbalance of the text–game relationship as perceived by the above and other players of *Always Sometimes Monsters* clearly unsettles the game's narrative and pace. This can potentially endanger the intactness of the diegesis, resulting in a negative attitude toward the game. In that respect, the game also does not fulfill the criterion of walking simulators being an "exploration-driven, character-focused adventure" (Lee and Morimoto 2021, 40), which poses the risk of disappointing player expectations not only toward the narrative, but also toward gameplay.

Research into this text–game relationship has previously been undertaken from many different angles. While videogame *paratexts* have attracted the interest of researchers in the recent past (see, e.g., Beil et al. 2021; Seiwald and Vollans 2023; Švelch 2020; Wolf 2006), intradiegetic game-text has only been marginally addressed, despite its presence in and key role for many games. One prominent direction taken in research into in-game text is the education perspective, in particular how text-in-games can stimulate the reading performance in (dyslexic) children (see, e.g., Bavelier et al. 2013; Bediou et al. 2018; Bejjanki et al. 2014; Franceschini 2013; Pasqualotto et al. 2022; Plass et al. 2020). These studies often do not distinguish between extradiegetic in-game text, i.e., text occurring on a different fictional plane to that of the in-game action and characters, and intradiegetic in-game text, i.e., text that occurs "naturally" in the gameworld and forms part of its construction, such as road signs or posters. Furthermore, the narratological concept, i.e., how text and game form a relationship and to what effect, has—apart from a few exceptions (see, e.g., Boluk and LeMieux 2017; Krampe 2023; Krampe et al. 2022)—hardly been addressed in research to date.

This excursus into the theoretical nature of text–game relationships as well as their status in (games) research leads to a question underpinning this chapter: Under which circumstances is intradiegetic text metareferential? To answer this, arguably ambitious, question, the discussion that follows looks at in-game text from a narratological and a ludological perspective to determine the circumstances under which the presence of text in games constitutes a metareference, and if this metareference is self-reflexive. At the core of this research is the question how the act of reading in gameworlds can form a metareference rendering the construction of the game itself by indicating that any artifact requires the recipient's active engagement. In this sense, the incorporation of written text in videogames emphasizes the status of the game as a creation, while it also affects the player's engagement with the game. Metareference here is thus not only understood as a game's reference to itself but also as general references to the textuality of text and to a game's status as an artwork (see Jannidis 2009, 544).

Part II: Forms of Intradiegetic Texts in Videogames

Intradiegetic text in videogames can take on a multitude of forms because any mode of writing we can encounter in reality can also occur within the fictional realms of a game. At the same time, the quantity and quality of text varies and is often mapped onto the kind of game it occurs in. If an in-game text self-reflexively emphasizes its textual status, the acknowledgment of a game as a created artifact, which needs to be engaged with by the player, is brought to the fore. To understand better how to distinguish between various degrees of self-reflexivity, which, in turn, influences if a text within a game is considered a metareference or not, case studies are analyzed, ranging from least to most text.

Short Non-Narrative Notes

Short non-narrative notes are found in the majority of games. Quite often, however, players do not pay a lot of attention to them because they are also present in our reality. Examples are traffic signs or notes such as "Do not enter." They often also follow a pattern of representation we are familiar with, for example, the hexagonal shape of a stop sign, framed in white, with white letters on a red background. The text found in *Control* mostly resembles the one we may find in a similar situation in reality: a shelter hatch stating the maximum occupancy or a door carrying the label "Emergency Supply Storage." These instances are not metareferential because this kind of text does not necessarily draw the player's attention to the fact that the game is constructed. *Resident Evil 4*, by contrast, includes clever puns that play with the idea of medium-specific characteristics. Throughout the game, bounty notes can be found, which not only function as small diversions from the otherwise horror game content, but also pay gemstones that can be used to buy unique items and upgrades if the player successfully completes them. One such bounty call is labelled "Egg Hunt," which tasks players to find a golden chicken egg. As this bounty hunt instruction is an Easter Egg—a hidden feature within the game—in the game universe, finding the "real," in-game egg is not only nominative determinism, but also an explicit reference to a prominent game feature.

While this incorporation of a short non-narrative note is partly self-reflexive, games may also be more explicit. The—arguably by now canonical (see, e.g., Backe and Thon 2019; Şengün 2017; Sonderman 2021; Waszkiewicz 2024)—overtly metareferential game *The Stanley Parable* includes notes that are visually presented in a conventional fashion, but their content is highly self-reflexive. In one sequence, for example, the playable character enters a dark room, when suddenly the words "The Stanley Parable" appear in bold, white letters. This is only one of many metareferential elements in the game, and jointly they have the effect that *The Stanley Parable* forms what Stefan Schubert calls an "unstable textualit[y]" (2019, 204). Below this reference to itself, the player enters a gallery, and when walking down the stairs discovers a museum containing key artifacts from the game, such as Stanley's computer. The game's *Ultra Deluxe* re-issue features many additional self-reflexive metareferences, such as a leader board (see Figure 9.1), stating the

Figure 9.1 Leader board in *The Stanley Parable: Ultra Deluxe*, framing the game as a progression in your career.

player's name and their "superior," i.e., the player in the rank above them. This labeling of their competitor is directly taken from the hierarchical structure underpinning Stanley's existence in the game, putting the player even more neatly into Stanley's shoes.

Diaries, Notebooks, and Files

While short non-narrative notes can create metareferential flashes, more extensive text in the form of diaries, notebooks, and files can develop more elaborate metareferences, while they may also serve as framing devices for the game's narrative. *Uncharted 4: A Thief's End* features notebooks that are vital for the protagonist, Nathan Drake, in the course of his actions. The pages are interactive and thus function as a scrapbook that allows the player to try out various options before committing in-game, such as when tiles need to be rotated in a specific way to crack a code. While Drake may also do so on the circular device itself, the notebook includes hints on the sides of the tiles that suggest how they should be arranged. Due to this, the notebook is not only embedded within the diegesis of the game, but also sets up a bridge to the player's reality. This is achieved by breaching the borders of what is possible within and outside of the gameworld, yet without breaking the fourth wall or hindering the player's engagement with or immersion in the game (see Ermi and Mäyrä 2005; Thon 2008). A similar mechanism can be found in *Silent Hill 4: The Room*, in which notebook entries frequently direct the next steps that players take. The visual depiction underlines the

Figure 9.2 Clue board in *Alan Wake 2*. Players can connect the individual pieces of evidence with the help of a (literal) red thread.

special status of this kind of text: The letter, in the sense of the object, is in the background, and the letters, in the sense of characters, are written in brown and typed in the foreground. This visual cue guides the player by emphasizing the kind of textual quality associated with this kind of writing, thus also already triggering expectations toward its content.

While these two examples are fairly static because they are unalterable representations, it is also possible to make diaries, notebooks, and files interactive. One of the key tasks for the player to complete in *Alan Wake 2* is to piece together evidence in a logical manner to escape the dark underworld of Cauldron Lake, located near the fictional town of Bright Falls. This is done in two interwoven stories. On the one hand, we find Wake writing a horror story while being trapped underneath Cauldron Lake for 13 years. On the other hand, we follow the narrative arch of FBI agent Saga Anderson, who tries to uncover mysterious cases in Bright Falls, and who eventually gets sucked into Wake's horror story (see also the analysis of *Alan Wake 2* in the the chapter by Waszkiewicz in this volume). The players must work their way through each element of both stories, but they may determine the order in which they want to do so based on the diaries, notebooks, and files in the game. These need to be organized on a virtual board (see Figure 9.2) to trace the story's development. That way, these fragments not only feature as artifacts in the story but determine how it progresses. This text–game relationship is highly self-reflexive because the texts appearing in the game not only support the gameworld, but determine how it is structured, while the novel of the first gameworld becomes the second gameworld, forming a Chinese-box structure.

Two-Way Communication

Longer notes can also suggest or encourage a two-way communication if they take on the form of letters, emails, and text messages. That way, they can be used to form a relationship between individual characters or suggest how the authors of such notes might have behaved toward the playable character. Many games make use of other digital modes of communication, which lends a sense of authenticity to the way in-game characters engage with each other. In *Fears to Fathom: Home Alone*, the player assumes the role of 14-year-old Miles, who is home alone while his parents are out of town for work. It soon becomes evident that a mysterious person is outside the house, but Miles has a hard time spotting them. He then receives a message from his mother, warning him about this person as she has received a photo from a neighbor who saw someone peeping through Miles's windows. The photo is shared with the player in Miles's chat with his mother, who then sends a chain of messages, urging Miles to lock all outside doors and hide in his bedroom to wait for the police to arrive. While these texts have a significant impact on the player's subsequent actions, their mode of representation and content (at least within this horror gameworld) is very conventional and not self-reflexive.

If the content of such and similar notes holds up a mirror to the gameworld, however, we are faced with a degree of self-reflexivity that can be considered a metareference. In *Gone Home*, an epistolary exchange between Sam and Lonnie, depicted below (see Figure 9.3), takes on the form of notes many of us exchanged with our school friends during class. The content of the letter is the cult movie *Pulp Fiction* (1994), highlighting its gruesome violence and graphic depictions, but equally emphasizing its artistic value.

The film and the game share that both push the boundaries of art and entertainment to create a new mode of representation. For example, in *Gone Home*, the player can roam the house and engage with objects without having any specific goal to work toward (see Şengün 2017, 31). In *Pulp Fiction*, the events are grouped in scenes that are randomly organized, forcing the audience to create a logical sequence in their reception process. In this sense, referencing *Pulp Fiction* in the letter creates a metareference to the overarching question of modes of representation and engagement available to entertainment media.

Games can also include artifacts suggesting two-way communication that refer to themselves in order to make their metareferential characteristic more apparent. Like *Gone Home*, *Dear Esther* is a walking simulator, but in this game, letters that are read aloud by a troubled-sounding narrator make up the sole component of the narrative. Between each playthrough, the audio fragments vary, subsequently altering the kind of narrative players encounter. According to Dawn Stobbart, this "highlights the need for repeated interactions with some videogames to understand their narratives" (2019, 104) because textual variation provides different perspectives. Some texts even reference themselves and the act of writing. One letter reads, "Donnelly did not pass through the caves. From here on in, his guidance, unreliable as it is, is gone from me. I understand now that it is between the two of us, and whatever correspondence can be drawn from the wet rocks." The idea of "guidance" here has a double meaning: Donnelly, who previously charted

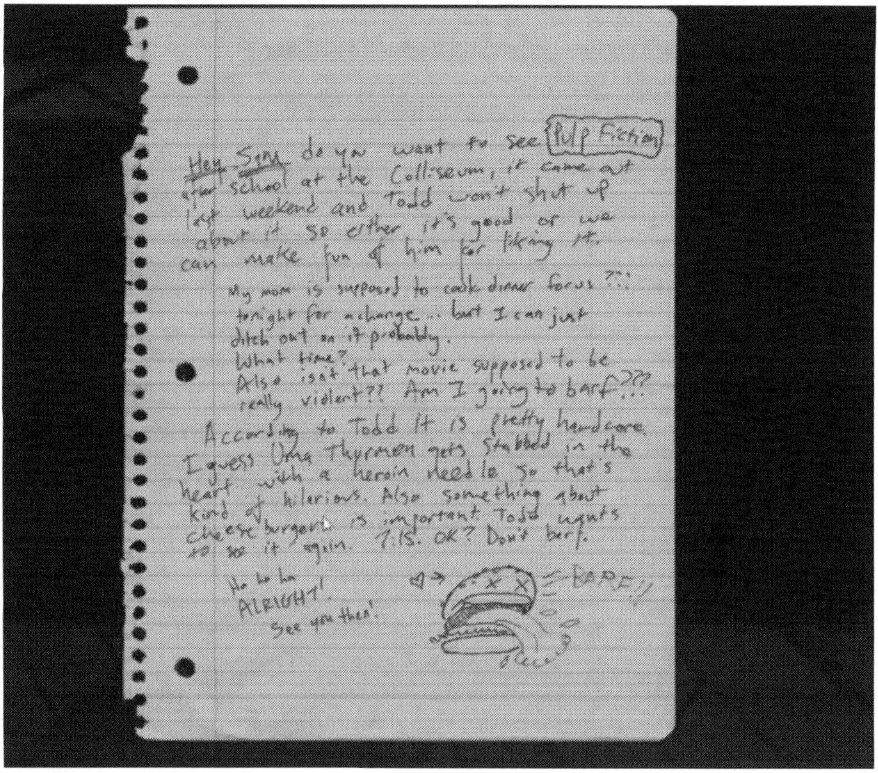

Figure 9.3 Handwritten epistolary exchange between Sam and Lonnie in *Gone Home*.

the island, was guiding the letter's author through the terrain, but he also guided the player's awareness of the gameworld. As his account is now proclaimed as "unreliable," the game narrative so far is called into question. In addition, this letter refers to itself as an artifact that may or may not be retrieved (and thus read, as the player does just now). With this metareference, the game suggests that it is acutely aware of its artifactuality and the necessity for someone to engage with it in order to exist.

Books

While the last two groups of texts are already very extensive, some games even push this textual length further by including whole books. The degree of self-reflexivity as well as the kind of metareference (if any) constituted by the inclusion of books in games heavily depends on the mode of interactivity afforded to the player in their engagement with the artifact. For example, *The Last of Us* (2013), *The Last of Us: Left Behind* (2014), and *The Last of Us II* (2020) feature two books that become important in the story: "No Pun Intended" and "No Pun Intended: Volume Too." For Ellie, these books not only form one of her few personal possessions, but also allow her to get a glance into a world she never knew. Puns, such as "A book just fell on my head, I only have my shelf to blame" or "Bakers trade bread recipes on a knead-to-know basis" become less effective in a world that neither has libraries nor professions in a traditional sense. However, despite the prominence of the references made to these books throughout the game, they lack a degree of self-reflexivity—mainly but not solely because players cannot read them themselves, but only via Ellie—and thus also a meta-perspective onto concepts such as artifactuality and fictionality.

If players themselves are allowed to engage with the in-game book, (self-) reflexive metareferences can be established, particularly if the engagement with books mirrors the engagement with games. The sandbox game *Minecraft* owes a large degree of its popularity to the fact that players can freely create and alter their surroundings in the virtually infinite terrain offered to them. Within the game, players can collect and enhance books. Some books have practical use within the game, such as Enchanted Books, which can be used to enchant other items; for example, a book paired with an ink sac and a feather results in "book and quill," which can be written in. Players can write, copy, and paste up to 79,800 (Java Edition) or 12,800 (Bedrock Edition) characters in any book (Minecraft Wiki 2023). Furthermore, authors can sign and give a title to a book they wrote in-game. These possibilities in the context of writing within the game mirror the creativity of sandbox games, and thus suggest that the player's creativity is needed for the game. Put differently, the act of creating the gameworld is rendered via a metareference in the act of creating text, albeit on a smaller scale.

If the book and the game narrative move closer or even align, the metareferential link between them is much stronger. Similar to *Alan Wake 2* discussed above, *Alan Wake* puts a book at the core of its story (see Thon 2016, 113–117). The game follows the eponymous bestselling thriller writer Alan Wake, whose wife disappears during their vacation in Bright Falls, Washington. While trying to uncover the mystery of her disappearance, Wake experiences sequences from his latest novel, "Departure," but he cannot remember writing it. In its story, the game utilizes typical thriller novel structures, such as cliffhangers and plot twists. From a gameplay perspective, the game is split into action-driven sequences happening at night, which are balanced out by calmer, narrative-heavy sequences set in the daytime. In the world, the player can find readable pages from the manuscript, but they are not in order, and hence mirror the chaos of the world Wake—and the player—finds himself in. The content of these pages varies, but they often foreshadow events that have yet to happen, and subsequently influence the player's next steps. Michael Fuchs has noted that this has a unique effect on the game's diegesis:

> Not only does the past narration create an uncanny effect here, as past, present, and future eerily become one, but, moreover, the conflation of temporal levels goes hand in hand with a conflation of diegetic levels, as the embedded narrative embodied by the manuscript pages (which is, in fact, not only embedded in the game, but at the same time embeds the story of the game) not simply foreshadows, but, indeed, performs the diegetic action.
>
> (Fuchs 2016, 44–45)

Furthermore, the Dark Presence, a power threatening the people of Bright Falls, intends to use Alan's writing as a means to escape Cauldron Lake, alluding metaphorically to the idea of fiction as escapism. To destroy the Dark Presence, Alan must write because he realizes that his ideas become reality. The fact that the fictional novel slowly reveals itself to be the gameworld forms a significant metareference to the act of creation, formation, reception, and criticism of artifacts. The player needs to engage with the book to gain a better understanding of the gameworld, and hence the tie between writing, reading, and playing is strong.

Text as Game Elements

The final group of games addressed here are those that rely on text as game elements, i.e., games that use text as its intradiegetic building blocks within its visual narrative world, but *not* text-based games that do not draw on visuals, such as *Zork*. In 2017, a videogame, or rather a visual novel, attracted the attention of people from many different backgrounds, and often also "non-gamers": *Bury Me, My Love*. The game follows the text messages sent between Nour and Majd while Nour tries to make her way to Europe to flee the war in Syria. The player has to choose Majd's replies to Nour's messages to give her advice on her next steps. Instead of presenting a visual narrative, the game centers on the text messages, interspersed with occasional photos of what Nour witnesses, such as the destruction of Damascus or the ocean of tents in the refugee camps as well as selfies from Nour and Majd. Although the game heavily builds on text, none of the messages are self-reflexive, thus they do not constitute metareferences to the act of reading or the act of writing.

More visual elements are found in the narrative adventure game *Heaven's Vault*, which focuses on the decryption of old glyphs. The player is presented with combinations of glyphs, which the main character, Aliya Elasra, and her robot assistant, Six, must translate into English. Instead of a surrounding that can be navigated, the player is presented with painted image frames and dialogue, hence placing the experience neatly between a game and a novel. In comparison to *Bury Me, My Love*, *Heaven's Vault* reflects on the act of reading, which implicitly also alludes to the act of playing as reception. However, while reflection is present, the game is lacking a meta-perspective, and hence while it constitutes a reference to writing and reading, the game does not form a metareference.

The final game analyzed here, *Stories Untold*, however, shifts the text–game relationship to a metalevel. In the opening scene, the player is presented with a computer screen displaying the loading screen of the intradiegetic game "The House Abandon," subtitled "Interactive Horror Adventure," which the player is invited to play. Soon, a narrative sequence appears, to which the player is invited to answer, but without any instructions of how to do so. Players must subsequently draw on their knowledge of text-based games, such as *Zork*, i.e., to type commands corresponding to a specific form, in order to be able to take part in that text adventure. The player in the game *Stories Untold* navigates the player in the game "The House Abandon," who roams his old house. In his room, he finds his old computer with a game on it,

Figure 9.4 The computer containing "The House Abandon" in *Stories Untold.*

and when the in-game player is tasked to input the cassette, the game crashes. The new loading screen shows the loading screen of "The House Abandon," but upside down and with the writing "Get out" scribbled over it (see Figure 9.4).

The game-within-the-game restarts, but this time it is more sinister. At the same time, the player's surrounding gets more eerie due to a thunderstorm happening outside. Soon, the onscreen text mirrors the occurrences in the player's fictional world, such as when the screen reads "Behind the door, a phone starts to ring," the phone in the visual gameworld starts to ring as well. The text and the world of *Stories Untold* move closer together and soon overlap. The two fictional layers of the game and the game-within-the-game cross over because the player controls the in-game character, who, in turn, controls what happens in the game-within-the-game by reading and writing out commands. In this very overt reference to the written word and the act of writing, the game as a whole becomes a metareference as the game-within-the-game, its world, its actions, and its character can only exist if it is written. The act of playing, the question of gameworld building, fictionality, and rules as well as the relationship between the player and the game are all addressed through this writing, distorting the notions of what is real and what is invented (see also the chapter by Krampe in this volume).

As the discussion of these case study games has shown, the incorporation of text in videogames possesses great potential for making the gameworld more approachable and tangible. However, it is important to emphasize that not all inclusions of text in gameworlds are also metareferences. This status very much depends on the degree of self-reflexivity of the text included within a game, i.e., whether it highlights and references its textual status, either implicitly or explicitly, and thus also suggests the textuality of the game. As this analysis has shown, the ability for self-reflexivity and metareferentiality is therefore not a question of textual quantity (length) or quality (genre), but instead one of signposting its own status as text. This idea draws on the production side of metareferences in the game, either in the form of text placed in a game by game makers, which is mostly unalterable, e.g., the note on the tent in *Firewatch* referenced above, or created by the player within the gameworld, e.g. when Saga Anderson assembles text snippets to create a meaningful story in *Alan Wake 2*. However, in order to fully understand their functionality, it is also important to understand their reception. Therefore, as outlined in the theoretical part of this chapter, the perspective of the player, their potential engagement with metareferences as well as the role of game genres and pacing when engaging with them, are crucial for the text–game relationship.

Conclusion: Texts in Games as Metareferences

The intricate relationship between text and videogames unveils a complex interplay between narrative construction, player engagement, and the inherent textual nature of videogames as a medium. As outlined throughout this chapter, the incorporation of text within videogames serves multiple purposes, from enhancing immersion and authenticity to shaping gameplay mechanics and narrative progression. Through an exploration of extradiegetic and intradiegetic texts, the theoretical section of this chapter has delved into how these textual elements contribute to the overall gaming experience. The focus was placed on intradiegetic texts, which immerse players within the gameworld, offering narrative depth and interactive storytelling opportunities.

The theoretical section of this chapter proposed metareferentiality as a concept that highlights instances where in-game texts explicitly or implicitly reference their own textual status or the unique characteristics of videogames as a medium. It has been made clear that not all texts incorporated in games generate metareferences, but that their degree of self-reflexivity and/or explicitness regarding their textual status evolves texts from references to metareferences. These metareferences add layers of meaning and invite players to actively participate in the meaning-making process. Genre expectations and pacing further influence the reception and impact of in-game texts, underscoring the importance of aligning textual elements with player preferences and gameplay dynamics. As games continue to evolve and diversify, understanding the nuanced role of text within the gaming landscape becomes increasingly essential for game researchers and game developers. The practical exploration of various kinds of text, forming the second section of this chapter, has shown that the incorporation of a text in a game does not always constitute a metareference. It was proposed that self-reflexivity should be seen as a spectrum, which is also influenced by the player's engagement with and interpretation of a game.

Ultimately, this exploration of the text–game relationship has shed light on the intricate interplay between textual and verbal narrative, gameplay, and player agency, paving the way for future research and innovation in the realm of interactive storytelling.

Works Cited

Alan Wake. 2010. Remedy Entertainment/Microsoft Game Studios. Xbox 360.
Alan Wake 2. 2023. Remedy Entertainment/Epic Games Publishing. PlayStation 5.
Always Sometimes Monsters. 2014. Vagabond Dog/Devolver Digital. Microsoft Windows.

Backe, Hans-Joachim, and Jan-Noël Thon. 2019. "Playing with Identity: Authors, Narrators, Avatars, and Players in *The Stanley Parable* and *The Beginner's Guide*." *DIEGESIS: Interdisciplinary E-Journal for Narrative Research* 8 (2): 1–25.

Bavelier, Daphne, C. Shawn Green, and Mark S. Seidenberg. 2013. "Cognitive Development: Gaming Your Way Out of Dyslexia?" *Current Biology* 23 (7): 282–283.

Bediou, Benoit, Deanne M. Adams, Richard E. Mayer, Elizabeth Tipton, C. Shawn Green, and Daphne Bavelier. 2018. "Meta-Analysis of Action Videogame Impact on Perceptual, Attentional, and Cognitive Skills." *Psychological Bulletin* 144 (1): 77–110.

Beil, Benjamin, Gundolf S. Freyermuth, and Hanns Christian Schmidt, eds. 2021. *Paratextualizing Games: Investigations on the Paraphernalia and Peripheries of Play*. Bielefeld: transcript.

Bejjanki, Vikranth R., Ruyuan Zhang, Renjie Lee, Alexandre Pouget, C. Shawn Green, Zhong-Lin Lu, and Daphne Bavelier. 2014. "Action Videogame Play Facilitates the Development of Better Perceptual Templates." *PNAS* 111 (47): 16961–16966.

Boluk, Stephanie, and Patrick LeMieux. 2017. *Metagaming: Playing, Competing, Spectating, Cheating, Trading, Making, and Breaking Videogames*. Minneapolis: University of Minnesota Press.

Bury Me, My Love. 2017. The Pixel Hunt/Arte France, Plug in Digital. iOS.

Call of Duty: Black Ops Cold War. 2020. Treyarch, Raven Software/Activision. PlayStation 4.

Coleridge, Samuel Taylor. 2014 [1817]. *Biographia Literaria*, edited by Adam Roberts. Edinburgh: Edinburgh University Press.

Control. 2019. Remedy Entertainment/505 Games. PlayStation 4.

Dear Esther. 2012. The Chinese Room. Microsoft Windows.

Ensslin, Astrid. 2014. "Playing with Rather Than by the Rules: Metaludicity, Allusive Fallacy, and Illusory Agency in *The Path*." In *Analysing Digital Fiction*, edited by Alice Bell, Astrid Ensslin, and Hans Rustad, 75–93. New York: Routledge.

Ermi, Laura, and Frans Mäyrä. 2005. "Fundamental Components of Gameplay Experience: Analysing Immersion." In *Proceedings of DiGRA 2005: Changing Views—Worlds in Play*, 1–14.

Fears to Fathom: Home Alone. 2021. Rayll. Microsoft Windows.

Ferri, Gabriele, Giovanni Caruso, Mauro Salvador, Riccardo Fassone, and Stefano Gualeni, eds. 2016. "Games on Games: Game Design as Critical Reflexive Practice." *GAME: The Italian Journal of Game Studies* 5: n.pag.

Fest, Bradley J. 2016. "Metaproceduralism: *The Stanley Parable* and the Legacies of Postmodern Metafiction." *Wide Screen* 6 (1): 1–23.

Final Fantasy VI. 2015 [1994]. Square. Microsoft Windows.

Firewatch. 2016. Campo Santo/Panic. PlayStation 4.

Franceschini, Sandro, Simone Gori, Milena Ruffino, Simona Viola, Massimo Molteni, and Andrea Facoetti. 2013. "Action Videogames Make Dyslexic Children Read Better." *Current Biology* 23 (6): 462–466.

Fuchs, Michael. 2016. "A Different Kind of Monster: Uncanny Media and *Alan Wake*'s Textual Monstrosity." In *Contemporary Research on Intertextuality in Video Games*, edited by Christophe Duret and Christian-Marie Pons, 39–53. Hershey: IGI Global.

Genette, Gérard. 1991. "Introduction to Paratext." *New Literary History* 22 (2): 261–272.

Genette, Gérard. 1997. *Paratexts: Thresholds of Interpretation*. Cambridge: Cambridge University Press.

Gone Home. 2013. The Fullbright Company. Microsoft Windows.

Gray, Jonathan. 2010. *Show Sold Separately: Promos, Spoilers, and Other Media Paratexts*. New York: New York University Press.

Gualeni, Stefano. 2016. "Self-Reflexive Videogames: Observations and Corollaries on Virtual Worlds as Philosophical Artifacts." *GAME: The Italian Journal of Game Studies* 5: n.pag.

Heaven's Vault. 2019. Inkle. PlayStation 4.

Huizinga, Johan. 1955. *Homo Ludens: A Study of the Play-Element in Culture.* Boston: Beacon Press.

Jannidis, Fotis. 2009. "Metareferences in Computer Games." In *Metareferences across Media*, edited by Werner Wolf, 543–565. Amsterdam: Rodopi.

Kagen, Melissa. 2022. *Wandering Games*. Cambridge, MA: MIT Press.

Krampe, Theresa. 2023. "Rewriting Rules, Changing Worlds: Diegetic and Ludic Forms of Metareference in *The Magic Circle.*" *Frontiers of Narrative Studies* 9 (1): 137–157.

Krampe, Theresa, Stephanie Lotzow, and Jan-Noël Thon. 2022. "Playful Poetics: Metareferential Interfaces in Recent Indie Games." *Poetics Today* 43 (4): 729–771.

The Last of Us. 2013. Naughty Dog/Sony Computer Entertainment. PlayStation 3.

The Last of Us: Left Behind. 2014. Naughty Dog/Sony Computer Entertainment. PlayStation 4.

The Last of Us Part II. 2020. Naughty Dog/Sony Computer Entertainment. PlayStation 4.

Lee, Nicole, and Ken Morimoto. 2021. "Walking Curricular Paths in the Virtual: *The Stanley Parable* and *Minecraft.*" In *Walking with A/r/tography*, edited by Alexandra Lasczik, Rita L. Irwin, Amy Cutter-Mackenzie-Knowles, David Rousell, and Nicole Lee, 39–58. Cham: Palgrave Macmillan.

Minecraft. 2011. Mojang Studios. macOS.

Minecraft Wiki. 2023. "Book and Quill." *Minecraft Wiki*, November 16, 2023. https://minecraft.fandom.com/wiki/Book_and_Quill?action=history.

Neale, Steve. 2000. "Questions of Genre." In *Film and Theory: An Anthology*, edited by Robert Stam and Toby Miller, 157–178. Cambridge: Blackwell Publishers.

Pasqualotto, Angela, Irene Altarelli, Antonella De Angeli, Zeno Menestrina, Daphne Bavelier, and Paola Venuti. 2022. "Enhancing Reading Skills through a Videogame Mixing Action Mechanics and Cognitive Training." *Nature Human Behaviour* 6: 545–554.

Plass, Jan L., Richard E. Mayer, and Bruce D. Homer, eds. 2020. *Handbook of Game-Based Learning*. Cambridge, MA: MIT Press.

Pulp Fiction. 1994. Director Quentin Tarantino. USA: Miramax Films.

Resident Evil 4. 2005. Capcom Production Studio/Capcom. GameCube.

Schubert, Stefan. 2019. *Narrative Instability: Destabilizing Identities, Realities, and Textualities in Contemporary American Popular Culture.* Heidelberg: Winter.

Seiwald, Regina. 2019. "Games within Games: The Two (or More) Fictional Levels of Videogames." In *Videogame Sciences and Arts*, edited by Nelson Zagalo, Ana Isabel Veloso, Liliana Costa, and Óscar Mealha, 18–31. Cham: Springer.

Seiwald, Regina. 2022. "Creating Game History: Intertextuality and the Formation of a Collective Memory of Games." In *Video Game Art Reader: Version_4.1.2022*, edited by Tiffany Funk, 59–76. Chicago: VGA Gallery.

Seiwald, Regina, and Ed Vollans, eds. 2023. *(Not) In the Game: History, Paratexts, and Games.* Berlin: De Gruyter.

Şengün, Sercan. 2017. "Ludic Voyeurism and Passive Spectatorship in *Gone Home* and Other 'Walking Simulators'." In *Video Game Art Reader: Version 1.1.2017*, edited by Tiffany Funk, 30–42. Chicago: VGA Gallery.

Silent Hill 4: The Room. 2004. Team Silent/Konami. Microsoft Windows.

Sonderman, Braxton. 2021. *Against Flow: Video Games and the Flowing Subject.* Cambridge, MA: MIT Press.

The Stanley Parable. 2013. Galactic Cafe. macOS.

The Stanley Parable: Ultra Deluxe. 2022. Crows Crows Crows. macOS.

Stobbart, Dawn. 2019. *Videogames and Horror: From* Amnesia *to* Zombies, *Run!* Cardiff: University of Wales Press.

Stories Untold. 2017. No Code/Devolver Digital. macOS.

Švelch, Jan. 2020. “Paratextuality in Game Studies: A Theoretical Review and Citation Analysis.” *Game Studies: The International Journal of Computer Game Research* 20 (2): n.pag.

Thon, Jan-Noël. 2008. “Immersion Revisited: On the Value of a Contested Concept.” In *Extending Experiences: Structure, Analysis, and Design of Computer Game Player Experience*, edited by Amyris Fernandez, Olli Leino, and Hanna Wirman, 29–43. Rovaniemi: Lapland University Press.

Thon, Jan-Noël. 2016. *Transmedia Narratology and Contemporary Media Culture*. Lincoln: University of Nebraska Press.

Todorov, Tzvetan. 1976. “The Origin of Genres.” *New Literary History* 8 (1): 159–170.

Uncharted 4: A Thief's End. 2016. Naughty Dog/Sony Computer Entertainment. PlayStation 4.

Waszkiewicz, Agata. 2024. *Metagames: Games about Games*. New York: Routledge.

wayne. 2014. “Worth It?” *Steam*, August 14, 2014. https://steamcommunity.com/app/274310/discussions/0/340951318090305491/.

What Remains of Edith Finch. 2017. Giant Sparrow/Annapurna Interactive. PlayStation 4.

Wolf, Mark J.P. 2010. *The Medium of the Videogame*. Austin: University of Texas Press.

Wolf, Werner. 2006. “Introduction: Frames, Framings, and Framing Borders in Literature and Other Media.” In *Framing Borders in Literature and Other Media*, edited by Walter Bernhart and Werner Wolf, 1–40. Amsterdam: Rodopi.

Wolf, Werner. 2009. “Metareference across Media: The Concept, Its Transmedial Potentials and Problems, Main Forms, and Functions.” In *Metareference across Media: Theory and Case Studies*, edited by Werner Wolf, 1–85. Amsterdam: Rodopi.

Zork: The Great Underground Empire. 1982 [1980]. Infocom. Microsoft Windows.

10 "The Name of the Reader"

Constructing the Bookish Player in *Pentiment*

Kübra Aksay, Simone Blessing, Astrid Ensslin, Sebastian R. Richter, and Fiona S. Schönberg

In this chapter, we explore how Pentiment *(2022) serves as an example of a metareferential medium par excellence by remediating the paradigm shift from medieval oral and manuscript culture to Early Modern print culture. Our central question asks how the game's engagement with "bookishness" (see Pressman 2020) and the materiality of books enables it to function as a multidimensional, medium-reflexive narrative device. We argue that* Pentiment *transforms the book into a protagonist by fostering object-oriented intersubjectivity through the "ludex" (or book-in-the-game; see Milligan 2019) that invites players to become bookish players. This transformation enables players to engage with the game's layered narratives, drawing on intertextual and intermedial references to literary works, particularly Umberto Eco's* The Name of the Rose *(1983 [1980]). Our methodology combines ludonarrative analysis with media theory, focusing on the game's remediation of medieval book production—transcription, illumination, and analog printing—and its thematic engagement with the political and intellectual shifts of the Reformation (see Eisenstein 1980). This analysis is significant for critical conversations around metareferentiality in games, demonstrating how* Pentiment *reflects historical shifts while redefining the relationship between players and textual media, offering new insights into the role of books in interactive storytelling.*

Introduction

In this chapter, we examine the late medieval murder mystery point-and-click game *Pentiment* (2022) as a metareferential videogame par excellence. Metareference, according to Werner Wolf (2009), refers to transmedial, "self-reflexive elements that a text or artifact may use to comment on itself or the media system it is embedded in" (quoted in Krampe et al. 2022, 735). Such elements can include intermedial references to computational technologies, books and other written documents, movies, photographs, music, and other media, often creating metaleptic and/or recursive effects aimed to evoke a metafictional, metamedial, or otherwise critical, reflexive stance in the audience. In videogames specifically, metareferential

DOI: 10.4324/9781003538592-10

designs can create metaludic effects that foreground medium-specific elements of games and play as well as practices that are part of game culture and the game industry at large. Metaludic effects thus engage players in interrogating their own activities and expectations as narrative-ergodic agents vis-à-vis medium and work-specific aesthetics (see Boluk and LeMieux 2017; Ensslin 2013).

Set in early-16th-century Upper Bavaria, in the fictional village of Tassing and the equally fictional Benedictine Kiersau Abbey, *Pentiment* tells the story of Andreas Maler, a journeyman artist from Nuremberg, who investigates a series of murder mysteries over a time span of 25 years. The game allows players to shape Andreas's personal history through dialogue choices, affecting the resolution of mysteries. After his presumed death following an attempt to rescue books from the flames of the burning Abbey, the player takes on the identity of printer and artist Magdalene Druckeryn, who eventually discovers Tassing's mysterious past. With Andreas, who has returned from hermitage, she goes on to reveal who was behind the numerous murders. It turns out, however, that the key reference point and source of the mystery is a book that chronicles the history of the village.

Pentiment draws on a plethora of scholarly and narrative materials, both historical and contemporary (see AKGWDS 2023). At a macro level, the game remediates the grand-narrative paradigm shift from medieval oral and manuscript culture to Early Modern print culture in Europe, including political upheavals associated with the dawn of the Reformation and the Peasant Wars, as well as the shift from performative, oral culture and cyclical thinking to the linearization of rational thought facilitated by the popularization of print in the early Renaissance (see Eisenstein 1980). The game further references legends from the village's Celtic origins, from early Christianity, and Roman mythology, and it embeds pages from a variety of illuminated manuscripts, directly inspired by material from real-life archives like the Bavarian State Library in Munich and the Bodleian Library in Oxford as layered interfaces (see Book Historia 2022). Its arguably most popular and pervasive transmedial and intertextual metareference is to Umberto Eco's *The Name of the Rose* (1983 [1980]), from which it borrows numerous themes, spatial concepts, genre elements, character types, and not least a focus on late medieval manuscript culture, the dawn of the Gutenberg Age, and a concomitant emphasis on the materiality and spatial context of the codex (see Hernandez 2024; Kennedy 2023; Kleinerman and Haynes 2023; Mukherjee 2024; Ryan 2021; Thon 2023; Wright 2024).

Against the backdrop of *Pentiment*'s multiple metareferences and specifically the frame of Eco's iconic novel, which is often cited as "a prime example of postmodern literature" (Philip 2023, 42) due to its diverse reflexive, metaleptic, and intertextual elements, we construe the concept of the bookish player as a possible implied audience for videogames such as *Pentiment*. The term "bookishness" (see Pressmann 2020), which serves as our key theoretical lens, reflects an object-led rather than simply object-oriented approach to narrative media design. In object-oriented narratives across media, according to literary scholar Marco Caracciolo, "an object takes center stage and partly pushes plot beyond its anthropocentric comfort zone" without however "completely eradicat[ing] the human element in the narrative" (2020, 46). While Caracciolo's use of the term reflects a primarily thematic meaning of "object," our reading of *Pentiment* assumes a more pervasive, trans-diegetic role of the ludex, or "book-in-the-game" (see Milligan 2019): Not only does it play a key part in the plot, lending it "overall thematic coherence" (Caracciolo 2020, 47), but it transgresses various diegetic boundaries. The ludex as a unique, playable artifact and metamedium forms the material and aesthetic foundation of the game itself. We therefore prefer the term "object-led" because, as we will elaborate in the following sections, it signifies the medial transformation from represented codex to multiply functionalized and narrativized ludex. The book-as-object literally constructs a bookish player on a referential, thematic, narrative, aesthetic, material, *and* ludic-interactive level (see also the chapter by Caracciolo in this volume).

Applying an object-led approach to our analysis of *Pentiment*, we argue that the ludex as a ludonarrative agent and multidimensional metareference translates into a variety of functions and roles that cumulatively transcend the conventional ludexical function as a playable object of interaction and a container of "embedded narratives" (see Jenkins 2004). The overall narrative structure of the game presents the book as a protagonist constructed in communication between the bookish player and the game. As a multidimensional, continuous, and cohesive narrative device, the ludex agens creates connectivity, thus engendering a horizontal relationship between humans and bookish objects. Yet the layered structure of the game, which evokes the titular "pentimento" (Italian for "repentance"), also evokes a vertical form of interaction, of permeating and revealing the carefully applied, vertical layers of correction and cover-up that the art historical term "pentimento" alludes to. *Pentiment* calls for a forensic style of play that not only aligns with the game's murder mystery theme but evokes processes of physical overwriting, erasure, and recovery, which manifest themselves in many aspects of (dialogic) gameplay. Our analysis of the metareferences in *Pentiment* thus focuses on the book as an unlikely, surprising, and emergent protagonist, as an archaeological space, as a framing device and interface, as a mechanic, as a metagame, and as an encyclopedia. To do justice to the richness of the presented text, we have chosen a rather broad approach that examines the game from a wide variety of theoretical approaches.[1] We argue that the game affords intersubjective communication with an imagined (encoded) and real-life (paratextual) bookish player to unfold its events, stories, and literary references across multiple layers of representation and medial spaces (see Punday 2017).

In the Beginning Was the Book

To be "bookish," as a term, has long outgrown the scholarly bubble where Jessica Pressman originally coined it. It has been used in non-academic, book-loving communities, such as *BookTok*, as a means of self-identification. Bookishness, by definition, extends this idea of being "bookish" beyond conventional reading habits, as it encapsulates an identity forged through a tangible closeness to books (see Pressman 2020, 10). Rather than being rendered superfluous by the digitalization of our culture, the expansion of medial forms has emphasized the ongoing importance of books as iconographic signifiers of reading, and as objects that allow reading others and being read as a member of this community (see Pressman 2020, 24).

Pressman's concept challenges traditional author-reader dynamics—especially so when it is applied to videogame narratives. Bookishness can and should be applied to the digital sphere as well as to the physical book. This is where Milligan's concept of the ludex is useful. As an extension of the codex, the ludex describes "that category of book-bound and book-adjacent reading objects found in digital games" (Milligan 2019, 3) and is helpful in understanding the evolving relationship between reading and playing.

As explained in the previous section, the title of *Pentiment* immediately makes the game's metareferential and bookish orientation explicit. The game requires the player to excavate hidden layers in its narrative, an aspect which we elaborate on in the last section of this chapter. We furthermore distinguish between three books-in-the-game, or ludices in our chapter, all of which are central to but fulfill different roles in *Pentiment*.[2] The first is an illuminated manuscript which serves as the game's interface and reading space. Its animated footnote function provides a hypertextual glossary about place names and characters in the story, and it allows players to delve into imaginary worlds that represent dreams and other mental and textual spaces of the protagonist and other characters. The second is the player character's journal, where important events, conversations, and findings are recorded. This journal stays consistent even when the player character, thus the owner of the journal, changes from Andreas to Magdalene in the third act of the game, implying that it is linked to the player rather than a specific character and their thoughts.

In addition to the manuscript and the journal, there is a third ludex in the game: "Historia Tassiae," a history book that reveals itself to be the connective, diegetic tissue of the overarching narrative. While the manuscript seems to have been written by Sister Amalie of Völklingen (as revealed by her signature at the end of the game),[3] the book "Historia Tassiae" remains unread throughout the game, even though it is implied to contain the secret to the mystery that the story revolves around. All three books—the manuscript, the journal, and the history book—and the way the player interacts with them lead the "reader-player" (Ensslin 2014, 92) to question if perhaps they have been placed in the role of a fictional author as well. The characters themselves never have the opportunity to read the manuscript that accompanies the player throughout *Pentiment*, and the book is both an interface and a core narrative device in one.

"Historia Tassiae" is first mentioned at a relatively early stage in the game. Its actual significance, however, is not revealed until the very end when some light is shed on the story's central mysteries. At this point, the book changes from one puzzle piece among many to a chronicle that retrospectively ties all the storylines together. This directly links the game to one of its main literary influences, Eco's *The Name of the Rose*, where an allegedly lost book is also the reason for multiple deaths. In both works, the principal antagonist aims to destroy the knowledge contained in the book in the hopes of maintaining a (religious) status quo and preventing an upset to the order of things. In both cases, the attempt at concealing this from the world also comes with the destruction of architectures of knowledge (i.e., burning libraries, collapsing temples). This can be read as a criticism of the role that the book has historically played in the Christian domestication of pagan cultures (see Pressman 2020, 32). The threat that the book poses in *Pentiment* is the interpretation of cultural history that it stores like the buried knowledge about Tassing's past and the interpretation of its legends. Another reading might suggest that the book adopts the narrative silhouette of a mysterious agent, a cryptic character in its own right with motivations and agency, which we might refer to as ludex agens. The concealed threat contained in the history book motivates the murders in the storyline of the game, placing the book in an active rather than merely passive role.

Like Eco's *The Name of the Rose*, the narrative in *Pentiment* is layered. It can be read as a detective story with a dubiously conclusive ending, but it can also be read as a starting point for a deep dive into medieval religious culture, identity (crises), historical events, and artworks. While the intertextuality in *The Name of the Rose* is limited to text and a few maps, *Pentiment* also makes use of the visual aspect (see Figure 10.1).

In some cases, it also seems to translate certain descriptive passages in Eco's novel into artwork, such as the "monsters" that appear on the book pages in the game and that are described in *The Name of the Rose* (see Eco 1983, 48). The role of the book as a gateway into a multitude of other texts further indicates how it will need a bookish reader-player to gain an appreciation of the full extent of the narrative.

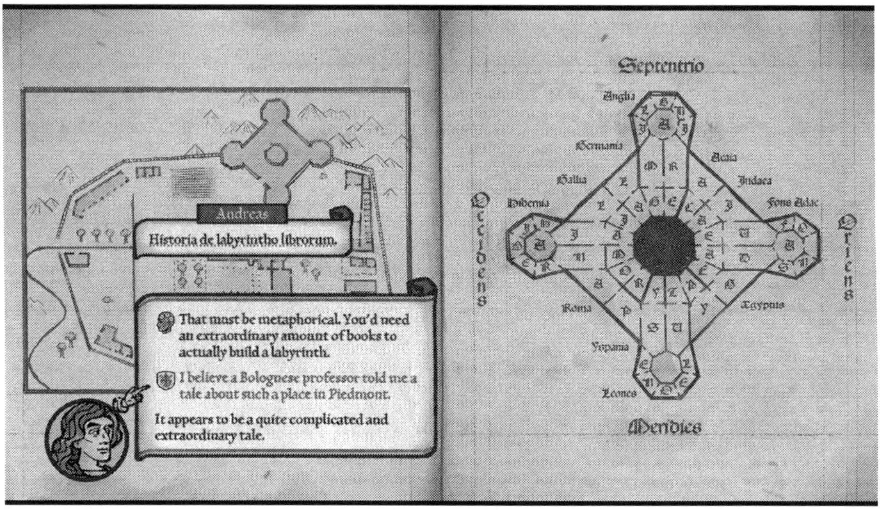

Figure 10.1 Reference to *The Name of the Rose* as well as to Eco in *Pentiment* (Act I).

Physically Bookish

While *Pentiment* employs the illuminated manuscript as a framing device for its entire story, the game also includes several other ludices within the embedded story inside this manuscript, and these different ludices exhibit a continuous intertext by consistently referring to each other. As we explained earlier, the player is unaware of how and by whom the manuscript was written until the end of the game, and the player's interaction with it (in terms of game mechanics) might seem to be limited to using it as a portal to the metadiegetic level.[4] However, the manuscript is not merely presented at the beginning and end of the story, as a traditional framing device would be (see Fludernik 1996, 343). At any point during play, the player can bring the pages of the manuscript back—e.g., by pausing the game, albeit with a partial view of it. The manuscript depicts a still image of the current scene from the game surrounded by marginalia, mainly filled with drolleries and pages of text summarizing the events during the current part of the game, written in Latin. In addition to the pause screen, the manuscript is shown each time the setting in the embedded story changes, showing an animation of the manuscript pages turning. The manuscript also serves as a glossary holding annotations. Clicking on rubricated[5] words in dialogues within the inner story again zooms out to the manuscript pages, with definitions of terms or pictures of characters in the margins and manicule pointing to the rubricated words they describe. This codexical function also extends to Andreas's journal, later taken over by Magdalene, which serves a similar role within the framed narrative. As the player characters[6] gradually encounter the 157 other characters in the game (see Kennedy 2023),[7] information about these characters is recorded in the in-game journal. Besides character information, the journal also contains diary entries, a map of Tassing, a glossary, and an ex-libris page that reminds the player of their chosen background and traits. Although the glossary functions of the journal and the manuscript overlap to some degree, and both ludices simultaneously contain the story and are contained within the story,[8] the player interacts with them on different levels. Remarkably, when the journal is accessed in the game, it does not automatically occupy the entire screen. Instead, it is depicted as lying atop the open pages of the manuscript (see Figure 10.2).

This visual arrangement suggests that the journal exists both within the narrative of the manuscript and alongside it in the three-dimensional space of the outer story layer. This interaction can be interpreted as a metalepsis, blurring the boundaries between the narrative levels and enhancing the player's involvement in them. The image of the two books together (as in Figure 10.2) also implies that Sister Amalie, who signs the manuscript at the end of the game, uses Andreas's journal as a source to complete her retelling of the events. Players can choose to view the journal in full screen once it is open, but the initial presentation of it atop the manuscript will reappear every time the journal is produced.

Material representations of bookishness in *Pentiment* also include items such as letters, notes, and pages from other manuscripts that the players can interact

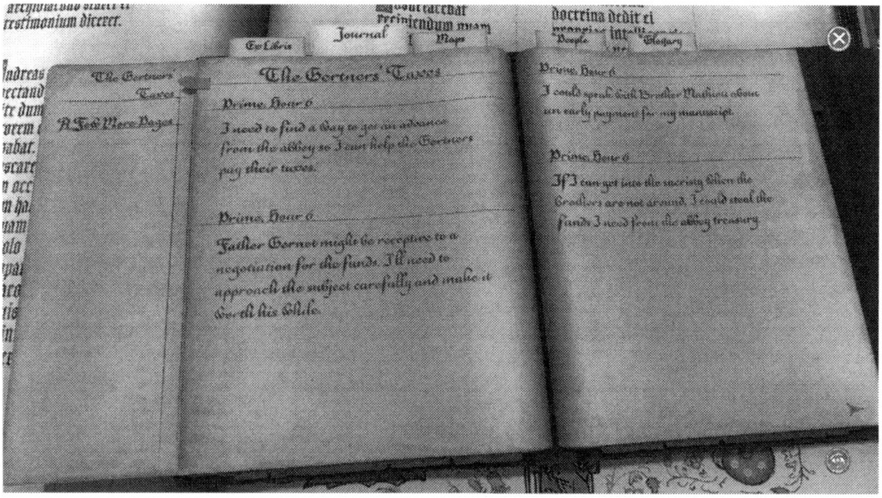

Figure 10.2 Andreas's journal placed on top of the partially visible illuminated manuscript in *Pentiment*.

with (see also the chapter by Thon in this volume). Considering the number of such objects within the game, in addition to the narrative significance of the in-game journal to the retelling of the story by Sister Amalie (as implied during the ending), *Pentiment* becomes akin to what Melissa Kagen refers to as an "archival adventure" (2020, 1008).[9] After all, the player characters' main actions in the game are walking, talking, and interacting with the bookish objects found in the game spaces, whether it is reading or examining these materials or indeed writing them. The gameplay allows and encourages a close inspection of the material with mini-games and puzzles requiring an examination of archival objects and inter-references between different ludices. For instance, the volvelle puzzle in the first act can be solved by inspecting another ludex found in the abbey's library and using it as a reference to decipher the volvelle code. Therefore, it can be argued that *Pentiment* simulates not only the aesthetics of the medieval manuscripts but also the practices of a historian interacting and interpreting historical material to reconstruct the game's narrative (see Kagen 2020, 1012; Swallow 2023, 9).

Many of the written materials found in the game include legible texts represented on their in-game assets (see also the chapter by Seiwald in this volume), with their legibility at times directly relevant to the gameplay challenges (as in some of the puzzles and minigames). However, while the illuminated manuscript and several other texts in the game are written in Latin or German, the player character's journal is always in the vernacular (plain English, or any other language selected by the player to play the game in). Thus, the ludices found in the game can include text with both varying legibility and readability. As the player character's journal serves as a reminder of relevant events, characters, and the player's current quests (and therefore has a significant mechanical role in aiding the player), the direct vernacular language in it appears to be a deliberate design choice, prioritizing the player's comprehension of the journal. By contrast, the text in most other ludices is often much more complex and cryptic, even when they include completely legible texts. Perhaps the most explicit example of *Pentiment*'s commentary on legibility and readability can be seen in the scenes following Magdalene's first encounter with "Historia Tassiae" in the game's third act. Magdalene, even when she has the Polyglot skill,[10] cannot comprehend the whole text, both because the Latin in it is too complex and because, as is noted in Act III of *Pentiment*, "the book is in bad condition after sitting in a peasant's drawer for so long." Magdalene can ask other characters to translate it, but eventually, all characters will reject helping her, causing the book to be unreadable, despite being mostly legible, and thus saving the book's importance in the history of Tassing for the revelation at the end of the game. The player character's inability to read the text, as a result, becomes a reading itself (see Milligan 2019, 7), while, at the same time, enhancing the sense of materiality and "otherness" of the medieval book, by presenting it as a "unique document with its own provenance history" (Swallow 2023, 9–10). Similarly, visible parts of the Latin text on the illuminated manuscript pages are legible, but the whole text cannot be read as the pages are both obscured by the journal and partially outside of the frame (see Figure 10.2).

Drawing on Bard Swallow's (2023) analysis of the representations of medieval books in the *Dragon Age*, *The Elder Scrolls*, and *The Witcher* series, we argue that the material representations of books in *Pentiment* extend beyond the manuscript as a "trope of medievalism" (Swallow 2023, 2) found in many medieval role-playing games. The degree of legibility of each text found in the game contributes to the materiality of the ludex in *Pentiment*, emphasizing that these details go beyond mere textual representation. The game's detailed visual representation of texts also allows it to include many references to writing and printing culture. In addition to the visual features such as marginalia found in the manuscripts, the dialogues in the game are represented within speech scrolls akin to those in medieval paintings, which are filled with text as the characters speak, implying the unfolding of the dialogue as the reader-player interacts with the game. The animation of the text in speech bubbles is accompanied by sound effects aurally representing the actions of scribbling, erasing, and printing, and occasionally shows spelling errors and splattering ink (when the characters express anger). With these representations, the game places speech and non-verbal communication in a material and bookish context, and conveys, at a microstructural level, the paradigm shift from oral to print culture (see Eisenstein 1980).

Pentiment also utilizes a set of distinct fonts (referred to as "scripts" in the game menu) that vary depending on the background of each character. For instance, Andreas, who has a university education, uses the "humanist script" in his speech bubbles and writing, while most of the villagers without a formal education use the "peasant script." This variety in *Pentiment*'s scripts and the animation of them being written during the game emphasizes the materiality of text and "the physicality of writing" (Sawyer quoted in Fenlon 2022, n.pag.). The highly skeuomorphic design of the journal also reflects this physicality, although the material object in the case of the journal does not have any features specific to the historical period in the game. As Obsidian design director Josh Sawyer notes in an interview, the game designers relied on one of Sawyer's physical journals to try to visually simulate its parts such as pages and tabs, and the player's interaction with them through the journal's animation (see Book Historia 2022). To locate a particular reference in the journal, the player must flip its pages, which means watching the animations for each page turning and the part of the pages with a table of contents for each section unfolding and folding back. The journal's design is evocative of a physical journal to a degree that can be damaging to its function of assisting the player to quickly return to already acquired pieces of information.

Bookish Spatiality

Pentiment also presents a particular spatial situation in the way that the reader-player can locate themselves in relation to the game. Most role-playing games strive, in some way, to create what Werner Wirth and colleagues define as a "spatial presence experience" as "[an] experience, during which perceived self-location and, in most cases, perceived action possibilities are connected to a mediated spatial environment and mental capacities are bound by the mediated environment instead of reality" (2007, 497). However, *Pentiment*, in line with the game's bookish, page-like interface, Tassing, as it is presented for the player to see, is quite literally flat, and it affords the player no space within it.

Tassing, and the systems that afford the player's interaction with and traversal through it, are designed through and through to prevent the formation of the spatial presence experience Wirth and colleagues refer to. That begins with the perspective—a flat side view, with the entire depth of the gameworld plainly visible on paper-in-the-game, and a skewed perspective that is less concerned with a detailed or conventionally realistic depiction of people and objects in a manner familiar to the player than it is with evoking (though not exactly replicating) the stylistic trappings of medieval art and manuscript illuminations.

Similarly, navigating Tassing is far from seamless—the play space, as it is presented to the player, is divided into individual slides and screens with fixed camera angles, so the player, forced into an outsider's view, will be hard-pressed to ever self-locate within this diegesis. Both the navigation through the game and the complete range of interaction possibilities are not informed by the spatial environment but rather accessed through the interface, both through interaction icons and interface transitions.[11] The same goes for temporal navigation. The passage of game-time in *Pentiment* is tightly regimented through an interface that aesthetically evokes the period with the way that it organizes diegetic days. However, despite this thematic evocation, this interface, too, exists distinctly outside the spatial environment that Andreas and Magdalene inhabit. Time does not pass in accordance with how long the player takes or follows an organic cycle, the likes of which can be found in many contemporary open-world games. Instead, the day is divided into scenes via an interface following the Christian practice of canonical hours, as well as, incidentally, the sectioning of Eco's *The Name of the Rose*. Even the flow of information on characters and places, a vital part of how the player's interactions with the diegetic world are informed, is regulated primarily through elements of the interface, ranging from subtle changes in the way the characters are drawn to the font of their speech bubbles. The speech bubbles themselves represent a constant intrusion of extradiegetic elements superimposed on the two-dimensional side view of Tassing and its inhabitants. As noted in the previous section, even the game menu itself frequently bleeds into view. The preceding analysis demonstrates the multiple ways in which *Pentiment* discourages the player from locating themselves within the flat and narrow play space of Tassing. However, to borrow terminology from Michael Nitsche, the Bavarian village seems to be the sum total of the "*mediated space*" (2008, 16; original emphasis)[12] in contradistinction to the "*play space*" (2008, 16; original emphasis), which describes Tassing, its abbey, and the surrounding ruins. The space that *Pentiment* mediates perhaps extends beyond the pages that seem to be the space Andreas and Magdalene traverse.

In *Pentiment*'s opening scene, the rock that scrapes away the opening lines of *The Name of the Rose* (written in Latin on the illuminated manuscript pages) is not wielded by Andreas's hand but is rather guided by player input alone. Similarly, the edges of the book that have been defaced, and the table it is lying on, visible just at the edge of the frame, are rendered with significantly higher graphical fidelity than the events in Tassing ever are. This suggests that there is another plane to the diegesis of *Pentiment*. One that, to refer to Nitsche's theory once again, exists somewhere between the second and third (and arguably fourth) of the analytical planes. That is to say, between the "*mediated space* as defined by the presentation [...] including the cinematic form of presentation" and the "*fictional space* that lives in the imagination" (Nitsche 2008, 16; original emphases), *Pentiment* creates another plane of space: one where the book, its illuminations, and the stories contained therein are merely part of a diegetic artifact—a book that is being handled, read, and investigated by an unseen reader just outside the frame. This plane assigns a role to the reader-player that they can spatially insert themselves into. This plane is not entirely outside of the *mediated space*, as its visual representation still exists in the background of menus and within the movements of the in-game camera perspective. Especially in a zoomed-out view (see Figure 10.2), the book that contains Tassing and the story that unfolds in it is visible, as are some hints of the table it rests on. Yet this existence remains, at least partially and by implication, in a *fictional space*—the hand that turns the page is invisible and has to be imagined. Unlike the characters inhabiting Tassing, the figure of the reader remains undisclosed—or perhaps, open.

The two-dimensional images that represent Tassing seem to reject experiences of spatial presence, but this 2.5th plane[13] between mediated and fictional space does not. This plane offers an accurate, arguably first-person perspective onto a three-dimensional diegetic artifact that merely contains flat images. Many of the interface elements that intrude upon the fully mediated plane no longer create distance—on the contrary, annotations and drolleries on the margins of the page outside of the image frame, speech bubbles with distinct fonts, blemishes in the drawings,[14] faded-out woodcuts, and similar elements all strengthen the believability of the book as a diegetic object—one which the player is indeed looking at from the outside. Even though the player cannot locate themselves in Tassing, they may very well imagine themselves sitting at a desk, looking down at a book, trying to coax meaning from old drawings, and watching the writing come to some amount of life before their eyes. The previously described idiosyncrasies, then, become merely shorthand for this interaction, which is heavily shaped, bound, and informed by the perceived environment—that of a reader.[15]

The story of *Pentiment*, taken as a whodunnit crime story, has no true resolution—the motive becomes clear by the end, but which hand actually struck the killing blows is very much left ambiguous. Throughout the game, Andreas and Magdalene are kept distant from the player and display a fair amount of agency of their own, distinct from what the player may choose for them. But if we look at the story, under the assumption of the 2.5th plane—one that sits between the player and the mediated space—there is a case to be made that Andreas and Magdalene are not the player characters at all. The player character, an inhabitant of the 2.5th plane, is instead the invisible reader in the sense of an ideal form of bookish reader-player, reading and engaging with a digital book, flipping from page to page, searching for meaning in the illuminations.

Metaludicity of *Pentiment*

The concept of the reader-player surpasses the boundary between players and a book as a playable object (narrative instance), which will be explored through the lens of *metaludicity* (see Ensslin 2013). This concept is intricately tied to the theory of metalepsis (see Schaeffer 2005, 330). The word *lepsis* (Greek for "seizure") highlights the notion of crossing boundaries, which can be seen in both traditional and interactive narratives.

As a "passage from one narrative level to another" (Genette 1980 [1972], 243) or "between two worlds" (Genette 1980 [1972], 245), the notion of metalepsis can further explain what it means to participate in an interactive narrative like *Pentiment* (see also Bell and Alber 2012; Ensslin and Bell 2021, ch. 2.). Other theoretical frameworks describe logical inconsistencies between the layers as "also be[ing] located within ontologically disconnected subworlds" (Thon 2016, 64). This interpretation proves problematic in *Pentiment* for the following reasons: In the game the subworlds are not separate but interconnected through the reader-player's interaction with the manuscript. These layers are logically consistent, though their truth can be questioned. Moreover, the player character in the game, not just the reader-player, can cross the layers as exemplified in the following narrative sequence.

Right after the game's opening scene with the palimpsest (see also the chapter by Waszkiewicz in this volume on the concept of the palimpsest in a game studies context), Andreas's story begins in a dream sequence where he interacts with allegorical figures. This dream sequence, which lacks interactivity except for dialogue options, mirrors the allegorical openings of medieval theater (see Watkins 1999, 767). The transition from the dream to the "real" world is achieved through another allegory; the "ship of fools," which symbolizes a literal transgression between Andreas's dream and his waking life. This transition clarifies the metaleptic nature of the game, as it blends the narrative layers, suggesting the reader-player is not simply interacting with the world of Tassing but also with a fiction within fiction.

Initially, the dream sequence can create a sense of disconnection from the extradiegetic manuscript. The game begins with a metaphorical representation of Andreas's mind-space, not the village of Tassing. As the player progresses through the dream sequence, the manuscript's extradiegetic nature becomes less tangible. Before the player can connect these layers, they are immediately placed into a completely different space, where they control Andreas. This shift between layers might initially make the reader-player question the consistency of the narrative.

The palimpsest scene, which presents a first-person perspective of interacting with a book, is quickly followed by a theatrical-style scene with Andreas as the protagonist, mirroring the structure of medieval plays. The reader-player, in a sense, navigates between these layers much like flipping through a manuscript, unsure of whether they are exploring fiction or fact. This metaludic play—oscillating between narrative layers and constantly interacting with the text as both a researcher and participant—becomes a fundamental part of *Pentiment*.[16]

Josh Sawyer introduces the idea of a fragmented history in *Pentiment* (see Sawyer 2023, 00:05:57), where the reader-player must solve a murder while reconstructing history. This process, connected to Umberto Eco's method as a semiotician, mirrors the role of piecing together facts from historical sources. The reader-player, while engaging with the game's narrative, assumes the role of both participant and researcher, further reinforcing the metaleptic interaction with the text. Their actions—researching, exploring, and reconstructing—are both real and simulated, creating a paradoxical yet meaningful connection to the game's narrative.

While the actions of the reader-player are genuine in the game's environment, they are also a simulation because the historical manuscript being explored is a digital remediation. Thus, the reader-player performs actions that feel real within the context of the game but are still part of a constructed, fictional world. This participatory role mirrors the audience of a theatrical performance, with the crucial distinction that here, the player is not a passive observer but an active performer in the narrative.

The metaludic dimension of *Pentiment* becomes even more evident in the third act of the game, when Andreas returns to Tassing and reflects on the village's hidden history. In a key dialogue with Magdalene, Andreas says:

> Tassing's real history is at odds with the story we've all been told. It's been covered, bit by bit, layer by layer until it could no longer be seen. But it's still here. It's always been here, hidden beneath our feet. And it's still protected, haunted by the specter of death that has hung over this place for generations.

This search for a "real history" mirrors the reader-player's own role in uncovering the murder mystery. Just as Andreas seeks the truth about Tassing, the player seeks the truth through interactive play. The force behind the solution of the riddle is the specter of death who threatens to expose the layers of its history. It is symbolically tied to the reader-player's quest to uncover narrative threads that might otherwise remain hidden. The reader-player's decisions—about murder weapons, motives, and alibis—are pivotal in shaping the narrative. Each choice determines a different path, and certain parts of the story remain hidden in subsequent playthroughs, reflecting the game's temporal and spatial restrictions. The reader-players are unable to have a look inside the "Historia Tassiae" or individual parts of the manuscript. These restrictions are also reflected in the game through meal scenes, as it is impossible to talk to all characters and uncover all clues they could share, the player has to choose who to share a meal with three times every in-game day. Additionally, the decisions regarding the murder weapon, motive, and missing alibi during the accusation scene define a chosen path. Similar perspectives in reading and playing are possible while there are similar story parts, which remain hidden in a first play. Also worth mentioning is the self-referential pointer to the labyrinth as the sublime underground of Tassing.[17] The "Lady of the Labyrinth," as referred to by the "Our Lady of the Labyrinth" church in the game, alludes to the (also sexually connoted) symbol of pre-Christian culture and to the game's exploration of historical layers. This labyrinth serves as a metaphor for the complex layers of history and narrative that the player must navigate. The reference alludes to Janet H. Murray's idea of agency as spatial navigation and orientation in "liberation from the tyranny of the author" (2001, 133).

The reader-player, like a historian, must navigate the labyrinth of Tassing's history, uncovering truths hidden within the layers of the village's past. The game's structure forces the reader-player to leap between metaludic layers of exploration, research, and reconstruction, all while engaging with the village's history in a constantly shifting narrative. At the game's conclusion, Magdalene's mural of Tassing's history becomes a symbol of the player's involvement in constructing the past. The player's decisions determine which historical events and figures are included in her painting, highlighting the active role of the reader-player in shaping the narrative. This shifting role—investigator, historian, and researcher—demonstrates *Pentiment*'s metaludic qualities. The reader-player oscillates between multiple layers, reconstructing the history of Tassing and engaging with the narrative from different perspectives. This also reflects the question of truth in the reconstructed history (see Figure 10.3).

While the basic metaludic game mechanics (as explained in the third section) endeavor to reconstruct events, players become critical observers of history,

Figure 10.3 Truth is also discussed in the scriptorium by referencing disruption through Enlightenment and Reformation.

representation, and narrative. In this form, the reader-player's participation in the narrative layers of *Pentiment* not only takes place from the extradiegetic perspective but also forms frameworks and new layers of narratives that are built upon each other or destroyed. As a layer is overwritten or exceeded, the leap into the metalepsis occurs.

The manuscript is comparable to an unreliable narrative instance or source[18] and, in this case, as an equally unreliable ludex agens in constant intersubjective exchange with the players. Both the players and the historical source are absent and present. In *Pentiment*, "bookishness" means bringing fictional knowledge from diaries, manuscripts, and narratives to the players as readers as a ludex of subjective[19] information. The latter examines the layers of Tassing's history, even though they can never read the "Historia Tassiae," by learning more about the fictional place in exchange with the characters, places, and interfaces and thus becoming part of Amalie's manuscript themselves.

Concluding Remarks

This chapter demonstrated the multiple layers and dimensions in which a bookish player is constructed in *Pentiment*. To derive full satisfaction from playing this game, a multi-faceted metareferential stance is required, one that does not just reflect an appreciation of the novelty of the bibliophilic interface design, but indeed an acknowledgment of the many references to existing medieval and meta-medieval art, literature, and media. Playing *Pentiment* affords a scholarly, analytical, inquisitive, and intertextual attitude—one that will detect the metareferential sources, or at least be ready to identify, interrogate, and interpret them within the narrative and ludic backdrop of the game and its palimpsestic settings.

That being said, we have argued that the game goes beyond a merely referential or structural, cohesion-evoking level when it comes to the role of its central object, the playable codex, or ludex. In an analytical approach that we have referred to as object-led rather than object-oriented, we have shown how the ludex agens in *Pentiment* assumes aspects of agency, ontological and diegetic diversity, continuity, and permanence. At a figurative level, it also adopts a paradigmatic quality, placing itself in a transformative historical context that is shaped by its medial and material affordances not unlike the transformations we are witnessing at the dawn of the age of pervasive artificial intelligence.

How the game constructs a bookish player harks back to a time when information and authority seemed to be in human hands (or at the least in some people's hands), taking over from another superhuman source of authority—that of an assumed, all-empowered divine voice. In reconstructing this divine voice as truth, the reader-player seems to fail, as this chapter aims to show. In analyzing the presented book culture, spatiality, and metaludic aspects of a reader-player attempting to find a factual story, *Pentiment* refers to an indifferent knowledge culture that is highly topical, and deeply reminiscent of contemporary debates surrounding the increasingly blurry boundaries between fact and fiction.

Notes

1 One might even argue that this chapter presents a form of deliberate metareferential interconnection between five authors from different academic fields and backgrounds.

2 For the purposes of this chapter, all of these books are also considered to be diegetic documents.

3 The surname "Völklingen" from German "Volk" (Engl. "folk") seems significant, because almost all of the other surnames in the game mark professions, such as Druckeryn (printer) or Maler (painter).

4 In the sense of narrative levels defined by Genette (1980 [1972]; see also Ryan 1986; Thon 2016).

5 As in medieval manuscripts, the majority of highlighted words appear in red in the game's dialogues. While many of these highlighted words are terms found in the in-game glossary, "divine words" such as the word "God" are rubricated for emphasis but do not have glossary definitions. Occasionally, blue and green are used instead of red for emphasis, e.g., for the word "God" when it is spoken by Lorenz Rothvogel, who is not religious (see Sawyer 2022).

6 We use the term "player character" to refer to the characters controlled by the player in the game, and deliberately avoid other terminology such as "avatar" (see, e.g. Klevjer 2022) or "playable figure" (see Vella 2015) to refer to these characters. Among the different understandings of the concept, Fernández-Vara's definition of player character as "mediator between the player and the world" (2011, n.pag.) is particularly useful for our main arguments in this chapter.

7 Ironically, an early version of the game had a bug that made the journal provide too much information about the characters, revealing future events in the game (see Young 2022).

8 As shown in the ending, the manuscript is written by a character in the game. Andreas's journal, by contrast, is carried with him throughout the game, in some parts of the game other characters comment on the journal.

9 Kagen further explores this concept in relation to walking simulators in her more recent work *Wandering Games* (2022), particularly in her analysis of the videogame *Return of the Obra Dinn* (2018).

10 "Polyglot" is one of the options that can be selected by the player as Magdalene's "reading interest," as part of player her background customization in the beginning of Act III.

11 The only exceptions are the food scenes and the minigames, which take place in a first-person view, and seem to hold their own, largely unrelated place in the dramaturgy of the game.

12 Specifically, to borrow Nitsche's taxonomy of the "five main conceptual planes for the analysis of game spaces" (2008, 15): The "rule-based" (that is the mechanics and code), the "mediated" (that is the cinematic form and presentation), the "fictional" (that lives in the player's imagination), "play" (meaning the physical space containing player and hardware), and "social" spaces (that is the interaction between players).

13 So called because in accordance with Nitsche's model, it would have to be somewhere in the distance between the second plane (of aesthetically mediated space) and the third plane (the player's imagination).

14 For instance, many older characters are drawn faded and scuffed when compared to the sharp lines of younger characters.

15 It bears mention that this spatial experience (sitting at a desk, interacting with a literary artifact) resembles the position the player is likely to be in closely enough that an argument could even be made that this metadiegetic plane begins scraping the walls of the *play space* as well.

16 Switching through the layers (or planes) is a form of philosophical thinking that is examined in Deleuze and Guattari 1996.

17 It can be viewed as a reference to the fundamental structure of videogames, as the labyrinth has played a significant cultural role throughout the history of these games (see also Rauscher 2018, 18).

18 The unreliable narrator in videogames is discussed by scholars such as Roe and Mitchell (2019) or Saroğlu (2023). For the purposes of this chapter, it is only relevant that the manuscript is a narrating source, whose origin is indifferent, and which is produced by the reader-player during gameplay.

19 The information is based on experience, which inherently implies subjectivity. Additionally, the reconstruction of history and the solution of the murder are incomplete, as only fragments are available. It is therefore necessary for the players to rebuild these fragments into a new narrative, a process that can be informed by performance theory as discussed by Fischer-Lichte and others (2012, 55; see also Leeker 2016, 160). In this instance, there are interrelationships between the reader-player and Leekers's term of "actor-agents" (2016, 160), which will not be examined in depth here.

Works Cited

AKGWDS. 2023. "Interview and Q&A with Josh Sawyer, Game Director of *Pentiment*." *YouTube*, May 8, 2023. www.youtube.com/watch?v=mptRooNj0Dg.

Barthes, Roland. 1972. *Mythologies*. New York: The Noonday Press.

Bell, Alice, and Jan Alber. 2012. "Ontological Metalepsis and Unnatural Narratology." *Journal of Narrative Theory* 42 (2): 166–192.

Boluk, Stephanie, and Patrick LeMieux. 2017. *Metagaming: Playing, Competing, Spectating, Cheating, Trading, Making, and Breaking Video Games*. Minneapolis: University of Minnesota Press.

Book Historia. 2022. "*Pentiment* Q&A with Josh Sawyer | How Did Books Influence the Game?" *YouTube*, December 7, 2022. www.youtube.com/watch?v=FHFKCS3AgZg.

Caracciolo, Marco. 2020. "Object-Oriented Plotting and Nonhuman Realities in DeLillo's *Underworld* and Iñárritu's *Babel*." In *Environment and Narrative: New Directions in Econarratology*, edited by Erin James and Eric Morel, 28–66. Columbus: Ohio State University Press.

Deleuze, Gilles, and Felix Guattari. 1996. *What Is Philosophy?* New York: Columbia University Press.

Eco, Umberto. 1983 [1980]. *The Name of the Rose*. San Diego: Harcourt.

Eisenstein, Elisabeth L. 1980. *The Printing Press as an Agent of Change*. Cambridge: Cambridge University Press.

Ensslin, Astrid. 2013. "Playing with Rather Than by the Rules: Metaludicity, Allusive Fallacy, and Illusory Agency in *The Path*." In *Analyzing Digital Fiction*, edited by Alice Bell, Astrid Ensslin, and Hans Rustad, 75–93. New York: Routledge.

Ensslin, Astrid. 2014. *Literary Gaming*. Cambridge, MA: MIT Press.

Ensslin, Astrid, and Alice Bell. 2021. *Digital Fiction and the Unnatural: Transmedial Narrative Theory, Method, and Analysis*. Columbus: Ohio State University Press.

Fenlon, Wes. 2022. "How *Pentiment*'s Hand-Crafted Fonts Give Pen and Ink a Voice." *PC Gamer*, November 15, 2022. www.pcgamer.com/how-pentiments-hand-crafted-fonts-give-pen-and-ink-a-voice/.

Fernández-Vara, Clara. 2011. "The Paradox Between Player Control and Player Character in Adventure Games." *Paper presented at the International Communication Association (ICA) Conference*. Boston, May 25, 2011.

Fischer-Lichte, Erika. 2012. *Performativität: Eine Einführung*. Bielefeld: transcript.

Fludernik, Monika. 1996. *Towards a 'Natural' Narratology*. London: Routledge.

Genette, Gérard. 1980 [1972]. *Narrative Discourse: An Essay in Method*. Ithaca, NY: Cornell University Press.

Hernandez, Luke. 2024. "Digital Pedagogy and *Pentiment* (2022): Playing with Critical Art History." *Digital Rhetoric Collaborative*, April 13, 2024. www.digitalrhetoriccollaborative.org/2024/04/13/digital-pedagogy-and-pentiment-2022-playing-with-critical-art-history/.

Jenkins, Henry. 2004. "Game Design as Narrative Architecture." In *First Person: New Media as Story, Performance, and Game*, edited by Noah Wardrip-Fruin and Pat Harrigan, 118–130. Cambridge, MA: MIT Press.

Kagen, Melissa. 2020. "Archival Adventuring." *Convergence* 26 (4): 1007–1020.

Kagen, Melissa. 2022. *Wandering Games*. Cambridge, MA: MIT Press.

Kennedy, Hannah. 2023. "Deep Dive: Behind the Evocative Medieval Manuscript Art of *Pentiment*." *Game Developer*, January 25, 2023. www.gamedeveloper.com/art/deep-dive-the-art-of-pentiment.

Kleinerman, Danielle and Chiara Haynes. 2023. "Regret in Play and in Paint: Authorship, Narrative, and Intertextuality in *Pentiment* (2022)." In *Proceedings of DiGRA 2023: Limits and Margins of Games*, n.pag.

Klevjer, Rune. 2022. *What Is the Avatar? Fiction and Embodiment in Avatar-Based Singleplayer Computer Games*. Revised and commented ed. Bielefeld: transcript.

Krampe, Theresa, Stephanie Lotzow, and Jan-Noël Thon. 2022. "Playful Poetics: Metareferential Interfaces in Recent Indie Games." *Poetics Today* 43 (4): 729–771.

Leeker, Martina. 2016. "Performativierung des Raumes: Wissens- und technikgeschichtliche Aspekte zeitgenössischer Bühnenräume." In *Bühne: Raumbildende Prozesse im Theater*, edited by Norbert Otto Eke, Ulrike Haß, and Irina Kaldrack, 149–170. Munich: Fink.

Milligan, Chloe Anna. 2019. "From Codex to Ludex: Paper Machines, Digital Games, and Haptic Subjectivities." *Publije* 1: n.pag.

Mukherjee, Hyrania. 2024. "'Veritas Omnia Vincit': A Brief Survey of Truth, Power, and History in *Pentiment*." *Knowledge Commons Works*, January 1, 2024. https://doi.org/10.17613/n6ya-1y27.

Murray, Janet H. 2001. *Hamlet on the Holodeck: The Future of Narrative in Cyberspace*. Cambridge, MA: MIT Press.

Nitsche, Michael. 2008. *Video Game Spaces: Image, Play, and Structure in 3D Worlds*. Cambridge, MA: MIT Press.

Pentiment. 2022. Obsidian Entertainment/Xbox Game Studios. Microsoft Windows.

Philip, Michelle. 2023. "Deconstructing the Narrative of the Fragmented Self in Umberto Eco's *The Name of the Rose*." *Gap Bodhi Taru: A Global Journal of Humanities* 6 (1): 42–44.

Pressman, Jessica. 2020. *Bookishness: Loving Books in a Digital Age*. New York: Columbia University Press.

Punday, Dan. 2017. "Space across Narrative Media: Towards an Archaeology of Narratology." *Narrative* 25 (1): 95–112.

Rauscher, Andreas. 2018. "Raum." In *Game Studies*, edited by Benjamin Beil, Thomas Hensel, and Andreas Rauscher, 3–26. Wiesbaden: Springer.

Return of the Obra Dinn. 2018. 3909, LLC. Microsoft Windows.

Roe, Curie, and Alex Mitchell. 2019. "'Is This Really Happening?': Game Mechanics as Unreliable Narrator." In *Proceedings of DiGRA 2019: Game, Play and the Emerging Ludo-Mix*, n.pag.

Ryan, Marie-Laure. 1986. "Embedded Narratives and Tellability." *Style* 20 (3): 319–340.

Ryan, Marie-Laure. 2021. "Introduction: Four Types of Textual Space and their Manifestations in Digital Narrative." In *Digital Narrative Spaces: An Interdisciplinary Examination*, edited by Dan Punday, 1–19. New York: Routledge.

Saroğlu, Ömer Can. 2023. "Unreliable Narrator in Video Games." MA thesis, Bahçeşehir Üniversites Istanbul. https://zenodo.org/records/11617657.

Sawyer, Josh. 2022. "That Character Has Extremely Unorthodox Views, So I Chose to Use Blue Text to Highlight Divine Words for Their Act III Conversation." *Frog Helms Fan*

Club Tumblr, November 21, 2022. www.tumblr.com/jesawyer/701558529458339840/hi-josh-being-raised-in-the-church-it-was-not-a.
Sawyer, Josh 2023. "Mixing History and Fiction in *Pentiment*." *YouTube*, December 18, 2023. www.youtube.com/watch?v=mhZcNA16m8A.
Schaeffer, Jean-Marie. 2005. "Métalepse et immersion fictionelle." In *Métalepses: Entorses au pacte de la représentation*, edited by John Pier and Jean-Marie Schaeffer, 323–334. Paris: Éditions de l'école des hautes études en sciences sociales.
Swallow, Bard. 2023. "High Fantasy RPGs and the Materiality of the Medieval Book." *Games and Culture*, online first November 19, 2023. https://doi.org/10.1177/15554120231214331.
Thon, Jan-Noël. 2016. *Transmedial Narratology and Contemporary Media Culture*. Lincoln: University of Nebraska Press.
Thon, Jan-Noël. 2023. "Alles literarisch? Zur ästhetischen Komplexität gegenwärtiger Computerspiele." *Der Deutschunterricht* 76.4: 24–33.
Vella, Daniel. 2015. "The Ludic Subject and the Ludic Self: Analyzing the 'I-in-the-Gameworld." PhD thesis, IT-Universitetet i København.
Watkins, John. 1999. "The Allegorical Theatre: Moralities, Interludes, and Protestant Drama." In *The Cambridge History of Medieval English Literature,* edited by David Wallace, 767–792. Cambridge: Cambridge University Press.
Wirth, Werner et al. 2007. "A Process Model of the Formation of Spatial Presence Experiences." *Media Psychology* 9 (3): 493–525.
Wolf, Werner. 2009. "Metareference Across Media: The Concept, Its Transmedial Potentials and Problems, Main Forms and Functions." In *Metareference across Media: Theory and Case Studies*, edited by Werner Wolf, 1–85. Amsterdam: Rodopi.
Wright, Esther. 2024. "'Layers of History': History as Construction/Constructing History in Pentiment." *ROMchip: A Journal of Game Histories* 6 (1): n.pag.
Young, Rory. 2022. "*Pentiment* Hotfixes Glitched Journal Spoiling the Story." *Game Rant*, November 19, 2022. https://gamerant.com/pentiment-hotfix-glitched-journal/.

11 Metareference in Comics Games

Kieron Brown

This chapter explores the metareferential potential of comics games *or works that are institutionally and paratextually framed as videogames but incorporate comics features into their mechanics. In particular, the chapter focuses on three works recently released by independent videogame publisher Annapurna Interactive:* Florence *(2018),* Gorogoa *(2017), and* Storyteller *(2023). These games' unique approaches to maintaining comics characteristics entail significant deviation from the conventions of both media. While such experimental tendencies might initially predispose the works to metareferential effects, the chapter instead looks at specific points within the works displaying "framing discordances" (involving irony, ambiguity, contradiction, etc.) where the potential for meta-effects is likely to be at its strongest. This focus entails a consideration of both narrative and ludic forms of metareference as well as how narrative and ludic features may mitigate each other's metareferential potential via opportunities for immersion.*

Introduction

This chapter explores the "metareferential potential" (Wolf 2009, 8) of *comics games* or works that are institutionally and paratextually framed as videogames but incorporate comics features into their mechanics. In particular, the chapter focuses on three works recently released by independent[1] videogame publisher Annapurna Interactive: *Florence* (2018), *Gorogoa* (2017), and *Storyteller* (2023). These games' unique approaches to maintaining comics characteristics entail significant deviation from the conventions of both media. While such experimental tendencies might initially predispose the works to metareferential effects, the chapter instead looks at specific points within the works displaying "framing discordances," (involving irony, ambiguity, contradiction, etc.) where the potential for "metaization" (Wolf 2009, 3) or "medium-awareness" (Wolf 2009, 28) in the recipient is likely to be at its strongest. This focus entails a consideration of both narrative and ludic forms of metareference as well as how narrative and ludic features may mitigate each other's metareferential potential via opportunities for immersion. That said, let me begin with an introduction to the topic of framing, which will undergird my approach to immersion and metareference.

DOI: 10.4324/9781003538592-11

Framing, Immersion, and Metareference

Building on the work of theorists such as Gregory Bateson (1972) and Erving Goffman (1986), Werner Wolf describes frames as "basic orientational aids that help us to navigate through our experiential universe, inform our cognitive activities and generally function as preconditions of interpretation" (2006a, 5). These "culturally formed metaconcepts" (Wolf 2006a, 5) regulate the application of other concepts, which, in turn, tend to "gover[n] a plurality of sub-concepts and expectations" (Wolf 2006a, 4; see also Rumelhart 1980). Frames can thus be considered as cognitive categories (and subcategories) that enable individuals not only to identify given situations as distinct from others but also to know what to expect from them and how to act appropriately within them (or, as Wolf puts it, frames have an "interpretive, guiding and controlling function" [2006a, 6; see also Deterding 2013]). As opposed to frames, the term "framings" (Wolf 2006a, 6; see also Bal 2002; Deterding 2013) refers to "codings of abstract cognitive frames that exist or are formed within, or on the margins and in the immediate context of, the framed situation" (Wolf 2006a, 6). Framing thus refers to the signaling, application, and maintenance of frames. It has both an internal dimension, in that individuals necessarily classify situations, though often not consciously, and an external dimension, involving sets of social and material signals that provide reasons to apply the appropriate frame (see also Bateson on "metacommunicative messages" [1972, 178]; as well as Jahn [1997, 464]; and Rumelhart [1980, 41] on the "top-down" and "bottom-up" nature of framing processes).

As opposed to what Goffman termed "primary framework[s]," i.e., those situations deemed to be "real or actual, to be really or actually or literally occurring" (1986, 47), engaging with works of art and literature generally involves a "secondary framework" (Wolf 2006a, 14), which might for the current purpose be termed "representation." This overarching frame typically involves a set of high-level subsidiary frames, further determining the type of situation or context encountered. Drawing on Wolf (2006a), I propose that among the most significant of these interlinked key frames are "narrative," "medium," and "genre" (see Wolf 2014; Rajewsky 2010; Frow 2006 for uses of these terms, respectively, in the context of frames). These frames are often signaled by a range of institutional and paratextual framings (e.g., being published on the videogame distribution platform Steam; the subtitle "a graphic novel," etc.) as well as various work-based framings (e.g., the representation of magical creatures signaling that a work belongs to the fantasy genre).

When engaging with representational works, the recipient's awareness of these frames can remain latent, a phenomenon often discussed in terms of "immersion" (see Ryan 2015; Thon 2008; Wolf 2013b). In the context of "noninteractive" media, cognitive narrative theorists typically take immersion to entail a recipient's "recentering" (Ryan 2015, 73) of attention to a represented world as they are constructing it based on prompts within a work. For Marie-Laure Ryan (2015), this imaginative and interpretive process involves a combination of spatial, temporal, and emotional dimensions.[2] Videogames complicate this notion because they are not only often classifiable as narratives but are also considered to be interactive "simulations" (Frasca 2003, 222; see also Juul 2005; Ryan 2006; 2015; Thon 2016a; 2016b). Such works offer the recipient various forms of "agency" or the "power to take meaningful action" (Murray 1997, 126; see also Bódi 2023; Bódi and Thon 2020; Wardrip-Fruin et al. 2009). In overly simple terms, these additional possibilities for recipient action allow for represented situations in "game spaces" (the "spatio-temporal location of ludic events" [Krampe et al. 2022, 730]) and interfaces ("WIMP interface devices, menus, and extradiegetic overlays" [Krampe et al. 2022, 731]) that may not directly correspond to a work's storyworld (see Thon 2016a; 2016b).[3] While there are different ways to group and label the additional dimensions of immersion that the combination of narrative and interactive components enables (see Calleja 2011; Ermi and Mäyrä 2005; Thon 2008),[4] not all of which are relevant to the works I discuss, it is generally acknowledged that videogames offer opportunities for "ludic immersion" (Bell et al. 2018, 4; Ryan 2015, 246; Thon 2008, 36). This term refers to a more embodied form of absorption in an activity or challenge, as afforded by a videogame's system (see also Csíkszentmihályi on "flow" [1975, 11]; as well as Soderman [2021] for a critical perspective on flow in the context of videogames).

Although I cannot offer an extended exploration of how narrative and ludic forms of immersion interact and overlap, I assume that because interactive simulation can be considered representational, if not always corresponding to a narrative storyworld (see Jørgensen 2013; Ryan 2006; 2015; Thon 2016a; 2016b), the relationship between immersion and "distance" (Wolf 2013b, 22) may be comparable for narrative and ludic forms of engagement. The term "distance" refers to the "awareness 'from without' [...] that the illusion-inducing trigger is an artefact and a 'mere' representation" (Wolf 2013b, 22). This awareness may be activated by a range of recipient-based and work-based variables, including interference from the environment, a lack of familiarity with conventions, mistakes/error states and other perceived aesthetic weaknesses, as well as the presence of (assumed-to-be) intentionally deployed anti-immersive devices, the latter of which brings me to the topic of metareference.

All framings or "self-reference[s]" (Wolf 2009, 22)[5] within a work necessarily imply what Wolf calls a "meta-level" (2009, 22). As noted, this metalevel is often used in a "pragmatic" (Wolf 2009, 28) way, aiding access to and guiding attention toward what is framed. In contrast, metareference employs this metalevel to *reflect* on the mediality or representationality of the work in which it is found (or that of other works). For Wolf, these self-reflexive statements can function in "explicit" or "implicit" (2009, 37) ways. Explicit metareference occurs in linguistic works when they verbally refer to themselves (e.g., a narrator commenting on the process of telling stories), but primarily visual representations can also be explicitly metareferential if the reference is especially "obvious" or "(quasi-)denotational" (Wolf 2009, 45; e.g., a painting of a painter in the act of painting). Implicit metareference, in comparison, shares with most cases of irony the idea that the meta-statement goes entirely "unsaid" (Hutcheon 1994, 9), as it were. This typically involves experimentation or "salient deviation" (Wolf 2009, 40) from convention.

Neither variant of metareference is simply the result of features within works alone. These elements merely have metareferential potential, as successful metareference requires activation by a willing and able recipient and depends on various contextual factors. For example, Wolf (2009; 2013c) posits that the disruptive effects of metalepsis (a paradoxical transgression of the borders between ontologically distinct narrative levels or [sub]worlds) can be lessened through factors such as appropriate and sufficient genre framings (e.g., fantasy or science fiction), sustained repetition or habituation of the device, "naturalization" (Wolf 2013c, 118; see also Thon's "plausibilization" [2016a, 63]) strategies within works (e.g., locating transgressions within a "work within a work" or a dream sequence), as well as the degree of emotional involvement the work affords. As such, the "metareferential function" (Wolf 2009, 67) of a given feature may be too weak to be perceived or too dominated by the feature's "heteroreferential" (Wolf 2009, 54) function(s).

This suggests that while a variety of features might be posited as making self-reflexive statements "after the fact," for Wolf, metareferential potential has a processual basis (as is reflected by the more process-focused term "metaization" [2009, 12]). The notion of framing consistency (or, rather, the lack thereof) would then seem a key determiner of degrees of metareferential potential, as in, the more consistent a work's framings in terms of narrative, medium, and genre (and associated frames), the less metareferential it will likely seem. Metaization will then be more prone to occur when a work involves a form of discordance between frames and framings (whether through irony, ambiguity, contradiction, etc.; see also Wolf on "defamiliarized framings" [2006b, 295]). These framing discordances will typically involve not only deviations from preconceived expectations upon encountering a work (e.g., what features a given medium prototypically displays) but also deviations from expectations instilled dynamically as a work progresses (e.g., how a work uses and continues to use a given medial feature).

Once again, videogames offer a distinct set of concerns in this regard when compared to less kinesthetic forms of medial engagement. As well as features such as metalepsis (and other so-called "unnatural" [Alber 2016, 3] elements), parody, etc., which can be deployed across narrative media, metareference can reflect on (and be the result of) videogames typically being rule-based systems designed for goal-oriented interaction. As such, Theresa Krampe posits forms of "ludic metareference" (2023, 143; see also Ensslin on "metaludicity" [2013, 77]; and Fest on "metaproceduralism" [2016, 16]), examples of which include unconventional game mechanics, "obtrusive, variable, or otherwise conspicuous rules" (Krampe 2023, 142), fake malfunctions, and other withdrawals of expected or established forms of agency.

If both metareference and immersion can be characterized by shifts of attention and awareness, it stands to reason that a videogame's narrative and ludic elements may mitigate each other's metareferential potential. By this, I mean that the metareferential potential of ludic elements might be reduced in scope or span by consistent narrative framings and sustained opportunities for narrative immersion and that the metareferential potential of narrative elements might be weakened by consistent ludic framings that afford significant ludic immersion (see also Ensslin and Bell 2021).[6] For reasons that will become clear, I believe that the works I refer to as comics games offer a fruitful avenue for exploring degrees of metareferential potential and posing questions about the interrelations between narrative and ludic forms of metareference and narrative and ludic forms of immersion.

Comics Games

As Rauscher and colleagues have noted, the "conventionally distinct media" (2021, 6; see also Rajewsky 2010, 61; Thon 2014, 336) of comics and videogames have been influencing one another since the release of various Atari titles in the late 1970s and early 1980s. To account for the "complex synergies, interactions, and interrelations" (Rauscher et al. 2021, 3) between the two media that have taken place since then, the authors offer two overlapping types of interrelation. What they term "transmedia expansions" (Rauscher et al. 2021, 3) concerns instances in which examples of both comics and videogames adapt, expand the storyworlds of, or otherwise reimagine works from the "other" medium. The term "hybrid medialities," in contrast, refers to the ways in which examples of comics and videogames "borrow, adapt, and transform a diverse range of aesthetic, ludic, and narrative strategies conventionally associated with the 'other' medium" (Rauscher et al. 2021, 2, see also Backe [2021] for a critical perspective on the notion of hybrids).[7] While I acknowledge the metareferential potential of examples of the former type of interrelation (e.g., parodic elements and other salient "intermedial references" [Rajewsky 2010, 55]), this chapter focuses on the latter type of interrelation. Still, although the authors provide several examples of borrowed characteristics between the two media and write of hybrid medialities as a "continuum" (Rauscher et al. 2021, 5), the (approximate) positioning of comics games on such a continuum requires further elaboration. For this, I turn to the work of comics theorist Daniel Merlin Goodbrey.

Goodbrey uses the term "hybrid" to describe a set of self-developed and theorized works he calls "game comics" (2021, 45). A game comic "exhibits some of the key characteristics of a game and uses some of the key characteristics of the form of comics as the basis for its gameplay" (Goodbrey 2021, 45; see also Järvinen on game mechanics as "verbs" [2007, 263] linked to the rules and goals of a videogame; as well as Sicart 2008). While Goodbrey draws on Juul's "*classic game model*" (Juul 2005, 36; original emphasis)[8] to identify the videogame characteristics in question, the set of comics characteristics he proposes might be summarized as involving juxtaposed sets of narratively organized panels housing pictorial and often verbal content, from which recipients can draw meaning sequentially and nonsequentially at a pace of their own. With some work-specific caveats, then, examples of game comics may include not only Goodbrey's well-known prototypes (*A Duck Has an Adventure* [2013]; *Icarus Needs* [2013]; and *The Empty Kingdom* [2014]) but also titles such as *Framed* (2014) and *Framed 2* (2017), *All You Can Eat* (2017) and *vAPE Escape* (2019), *Breaking the 4th Wall* (2020), as well as the three titles published by Annapurna Interactive to be discussed shortly: *Florence*, *Gorogoa*, and *Storyteller*.

Yet, while I will broadly follow Goodbrey's conceptualization of game comics, I will not follow his terminology. Although Goodbrey's prototypical approach to videogame and comics features is compatible with a frame-based approach to individual media as conventionally distinct, he restricts his comics characteristics to what are often referred to as semiotic "modes," their "affordances" (Kress 2010, 47), and conventional uses. Although these modes are obviously crucial for identifying comics, the limitation downplays the significance of institutional and paratextual framing factors for questions of medial attribution (e.g., where and by whom a work is published, how accompanying [promotional] materials, author figures, industry publications, reviewers, commentators classify the work, etc.). The term "game comics" suggests that the works Goodbrey discusses are comics first and foremost (see Backe 2021). If this choice of term was not motivated by the perceived dominance of comics features (Goodbrey writes of game comics as displaying "true hybridization" [Goodbrey 2021, 48]), then the application of this label would be more appropriately based on those institutional and paratextual factors noted previously. Besides Goodbrey's prototypes, the above works were all published and received in a context more typical of videogames than comics.

I will thus use the term "comics games" to refer to works that may not be primarily institutionally or paratextually framed as comics but still make it clear that both "comics" and "videogame" are suitable frames of interpretation (see also Backe's term "comic-game" [2022, 286]; as well as Ng 2021).[9] In short, my focus is on videogames that are sufficiently "comics-like" (see Goodbrey 2017; Wilde 2015; Witek 2009; see also Beineke 2017) to affect how recipients approach and interpret them. Allowing for various points of overlap, then, one might evaluate how comics-like a work appears, from more peripheral examples that, for instance, mainly draw on visual styles associated with comics (e.g., *MadWorld* [2009]; *The Wolf Among Us* [2013]; *HiFi Rush* [2023]), via those that (also) employ comics-like elements as part of their scripted narrative sequences (e.g., *Max Payne* [2001]; *Gravity Rush* [2012]; *Riversiders* [2023]) and/or that borrow partially or intermittently from comics' conventional vocabulary as part of their gameplay/interfaces (e.g., *Comix Zone* [1995]; *XIII* [2003]; *What Remains of Edith Finch* [2017]; *Liberated* [2020]), to those here referred to as comics games, which largely maintain comics features for their durations and incorporate them in various ways into their mechanics (e.g., *Framed* and *Framed 2*; *All You Can Eat* and *vAPE Escape*; *Breaking the 4th Wall*; *Florence*; *Gorogoa*; *Storyteller*).

Again, without denying any metareferential potential that examples of less extensively integrated medial features may possess, comics games would seem particularly predisposed to meta-effects (in theory, rendering insights gained from their study somewhat applicable to the other kinds of medial interaction noted). While comics games typically entail some significant deviation from prototypical comics features or framings (e.g., movement, sound, loss of control of pacing, forms of agency, etc.), the restricting of gameplay by making it in some sense reliant on comics principles, when combined with various other genre conventions (e.g., *Framed* as a "noir-puzzle" game), has led to a set of works with diverse and often innovative sets of (narrative) mechanics (see also Backe 2022). Such games are thus likely to challenge the player's existing cognitive frames to varying degrees and, as such, are also liable to prompt a form of medium awareness.

Still, to the extent that the player perceives a given work as unconventional, they will likely also "tune" their active frames or "modify the variable constraints and default values [of frames] in the direction of the current experience" (Rumelhart 1980, 53). Providing this tuning of comics and videogame-related expectations occurs, comics games may not routinely prompt metaization. In other words, I assume that via an initial period of work-provided instruction and/or player experimentation (see Wardrip-Fruin et al. 2009), these works' framings may be experienced as consistent enough to allow for significant narrative and ludic immersion, thus potentially limiting metareferential potential. While it then might not be particularly revealing to focus on this initial metareferential potential alone, I would argue that it serves as a productive base from which to consider the (mitigation of) meta-effects caused by further framing discordances within the works. Once more, by the term "framing discordances," I refer to inconsistencies between frames and framings or ironic, ambiguous, contradictory, etc., elements (be they primarily narrative or ludic) that subvert the player's dynamically produced frame structures in some way. Each of the chosen case studies offers forms of these framing discordances: these are primarily ludic in *Florence*, via various unfulfilled invocations of agency, and primarily narrative in *Gorogoa* and *Storyteller*, through the representation of impossible spaces and temporalities in the former and various elements that can be considered parodic in the latter.

Florence *(2018)*

Florence is the celebrated first (and to date only) work from the Australian studio Mountains.[10] This comics game invites the player to accompany 25-year-old Florence Yeoh through 20 short "chapters," from an initially humdrum work/life routine via a burgeoning romantic partnership with cellist Krish Hemrajani and the dissolution of their relationship into a subsequent period of personal and professional growth. Throughout various sequences of narrative panels/screens, *Florence* offers frequent instances of touchscreen-based interactivity or "minigames" (see Juul 2010, 117–118) in which the player must carry out actions corresponding in various ways to those of the main character. In doing so, *Florence* distances itself from various videogame characteristics. While it does require kinesthetic or "nontrivial effort" (Aarseth 1997, 1) from the player, it offers little in the way of goals, associated challenges, and meaningful choice. Such omissions would, however, seem somewhat compatible with comics features, the use of which I will briefly outline.

Like various webcomics (see Batinić 2016; Kleefeld 2020; Kukkonen 2014; see also Aggleton 2019; Wilde 2015), *Florence* deploys many of its hand-drawn

Figure 11.1 The player scrolls through the panels in *Florence*.

narrative pictures in the form of single-panel screens. Still, the work occasionally adopts scrolling comics-like layouts (see Figure 11.1) and often also features combinations of an inclusive panel depicting Florence and an inset panel housing interactive elements or vice versa (see Figure 11.2). While *Florence* features a near-constant soundtrack (composed by Kevin Penkin and primarily consisting of piano and cello arrangements), most of the soundtrack is what Goodbrey describes as "ambient" (2017, 156), with the sound only occasionally becoming responsive to the player's actions. As is also atypical of traditional comics, *Florence*'s pictorial elements are not always static: The game frequently employs subtle

Figure 11.2 As Florence looks at a phone in the inclusive panel, the (interactive) contents of the phone's screen are displayed in the inset panel.

looped GIF-like animations and includes various player-instigated movements. These latter movements include those taking place in the inset/inclusive panels (where the player's movements correspond with Florence's), those resulting from various single-panel interactions (e.g., dragging and dropping elements), and panel transitions. This means that the "indefinite, abstract time" (as opposed to "concrete, measurable time" [Groensteen 2013, 70]) of comics is maintained for large portions of the game, and the player generally retains control of pacing. Finally, regarding verbal-pictorial combinations, *Florence* features little text but otherwise makes pronounced use of speech balloons.

Moving on to *Florence*'s metareferential potential, creative director Ken Wong has noted that the Mountains team wanted the work to "evoke emotions; to bring the player into the emotional journey" (Sim 2019, n.pag.). Consequently, "an explicit goal for the player is not important, and neither is choice" (Sim 2019, n.pag.). These suggestions point to a tension between the heteroreferential and metareferential functions of various of *Florence*'s mechanics. On the one hand, Wong's comments evoke Marie-Laure Ryan's proposal that while "narrative interest regards characters as persons, ludic interest regards them as means to an end" (2015, 249) or the notion that although significant player freedom does not necessarily prohibit emotional immersion, it does endanger it. As such, *Florence* deploys most of its mechanics as disarmingly simple metaphors for its protagonist's state of mind. On the other hand, *Florence* does not simply omit videogame conventions such as goals, challenges, and significant amounts of choice. Instead, it actively thematizes these missing elements to the extent that it is also possible to interpret *Florence* as an extended (ludic) metareferential reflection weighing in on longstanding debates about the potential reconciliation between storytelling and agency (see Ryan 2015), a frequent target of metareferential devices in videogames (see Backe and Thon 2019; Krampe 2023; Krampe et al. 2022).

The tension between emotional investment and metareferential potential can be demonstrated via a brief discussion of the game's use of puzzle-like elements, including its celebrated jigsaw-based dialogue mechanics. When Florence and Krish interact, the player must assemble some notably simple jigsaw puzzles to produce speech balloons, which, though empty of linguistic elements, represent conversations/arguments. In the chapter "First Dates," the game initially requires the player to assemble eight puzzle pieces to produce Florence's speech balloons, which are a similar color to that worn by Krish (see Figure 11.3). This signals Florence's nervousness, and that she is thinking about what to say, perhaps how to impress Krish, who replies almost instantly and thus appears more confident. As Florence and Krish get to know each other over three dates, the puzzles consist of fewer pieces and take less time to complete, indicating that Florence is becoming more comfortable and thinking less about her replies. In fact, the final instance of dialogue in this chapter is not classifiable as a puzzle at all. The task simply requires the player to relocate one oblong shape into the corresponding location, after which Florence and Krish share their first kiss. The game will employ variations on this mechanic to represent conflict in later chapters in which the standard jigsaw piece shapes become more angular ("Groceries"), and the associations turn toward the progressive ease with which the characters can hurt one another's feelings ("Fight"; see Figure 11.4).

If puzzles typically involve "a problem in need of a solution" (Fernández-Vara 2009, 6), *Florence*'s puzzles do not comfortably fit the description, as they offer very little in terms of challenge. In invoking such a "quintessential" ludic form as the jigsaw puzzle in this way, *Florence* would seemingly wish to draw attention to what it lacks compared to various other games, thus potentially amounting to

Figure 11.3 Dialogue mechanic in *Florence*'s "First Dates" chapter.

a form of ludic metareference. However, that these comics-related puzzles are so simple, accessible, and so easily mapped to the mental state of the game's main character may detract from any meta-effects that this apparent self-reflection might have. This possible mitigation of metaization potentially extends to instances when the work breaks from its established patterns and thematizes agency via its denial. For example, the puzzle motif is used twice outside the context of dialogue later in the game as the couple's relationship starts to break down. In one instance, the player is prompted to assemble a jigsaw-like picture of Florence and Krish facing away from each other in bed, while in the other, they are tasked with reassembling the pieces of a torn picture of the couple embracing. Unlike the dialogue puzzles, neither of these tasks can be completed: In the first case, the puzzle pieces have sockets without any corresponding tabs and vice versa (leaving a comics-like

Figure 11.4 Dialogue mechanic in *Florence*'s "Fight" chapter.

"gutter" between the two characters), and in the second, the partially reassembled torn pieces of paper slowly move apart. Though the latter example quite knowingly involves a light form of challenge, the player's efforts cannot be successful. The game will ultimately progress once these torn fragments are "close enough" to each other (incidentally, also somewhat resembling a traditional comics page).

It might then follow that these elements should have a higher degree of metareferential potential than the relatively consistent use of the dialogue mechanic. However, although these puzzle-like features may not amount to problems in need of solutions, they do *represent* problems in need of solutions. These anti-puzzles occur at the game's emotional high point (or low point), and the player's failed efforts quite clearly correspond to *Florence*'s doomed efforts to fix the relationship. Thus, even when the game appears to deviate from its own established practices, it does so for extremely evident metaphorical reasons. In sum, if not neutralizing the metareferential potential of its elements (given that the work appears to frequently point to how it *is not* using certain ludic elements), *Florence* opposes it with a strong heteroreferential or narrative function. While I have primarily focused on *Florence*'s use of puzzle-like components here, the work's various mechanics are typically quite easily reconciled with its narrative elements. Questions of "representational correspondence" (Currie 2007, 59) thus remain unproblematic (if undetailed). This is less clearly the case for Jason Roberts's *Gorogoa*, in which the use of comics-like mechanics results in significant narrative ambiguity or "unnatural" elements, which, via their logical impossibility, appear to be probable candidates for encouraging metaization.

Gorogoa *(2017)*

Gorogoa can be described as a puzzle/adventure game in which the player manipulates a 2×2 grid of changeable panels filled with spatially, temporally, and ontologically discontinuous representational content until the panels achieve visual continuity and influence one another. The individual panels (the puzzle pieces) represent parts of an elliptical narrative ostensibly featuring one unnamed individual at various points in their life, which they have dedicated to seeking knowledge of the eponymous god-like creature Gorogoa. These versions of the protagonist appear to include a child whose initial pursuit of Gorogoa leaves them permanently injured, a teen attempting to study during wartime as bombs hit the city around them, an older student diligently researching in an apparent period of political calm, a middle-aged scholar still intent on understanding the incident from their youth, and an incarnation of the protagonist in old age recollecting the various moments of their life. The player's task is to guide the youngest version of this character through various panels as they try to enact a ritual discovered upon first encountering Gorogoa (see Figure 11.5). This involves searching for five fruits to serve as an offering, a gesture the creature initially (and violently) rejects but seemingly later accepts once the character revisits the task in old age.

Gorogoa offers two broad types of mechanics: those that involve exploring various in-panel game spaces (which one can reasonably assume to largely correspond with those of the game's storyworld[s], but not without significant ambiguity) and those taking place at the level of the interface, where panels are manipulated and combined. In the first case, the player can zoom in and out of the contents of panels via parallax (changing the perspective of a scene; see Figure 11.6) and pan through in-panel space from side to side and up and down via prompts. In the second case, the player can move panels around the grid, occasionally stack panels on top of one another (changing the in-panel environment, often to provide doorways or other spaces that the child can traverse; see Figure 11.7), as well as unstack or split panels apart (frequently revealing the lifted panel as a partly transparent facade and exposing a layer of content underneath; see Figure 11.8). Achieving the correct configuration of panels triggers an animated sequence, during which the system momentarily takes control from the player, ultimately

Figure 11.5 The child discovers the ritual in *Gorogoa*.

Figure 11.6 Zooming into a single panel in *Gorogoa* (depicted consecutively).

resulting in additional game space to explore. For example, the first puzzle in the game involves aligning panels in such a way that a crow taking flight in the top-left panel of the grid triggers an apple to fall in the top-right panel, which lands in the child's bowl in the bottom-right panel of the grid (see Figure 11.9 for a static recreation of this process).

Figure 11.7 Stacking panels in *Gorogoa*.

Figure 11.8 Unstacking panels in *Gorogoa*.

In terms of established videogame conventions, *Gorogoa* takes significant cues from adventure games (e.g., *Myst* [1993]), which, according to Fernández-Vara (2014, 233), are prototypically characterized by their story-driven nature, the use of a player character, encouragement of exploration, puzzle-solving-focused gameplay, and interaction based mainly on object manipulation and spatial navigation. *Gorogoa* distinguishes itself from these games via what Roberts calls the "no touching rule" (GDC 2018, 00:30:25–00:30:26), which refers to the notion that the only way for the player to progress is by combining two or more panels. In Roberts's apt phrasing, "instead of puzzles inside of a story, it's a story suspended inside a puzzle" (GDC 2018, 00:39:19–00:39:25). As this suggests, the result is a highly fragmentary nonlinear narrative. While a certain amount of spatial navigation is possible, *Gorogoa* forgoes the use of a player character, meaning that the player's actions do not directly correspond with those of the youngest version of the protagonist. This separation renders the notion of object manipulation applicable only to the panels or interface itself, which brings me to *Gorogoa*'s comics-like features.

Roberts has noted on multiple occasions that the project that would eventually become *Gorogoa* was initially intended to be an interactive comic. Although the resulting "multi-panel game design" (IGDA Taiwan 2018, 00:05:52–00:05:53) complicates this initial link, the game retains various comics-like features (see also Seller 2018). For example, *Gorogoa* decidedly deviates from sequential panel organization, but it does entail connection-making at the level of layout or panel networks. In this respect, it is not dissimilar to the still marginal field of abstract comics (see Baetens 2011; Molotiu 2009; Rommens 2019). The game employs

Figure 11.9 Crow puzzle solution and animation (*Gorogoa*).

occasional looped in-panel animations, as well as ambient music (by Joel Corelitz) and sound effects (by Eduardo Ortiz Frau) that maintain abstract time. In addition, while the exploratory options provided to the player involve rudimentary movement, this movement is not "free." These aspects ensure that much of the game entails the player's interaction with changeable but mostly static representational elements. Thus, besides a few time-sensitive challenges, none of which are particularly punishing, *Gorogoa*'s gameplay generally leaves the player in control of pacing. While the same cannot be said about its inter-puzzle animations, as with *Florence*'s panel transitions, these animations are only triggered by the player's effort. Lastly, *Gorogoa* does not often feature readable text but does use thought balloons, which typically house additional interactive pictorial content.

While *Gorogoa* could be interpreted as an extended commentary on the notion of framing itself (see GDC 2018, 00:04:25–00:09:32), my focus in terms of likely high points of metareferential potential is on how *Gorogoa*'s unique set of comics-like mechanics often leads to a form of narrative ambiguity beyond the significant nonlinearity of its storytelling. As the protagonist is not the player's avatar, the player's activity is less narrativizable than the puzzles of more conventional adventure games might be. As the player solves the puzzles, drawing on elements from other times/places to allow the child to collect the five fruits, the child seemingly does not have to commit much effort (see Figure 11.9). This often makes it difficult to surmise what, if anything, the child is supposed to be doing. While this vagueness on its own might not be overly disruptive given that there appears to be some narrative motivation for it (the child's presumptuousness and lack of sustained effort offer a plausible reason why Gorogoa rejects the initial offering), it is not the only ambiguity that stems from Roberts's decision to forgo the link between player and primary character.

Likely more troubling in this regard is the lack of logical restriction on the player's movements and how panels can connect. For example, the player can zoom into the thought balloons of the various versions of the protagonist, whether these reflect the content of a representation the character is engaging with or a memory. They may also "enter" representations on walls (see Figure 11.9), such as a pattern on a china plate or a part of the various mandala-like decorations within the game (see also Ensslin and Bell on "impossible zooming worlds" [2021, 85]). The resulting panels can then connect to and influence others whose content should represent distinct ontological levels according to widely shared representational conventions. The result is a set of "impossible" (Ensslin and Bell 2021, 86) spaces and temporalities that occasionally even see the youngest version of the protagonist included in the same space and time as an older version of themselves. In short, the extent of representational correspondence at play here becomes quite difficult to discern.

Although apparent logical impossibilities such as these are considered to be frequent sources of metareferential effects across media (see Alber 2016; Ensslin and Bell 2021; Thon 2016a; Wolf 2009), I would argue that two main factors may mitigate against prolonged or repeated metareferential reflection in this case, both linked to *Gorogoa*'s gameplay. The first factor is whether the player interprets

Gorogoa's combination of narrative and ludic elements as a representation of a mental process. The untethered movements and transitions provide the game with a dream-like quality that has been noted by reviewers (see, e.g., Chan 2017; Webster 2017a), a quality that, as Roberts has once again observed, might also correspond to memory (see GDC 2018, 00:36:48–00:37:22). As the player encounters various versions of the protagonist at different ages throughout the game, the gameplay is perhaps akin to the process of searching through memories and rearranging them in retrospect, necessarily being unable to change the course of action (as the protagonist's frequent memories of falling from a tower make clear) but making new connections between fragments of experience and attempting to come to the "right" conclusions. It could then be argued that the game invites a naturalization or plausibilization of the apparent disconnect between narrative and mechanics, especially as certain thematic associations become apparent (e.g., the value of persistence). To whom the player is to ascribe this hypothetical memorial activity is debatable, the most likely option being the oldest incarnation of the protagonist who appears to make a successful offering to Gorogoa. However, as their activity is implicated in the player's machinations, the aforementioned strangeness is not obviously plausibilized by the work itself.

The second factor potentially countering metaization is the game's consistent ludic framings, despite the often surprising ways panels connect. Roberts's attempts to hide *Gorogoa*'s "seams" (IGDA Taiwan 2018, 00:36:16) or the means of connecting panels via the inclusion of various (hand-drawn) obscure objects and buildings amounts to a deliberate blurring of the "narrative" and "ludic functions" (Thon 2016a, 183) of the game's elements. The player is thus likely to spend much of their playing time experimenting, oscillating between attention paid to *Gorogoa*'s in-panel game spaces and its paneled surface layer or interface. While this oscillation itself might superficially resemble the process of metaization, routinely encouraging an "outside view" of the game spaces, this does not seem akin to the "rational distance" that "presupposes that a recipient is aware of the nature, forms and conventions of the signifying systems and media in question" (Wolf 2009, 28).

Instead, *Gorogoa*'s consistent mechanics suggest that this repeated pseudo-distance is supposed to be habitualized and contained, thus also discouraging attention from being paid to any one element for too long. When combined with the one-way nature of the puzzle transitions, which effectively urges the player forward, this implies that the player is not meant to dwell on as much as simply tolerate the work's narrative ambiguity (see also Alber's "Zen way of reading" [2016, 48]). Indeed, reviewers have described the experience of playing *Gorogoa* as "soothing" (Webster 2017a, n.pag.) and "meditative" (Chan 2017, n.pag.; Faulkner 2017, n.pag.; Wilson 2018, n.pag.), implying that distanced metareferential reflection may have been held in abeyance by ludic immersion (see also Kuijpers et al. on "artifact absorption" [2017, 33] or absorption based on the formal features of literary works). This possible mitigation of distance by consistent (if irregular) game mechanics and opportunities for ludic immersion is an idea that will carry through into the discussion of my third example, *Storyteller*,[11] which would appear to incorporate a form of metaization into its gameplay.

Storyteller ***(2023)***

Storyteller is a reactive puzzle game developed by Daniel Benmergui with art and design support from Jeremias Babini and music and sound effects by musician and playwright Zypce. While different incarnations of the game have existed since 2008, the 2023 version presents the player with brief plot descriptions and requires them to construct narrative comics corresponding to those descriptions. The player does so by dragging and dropping elements from toolboxes of characters and scenarios (or "scenes") into preset numbers of empty panel slots. The placement and arrangement of these characters and scenarios within the panels dynamically determines how a story unfolds. At the time of writing, the player can initially select from 60 self-contained levels (15 of which have bonus prompts) across 14 readily accessible "chapters," which link the levels by theme. These levels either offer original combinations of settings and characters within recognizable genres (e.g., fairy tale, murder mystery) or variations on well-known stories (e.g., Bram Stoker's *Dracula* [1897] and Samuel Beckett's *Waiting for Godot* [1954]).

In terms of the extent to which *Storyteller* maintains comics features, the sequentiality of panels is required by the game's "continuity engine" (InsideCreativeGaming 2021, n.pag.), which checks for various criteria as each panel is placed/removed. Yet, the notion of nonsequential or networked panel relationships is also made salient through the game's reactive nature (a change in one panel may lead to instant changes in others). Like the other comics games discussed, *Storyteller* employs ambient soundtracks and occasional looped animations. In addition, more "active" animations and sound effects occur as and when the player makes changes. However, once these latter animations have alerted the player to how the system has interpreted their behavior, the elements become largely static. Benmergui has explicitly linked the reactive nature of the game to the abstract time of comics (see Johnson 2012; see also Romero 2023), with the player being free to spend as much or as little time constructing the comics as they wish. Finally, other than level titles/plot prompts, toolbox labels, and one scenario that establishes familial ties between characters, *Storyteller* rarely uses text but does employ other conventional comics features such as thought/speech balloons and various forms of expressive symbols (or "emanata" [Walker 2000, 28]).

Moving on to *Storyteller's* metareferential potential, several of the game's prompts (and the stories that fulfill those prompts) could be considered parodic. Parody as "repetition with critical distance" (Hutcheon 2000, 6) can be said to involve a discordance between the frames evoked by its borrowed features and the framings of the current context.[12] For example, the levels in "Chapter 10: Genesis" are loosely based on the biblical tale in which Adam and Eve are expelled from the Garden of Eden after the latter is tempted by a serpent and both eat the fruit of the prohibited tree of knowledge. The first of these, a three-panel tutorial-like level titled "Temptation," offers the prompt "Eve Rejects Apple," refashioning the story of the "original sin" and evidently also acknowledging the gender-based connotations of the original story.[13] The level requires the player to first place Adam in the "tempt" scenario, where he will accept the snake's offering, and to have Eve witness Adam's subsequent punishment by a compass-like eye in the sky in the "judgment" scenario. When the player then places Eve in the "tempt" scenario, she will emit a speech balloon referencing Adam's fate and will reject the apple (see Figure 11.10). Within the same biblical setting, the level "Vengeance," which includes the prompt "Friedrich Takes Revenge," riffs on the moral implications of a waning of Christian belief evoked by the famous Nietzsche line that "God is dead. God remains dead. And we have killed him" ([1882] 2001, 120). The level requires the player to have the character of Friedrich (Nietzsche) first become romantically entangled with Eve in the "love" scenario, to later place Eve in the "tempt" and "judgment" scenarios, and to have Friedrich witness the resulting punishment. After this, Friedrich will be willing to take arms if placed in the "gun" scenario and will proceed to *literally* kill this "God" when placed in the "judgment" scenario (see Figure 11.11).

If these examples ironically "trans-contextualize" (Hutcheon 2000, 41) specific works, the elements in *Storyteller*'s toolboxes are often generic in all respects. As the levels progress, characters and scenarios from distinct chapters are combined in the available toolboxes, leading to various would-be anachronisms or mismatches (e.g., the gun used by the already out-of-place Friedrich was first introduced in levels evoking a 20th-century murder mystery setting). While these levels ultimately rely on the logic of cause and effect (a result of the game's continuity engine), the combination of game pieces appears somewhat arbitrary. This potentially points to the conventional nature of genre, *Storyteller*'s levels amounting to a suggestion along the lines of "conventions could always be different," which brings me to the notion that *Storyteller*'s mechanics might inherently invite a certain form of metaization.

Storyteller's narratives are not only constructed in the imaginative and interpretive sense but are constructed in a more literal way within a two-dimensional

Figure 11.10 "Temptation"/"Eve Rejects Apple" prompt and solution (*Storyteller*).

Figure 11.11 "Vengeance"/"Friedrich Takes Revenge" prompt and solution (*Storyteller*).

interface.[14] The player is thus always "outside" the stories that they are building. In other words, although the game's mechanics require ongoing narrativization, they do not encourage significant narrative immersion. This is reflected by the game's Steam page, which suggests that *Storyteller*'s "comic-panel design and charming animations allow for experimentation within the *framing* of its many stories" (Steam 2023, n.pag.; my emphasis), as well as Boelman and König's educationally oriented proposal that *Storyteller* serves as a "playground for experimenting with the plot logic of a story" (Boelmann and König 2023, 14; my translation).

Storyteller's levels typically allow for multiple solution pathways (if not always alternative solutions), leaving the resulting comics somewhat open in terms of "who did what to and with whom, when, where, why and in what fashion" (Herman 2002, 5). Beyond this, however, Benmergui notes that:

> you can do anything that the toolbox allows [...], so if you go off [...] the main path of trying to solve the puzzles, you can create some really weird situations [...]. We tried to find them all and have something to give you in exchange for them. Maybe it's just [...] a custom animation, custom sound, or an achievement.
> (Waypoint Radio 2023, 01:24:40–01:25:08)

Storyteller thus incentivizes the player's subversion of generic and story-specific frames, potentially amounting to the player's own form of "repetition with critical distance" (Hutcheon 2000, 6). In doing so, it also encourages them to experiment with the system's limitations and discover what would-be stories the designers have anticipated.

For example, continuing the biblical theme above, the level "Repentance" features the prompt "Adam Watches His Love Die," which admits two solutions: one where Eve is tempted and then punished in front of Adam and one where Adam tempts Eve and is punished but is later resurrected via the "revive" scenario to then witness Eve's punishment. Quite apart from these two "tasked" solutions, however, the player may, for example, also wish to see how Eve would react to Adam's leading her into temptation and her subsequent punishment by reviving her and placing her in the "love" scenario with Adam. Once placed, she will glare at Adam and emit a squiggly line signaling her disgruntlement. The player might wish to see what happens if they put two punished characters back within a panel without first being revived. If they do so, the characters will appear as two ashen statues. In addition, the player might wish to have the characters only eat apples in successive panels, which will eventually lead to them struggling with indigestion (see Figure 11.12; note that if this experimentation takes place after completing all the levels, the player will also receive the stamps "Original Fight," "Dust to Dust," and "Gluttony").

Given that the game's invitation to "play with" story elements appears to require a form of metaization, to what extent is ludic immersion likely to be disrupted here as well? While the disruption of ludic immersion can certainly have interesting metareferential effects, I would pose that nothing in the design of *Storyteller* appears to be intentionally obstructive to the gameplay experience. For example, Benmergui's insistence on instant reactivity and the sustained use of abstract time ensures that the player does not have to wait to see the result of their actions or

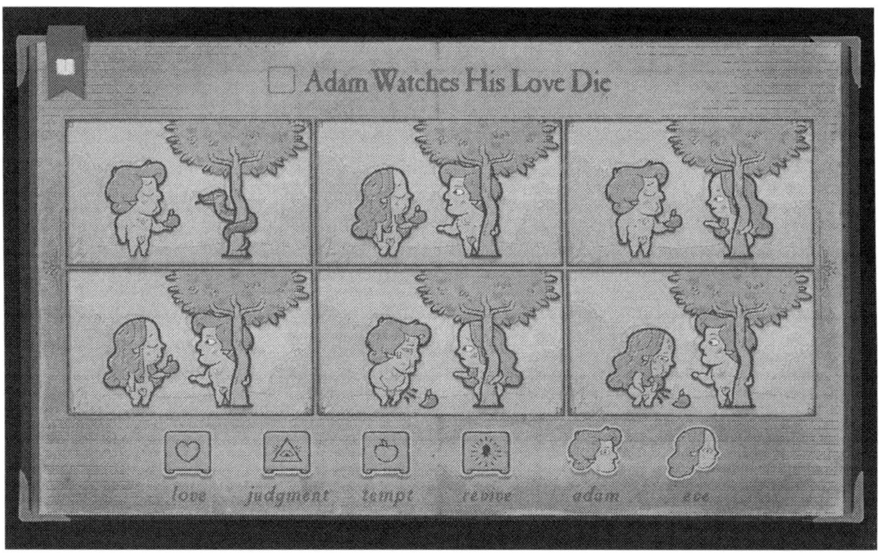

Figure 11.12 "Repentance"/"Adam Watches His Love Die" level experimentation (*Storyteller*).

retrace their steps when they inevitably reach a limit of the system or a mismatch between their comics-related expectations and the system's reaction. They can simply try something new. Even the game's potentially metareferential "error states" (Eggplant 2023, 00:21:23–00:21:24), which are triggered when the player places characters in panels without established continuity (e.g., when characters shrug as if to ask the player "why have you put me here?"), were reportedly included for the instructive value they offer. *Storyteller* might then involve something similar to what Braxton Soderman terms "critical instances" (2021, 151) in metareferential videogames. Although I am dubious about Soderman's proposal that such critical instances tend to quash the kind of outward-facing criticality that leads to social action, the term rather fittingly "alludes to distance, but it foregrounds that the reflection that these activities generate turns inward, back toward the activity that created it" (Soderman 2021, 151). This seems an apt description of *Storyteller*'s apparent capacity to incorporate metareferential reflection via consistent opportunities for ludic immersion.

Conclusion

This chapter has adopted a frame-based approach to exploring the metareferential potential of comics games, with a particular focus on *Florence*, *Gorogoa*, and *Storyteller*. These works' experimental combinations of medial features were assumed to predispose them to meta-effects. Nevertheless, as framing factors shape ongoing metareferential potential, the chapter instead focused on specific points in the works displaying additional forms of framing discordances or ironic, ambiguous, contradictory, etc., elements where the potential for metaization was likely to be particularly high. This focus involved a consideration of how consistent narrative framings and opportunities for narrative immersion may mitigate the metareferential potential of ludic framing discordances, as well as how consistent ludic framings and opportunities for ludic immersion may weaken the metareferential potential of narrative framing discordances.

While *Florence* was noteworthy for thematizing agency through flouting game characteristics such as goals, challenges, and significant choice, I argued that the accessibility of the game's metaphorical mechanics and resulting opportunities for emotional immersion might lessen any disruptive effects its nonstandard use of puzzle elements might have. *Gorogoa*'s comics-like mechanics, which sever the link between player and primary character, were shown to lead to various impossible spaces and temporalities, the likes of which are widely held to have high metareferential potential. I nonetheless posited that *Gorogoa* counters this potential metaization through its consistent use of game mechanics, which encourage player experimentation. *Storyteller*, the gameplay of which consists of constructing rudimentary comics narratives in service of puzzles based on story prompts, turned out to involve a form of metaization inherently: Here, the player "plays with" story conventions and tests the possibilities of the system, though this form of metareferential awareness appeared to be quite compatible with ludic immersion, owing to *Storyteller*'s prioritization of obstacle-free gameplay. Although deemed productive for hypothesizing about metareferential potential, these games' extensive use of comics features notably restricts the kinds of agency available to the player. As such, the suggestions made here could be supported by studies focusing on metareferential videogames with a more diverse set of mechanics.

Notes

1 While the notion of "independence" is quite difficult to delimit in the context of videogames (see Lipkin 2013; Ruffino 2013), attempts to do so often involve opposing not only the production contexts of videogames but also their formal/aesthetic features to those of "mainstream" games, i.e., both large-budget AAA titles and smaller "casual" (Juul 2019, 6) games played by broad audiences. For Jesper Juul, one of the most salient aesthetic signals of independence is the "Independent Style," which involves "a representation of a representation" and "uses contemporary technology to emulate low-tech [...] graphical materials and visual styles" (2019, 38; see also Thon 2020; and the chapter by Thon in this volume). This is quite in line with each of the examples discussed in this chapter, which not only draw on the formal features of comics but also emulate the materiality of print media to some extent.

2 For Ryan, "spatial immersion" (2015, 86) concerns the recipient's response to a work's setting and is encouraged by delineations of space that result in a "stable geography" (2015, 91). "Temporal immersion" (2015, 86) involves the recipient's response to the unfolding of a story and involves different forms of suspense (e.g., "what," "who," and "how" [2015, 103]). Lastly, "emotional immersion" (Ryan 2015, 106) pertains to the recipient's empathic responses to characters and their circumstances.

3 As Bódi and Thon suggest, this "adds a considerable layer of additional complexity to traditional notions of 'representational correspondence'" (2020, 160n6). The term "representational correspondence" here refers to the observation that "within a domain defined by the genre [and medium] of the work, certain features of the representation serve to represent features of the things represented" (Currie 2007, 59; see also Currie 2010). Game spaces as simulated environments typically entail processes of "representational reasoning" (Thon 2016a, 111) distinct from, yet interrelated with, that of the representation of storyworlds. For example, a procedurally generated configuration of obstacles (e.g., rocks, trees, etc.) or a floating arrow pointing the player in the right direction may be represented as part of a game space but not a work's storyworld. According to Jørgensen (2013), elements such as these would nonetheless be classifiable as "ecological" and "emphatic" kinds of information, respectively. The former refers to information "correspond[ing] to how information exists in the real, physical environment" (Jørgensen 2013, 79), while the latter refers to information "represented by way of symbols, color filters and other features that are not represented in a verisimilar manner" (Jørgensen 2013, 80). While these terms are potentially helpful for describing game space elements, Jørgensen forgoes the term "game space," instead proposing the term "gameworld" (2013, 1) to refer to a work's combined total of game spaces and interfaces. I avoid this term primarily because of potential confusion with both the term "storyworld" and Kendall Walton's term "game world" (1990, 216; the recipient's realm of imaginative and interpretive activity when engaging with various "props" within representational works) and because Jørgensen's focus on the latter regarding videogames' narrative elements leaves the former somewhat under-elaborated (see also Thon on the "intersubjectively valid" [2016a, 55] comprehension of storyworlds).

4 Ermi and Mäyrä's widely cited "gameplay experience model" (2005, 1) proposes three overlapping dimensions of immersion. The first is "sensory immersion," which refers to the "audiovisual execution" of games and how various technologies may overpower sensory interference from the player's environment, thereby allowing them to become "entirely focused on the game world and its stimuli" (Ermi and Mäyrä 2005, 7). The second dimension is "challenge-based immersion" (based on Csíkszentmihályi's flow), which is often facilitated by a "satisfying balance of [mental and motor-based] challenges and abilities" (Ermi and Mäyrä 2005, 7). The third and final dimension is "imaginative immersion" (Ermi and Mäyrä 2005, 8), which involves the player's absorption regarding a game's story-related elements, including empathizing with characters. Thon (2008) offers a more overtly attention-centered multidimensional model of immersion in videogames, focusing primarily on avatar-based games. Drawing on Ryan's notion of recentering, Thon posits that immersion involves a player shifting their attention to parts of a videogame's structure as they build mental representations or "situation models" (2008, 33) of those structures. Immersion may then involve shifts of attention to (1) explorable game spaces ("spatial immersion" [Thon 2008, 35]), (2) the possibilities for action within game spaces and the various kinds of challenges involved ("ludic immersion" [Thon 2008, 36]), (3) the unfolding of a game's story (including scripted narrative segments as well as relevant ludic events; "narrative immersion" [Thon 2008, 37]), as well as (4) the "social space that is constituted through the communication and social interaction between the players" ("social immersion" [Thon 2008, 39]). Another multidimensional model is provided by Calleja (2011), who, aiming to counter "*monolithic perspectives*" (2011, 33; original emphasis) on immersion, proposes the alternative terms "involvement" (2011, 2) and "incorporation" (2011, 3). Calleja posits six dimensions of involvement: "kinesthetic," "spatial," "shared," "narrative," "affective," and "ludic" (Calleja 2011, 4). These foci of attentional resources operate on a "continuum of attentional intensity" (Calleja 2011, 33) from "conscious" to "internalized" (Calleja 2011, 45). As the internalization of a dimension occurs, it requires incrementally less attentional resources, and the player can attend to multiple dimensions simultaneously. This may then lead to incorporation or instances when "the player incorporates (in the sense of internalizing or assimilating) the game environment into consciousness while simultaneously being incorporated through the avatar" (Calleja 2011, 169). Finally, this incorporation often "slip[s] back into involvement the moment any dimension requires the player's full, conscious attention" (Calleja 2011, 171).

5 Wolf notes that the term "self-reference" refers to "all kinds of internal references or relations within one and the same system" (Wolf 2013a, 191n15), where "system" may refer to an individual work, its genre, its medium, etc. Metareference, in contrast, is "a special case of self-reference that mobilizes the cognitive activity of the recipient: it makes [them] 'reflect' on the text as such, on its textuality, fictionality, etc." (Wolf 2013a, 191n15). Self-referential and metareferential elements might then be aligned with *framings* and *self-reflexive framings*.

6 Although the distinction between narrative and ludic forms of immersion on which I base various of my observations has found some empirical support (see Bell et al. 2018), and while I do occasionally draw on anecdotal support from paratextual sources (e.g., quotes from author figures and reviewers), I have not conducted any empirical research regarding the reception of these works. Nevertheless, the cognitively oriented, frame-based approach adopted, paired with careful analysis, intends to highlight the complex and sometimes conflicting responses invited by the set of (hypothetically) intentionally designed works studied. With these plausible responses and effects elaborated, the proposals made throughout the chapter could be complemented by more social science–oriented methods.

7 The prototypical features of videogames would seem more "capable of 'reproducing' or 'remediating' the multimodal configurations characteristic" (Thon 2016a, 108) of comics than vice versa. For example, works such as *Adventuregame Comics: Leviathan* (Shiga 2022) and the highly metareferential *You Are Deadpool* (Ewing et al. 2018) may introduce a limited form of the rules, goals, and emergent behaviors associated with games, but as Rauscher and colleagues (2021) once more note, these works tend to resemble non-digital games more than videogames. Webcomics, in contrast, appear more capable of remediating the multimodal configurations typical of videogames, to the extent that some comics theorists have suggested that interactivity beyond scrolling and clicking/tapping to summon panels might result in a form of playability (see Boudissa 2016) that threatens to "turn digital comics into games" (Dittmer 2015, n.pag.; see also Groensteen 2013; Batinić 2015), with Thierry Groensteen referring to interactivity as the "Gateway to the Gaming World" (Groensteen 2013, 72). However, it is not necessarily evident that there should be a default connection between interactive comics (e.g., *Nawlz* [Campbell 2009]; *Murat* [Motiv 2014]) and videogames without the former displaying sufficient additional videogame framings (e.g., *Homestuck* [Hussie 2018]).

8 For Juul, a game is prototypically "a rule-based system with a variable and quantifiable outcome, where different outcomes are assigned different values, the player exerts effort in order to influence the outcome, the player feels emotionally attached to the outcome, and the consequences of the activity are negotiable" (2005, 58).

9 Despite significant comics-oriented framings within and surrounding each of the works I discuss, I acknowledge that the frame of "comics" may not be evoked for all players. While it seems implausible that players would not recognize *Storyteller*'s comics-like qualities, *Florence* might be interpreted in terms of the "vignette games" (short, evocative works that typically eschew "traditional videogame objectives, challenges or rewards" [Henderson and Iacovides 2020, 2]) that inspired it, such as Jenny Jiao Hsia's *Morning Makeup Madness* (2016). Despite its often conspicuous lack of text, *Florence* has also been likened to a "visual novel" by some reviewers and commentators (see, e.g., Gibbons 2018; Webster 2017b). These games typically do not "include action elements and [are] therefore able to unfold at a deliberate pace" (Cavallaro 2010, 9). They also often communicate their stories via (and accompany their typically menu-based opportunities for interaction with) "static images of characters, background art, sound effects, (SFX) feedback, and soundtracks" (Camingue et al. 2021, 11). In terms of *Gorogoa*, Backe, for example, writes that although interpreting the work's mechanics in terms of comics is "not wrong," *Gorogoa* also implies a "legacy of physical puzzles, from slide puzzles to Rubik's Cube" (2021, 75; see Game Dev Graz [2019] for a list of Roberts's influences when making *Gorogoa*). Still, I assume that even if players do not perceive the elements I describe as comics-like as such, the works are still likely to be perceived as deviating from existing videogame genre frames to some extent.

10 The status of Mountains is uncertain following accusations aimed at Wong of abusive behavior toward the other members of the studio. Wong publicly apologized in August 2019 (see Batchelor 2019).

11 I focus on the updated version of *Storyteller* (September 2023). Notable departures from the long-awaited launch version include an optional thespian-like narrator, who voices the titles of levels, and a "secret stamp collection" that offers a set of additional goals/rewards (replacing what were initially Steam achievements). Various of the launch version's levels were also modified, and others added, including a set of "devil" levels unlocked after completing the core prompts. These variations on existing levels feature a devil character who changes the behaviors of each scenario. While Benmergui has

described this feature as "meta" (Eggplant 2023, 01:03:23), to my mind, these levels do not amount to a particularly large departure from *Storyteller*'s regular gameplay.

12 At other times, it may be the choice of content itself in the context of videogames that might amount to parody. For example, the level "Godot," featuring the prompt "Tiny and Hatey Wait Forever," gestures toward Beckett's play *Waiting for Godot*, a story decidedly unfit for adaptation in videogame form given that "nothing happens. Nobody comes, nobody goes. It's awful!" (Beckett 1954, 27).

13 As this might already have suggested, *Storyteller*'s various possibilities in terms of solutions are not neutral. This level could thus be considered an example of what Frasca calls "simulation rhetoric" (Frasca 2003, 225; see also Bogost [2007, 3] on "procedural rhetoric"), which refers to the notion that games convey ideology through adding or omitting various rules. That said, a broader consideration of identity representation in *Storyteller* is beyond the scope of this chapter.

14 *Storyteller*'s interface is stylized as an ornately decorated fairy tale storybook featuring woodcut-like illustrations. The initial and concluding interface features might imply that the player's various actions correspond in some way to events within a (minimally represented) storyworld. For example, once the player completes the challenges, they reach a "ceremony" screen, where they must drag a crown onto a pedestal. This triggers an animation during which the shadow of the crown emerges on the page, metareferentially implying the player themselves is being crowned. These framings could indicate that the player controls an unseen character manipulating a magical artifact within a storyworld and that their various machinations on a two-dimensional plane (via clicking, dragging, swapping, etc.) may represent the creativity of the unseen character filling the book. Still, not only is the player's presence not evoked in narrative terms throughout, but the book itself appears to be floating in a void of sorts, suggesting that little effort was made to sustain the frame of narrative outside of the individual levels.

Works Cited

Aarseth, Espen J. 1997. *Cybertext: Perspectives on Ergodic Literature*. Baltimore: Johns Hopkins University Press.

Aggleton, Jen. 2019. "Defining Digital Comics: A British Library Perspective." *Journal of Graphic Novels and Comics* 10 (4): 393–409.

Alber, Jan. 2016. *Unnatural Narrative: Impossible Worlds in Fiction and Drama*. Lincoln: University of Nebraska Press.

All You Can Eat. 2017. Gamechuck. Microsoft Windows.

Backe, Hans-Joachim. 2021. "Game-Comics and Comic-Games: Against the Concept of Hybrids." In *Comics and Videogames: From Hybrid Medialities to Transmedia Expansions*, edited by Andreas Rauscher, Daniel Stein, and Jan-Noël Thon, 60–83. New York: Routledge.

Backe, Hans-Joachim. 2022. "Who Controls the Speech Bubbles? Reflecting on Agency in Comic-Games." In *Comics and Agency*, edited by Vanessa Ossa, Jan-Noël Thon, and Lukas R. A. Wilde, 283–299. Berlin: De Gruyter.

Backe, Hans-Joachim, and Jan-Noël Thon. 2019. "Playing with Identity Authors, Narrators, Avatars, and Players in *The Stanley Parable* and *The Beginner's Guide*." *DIEGESIS: Interdisciplinary E-Journal for Narrative Research* 8 (2): 1–25.

Baetens, Jan. 2011. "Abstraction in Comics." *SubStance* 40 (1): 94–113.

Bal, Mieke. 2002. *Travelling Concepts in the Humanities: A Rough Guide*. Toronto: University of Toronto Press.

Batchelor, James. 2019. "Ken Wong Apologises Following Accounts of Abuse from Former Employee." *GamesIndustry.biz*, August 29, 2019. www.gamesindustry.biz/ken-wong-apologises-following-complaints-of-abuse-from-former-employee.

Bateson, Gregory. 1972. *Steps to an Ecology of Mind: Collected Essays in Anthropology, Psychiatry, Evolution, and Epistemology*. New York: Ballantine Books.

Batinić, Josip. 2016. "'Enhanced Webcomics': An Exploration of the Hybrid Form of Comics on the Digital Medium." *Image [&] Narrative* 17 (5): 80–91.

Beckett, Samuel. 1954. *Waiting for Godot: A Tragicomedy in Two Acts*. New York: Grove Press.

Beineke, Colin. 2017. "On Comicity." *Inks: The Journal of the Comics Studies Society* 1 (2): 226–253.

Bell, Alice, Astrid Ensslin, Isabelle Van Der Bom, and Jen Smith. 2018. "Immersion in Digital Fiction." *International Journal of Literary Linguistics* 7 (1): 1–22.

Bódi, Bettina. 2023. *Videogames and Agency*. New York: Routledge.

Bódi, Bettina, and Jan-Noël Thon. 2020. "Playing Stories? Narrative-Dramatic Agency in *Disco Elysium* (2019) and *Astroneer* (2019)." *Frontiers of Narrative Studies* 6 (2): 157–190.

Boelmann, Jan M., and Lisa König. 2023. "*Storyteller* als Puzzlegame—Spielend Handlungslogik Verstehen in jüngeren Klassenstufen." *Praxis Deutsch* 298: 14–18.

Bogost, Ian. 2007. *Persuasive Games: The Expressive Power of Videogames*. Cambridge, MA: MIT Press.

Boudissa, Magali. 2016. "Typologie des Bandes Dessinées Numériques." In *Bande Dessinée et Numérique*, edited by Pascal Robert, 79–99. Paris: CNRS Éditions.

Breaking the 4th Wall. 2020. 11Sheep. Android.

Calleja, Gordon. 2011. *In-Game: From Immersion to Incorporation*. Cambridge, MA: MIT Press.

Camingue, Janelynn, Elin Carstensdottir, and Edward F. Melcer. 2021. "What Is a Visual Novel?" In *Proceedings of the ACM on Human-Computer Interaction 5 (CHI PLAY)*, 1–18.

Campbell, Stu. 2008. *Nawlz*. https://web.archive.org/web/20080913153416/http://www.nawlz.com/.

Cavallaro, Dani. 2010. *Anime and the Visual Novel: Narrative Structure, Design and Play at the Crossroads of Animation and Computer Games*. Jefferson: McFarland & Co.

Chan, Stephanie. 2017. "*Gorogoa* Review—A Brief but Beautiful Foray into an Otherworldly Mystery." *VentureBeat*, December 14, 2017. https://venturebeat.com/games/gorogoa-review-a-brief-but-beautiful-foray-into-an-otherworldly-mystery/.

Comix Zone. 1995. Sega Technical Institute/Sega. Sega Genesis.

Csíkszentmihályi, Mihaly. 1975. *Beyond Boredom and Anxiety*. San Francisco: Jossey-Bass Publishers.

Currie, Gregory. 2007. "Both Sides of the Story: Explaining Events in a Narrative." *Philosophical Studies* 135 (1): 49–63.

Currie, Gregory. 2010. *Narratives and Narrators: A Philosophy of Stories*. Oxford: Oxford University Press.

Deterding, Sebastian. 2013. "Modes of Play: A Frame Analytic Account of Video Game Play." PhD thesis, University of Hamburg.

Dittmar, Jakob, F. 2015. "Experiments in Digital Comics: Somewhere between Comics and Multimedia Storytelling." *Comics Forum*, March 14, 2015. https://comicsforum.org/2015/03/14/experiments-in-digital-comics-somewhere-between-comics-and-multimedia-storytelling-by-jakob-f-dittmar/.

A Duck Has an Adventure. 2013. Daniel Merlin Goodbrey/E- merl. https://e-merl.com/stuff/duck.html.

Eggplant. 2023. "113: On Top of the Fires of Hell w/ Daniel Benmergui (*Storyteller*)." *Eggplant*, April 9, 2023. https://eggplant.show/website/113-on-top-of-the-fires-of-hell-w-daniel-benmergui-storyteller.

The Empty Kingdom. 2014. Daniel Merlin Goodbrey/E-merl. www.e-merl.com/kingdom.html.

Ensslin, Astrid. 2013. "Playing with Rather Than by the Rules: Metaludicity, Allusive Fallacy, and Illusory Agency in *The Path*." In *Analyzing Digital Fiction*, edited by Alice Bell, Astrid Ensslin, and Hans Rustad, 75–93. New York: Routledge.

Ensslin, Astrid, and Alice Bell. 2021. *Digital Fiction and the Unnatural: Transmedial Narrative Theory, Method, and Analysis*. Columbus: Ohio State University Press.

Ermi, Laura, and Frans Mäyrä. 2005. "Fundamental Components of the Gameplay Experience: Analysing Immersion." In *Proceedings of DiGRA 2005: Changing Views—Worlds in Play*, 1–14.

Ewing, Al, Salva Espin, and Paco Diaz. 2018. *You Are Deadpool*. New York: Marvel Comics.

Faulkner, Jason. 2017. "*Gorogoa* Review—Short Visual Sensation." *Game Revolution*, December 18, 2017. www.gamerevolution.com/review/360371-gorogoa-review-short-visual-sensation.

Fernández-Vara, Clara. 2009. "The Tribulations of Adventure Games: Integrating Story into Simulation through Performance." PhD thesis, Georgia Institute of Technology.

Fernández-Vara, Clara. 2014. "Adventure." In *The Routledge Companion to Video Game Studies*, edited by Mark J.P. Wolf and Bernard Perron, 232–240. New York: Routledge.

Fest, Bradley J. 2016. "Metaproceduralism: *The Stanley Parable* and the Legacies of Postmodern Metafiction." *Wide Screen* 6 (1): 1–23.

Florence. 2018. Mountains/Annapurna Interactive. Android.

Framed. 2014. Loveshack Entertainment/Noodlecake Studios. Android.

Framed 2. 2017. Loveshack Entertainment/Noodlecake Studios. Android.

Frasca, Gonzalo. 2003. "Simulation versus Narrative: Introduction to Ludology." In *The Video Game Theory Reader*, edited by Mark J.P. Wolf and Bernard Perron, 221–235. New York: Routledge.

Frow, John. 2006. *Genre*. London: Routledge.

Game Dev Graz. 2019. "The Making of *Gorogoa*—Jason Roberts @ TU Graz." *YouTube*, June 3, 2019. www.youtube.com/watch?v=gRbFZm8ZvcM.

GDC. 2018. "*Gorogoa*: The Design of a Cosmic Acrostic." *YouTube*, April 30, 2018. www.youtube.com/watch?v=rZrGoUhcSNo.

Gibbons, Brodie. 2018. "*Florence* Review—A Love Letter to Love." *Press Start*, February 16, 2018. https://press-start.com.au/reviews/tech/2018/02/16/florence-review-love-letter-love/.

Goffman, Erving. 1986. *Frame Analysis: An Essay on the Organization of Experience*. Boston: Northeastern University Press.

Goodbrey, Daniel Merlin. 2017. "The Impact of Digital Mediation and Hybridisation on the Form of Comics." PhD thesis, University of Hertfordshire.

Goodbrey, Daniel Merlin. 2021. "Game Comics: Theory and Design." In *Comics and Videogames: From Hybrid Medialities to Transmedia Expansions*, edited by Andreas Rauscher, Daniel Stein, and Jan-Noël Thon, 45–59. New York: Routledge.

Gorogoa. 2017. Jason Roberts/Annapurna Interactive. Microsoft Windows.

Gravity Rush. 2012. Japan Studio/Sony. PlayStation Vita.

Groensteen, Thierry. 2013. *Comics and Narration*. Jackson: University Press of Mississippi.

Henderson, Thryn, and Jo Iacovides. 2020. "'It's Just Part of Being a Person'—Sincerity, Support & Self Expression in Vignette Games." In *Proceedings of DiGRA 2020: Play Everywhere*, 1–4.

Herman, David. 2002. *Story Logic: Problems and Possibilities of Narrative*. Lincoln: University of Nebraska Press.

HiFi Rush. 2023. Tango Gameworks/Bethesda Softworks. Microsoft Windows.

Hussie, Andrew. 2018. *Homestuck*. www.homestuck.com/story.

Hutcheon, Linda. 1994. *Irony's Edge: The Theory and Politics of Irony*. London: Routledge.

Hutcheon, Linda. 2000. *A Theory of Parody: The Teachings of Twentieth-Century Art Forms*. Urbana: University of Illinois Press.

Icarus Needs. 2013. Daniel Merlin Goodbrey/E-merl. www.e-merl.com/icneeds.html.

IGDA Taiwan. 2018. "[2018 TGDF] Jason Roberts—*Gorogoa*: Weaving a Multidimensional Quilt." *YouTube*, November 14, 2018. www.youtube.com/watch?v=j-Oos6wwjwI.

InsideCreativeGaming. 2021. "PLAY21 Mini Let's Play: *Storyteller* with Daniel Benmergui." *YouTube*, November 8, 2021. www.youtube.com/watch?v=HTXhrqEv9nc.

Järvinen, Aki. 2007. "Games without Frontiers: Theories and Methods for Game Studies and Design." PhD thesis, University of Tampere.

Jahn, Manfred. 1997. "Frames, Preferences, and the Reading of Third-Person Narratives: Towards a Cognitive Narratology." *Poetics Today* 18 (4): 441–468.

Johnson, Jason. 2012. "The Indie Talks: Daniel Benmergui's *Storyteller* Lets You Make Webcomics, Simply by Playing." *Kill Screen*, February 23, 2012. https://killscreen.com/previously/articles/the-indie-talks-daniel-benmerguis-storyteller-lets/.

Jørgensen, Kristine. 2013. *Gameworld Interfaces*. Cambridge, MA: MIT Press.

Juul, Jesper. 2005. *Half-Real: Video Games between Real Rules and Fictional Worlds*. Cambridge, MA: MIT Press.

Juul, Jesper. 2010. *A Casual Revolution: Reinventing Video Games and Their Players*. Cambridge, MA: MIT Press.

Juul, Jesper. 2019. *Handmade Pixels: Independent Video Games and the Quest for Authenticity*. Cambridge, MA: MIT Press.

Kleefeld, Sean. 2020. *Webcomics*. New York: Bloomsbury.

Krampe, Theresa. 2023. "Rewriting Rules, Changing Worlds: Diegetic and Ludic Forms of Metareference in *The Magic Circle*." *Frontiers of Narrative Studies* 9 (1): 137–157.

Krampe, Theresa, Stephanie Lotzow, and Jan-Noël Thon. 2022. "Playful Poetics: Metareferential Interfaces in Recent Indie Games." *Poetics Today* 43 (4): 729–771.

Kress, Gunther R. 2010. *Multimodality: A Social Semiotic Approach to Contemporary Communication*. London: Routledge.

Kuijpers, Moniek M., Frank Hakemulder, Katalin Balint, Miruna Doicaru, and Ed S. Tan. 2017. "Towards a New Understanding of Absorbing Reading Experiences." In *Narrative Absorption*, edited by Frank Hakemulder, Moniek M. Kuijpers, Ed S. Tan, Katalin Bálint, and Miruna M. Doicaru, 29–47. Amsterdam: John Benjamins Publishing Company.

Kukkonen, Karin. 2014. "Web Comics." In *The Johns Hopkins Guide to Digital Media*, edited by Marie-Laure Ryan, Lori Emerson, and Benjamin J. Robertson, 521–524. Baltimore: Johns Hopkins University Press.

Liberated. 2020. Atomic Wolf/Walkabout. Microsoft Windows.

Lipkin, Nadav. 2013. "Examining Indie's Independence: The Meaning of 'Indie' Games, the Politics of Production, and Mainstream Co-Optation." *Loading…: The Journal of the Canadian Game Studies Association* 7 (11): 8–24.

MadWorld. 2009. Platinum Games/Sega. Nintendo Wii.

Max Payne. 2001. Remedy Entertainment/Gathering of Developers. Microsoft Windows.

Molotiu, Andrei, ed. 2009. *Abstract Comics: The Anthology: 1967–2009*. Seattle: Fantagraphics.

Morning Makeup Madness. 2016. Jenny Jiao Hsia/*QDork*. https://q_dork.itch.io/morning-makeup-madness.

Motiv. 2014. *Murat*. https://web.archive.org/web/20140702144518/http://nonstopbar.com/.

Murray, Janet. 1997. *Hamlet on the Holodeck: The Future of Narrative in Cyberspace*. New York: The Free Press.

Myst. 1993. Cyan, Inc./Broderbund. Microsoft Windows.

Ng, Carmen. 2021. "Interfacing Comics and Games A Socio-Affective Multimodal Approach." In *Comics and Videogames: From Hybrid Medialities to Transmedia Expansions*, edited by Andreas Rauscher, Daniel Stein, and Jan-Noël Thon, 29–44. New York: Routledge.

Nietzsche, Friedrich. 2001. *The Gay Science: With a Prelude in German Rhymes and an Appendix of Songs*. Cambridge: Cambridge University Press.

Rajewsky, Irina. 2010. "Border Talks: The Problematic Status of Media Borders in the Current Debate about Intermediality." In *Media Borders, Multimodality and Intermediality*, edited by Lars Elleström, 51–68. London: Palgrave Macmillan.

Rauscher, Andreas, Daniel Stein, and Jan-Noël Thon. 2021. "Introduction: Comics and Videogames." In *Comics and Videogames: From Hybrid Medialities to Transmedia Expansions*, edited by Andreas Rauscher, Daniel Stein, and Jan-Noël Thon, 1–14. New York: Routledge.

Riversiders Demo. 2023. Hoot Like an Owl. Microsoft Windows.

Romero, Adrienne. 2023. "*Storyteller* Interview: Dev Talks 15-Year Journey for Its Twisted Classic Stories." *Game Rant*, March 25, 2023. https://gamerant.com/storyteller-interview-development-history/.

Rommens, Aarnoud. 2019. "Introduction." In *Abstraction and Comics = Bande Dessinée et Abstraction*, edited by Aarnoud Rommens, Benoît Crucifix, Björn-Olav Dozo, Erwin Dejasse, and Pablo Turnes, 25–61. Brussels/Liège: La Cinquième Couche/Presses Universitaires de Liège.

Ruffino, Paolo. 2013. "Narratives of Independent Production in Video Game Culture." *Loading…: The Journal of the Canadian Game Studies Association* 7 (11): 106–121.

Rumelhart, David E. 1980. "Schemata: The Building Blocks of Cognition." In *Theoretical Issues in Reading Comprehension: Perspectives from Cognitive Psychology, Linguistics, Artificial Intelligence and Education*, edited by Rand J. Spiro, Bertram C. Bruce, and William F. Brewer, 33–58. Hillsdale: Lawrence Erlbaum Associates.

Ryan, Marie-Laure. 2006. *Avatars of Story*. Minneapolis: University of Minnesota Press.

Ryan, Marie-Laure. 2015. *Narrative as Virtual Reality 2: Revisiting Immersion and Interactivity in Literature and Electronic Media*. Baltimore: Johns Hopkins University Press.

Seller, Merlyn. 2018. "Dear Player: *Gorogoa* and the Language of Comics." *Dear Player*, February 10, 2018. www.dearplayer.org/blog/2018/2/10/dear-player-gorogoa-and-the-language-of-comics.

Shiga, Jason. 2022. *Adventuregame Comics 1: Leviathan*. New York: Amulet Books.

Sicart, Miguel. 2008. "Defining Game Mechanics." *Game Studies: The International Journal of Computer Game Research* 8 (2): n.pag.

Sim, Andrea. 2019. "Artist, Art Director & Designer Ken Wong on Immersive Storytelling in the Digital Medium." *Female Singapore*, January 14, 2019. www.femalemag.com.sg/culture/ken-wong-mountains-interview-florence-creative-director/.

Soderman, Braxton. 2021. *Against Flow: Video Games and the Flowing Subject*. Cambridge, MA: MIT Press.

Steam. 2023. "Storyteller." *Steam*, March 23, 2023. https://store.steampowered.com/app/1624540/Storyteller/.

Stoker, Bram. 1897. *Dracula*. London: Archibald Constable & Co.

Storyteller. 2023. Daniel Benmergui/Annapurna Interactive. Microsoft Windows.

Thon, Jan-Noël. 2008. "Immersion Revisited: On the Value of a Contested Concept." In *Extending Experiences: Structure, Analysis and Design of Computer Game Player Experience*, edited by Fernandez Amyris, Olli Tapio Leino, and Hanna Elina Wirman, 29–43. Rovaniemi: Lapland University Press.

Thon, Jan-Noël. 2014. "Mediality." In *The Johns Hopkins Guide to Digital Media*, edited by Marie-Laure Ryan, Lori Emerson, and Benjamin J. Robertson, 334–337. Baltimore: Johns Hopkins University Press.

Thon, Jan-Noël. 2016a. *Transmedial Narratology and Contemporary Media Culture*. Lincoln: University of Nebraska Press.

Thon, Jan-Noël. 2016b. "Narrative Comprehension and Video Game Storyworlds." In *Video Games and the Mind: Essays on Cognition, Affect and Emotion*, edited by Bernard Perron and Felix Schröter, 15–31. Jefferson: McFarland.

Thon, Jan-Noël. 2020. "Analyzing Indie Aesthetics." In *Proceedings of DiGRA 2020: Play Everywhere*, 1–4.

vAPE Escape. 2019. Gamechuck. Microsoft Windows.

Walker, Mort. 2000. *The Lexicon of Comicana*. Lincoln: iUniverse.

Walton, Kendall L. 1990. *Mimesis as Make-Believe: On the Foundations of the Representational Arts*. Cambridge, MA: Harvard University Press.

Wardrip-Fruin, Noah, Michael Mateas, Steven Dow, and Serdar Sali. 2009. "Agency Reconsidered." In *Proceedings of DiGRA 2009: Breaking New Ground: Innovation in Games, Play, Practice and Theory*, 1–9.

Waypoint Radio. 2023. "*Storyteller* Interview, *Redfall*, and More *Counter-Strike*." *Vice*, April 6, 2023. www.vice.com/en/article/ak3ddb/storyteller-interview-redfall-and-more-counter-strike.

Webster, Andrew. 2017a. "This Soothing, Intricate Puzzle Game Will Make You Feel Like a Genius. *The Verge*, December 14, 2017. www.theverge.com/2017/12/14/16774194/gorogoa-game-review-iphone-switch-steam.

Webster, Andrew. 2017b. "*Florence* Is a Game about Love from the Designer behind Monument Valley." *The Verge*, October 24, 2017. www.theverge.com/2017/10/24/16533918/florence-iphone-game-announce-ken-wong-interview.

What Remains of Edith Finch. 2017. Giant Sparrow/Annapurna Interactive. Microsoft Windows.

Wilde, Lukas. 2015. "Distinguishing Mediality: The Problem of Identifying Forms and Features of Digital Comics." *Networking Knowledge: Journal of the MeCCSA Postgraduate Network* 8 (4): 1–14.

Wilson, Craig. 2018. "*Gorogoa*." *Split Screen*, April 8, 2018. https://split-screen.net/gorogoa/.

Witek, Joseph. 2009. "The Arrow and the Grid." In *A Comics Studies Reader*, edited by Jeet Heer and Kent Worcester, 149–156. Jackson: University Press of Mississippi.

The Wolf Among Us. 2013. Telltale Games. Microsoft Windows.

Wolf, Werner. 2006a. "Introduction: Frames, Framings and Framing Borders in Literature and Other Media." In *Framing Borders in Literature and Other Media*, edited by Werner Wolf and Walter Bernhart, 1–40. Amsterdam: Rodopi.

Wolf, Werner. 2006b. "Defamiliarized Initial Framings in Fiction." In *Framing Borders in Literature and Other Media*, edited by Werner Wolf and Walter Bernhart, 295–328. Amsterdam: Rodopi.

Wolf, Werner. 2009. "Metareference across Media: The Concept, Its Transmedial Potentials and Problems, Main Forms and Functions." In *Metareference across Media: Theory and Case Studies*, edited by Werner Wolf, 1–85. Amsterdam: Rodopi.

Wolf, Werner. 2013a. "Aesthetic Illusion as an Effect of Lyric Poetry?" In *Immersion and Distance: Aesthetic Illusion in Literature and Other Media*, edited by Werner Wolf, Walter Bernhart, and Andreas Mahler, 183–233. Amsterdam: Rodopi.

Wolf, Werner. 2013b. "Introduction." In *Immersion and Distance: Aesthetic Illusion in Literature and Other Media*, edited by Werner Wolf, Walter Bernhart, and Andreas Mahler, 1–62. Amsterdam: Rodopi.

Wolf, Werner. 2013c. "Unnatural Metalepsis and Immersion: Necessarily Incompatible?" In *A Poetics of Unnatural Narrative*, edited by Jan Alber, Henrik Skov Nielsen, and Brian Richardson, 113–141. Columbus: Ohio State University Press.

Wolf, Werner. 2014. "Framings of Narrative in Literature and the Pictorial Arts." In *Storyworlds across Media*, edited by Marie-Laure Ryan and Jan-Noël Thon, 126–147. Lincoln: University of Nebraska Press.

XIII. 2003. Ubisoft Paris Studio/Microids. Microsoft Windows.

12 Postdigital Aesthetics in Recent Indie Games

Jan-Noël Thon

Rather than focusing exclusively on metareference in videogames, this chapter concludes the present volume by expanding its theoretical and analytical scope toward what is here conceptualized as the postdigital aesthetics of videogames in general and indie games in particular. To this end, the chapter begins by exploring the concept of the postdigital, heuristically distinguishing four domains of postdigital aesthetics that can be specified as the aesthetic intensification of the digital, the aesthetic transfer from the digital to the nondigital, the aesthetic intensification of the nondigital, and the aesthetic transfer from the nondigital to the digital. This is followed by an explication of what the "aesthetics" in "postdigital aesthetics" refers to, with a particular focus on those medial representations that foreground their own mediality, materiality, and aesthetic form as opposed to their representational content and thus follow the logic of hypermediacy rather than the logic of immediacy. The chapter then turns toward the area of videogames, and more specifically indie games, analyzing different instantiations of the aesthetic intensification of the digital and the aesthetic transfer from the nondigital to the digital in the (highly canonical) indie games Proteus *(2013),* Pony Island *(2016),* Cuphead *(2017), and* What Remains of Edith Finch *(2017).*

Conceptualizing (the Aesthetic Domains of) the Postdigital

The term "postdigital" was coined independently at the turn of the millennium by Cascone (2000), on the one hand, and Pepperell and Punt (2000), on the other. Cascone (2000) takes Negroponte's (1998) observation that the "digital revolution" is over as the starting point for the diagnosis of a specific "'post-digital' aesthetic" that manifests itself as an "aesthetics of failure" in electronic music. According to Cascone, this "aesthetics of failure" should be understood, at least in part, as "a result of the immersive experience of working in environments suffused with digital technology" (2000, 12) in that it incorporates "glitches, bugs, application errors, system crashes, clipping, aliasing, distortion, quantization noise, and even the noise floor of computer sound cards" (2000, 13). While Pepperell and Punt's (2000) exploration of the "postdigital membrane" as a means of overcoming the "binary thinking" they associate with digital technology is considerably more

DOI: 10.4324/9781003538592-12

wide-ranging than Cascone's comparatively narrow approach to the postdigital, the latter has turned out to be rather more influential than the former.[1] Accordingly, the notion of the postdigital and of a specifically postdigital aesthetics initially circulated primarily in the discourse fields of electronic music and media art. It has, however, received increasing academic attention since the 2010s and is now employed not only in artistic and practice-oriented contexts (see, e.g., Bishop et al. 2016; Paul 2016) but also in disciplines and research fields as diverse as sound studies (see, e.g., Ford 2023; Kouvaras 2016), literary studies (see, e.g., Abblitt 2018; Ludovico 2012), theater studies (see, e.g., Causey 2016; Papagiannouli 2022), media studies (see, e.g., Diecke et al. 2022; Murray 2020), and education research (see, e.g., Hayes 2021; Mathier 2023) as an alternative to more established terms such as "digit(al)ization," "mediatization," or "media convergence" (see, e.g., Balbi and Magaudda 2018; Hjarvard 2013; Jensen 2010). Based on the diagnosis of the increasing ubiquity of digital technology in everyday life that can already be observed in Cascone's remark that "[t]he tendrils of digital technology have in some way touched everyone" (2000, 12) as well as in Pepperell and Punt's argument that "the intellectual restrictions of the digital paradigm are now becoming unavoidable" (2000, 2),[2] much of the existing research on the postdigital stresses that "the historical distinction between the digital and the nondigital becomes increasingly blurred" (Berry 2014, 22; Berry and Dieter 2015b, 2; see also, e.g., Arndt et al. 2019; Contreras-Koterbay and Mirocha 2016; Jandrić et al. 2018; Jordan 2020).

The distinction between "the digital" and "the nondigital" that is invoked here evidently does not coincide with the more precise distinction in media theory and philosophy between "digital-in-the-sense-of-discrete" and "analog-in-the-sense-of-continuous" (see, e.g., Fazi 2019; Schröter 2004; but also Frigerio et al. 2013; Maley 2023), instead referring—less precisely, but more compatible with everyday usage—to the presence or absence of "computer technology," broadly conceived (see Cramer 2015; as well as, e.g., Cubitt 2006; Maley 2011). Moreover, the prefix "post" in the term "postdigital"[3] by no means denotes the end of the digital or the disappearance of digital technology—rather, it stresses the increased significance and fine-grained everyday integration of digital technology after the so-called digital revolution, which has led to a decreased saliency of the distinction between digital and nondigital technologies, practices, and artifacts in everyday life. That said, although the blurring of the boundary between digital and nondigital technologies, practices, and artifacts is a common thread throughout existing conceptualizations of the postdigital, these conceptualizations still differ substantially across disciplinary contexts as well as from scholar to scholar—and many contributions to the arguably still evolving research field do indeed seem to position the postdigital as an "umbrella term" or otherwise multilayered concept, and thus more or less systematically distinguish between or at least hint at the existence of distinct dimensions, aspects, or domains of the postdigital.

A good example of this would yet again be Cramer's work on the postdigital, which connects the term not only to a "[d]isenchantment with [the] 'digital'" and a "revival of 'old' media" (2015, 13) but also more generally to "the messy state of media, arts and design *after* their digitization" (2015, 19; original emphasis) that includes "hybrids of 'old' and 'new' media" (2015, 20) as well as "'old' media used like 'new media'" (2015, 21).[4] Yet, Cramer also emphasizes the critical potential of the postdigital, suggesting that "[w]e could metaphorically describe post-digital cultures as postcolonial practices in a communications world taken over by a military–industrial complex" (2015, 24). Similarly, Taffel distinguishes between five "applications of the trope of postdigitality, which refer to (1) a return of the analogue or move beyond discrete samples, (2) the revelation of seams and artifices within the otherwise smooth spaces of the digital, (3) the historical phase of technocultural development occurring after the digital revolution, (4) the rematerialization of digital technology and its integration into urban environments and (5) a way of escaping the fetishization of newness and upgrade culture" (2016, 325). Indeed, the term's iridescence would seem to be part of the appeal of the postdigital, not least because it allows for the integration of shifting theoretical positions with comparative ease (see, e.g., how the "postdigital" is conceptualized differently in Cascone 2000 and in Cascone and Jandrić 2021, or in Cramer 2015 and in Cramer and Jandrić 2021).[5]

For our present purpose, however, it mainly seems important not only to note that the ubiquity of digital technology has shifted, blurred, or dissolved the border between the digital and the nondigital (as well as between "being online" and "being offline"[6]) but also to ask which new(ish) practices, artifacts, and experiences such a shift, blurring, or dissolution of these established borders has led to. In order to articulate the resulting domains of the postdigital more precisely, I will follow Jordan's recent work on postdigital storytelling, though my focus here is more on the aesthetic than on the narrative aspects of these domains.[7] Jordan notes, first, "that the postdigital is a 'coming together,' a hybridisation of both the digital and the non-digital domains, and a denial of any implicit 'disjuncture' [...] in how we experience them"; second, "that this 'coming together' or hybridisation has two vectors: the movement of the non-digital to the digital and the digital to the non-digital" and that, therefore, "at the heart of the postdigital lies a more open and fluid negotiation between the digital and the non-digital"; third, that, "in this revised configuration of postdigitality, the postdigital operates from two states or positions: within or across the digital/non-digital nexus"; fourth, "that regardless of state or position (within or across the domains), the postdigital remains the dominant modality"; and, fifth, "that the non-digital domain is subordinate to the digital domain" (2020, 63). This is admittedly still quite abstract and Jordan himself does not offer particularly illuminating examples for everything this rather inclusive "definition" of the postdigital hints at, but it nevertheless provides a good starting point for understanding the latter's salient domains.

Drawing on the first three elements of Jordan's conceptualization of the postdigital in particular,[8] I would argue that a comprehensively conceptualized postdigital *aesthetics* can similarly be observed in four domains of the postdigital that are at least heuristically distinguishable from one another. First, the term "postdigital aesthetics" can refer to an aesthetic intensification of the digital that is already at the center of Cascone's (2000) influential conceptualization of postdigital aesthetics as an "aesthetics of failure" in electronic music, though both "postdigital aesthetics" and "aesthetics of failure" certainly expand well beyond primarily auditive media forms (see also, e.g., Betancourt 2017; Kane 2019; Menkman 2011 for further explorations of what is often discussed in terms of "glitch aesthetics" in visual and audiovisual media forms as well).[9] Second, it can refer to an aesthetic transfer from the digital to the nondigital that is, for example, often discussed with reference to James Bridle's (2011; 2012; 2013) notion of a "new aesthetic," and which includes the (re)production of recognizably "digital" patterns, designs, and surfaces in (supposedly) nondigital contexts (see also, e.g., several contributions in Berry and Dieter 2015a; as well as Contreras-Koterbay and Mirocha 2016; Hodgson 2019 for proposals to connect the "new aesthetic" to the concept of the postdigital).[10] Third, it can refer to an aesthetic intensification of the nondigital that would, for example, include the (considered) prioritization of nondigital technologies, practices, and artifacts in contexts in which digital technologies, practices, and artifacts would be more readily available (see, once more, Cramer 2015; as well as, e.g., various contributions in Wolf 2019).[11] Fourth and finally, it can refer to an aesthetic transfer from the nondigital to the digital that entails various ways in which digital aesthetic objects, medial artifacts, or, more specifically, medial representations across media forms may evoke, simulate, or otherwise recreate the conventionally recognizable aesthetics of nondigital media forms (see, e.g., Bolter and Grusin 1996; 1999 on "remediation"; Rajewsky 2005; 2010 on "intermedial references"; and Schröter 2019; 2023 on "transmaterialization").[12]

Conceptualizing Postdigital Aesthetics in Recent Indie Games

Having tentatively delineated the domains of *postdigital* aesthetics that I would describe as the aesthetic intensification of the digital, the aesthetic transfer from the digital to the nondigital, the aesthetic intensification of the nondigital, and the aesthetic transfer from the nondigital to the digital, I would also like to unpack in slightly more detail the conceptualization of *aesthetics* that underlies my approach. First, I should note that I am not primarily concerned with aesthetic judgments (or with the concept of art), nor with aesthetic properties such as beauty (or ugliness), though the analysis of postdigital aesthetics will arguably still need to focus on (particular) "aesthetically relevant properties" (Nanay 2016, 67) that make a difference with regard to aesthetic perception, aesthetic experience, or aesthetic appreciation.[13] Second, while I would consider aesthetic perception to be at the center of any appropriately "nonnormative" conceptualization of aesthetics, I do not suggest to conflate aesthetics with *aisthesis* (or aisthetics).[14] Rather, I would want to maintain a distinction between aesthetic and nonaesthetic (or functional, or pragmatic) perception that might, for example, be specified via the former's "self-referentiality" or "sensing self-awareness" that ties "[t]he special presence of the *object* of perception [...] to a special presence of the *exercise* of this perception" (Seel 2005, 31; original emphases).[15] Third, despite understanding aesthetics as a perceptual (or, more broadly, experiential) category, I am primarily concerned with the aesthetic form of medial artifacts to which a postdigital aesthetics can be attributed, and which broadly refers to the external *Gestalt* of such artifacts that is accessible to perception as a result of a "particular way of manipulating the materials [...] of its medium" (Eldridge 1985, 313) as opposed to their representational content.[16] Fourth and finally, since medial artifacts instigating aesthetic perception are made (at least partially) by humans (although aesthetic objects that are *not* artifacts do of course also possess an aesthetic form and can instigate aesthetic perception), aesthetic practice(s) as the "localized practices of artefactual construction" (Corner 2019, 108) that have brought the medial artifacts in question into existence would also need to be taken into account.[17] So, while my analytical focus is on postdigital aesthetics as a set of (particular) "aesthetically relevant properties" (Nanay 2016, 65) that can be attributed to (elements of) the aesthetic form of various medial artifacts, most if not all of which can be further specified as medial representations,[18] (postdigital) aesthetic forms are always connected to the (postdigital) aesthetic practices that these medial artifacts or medial representations are based on as well as to the (postdigital) aesthetic experiences that they afford their various recipients (and which will usually entail, but arguably cannot be reduced to aesthetic perception).

Against the background of the comparatively comprehensive conceptualization of postdigital aesthetics presented thus far, however, I would like to stress yet again that I am primarily concerned with a specific kind of medial representations here, namely those medial representations that foreground their own mediality, materiality, and aesthetic form as opposed to their representational content. This does not mean that medial representations not foregrounding their own mediality and materiality in an immediately noticeable way have no aesthetic form or cannot instigate aesthetic perception, but I would still maintain that there is a connection between the "sensing self-awareness" (Seel 2005, 31) of aesthetic perception and the self-referentiality of medial representations that foreground their own mediality, materiality, and aesthetic form. In line with the overall focus of the present volume, we could also describe the latter as a kind of metareference *sensu* Wolf, who conceptualizes the term as referring to "a special, transmedial form of usually non-accidental self-reference [...], which can extend [...] to the entire system of the media" and will at least potentially elicit a "corresponding 'meta-awareness' [...] in the recipient, who thus becomes conscious of both the medial [...] status of the work under consideration and the fact that media-related phenomena are at issue" (2009, 31).[19] Clearly, then, the distinction between the aesthetic form of medial representations and their representational content as well as the "self-referential" or "metareferential" foregrounding of the former can be specified further in various different ways.[20] One particularly influential conceptualization of this kind of foregrounding has been developed by J. David Bolter and Richard Grusin (1996; 1999), who not only argue, following Marshall McLuhan (1964), that so-called new media remediate the "content" and "form" of older media in various ways, but who also postulate a "double logic of remediation" (Bolter and Grusin 1999, 31), which amongst other things allows us to locate concrete medial representations between the poles of transparent "immediacy" and opaque "hypermediacy." While the term "immediacy" broadly refers to the deemphasizing of the aesthetic form of a medial representation compared to its representational content that "either [...] erase[s] or [...] render[s] automatic the act of representation" (Bolter and Grusin 1999, 33) and is often explained using the metaphor of a transparent window, the term "hypermediacy" refers to medial representations that foreground "acts of representation and mak[e] them visible," "multipl[y] the signs of mediation" (Bolter and Grusin 1999, 34), and thus draw our attention to their mediality, materiality, and aesthetic form. An interplay of transparent immediacy and opaque hypermediacy can be observed in very different medial representations across conventionally distinct media forms, but, as noted above, I would suggest that medial representations which emphasize the "logic of hypermediacy" more strongly than the "logic of immediacy" are particularly interesting for the question of postdigital aesthetics—and perhaps also tend to more readily instigate aesthetic as opposed to "merely" nonaesthetic, functional, or pragmatic processes of perception in their recipients.

Returning to the question of postdigital aesthetics, we can further observe that medial representations whose aesthetic form emphasizes the logic of opaque hypermediacy as opposed to the logic of transparent immediacy and, therefore, at least tend to privilege aesthetic as opposed to "merely" nonaesthetic, functional, or pragmatic perception can be found in a broad range of conventionally distinct media forms, including (digital as well as nondigital) literary texts, comics, animation, photography, films, series, and games.[21] Although other avenues of inquiry are certainly available, then, I would like to use the remainder of the present chapter to focus on the area of videogames, and more specifically on so-called indie games, which are usually produced by comparatively small teams of developers and distributed independently of large publishers.[22] Admittedly, the "independence" of indie games is yet another complex affair, but there is a broad consensus that at least *some* indie game developers use the creative control that tends to come with independently financing and publishing a videogame in order to make comparatively unusual aesthetic choices (when compared to the default aesthetics of mainstream videogames, that is), some (though not all) of which may result in what I would describe as postdigital aesthetics.[23] Despite a broad consensus that the aesthetic form of videogames in general and indie games in particular cannot be reduced to their audiovisual design,[24] the latter still tends to be foregrounded here, with scholars such as Garda and Grabarczyk (2016) focusing on nostalgic "retro style" as a core element of what players tend to recognize as a decidedly "indie" aesthetics and Juul developing the concept of a distinctly "independent style" as referring to "a representation of a representation" that "uses contemporary technology to emulate low-tech and usually cheap graphical materials and visual styles" (2019, 38; see also Juul 2014). Even without having to follow Juul in his assessment of these remediated aesthetic forms as "cheap" or indeed in his related argument that the use of "independent style" signals "small teams, authenticity, and honesty" (2019, 38),[25] it seems clear that the examples Juul gives of indie games using an "independent style," including early ones such as *And Yet It Moves* (2009), *Crayon Physics Deluxe* (2009), *VVVVVV* (2010), and *Fez* (2012), are located either in the domain of postdigital aesthetics that I would describe as the aesthetic intensification of the digital or in the domain of postdigital aesthetics that I would describe as the aesthetic transfer from the nondigital to the digital. While both the aesthetic intensification of the nondigital and the aesthetic transfer from the digital to the nondigital can perhaps also be observed in the postdigital aesthetics of nondigital games[26] such as *Pax Pamir: Second Edition* (2019) or *The Shivers* (2022), on the one hand, and *Pixel Tactics Deluxe* (2015) or *To the Death!* (2019), on the other, the following will thus primarily focus on the aesthetic intensification of the digital and the aesthetic transfer from the nondigital to the digital as two salient domains of postdigital aesthetics that can commonly be observed in indie games as a particularly "postdigital" subset of videogames. To this end, I will explore in more detail different instantiations of the aesthetic intensification of the digital and the aesthetic transfer from the nondigital to the digital in the (highly canonical) indie games *Proteus* (2013), *Pony Island* (2016), *Cuphead* (2017), and *What Remains of Edith Finch* (2017).

Postdigital Aesthetics as the Aesthetic Intensification of the Digital in *Proteus*

As noted above, the domain of postdigital aesthetics that I would describe as the aesthetic intensification of the digital includes a range of aesthetic practices that evoke, simulate, or remediate the mediality and materiality of digital media forms. Despite their different developers, game mechanics, and genre affiliations, the audiovisual aesthetics of indie games such as *Minecraft* (2011), *Terraria* (2011), *To the Moon* (2011), *Evoland* (2013), *The Escapists* (2015), *Undertale* (2015), *Stardew Valley* (2016), *Thimbleweed Park* (2017), *Celeste* (2018), *Blasphemous* (2019), *ScourgeBringer* (2020), or *Sea of Stars* (2023) are all saliently characterized by processes of remediation that remediate the aesthetics of older videogames and, in doing so, follow the logic of opaque hypermediacy rather than that of transparent immediacy. Evidently, the processes of remediation at play here do not usually involve a particularly faithful or complete recreation, emulation, or simulation of the audiovisual aesthetics of videogames from the 1970s, 1980s, or 1990s, and thus tend not to actually employ "low-resolution" graphics, sound effects, or music. Yet, they still do remediate certain aspects of what is perhaps best described as an "imagined […] video game aesthetics" (Braguinski 2018, 106), often making use of "pixelated" graphics and an overall sound design that imitates characteristics of "archetypal 8-bit-era video game music," such as "coarse tuning, primitive synthesis, few voices, inflexible note lengths, mechanical performance, and a lot of repetition" (Braguinski 2018, 109).[27] Even if these aesthetic practices and their resulting aesthetic forms are now so thoroughly conventionalized in the area of indie games that the extent to which they may still generate pronounced "hypermediacy effects" (or, indeed, afford the kind of "meta-awareness" [Wolf 2009, 31] that is usually considered to be a core element of metareference) might seem questionable, some of these indie games arguably foreground the respective processes of remediation more than others. Here, I want to focus on *Proteus*, an early walking simulator[28] that represents the changing seasons on a (partially) procedurally generated island[29] using rather striking "pixelated" graphics with a matching trance-like soundtrack (see also, e.g., Bohunicky and Milligan 2019; Golding 2013; Montembeault and Deslongchamps-Gagnon 2019; Muscat et al. 2016; O'Hara 2020; Vella 2013; Zimmerman and Huberts 2019 for a selection of existing research on *Proteus*).

Figure 12.1 The island that is visible in the distance at the beginning of *Proteus* (2013).

Despite being a comparatively early example of the decidedly "indie" genre of the walking simulator that pointedly subverts the generic conventions of the first-person shooter, *Proteus* already offers notably genre-specific gameplay. Once the player has clicked on the island-shaped silhouette depicted in the starting menu, each playthrough begins with the unnamed player-controlled character opening their eyes in what appears to be an ocean that is strikingly empty except for an island barely visible in the distance (see Figure 12.1). What initially appear to be the default WASD controls[30] are then used to move the player-controlled character through the three-dimensional game spaces,[31] though it is entirely possible (if perhaps not particularly interesting or satisfying) to move them away rather than toward the island, since they cannot drown and their movement is indeed represented less as swimming (or walking) and more as a slow kind of floating just above the ground (or the waves).[32] Despite the fact that *Proteus* represents its game spaces using a subjective point of view, with the position of the "virtual camera" closely corresponding to the spatial position of the player-controlled character, and the subjectivity of the resulting perspective being emphasized further by the opening and closing eyelids that mark the beginning and the ending of each playthrough (see also, e.g., Beil 2010; 2017; Thon 2009; 2016b, 221–326, on modes and markers of subjective representation in videogames and other media forms), *Proteus*'s gameplay is thus clearly very different from that of a first-person shooter. Still, some players may well be surprised that pressing the Shift or Space keys, respectively, does not result in the player-controlled character running or jumping (which would have been the expectation regarding the set of in-game actions and default key mappings for a first-person shooter in 2013), but rather slows down their already slow movement even further and lowers the point from which the game spaces are represented, suggesting that the player-controlled character sits down. At least initially, the players are also not given any specific game goals to fulfill, although having the player-controlled character move toward the island rather than away from it seems to be the expected choice here and the players will need to find a specific place marked by a stone circle in order to cycle through the seasons (from the initial spring via summer and fall to winter) and allow the player-controlled character to ascend toward heaven once winter has passed (see Figure 12.2).[33]

In any case, *Proteus*'s postdigital aesthetics do not predominantly emerge from its (reduced) game mechanics and (lack of) game goals. Instead, what makes *Proteus* noteworthy in the context of the present chapter is its unusual audiovisual aesthetics. Indeed, *Proteus*'s combination of "pixelated" graphics with flat colors that change from the light shades of green, yellow, brown, and pink that dominate the island during spring and summer (see Figure 12.3) to darker shades of green, orange, brown, and purple during fall (see Figure 12.4), before a blanket of white snow covers everything apart from a few buildings, stones, statues, and leafless trees during winter (in addition to color changes due to different weather conditions and different lighting conditions during the day/night cycle within each season) is certainly unconventional not only for the genre of the walking simulator but also for the broader set of indie games that employ a version of the aforementioned "pixelated" graphics. The resulting "pixelated abstract scenery" (Montembeault and Deslongchamps-Gagnon 2019, 10) may indeed "look[] like Kandinsky with a copy of MS Paint" (Golding 2013, n.pag.) or feel "like stepping into an installation of the artist James Turrell" (Zimmerman and Huberts 2019, 42) to some players, but I would maintain that, while its use of flat colors arguably does make *Proteus* appear more like a series of (digital) paintings than a traditional three-dimensional CGI environment, its visual aesthetics will still primarily be read as a remediation of the materiality, mediality, and aesthetic form of older videogames rather than that of nondigital artworks, let alone the decidedly nonrepresentational paintings

Figure 12.2 The stone circle that triggers a changing of the seasons in *Proteus* (2013).

Figure 12.3 Light shades of green, yellow, brown, and pink during spring (reproduced in gray scale).

Figure 12.4 Darker shades of green, orange, brown, and purple during fall (reproduced in gray scale).

of Wassily Kandinsky.[34] This visual dimension of the aesthetic intensification of the digital is also highlighted in the surrounding paratexts, with early critics already having noted that *Proteus*'s "visuals are [...] seemingly rendered via 70s computer technology" (Stuart 2013, n.pag.) and that its "art style looks like it'd be more at home inside a dusty Atari 2600 cartridge" (Grayson 2013, n.pag.; see also, e.g., Montfort and Bogost 2009 on the specific technological affordances of the

Atari 2600/Atari VCS), yet I would further like to emphasize here that *Proteus*'s aesthetic intensification of the digital saliently expands to its auditive dimension, resulting in a genuinely *audio*visual postdigital aesthetics (which also gels well with the fact that *Proteus* was co-designed by the game designer Ed Key and the composer David Kanaga, both of whom are credited in the title menu).

Indeed, early critics have consistently noted the foregrounded "digital qualities" of *Proteus*'s soundscape, highlighting the "slightly unsettling bleeps and bloops" (Grayson 2013, n.pag.) that make it "sound[] as though an outdated electronic synthesizer has created it" (Gamespot Staff 2013, n.pag.), or writing rather more evocatively about the presence of "an electronic riff," "a digitized clarinet," or a "frenzied cyber-fiddle" (Senior 2013, n.pag.). Beyond the distinctly "digital" qualities of much of *Proteus*'s soundscape, however, the way that the latter is generated is also particularly interesting. Put in a nutshell, most if not all sounds and sequences of sounds that *Proteus*'s players will hear in any given playthrough are connected to the objects within the game spaces, leading to a "procedurally generated soundtrack" that is arranged anew every time *Proteus* is played out of "a large vocabulary of [predefined; JNT] short musical gestures and atmospheric synthesizer textures" (O'Hara 2020, 37–38). Even if it would thus be possible to describe *Proteus*'s sound design as exclusively focusing on sound effects rather than music,[35] both the (sequences of) sounds that are connected to the individual objects within the procedurally generated game spaces and the overall soundscape that results from their spatial arrangement and proximity to the player-controlled character exploring the island (which allows us to describe *Proteus*'s soundscape not only as "diegetic" rather than "nondiegetic" but also as "nonlinear" rather than "linear" and as "dynamic" [i.e., "adaptive" or even "interactive"] rather than "nondynamic" [see Collins 2008, 125–127]) consistently have musical qualities attributed to them in the existing research and the surrounding paratexts. In what remains a particularly detailed analysis of its musical qualities,[36] O'Hara highlights that "*Proteus* mixes traditional sound effects (waves, wind, insects, birds) with musical imitations of environmental and animal sounds" (2020, 42), and Montembeault and Deslongchamps-Gagnon even describe it as an "acoustic safari" that encourages players "to hunt down new musical arrangements to contemplate" (2019, 11). *Proteus* thus appears as a particularly instructive example of an indie game located in the domain of postdigital aesthetics that I would describe as the aesthetic intensification of the digital. That said, I would also like to stress again that the latter should not be conceptualized as being limited to the use of "pixelated" graphics or supposedly 8-bit sound and music.

Postdigital Aesthetics as the Aesthetic Intensification of the Digital in *Pony Island*

Indeed, while the use of supposedly "low-resolution" audiovisual aesthetics has become widespread, indie games such as *Imscared: A Pixelated Nightmare* (2016), *David.* (2014), *Axiom Verge* (2015), *The Magic Circle* (2015), *Archimedes* (2016), *Doki Doki Literature Club!* (2017), *The Hex* (2018), *Break the Game* (2019), *The*

Cursèd Pickle of Shireton (2020), *There Is No Game: Wrong Dimension* (2020), *Inscryption* (2021), or indeed *Glitched* (forthcoming) take the aesthetic intensification of the digital even further in prominently remediating a range of visual and auditory "glitches," thereby yet more strongly foregrounding their own aesthetic form. Here, I want to explore these aesthetic practices using the example of *Pony Island*, a narratively complex and highly metareferential indie game[37] that not only follows the logic of hypermediacy in remediating a range of different "imagined aesthetics" of older videogames but also makes extensive use of visual and auditory "glitches" (see also, e.g., Barkman 2021; Edrei 2018; Gass 2024; Krampe et al. 2022; Schlarb 2019; Schoppmeier 2018; Waszkiewicz 2024, 65–69, for a selection of existing research on *Pony Island*).

Pony Island initially offers its players a fairly conventional, simple, and colorful title menu within which they can start a "New Game," enter an overlay menu entitled "Options," or read the "Credits," yet its decidedly postdigital aesthetics are foregrounded immediately after the players click on the "New Game" button. The colorful design of the initial title menu (which is also used for *Pony Island*'s pause menu) is replaced by a monochromatic title menu that is surrounded by the concave brown frame of "an old transistor screen" (Schlarb 2019, 206) and accompanied by a low humming noise, suggesting that *Pony Island* remediates the mediality and materiality of a considerably older videogame as well as diegetizing the system on which that videogame runs at least to some extent, which additionally foregrounds a notable "medial difference" between the actual videogame *Pony Island* and the fictional videogame Pony Island.[38] This is also emphasized by *Pony Island*'s creator Daniel Mullins, who notes that he "was most happy with [...] the mood" resulting from the combination of "the low, relentless humming of the machine with the gently shaking CRT-style graphics" (Daniel Mullins in Ruhland 2016, n.pag.), as well as by various early critics (see, e.g., Coleman 2016; Morrison 2016; Shea 2017; Walker 2016). No less interestingly, however, the monochromatic title menu turns out to be quite dysfunctional, with any attempt to click on the "Start Game" or "Credits" buttons resulting in nothing but a brief representation of manufactured "glitches" that manifest as visual and auditive "noise," and repeated clicking on the "Start Game" button even changing it to an "<ERROR>" button. Clicking on the "Options & Help" button reveals the following submenu to be thoroughly broken as well, thereby also presenting the first of many "hacking-themed" puzzle segments to the players (or, rather, the barely diegetized player-controlled character), who may proceed to "fix" the title menu by "messing around" in the (supposed) backend of the fictional Pony Island (see Figure 12.5). Alas, "fixing" the monochromatic title menu then prompts the irritated voice of an entity that initially "appears to be the programmer of Pony Island" (Schoppmeier 2018, 437) to address the player-controlled character, giving them access to the first of many side-scrolling segments in which they take control of one of the eponymous ponies (which later turn out to be souls trapped in limbo).

Having successfully completed this strikingly nonchallenging "pony-themed" side-scrolling segment (and having been showered with wholly undeserved praise after each of the rather short levels), the player-controlled character is asked to

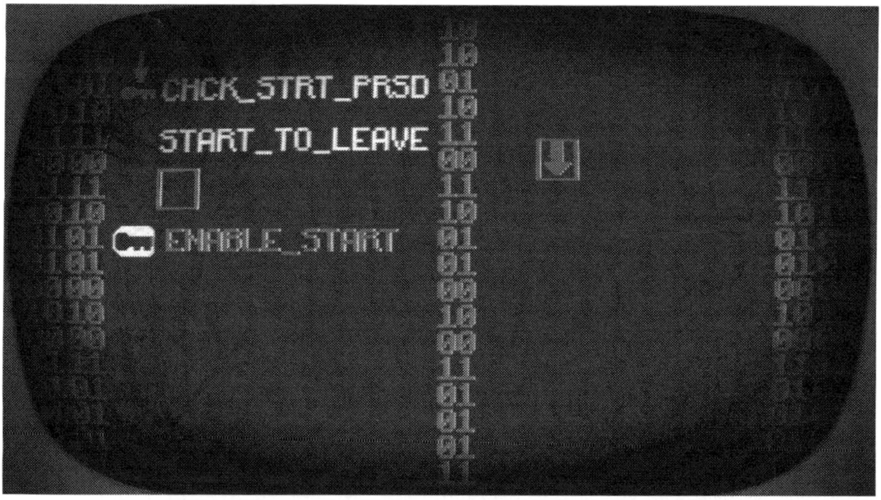

Figure 12.5 The first "hacking-themed" puzzle sequence in *Pony Island* (2016).

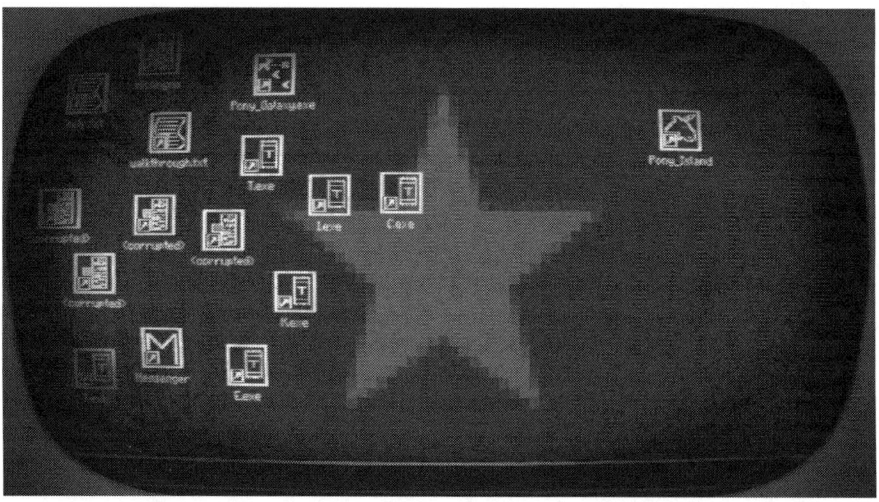

Figure 12.6 The "desktop" of the fictional arcade machine in *Pony Island* (2016).

"insert [their] soul to continue" playing, leading to another "hacking-themed" puzzle segment that results in the fictional Pony Island crashing and the player-controlled character gaining access to the "desktop" of the fictional arcade machine that might remind the players of the graphical user interfaces of older operating systems such as GEOS, AmigaOS, or various 1980s versions of Windows (see Figure 12.6). Much to the chagrin of Pony Island's creator, who now identifies himself as Lucifer (or "1U©iF#r"), a Hopeless Soul (or "h0peles$0uL") trapped in the fictional arcade machine then uses an instant messenger program to recruit the player-controlled character to its cause, tasking them (and, thus, the players) with deleting three "core files" that run in the background of Pony Island as the three rather demon-like daemons Azazel, Beelzebub, and Asmodeus, which Mullins succinctly describes as "the 'puzzle' boss," "the 'battle' boss," and "the 'fucks with you' boss" (Daniel Mullins in Ruhland 2016, n.pag.), respectively.

While it would go beyond the scope of this chapter to exhaustively unpack *Pony Island*'s complex narrative structure, I would still like to highlight the ways in which it combines the remediation of the aesthetics of older videogames with the remediation of different kinds of "glitches." As noted above, *Pony Island* generally employs "pixelated" text and graphics as well as supposedly 8-bit sound and music throughout the "hacking-themed" puzzle segments, the "pony-themed" side-scrolling segments, and the (even more clearly metareferential) "desktop-themed" puzzle segments, with the (entirely predetermined) "hacking-themed" puzzle segments also changing the gameplay of the "pony-themed" side-scrolling segments by adding a "pony laser," which is represented as "a projectile vomit of binary code, pixelation, and chromatic aberration" (Gass 2024, 18), to the set of available in-game actions (see Figure 12.7). All three kinds of gameplay segments also heavily employ the remediation of various kinds of "glitches," most of which are supposedly caused by the player-controlled character "hacking" Pony Island and successively deleting its "core files." After the player-controlled character has defeated the daemon Azazel, the pony that they control traverses an increasingly "glitchy," corrupted "world map" during what is identified as the "adventure mode." Eventually, the player-controlled character defeats the daemon Beelzebub and deletes the second "core file," which leads to them being knocked unconscious by a green gas emitted by the arcade machine. When the

Figure 12.7 The "pony laser" in a "pony-themed" side-scrolling segment in *Pony Island* (2016).

player-controlled character awakes in what appears to be some kind of largely empty arcade, they step toward a different arcade machine with a cobweb-adorned gray (rather than brown) case as well as an integrated keyboard and joystick that seems to have remained unused for some time.

Both the player-controlled character and the players are then presented with a decidedly more colorful and cheerful version of Pony Island that replaces Lucifer with the devil costume–wearing "Louey," the devil-shaped enemies of the side-scrolling segments with butterflies, the "pony laser" with a gust of wind, and the "hacking-themed" with "butterfly-themed" puzzle segments. Defeating "Louey" and solving another "hacking-themed" puzzle segment gives the player-controlled character access to the desktop of the gray arcade machine, the "recycling bin" of which contains a number of "discarded versions" of Pony Island, two of which are particularly interesting with regard to *Pony Island*'s postdigital aesthetics in that they remediate the aesthetics of older videogames in ways that are decidedly different from *Pony Island*'s dominant aesthetic form. "PI_Text_Based.exe," on the one hand, reconfigures both the initial "hacking-themed" puzzle segment and "pony-themed" side-scrolling segment as a remediation of the aesthetics of 1970s text adventures. "Pony_Island_3D.exe," on the other hand, reconfigures the "pony-themed" side-scrolling segments as a remediation of the aesthetics of early 1980s 3D videogames (see Figure 12.8) (although, apart from the whirring sound of an old hard drive booting up that accompanies all of the "discarded versions," the "current" Pony Island's sound and music remain unchanged). The "recycling bin" contains other "discarded versions," with "PonyIsland.Meta" reproducing the initial logo and title menu of the actual *Pony Island*, while "Devil_Island.exe" offers an inverted version of Pony Island that has the player-controlled character take control of a devil-like entity jumping

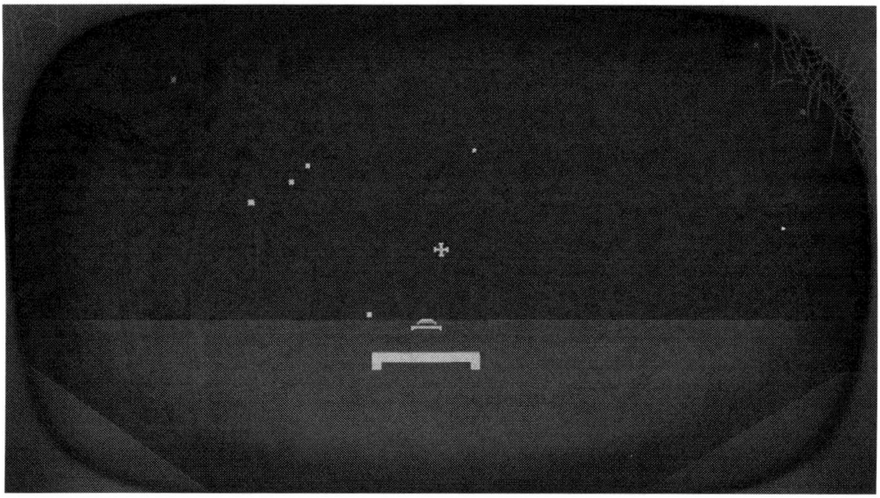

Figure 12.8 The rudimentary 3D graphics of "Pony_Island_3D.exe" in *Pony Island* (2016).

over obstacles and fighting a horde of ponies, but the text-based Pony Island and the three-dimensional Pony Island seem particularly noteworthy in terms of their contribution to the aesthetic intensification of the digital that characterizes *Pony Island*'s aesthetic form as a whole.

After the player-controlled character has defeated the daemon Asmodeus during an escalating sequence of "desktop-themed" puzzle segments that also further blur the line between the fictional operating system of the gray arcade machine and the actual operating systems on the players' computers that run *Pony Island* via a rather clever use of the Steam API, the remainder of *Pony Island* consists of an extended "pony-themed" side-scrolling segment during which the player-controlled character leads the pony-shaped souls that were trapped by Lucifer to freedom while a "system dump" is executed, with an increasingly "glitchy" audiovisual aesthetics reflecting the (supposedly) corrupted program files of the fictional Pony Island(s). Whether or not the player chooses to follow the Hopeless Soul's final metaleptic request to actually delete what the latter describes as "*Pony Island*'s rotten bits,"[39] then, *Pony Island*'s prolific remediation of the mediality and materiality of older videogames as well as its extensive use of manufactured "glitches" serve as helpful reminders of the range of aesthetic practices and forms that the domain of postdigital aesthetics that I would describe as the aesthetic intensification of the digital entails.

Postdigital Aesthetics as the Aesthetic Transfer from the Nondigital to the Digital in *Cuphead*

Just as indie games' use of "pixelated" graphics and supposedly 8-bit sound has become a highly conventionalized aesthetic practice located in the domain of postdigital aesthetics that I would describe as the aesthetic intensification of the digital, so do indie games also commonly remediate the mediality and materiality of nondigital media forms, which locates them in the domain of postdigital aesthetics that I would describe as the aesthetic transfer from the nondigital to the digital. If anything, examples of the latter are even more common (or at least more aesthetically diverse) than examples of the former, ranging from the remediation of pencils and crayons in indie games such as *Crayon Physics Deluxe*, *Neverending Nightmares* (2014), *Crayon Chronicles* (2015), and *Slay the Princess* (2023) via the remediation of watercolor and oil paint in indie games such as *Braid* (2008), *Gris* (2018), *Disco Elysium* (2019), and *Dordogne* (2023) to the remediation of paper and cardboard in indie games such as *And Yet It Moves*, *Lumino City* (2013), *Wildermyth* (2019), and *Papetura* (2021). In the following, however, I would like to zoom in on *Cuphead*, a run-and-gun game that is considered "a visual and auditory masterpiece" (Jung 2017, n.pag.) by many critics due to its still comparatively unusual combination of highly challenging shooter/platformer gameplay with a notably foregrounded and extensive remediation of the nondigital aesthetics of 1930s animation (see also, e.g., Anderson and Cullen 2023; Blamey 2021; Makai 2018; McGowan 2019; Scoggin 2023; Thibault 2016; Wood and Summerville 2019 for a selection of existing research on *Cuphead*).

Cuphead's unusual audiovisual aesthetics are introduced as early as the title screen, which consists of a minimally animated image of the protagonist Cuphead and his brother Mugman, who move ever so slightly to the tune while a barbershop quartet recounts the backstory of the game in the broadest of brushstrokes (see Figure 12.9). Once the players start a new game, *Cuphead* then uses a "framing device" that at first glance might seem somewhat similar to the arcade machines in *Pony Island*, as the opening and closing cutscenes each extensively represent a picturebook that in turn represents the beginning and the ending of the story of Cuphead and Mugman fighting the Devil for their souls (see Figure 12.10).[40] Yet,

Figure 12.9 The barbershop quartet sequence before the title screen in *Cuphead* (2017).

Figure 12.10 The picturebook from the opening cutscene in *Cuphead* (2017).

despite the picturebook indeed being remediated in great detail and doubtlessly constituting an example of the domain of postdigital aesthetics that I would describe as the aesthetic transfer from the nondigital to the digital, it is arguably best understood as an integral if slightly anachronistic part of *Cuphead*'s overall remediation of the "imagined aesthetics" of 1930s animation rather than the mediality and materiality of the primarily nondigital media form of the picturebook (see, e.g., the various contributions in Dammers et al. 2022; Kümmerling-Meibauer 2017; but see also, e.g., Al-Yagout and Nikolajeva 2017; Day 2024; Järvenpää 2021; Müller 2022 on picturebook apps/digital picturebooks), since using "storybooks" as narrative "framing devices" became increasingly popular toward the end of the 1930s, with canonical examples including Disney films such as *Snow White and the Seven Dwarves* (1937) or *Pinocchio* (1940).

Indeed, the following gameplay, which uses a "world map" that gives the players access to *Cuphead*'s numerous multi-phase boss levels, run-and-gun levels, ghost levels, and airplane levels (see Figures 12.11 and 12.12), not only consistently remediates the "imagined aesthetics" of 1930s nondigital animation practices with a particular focus on early rubberhose animation (see, e.g., Arnold 2017, 33–50; Ohmer 2019) but also includes a number of specific references to animated films such as *Swing You Sinners!* (1930), *Bimbo's Initiation* (1931), *King Neptune* (1932), *Snow-White* (1933), *Poor Cinderella* (1934), *A Picnic Panic* (1935), *Popeye the Sailor Meets Sindbad the Sailor* (1936), or *The Fresh Vegetable Mystery* (1939). Perhaps unsurprisingly, the remediation of 1930s animation is also repeatedly thematized in production- and reception-oriented paratexts, with lead game designer Jared Moldenhauer and art director Chad Moldenhauer in particular not having been shy to emphasize the effort it took to create *Cuphead*'s postdigital aesthetics, stressing not only that they "purposely run all of the animation at 24 frames per second" (Chad Moldenhauer in Peckham 2016, n.pag.) but also that, although the coloring was done digitally, everything else was "hand drawn on paper, hand-inked on paper, all the backgrounds are watercolor paintings, in some places there are actual physical models, and all the music of course is […] live-recorded" (Chad Moldenhauer in GameSpot 2017, 6:12–6:32).

The aforementioned observation that *Cuphead*'s postdigital aesthetics is not diegetized or fictionalized despite the use of the picturebook as a narrative "framing device" is further reinforced by the use of film-specific "title cards" with 1930 (or, rather, MXMIII) copyright dates before each of the individual levels as well as by the application of an additional "layer" of remediation in the form of a filter that adds scratches, dust particles, hairs, and light patches evidently meant to evoke the look of damaged nondigital film material, thus highlighting yet again 1930s animated films rather than picturebooks as the primary "source" of the aesthetic transfer from the nondigital to the digital that is at the center of *Cuphead*'s audiovisual aesthetics.[41] Indeed, this looped sequence of scratches, dust particles, hairs, and light patches is added to all segments of the indie game from the opening cutscene and the "world map" via the multi-phase boss levels, the run-and-gun levels, the ghost levels, and the airplane levels to the closing cutscene and the credits

Figure 12.11 Chauncey Chantenay from the Botanic Panic! boss level in *Cuphead* (2017).

Figure 12.12 Hilda Berg from the Threatenin' Zeppelin airplane level in *Cuphead* (2017).

sequence (with the cutscenes, the "world map," the "title cards," and the credit sequence also adding an "auditive filter" that remediates the crackling noise characteristic for early shellac records) and even remains present when players who have completed a full playthrough without shooting use the thereby unlocked option to change the visual representation of the gameplay from its original sprightly colors to a black-and-white color scheme that moves *Cuphead* even closer to many of the early 1930s animated films it aims to remediate (since early canonical films such as *Swing You Sinners!*, *Bimbo's Initiation*, and *Snow-White* were still presented in black-and-white, even as other films such as *King Neptune*, *Poor Cinderella*, and *A Picnic Panic* already used color).[42]

This decidedly foregrounded form of remediation has certainly contributed to *Cuphead*'s considerable commercial as well as critical success, with most if not all critics noting that it is "a brutal, exhausting game" (Pedroza 2017, n.pag.) that is "as frustrating as it is exhilarating" (Parkin 2017, n.pag.) and affords its players "hours spent in a highly focused, fervently determined, thoroughly delighted state" (Sullivan 2017, n.pag.) as well as echoing the production-oriented paratexts regarding *Cuphead*'s remediation of the "imagined aesthetics" of 1930s animation (in addition to the unusually challenging gameplay in itself perhaps best considered to be a remediation of the game mechanics of 1980s and 1990s run-and-gun videogames such as *Contra* [1987], *Mega Man* [1987], *Gunstar Heroes* [1993], and *Metal Slug* [1996]). That said, the analysis of *Cuphead*'s remediation of 1930s rubberhose animation is further complicated by the Moldenhauer brothers repeatedly noting that their design process was informed by them having "watched old VHS tapes of Popeye, Betty Boop, Silly Symphonies and more" (Chad Moldenhauer in Gilyadov 2017, n.pag.) as children. This is unpacked further by McGowan, who argues not only that *Cuphead*'s levels "generally appropriat[e] the length of a one-reeler cartoon" and that "[t]he jump from one stage to the next, with a variety of different locations, gameplay styles, and bizarre antagonists, calls to mind the eclectic mix of shorts found on many public domain animation videos" but also that "the intense difficulty of *Cuphead*'s gameplay means that one is forced to continually replay and master each level in order to progress, an act which itself elicits the almost-ritualized repeat viewings of VHS tapes—especially identified in titles marketed toward children—in an era when options for home entertainment were rather more limited" (2019, 21). McGowan also connects the filter that remediates the scratches, dust particles, hairs, and light patches of damaged nondigital film material to the supposed remediation of VHS tapes, noting that "most public domain video transfers—particularly in the VHS era—have been characterized as being derived from 'inferior' sources, such as well-worn theatrical copies or 16 mm dupes made for television" (2019, 22), though he also acknowledges that *Cuphead* does not actually go beyond the remediation of film-specific aesthetics as it does not, for example, remediate VHS-specific "markers" such as "tracking errors nor any instances of static or 'snow'" (2019, 23).[43]

Beyond the primarily visual aspects of its postdigital aesthetics discussed thus far, *Cuphead*'s auditive dimension is also particularly noteworthy, both because it demonstrates that, for aesthetic strategies located in the domain of postdigital aesthetics that I would describe as the aesthetic transfer from the nondigital to the digital, generating a notable "medial difference" is considerably more difficult in the auditive dimension than it is in the visual dimension of audiovisual aesthetics and because *Cuphead* arguably still manages to do so by remediating specific aspects of the sound and music that form an integral part of the "imagined aesthetics" of 1930s animation, while also employing aesthetic practices that further highlight the supposedly nondigital aesthetics of its vocalization, sound effects, ambient effects, and music. As, for example, Scoggin has explored in considerable detail, *Cuphead*'s "soundtrack (written by percussionist and composer Kris Maddigan) is [...] designed to sound like music typical of the period, focusing on various forms of then-contemporary jazz (i.e., hot jazz/big band), but also including barbershop quartets, waltzes, early jazz, and ragtime" (2023, 62), with hot jazz being consistently used for the multi-phase boss levels, while "the run and gun sections use a mix of ragtime and stride piano, and the other sections vary, depending on the context" (2023, 63). Despite the composer himself acknowledging that the result is "definitely anachronistic" (Kristofer Maddigan in McMillan 2017, n.pag.) to some extent, *Cuphead*'s music complements the (also at least partially anachronistic) visual design rather well, and although it was *recorded* digitally, StudioMDHR yet again repeatedly emphasized that all music was specifically *performed* nondigitally by an actual bigband (see, e.g., GameSpot 2017; Peckham 2016). No less importantly, the auditive dimension of *Cuphead*'s postdigital aesthetics is completed by "cartoony" sound effects and "tinny," "echoing" vocalization that would not sound out of place in a 1930s animated film (see also the additional remarks from one of *Cuphead*'s sound designers, Samuel Justice, in Kuzminski 2017).

Cuphead thus turns out to be a particularly notable example of an indie game whose audiovisual aesthetic form can be squarely located in the domain of postdigital aesthetics that I would describe as the aesthetic transfer from the nondigital to the digital, but it is still worth repeating that many other examples of such an aesthetic transfer can be found in the area of indie games, where we can observe not only a broad range of remediation processes remediating the nondigital aesthetics of, for example, pencil and crayon drawings, watercolor and oil paintings, paper and cardboard collages, comics and animation, or photographs and films but also fairly common occurrences of the aforementioned diegetization of fictional nondigital objects that serves to further emphasize the notable "medial difference" between the aesthetic form of the represented nondigital object and the aesthetic form of the representing digital videogame.

Postdigital Aesthetics as the Aesthetic Transfer from the Nondigital to the Digital in *What Remains of Edith Finch*

Even if the aforementioned "framing device" of the videogame-within-a-videogame that accompanies the aesthetic intensification of the digital in *Pony Island* as well as in a range of other highly metareferential indie games such as *The Magic Circle*, *CrossCode* (2018), *There Is No Game: Wrong Dimension*, and *Among Ashes* (2024) is not particularly rare, then, indie games perhaps even more commonly remediate the mediality and materiality of nondigital aesthetic objects that foreground the aesthetic transfer from the nondigital to the digital by diegetizing the objects in question at least to some extent, thereby underscoring the difference between the *represented* fictional nondigital object, on the one hand, and the *representing* actual digital videogame, on the other. While indie games such as *Armello* (2015), *Card Hunter* (2015), *Inscryption*, and *Trials of*

Fire (2021) focus on the remediation of nondigital "ludic objects" such as game boards, cards, and dice that primarily connect the aesthetic transfer from the nondigital to the digital to their ludic aesthetics, indie games such as *Gone Home* (2013), *Pyre* (2017), *Pentiment* (2022), and *The Plucky Squire* (2024) focus on the remediation of nondigital "narrating objects"[44] that often (but not always) take the form of books and primarily connect the aesthetic transfer from the nondigital to the digital to their narrative aesthetics (see also the chapters by Aksay et al. and Seiwald in this volume). In the following, I want to explore the diversity of how such remediated nondigital aesthetic objects can function as narrative "framing devices" by analyzing *What Remains of Edith Finch*, another walking simulator that remediates a particularly broad range of nondigital "narrating objects" in order to tell the stories of the deaths of the many members of the fictional Finch family (see also, e.g., Balduzzi 2024; Bozdog and Galloway 2020; Kagen 2020; Kirkland 2020; Krampe 2025, ch. 4; Mészáros 2022; or Thon 2025 for a selection of existing research on *What Remains of Edith Finch*).

Following a brief title sequence that uses a segment of Johann Sebastian Bach's cantata "Wir danken dir, Gott, wir danken dir" (1731) in order to foreground the otherwise rather more subtle (but still fully orchestrated and thus arguably yet again decidedly "nondigital") musical score that was composed by Jeff Russo in his first contribution to a videogame (see, e.g., Galas 2017; Kim 2017), *What Remains of Edith Finch*'s gameplay initially represents a character who later turns out to be Edith Finch's son Christopher reading a journal she has addressed to him before dying due to complications during childbirth, but then switches from representing the diegetic primary storyworld level on which Christopher reads Edith's journal to representing the hypodiegetic secondary storyworld level that is narrated by that very journal. Such a switch from the diegetic primary storyworld level to the hypodiegetic secondary storyworld level is not particularly unusual for a narratively complex videogame, but *What Remains of Edith Finch* goes much further than that, as the player-controlled Edith on the hypodiegetic secondary storyworld level narrated by the journal finds various other "narrating objects" that tell the stories of her prematurely deceased relatives in one way or another, and the nonnarratorial gameplay often (though not always) switches storyworld level yet again, representing the hypo-hypodiegetic tertiary storyworld levels established by these various "narrating objects."

The latter include Edith's maternal great-aunt Molly's journal, a View-Master-style stereoscope containing a series of sepia-tinted pictures illustrating the story of her maternal great-great-grandfather Odin's death, an essay by her maternal grandfather Sam that tells the story of his brother (and Edith's maternal great-uncle) Calvin's death, a horror comic that tells the story of Edith's maternal great-aunt Barbara's death, a farewell letter from Edith's maternal great-uncle Walter, who died soon after writing it, a collection of photographs that Edith's mother Dawn took of her (Dawn's) father Sam during a hunting trip right before Sam died, a letter from Sam about the death of his son Gregory, who was Edith's maternal uncle, a poem from Dawn, dedicated to Edith's maternal uncle Gus, a flip book from Edith's second older brother Milton depicting him creating a flip book that depicts his disappearance into one of his paintings (and thus represents not just a hypo-hypodiegetic tertiary but also a hypo-hypo-hypodiegetic quarternary storyworld level), a letter from the psychiatrist Dr. Emily Nuth about the suicide of Edith's first older brother Lewis (which also leads to a segment of gameplay representing not just the hypo-hypodiegetic tertiary storyworld level of Lewis's suicide but also the hypo-hypo-hypodiegetic quarternary storyworld level of his elaborate "inner life"), and, finally, a hypodiegetic version of Edith's journal as it is being written, in which she tells the story of finding a similar journal that her maternal great-grandmother Edie addressed to her before she "disappeared" or, rather more likely, died by suicide (which thus leads to yet another representation of not just a hypo-hypodiegetic tertiary but also a hypo-hypo-hypodiegetic quaternary storyworld level).

Even if this degree of narrative (or, rather, narratorial) complexity is certainly unusual, *What Remains of Edith Finch* still largely adheres to the generic conventions of the walking simulator in representing its game spaces from a first-person perspective and mainly using broadly "realistic" graphics that fall somewhere between "caricaturism" and "photorealism" on the spectrum of graphical styles in videogames identified by Järvinen (2002). At the same time, however, the aforementioned "narrating objects" often trigger extended voice-over narration as well as character dialogue (by Edith, Molly, Sam, Barbara, her boyfriend Rick, "Old Jack," Walter, Dawn, Sam's ex-wife Kay Carlyle, Dr. Emily Nuth, and Edie) that complement the respective gameplay segments, and *What Remains of Edith Finch* further foregrounds the mediality and materiality of the written words that were used to record many of the stories of the deaths of the members of the Finch family by having them accompany the voice-over narration not as conventional subtitles but as floating segments of text in different (narrator-specific) fonts that appear as if they were part of the (narrated) game spaces. There are also various other nondigital objects remediated in more or less detail, including countless family pictures, an increasingly "uncanny" number of books,[45] and many more nondigital objects that fulfill primarily narrative functions in the context of what is sometimes described as "environmental storytelling" (Jenkins 2004, 121) or "indexical storytelling" (Fernández-Vara 2011, n.pag.) as well as a music box, a pop-up book, and many more nondigital objects that are integrated into the (generally very simple) interaction puzzles that *What Remains of Edith Finch* confronts its players with, but it is clear that the latter's overall focus is on the individual family members' stories that were developed independently from each other, for the most part, and that *What Remains of Edith Finch*'s creative director Ian Dallas thus describes as "vignettes" (Ian Dallas in gamer_152 2018, n.pag.).[46]

Some of these "vignettes" are largely limited to representations of the hypodiegetic Edith interacting with the respective "narrating object," with the story of the death of Odin being narrated by Edith while she looks through the View-Master-style stereoscope containing a series of sepia-tinted pictures of Odin and his family (see Figure 12.13), whereas the story of the disappearance of Milton is represented without any spoken or written narration, with *What Remains of Edith Finch* employing only the handdrawn flipbook that Milton has created and that Edith is represented as flipping through (see Figure 12.14). As noted above, there is quite a bit of narrative complexity to be found here already, with the hypodiegetic flipbook representing a hypo-hypodiegetic Milton drawing a hypo-hypodiegetic flipbook that in turn represents a

Figure 12.13 Remediated stereoscope pictures in *What Remains of Edith Finch* (2017).

Figure 12.14 Remediated flipbook in *What Remains of Edith Finch* (2017).

hypo-hypo-hypodiegetic Milton painting a door on a canvas through which he then disappears,[47] but there are also various other "vignettes" (namely those telling the stories of Molly, Calvin, Barbara, Walter, Sam, Gregory, Gus, and Lewis) that trigger an additional switch of the gameplay, which then contributes to representing hypo-hypodiegetic tertiary or even hypo-hypo-hypodiegetic quarternary storyworld levels. Every one of these different "vignettes" is audiovisually, ludically, and narratively interesting in their own right, with the gameplay segments in question allowing the players to make the various player-controlled characters not just walk but also swing on a swing, climb a tree, fly through the sky, roll down a hill, dive through water, crawl on the floor, ride a boat, and operate various kinds of machinery (including a can opener, a camera, a kite, and two rather different guillotines). However, the "vignette" telling the story of the death of Barbara is particularly noteworthy in terms of *What Remains of Edith Finch*'s postdigital aesthetics.[48]

As with the other "vignettes," *What Remains of Edith Finch* makes extensive use of Barbara's cluttered room to "set the scene," with a film poster and cardboard cut-out of Barbara as well as various other memorabilia, awards, and books about (Hollywood) filmmaking emphasizing the importance that Barbara's acting career as a child star had for her (though the fact that it was rather short-lived is also underscored by a waitress uniform from Penelope's Diner with Barbara's name on it). That said, the salient "narrating object" representing the story of the 16-year-old Barbara's premature death in 1960 is not a film but a horror comic that (rather strangely) appears to have been professionally produced and published as early as October 1961. The story of Barbara's death that the horror comic tells is evidently also inspired by early horror films from the 1950s through to the 1970s, with the "vignette" even briefly using the Michael Myers theme from *Halloween* (1978), but despite the decidedly nondigital aesthetic practices that define this chapter in film history (including a rich tradition of "practical effects"; see also, e.g., Johnson 2009; Roche 2014), the primary object of remediation arguably remains the mediality and materiality of 1950s horror comics such as EC Comics' *Tales from the Crypt* series (1950–1955; see also, e.g., Whitted 2019; Yanes 2021).

Edith is initially represented as reading the comic in a way that seems quite similar to the "vignettes" representing the death of Odin and the disappearance of Milton (see Figure 12.15), yet once the players have made her turn the title page, they lose

Figure 12.15 Remediated horror comic in *What Remains of Edith Finch* (2017).

Figure 12.16 Gameplay integrated in a comics page in *What Remains of Edith Finch* (2017).

control of Edith, who continues to turn pages until the players are allowed to take control of Barbara, who in turn is represented as moving through various 3D game spaces that use cel shading to connect to a comics aesthetics, but still remain framed by the comics panels and the comics page (see Figure 12.16). Similarly, even if "Old Jack," the horror comic's pumpkin-headed narrator as well as the hypo-hypodiegetic Barbara, her boyfriend, and various other characters are fully voice-acted, *What Remains of Edith Finch* simultaneously employs comics-specific narration boxes, speech bubbles, and sound words to represent the narrator's and the characters' voices (see also, e.g., Forceville 2014; Thon 2021; and the chapter by Brown in this volume). This comics-specific framing of the gameplay is also foregrounded further by the representation repeatedly switching between the hypodiegetic Edith merely reading the comic (i.e., turning the page without the players' input) and the panels "coming to life" (i.e., the players taking control of the hypo-hypodiegetic Barbara). Hence, while some of the audiovisual qualities of the representation (including Barbara's famous "scream") clearly also remediate aspects of 1950s to 1970s filmmaking, the remediation of the mediality and materiality of 1950s comics seems more salient, at least aesthetically. In any case, even this necessarily brief analysis of *What Remains of Edith Finch* will have further demonstrated the diversity of how remediated nondigital "narrating objects" can function as narrative "framing devices" in indie games that are primarily located in the domain of postdigital aesthetics that I would describe as the aesthetic transfer from the nondigital to the digital.

Conclusion

Let me conclude, then, by underscoring yet again the diversity of a decidedly postdigital aesthetics as I have tentatively delineated it throughout the previous pages. Not only does this conceptualization encompass at least the four salient domains that I would describe as the aesthetic intensification of the digital, the aesthetic transfer from the digital to the nondigital, the aesthetic intensification of the nondigital, and the aesthetic transfer from the nondigital to the digital, all of which entail an emphasis on the logic of (opaque) hypermediacy as opposed to the logic of (transparent) immediacy that arguably tends to more readily instigate aesthetic as opposed to "merely" nonaesthetic, functional, or pragmatic processes of perception, but also can these different domains of postdigital aesthetics be observed in a broad range of conventionally distinct media forms that include (digital as well as nondigital) literary texts, comics, animation, photography, films, series, and games. The area of indie games that the present chapter focused on is thus only one of many potential avenues of inquiry into postdigital aesthetics, albeit one that is particularly productive with regard to at least two of the four salient domains of postdigital aesthetics heuristically distinguished above. Indeed, while the aesthetic forms of nondigital indie games such as *Pax Pamir: Second Edition*, *The Shivers*, *Pixel Tactics Deluxe*, or *To the Death!* may well be located in the domains of postdigital aesthetics that I would describe as the aesthetic intensification of the nondigital and the aesthetic transfer from the digital to the nondigital, respectively, digital indie games such as *Proteus*, *Pony Island*, *Cuphead*, or *What Remains of Edith Finch* more extensively demonstrate a variety of aesthetic practices that remediate the mediality and materiality of digital media forms via "pixelated" graphics, supposedly 8-bit sound, and manufactured "glitches" (and hence can be located in the domain of postdigital aesthetics that I would describe as the aesthetic intensification of the digital), on the one hand, and aesthetic practices that remediate the mediality and materiality of nondigital media forms such as pencil and crayon drawings, watercolor and oil paintings, paper and cardboard collages, comics and animation, or photographs and films (and hence can be located in the domain of postdigital aesthetics that I would describe as the aesthetic transfer from the nondigital to the digital), on the other.

Acknowledgments

Work on this chapter was supported by a Feodor Lynen Research Fellowship for Experienced Researchers from the Alexander von Humboldt Foundation (2023–2025), which funded several extended research stays at the Zurich Aesthetics Lab, University of Zurich, Switzerland.

Notes

1 One reason for this difference in impact between Cascone (2000), on the one hand, and Pepperell and Punt (2000), on the other, may also be that the latter's book largely reads like a rather meandering manifest consisting of a series of very wide-ranging claims, without necessarily providing much in the way of evidence. This already becomes visible in many of the "propositions" that Pepperell and Punt employ to open each of the "sections" of their book, and which include claims that "[t]he distinctions between the words 'human' and 'machine,' and between humans and machines, lose validity as meanings mutate in response to imagination and desire" (2000, 71), that "[t]he idea that

living things consist of organised energy is disavowed by conventional science" (2000, 107), that "[t]echnology can permit limited quantities of specific human energy to be recorded, stored and consumed" (2000, 143), and, of course, that "[t]he categories of logic, reason and the binary are absorbed and transcended in the postdigital membrane" (2000, 157). Hence, while Cascone certainly is no less of an artist than Pepperell and Punt are, the former's attempt to explore a "'post-digital' aesthetics" (Cascone 2000, 12) in electronic music is notably less freewheeling and, therefore, may have appeared more carefully argued and convincing in an academic context.

2 Interestingly, Pepperell and Punt also suggest that "the digital age is transitional and quite possibly short-lived" (2000, 163), which does not seem to have been a particularly accurate prediction as of yet (to the extent that Pepperell and Punt here seem to refer to the vanishing of digital technology or what they describe as "digital processing" [2000, 163] that is decidedly not an element of most if not all of the more recent conceptualizations of the postdigital), though it is arguably still possible that the "digital age" *will* turn out to be "short-lived" in that its end may well go hand in hand with the end of the Anthropocene as such (see, e.g., Clarke 2020; Gormley 2021; Holloway 2022; MacCormack 2020).

3 The term "post-digital" can therefore be compared with similar terms such as "poststructuralism," "postmodernism," "postcolonialism," or "postpunk" as well as "post-photography," "post-cinema," "postmedia," or "postinternet" (see, once more, Cramer 2015; as well as, e.g., Apprich et al. 2013; Denson and Leyda 2016; Guattari 1990; Hagener et al. 2016; Mitchell 1992; Olson 2011; Rothwell 2024; Shore 2014), because all of these "post-terms" broadly refer to the transformation of what has existed up to a point, while critically acknowledging that what has existed up to that point remains impactful despite this transformation. It is also worth noting here that the postdigital is commonly connected not only to arguments around "postinternet" (see, e.g., Paul 2016) and "postmedia" (see, e.g., Manovich 2014) but also to "metamodernism" (see, e.g., Jordan 2020).

4 As Cramer rightly notes, "when the term 'post-digital' draws critical reactions focusing on the dubious historico-philosophical connotations of the prefix 'post,' one cannot help but wonder about a previous lack of such critical thinking regarding the older (yet no less Hegelian) term 'new media'" (2015, 20). That said, the notion of "new media" has been problematized and historicized for at least as long as the notion of the postdigital exists (see, e.g., Hansen 2004; Manovich 2001) and is now quite unlikely to be used naïvely within media studies and beyond (see, e.g., Gitelman 2006; Jenkins 2006; as well as Levinson 2015; Scolari 2023).

5 Its merely tangential connection to the focus of the present chapter notwithstanding, it is worth noting that Jandrić and others have recently set up a surprisingly productive publication pipeline with Springer that has since churned out a rather impressive number of articles and books on the postdigital that arguably also exemplify a particularly postdigital trend within academic publishing. Admittedly, not all of these publications are as carefully copy-edited as one might have hoped and at least a few of them also seem to be the result of somewhat unusual academic practices such as unceremoniously promoting the supposed peer reviewers to co-authors, which would seem to subvert the peer review process (see, e.g., Arndt et al. 2019; Cormier et al. 2019), yet both the journal *Postdigital Science and Education* and the accompanying book series of the same name evidently do valuable work here, not least with regard to the documentation of the complex conceptual history of the postdigital.

6 Berry in particular emphasizes that "the ideas of 'online' or 'being online' have become anachronistic as a result of our always-on smartphones and tablets and widespread wireless networking technologies" (2014, 22). Even if the distinction between "the digital" and "the nondigital" should not be conflated with the distinction between "being online" and "being

offline," then, everyday notions of "the digital" are closely connected to "the Internet," and our experiences of the "postdigital condition" (see Berry 2015) are thus indeed likely to have been intensified by the "always-on/always-on-you" (see Turkle 2008) and "anytime-anywhere" (see Genner 2017) qualities of most if not all current online practices.

7 This does, however, not mean that narrativity or what could more broadly be described as the representational functions of the medial artifacts to which a postdigital aesthetics might be attributed would or should not play a role in their analysis. As I have discussed in considerably more detail elsewhere, prototypical narrative representations are representations of worlds situated in space and time as well as populated by characters (see, e.g., Thon 2016b; 2017; as well as Herman 2009; Ryan 2006) and such representations can be realized not only in, say, literary texts, comics, animation, photography, films, or series but also in videogames (see, e.g., Thon 2015; 2016a; as well as Domsch 2013; Ensslin 2014). Of course, not *all* videogames are (prototypical) narrative representations, but many arguably are—including those I will analyze in more detail below, albeit with some differences in degree. See also the more detailed discussion of (medial as well as narrative) representations in note 18.

8 It is worth noting here that I find Jordan's (2020) conceptualization of the postdigital helpful as a starting point for my own tentative delineation of four domains of the postdigital (and, by extension, of postdigital aesthetics), but do not mean to suggest a wholesale endorsement of Jordan's argument regarding what he describes as postdigital storytelling. In fact, I would not characterize Jordan's study as offering a particularly systematic or convincing account of postdigital storytelling, let alone one that would have narratological merit. For examples of the kind of rigor that one should expect from theoretical work in this space, see, e.g., Ensslin and Bell 2021; Punday 2019. For an example of how a more practice-oriented approach might look, see Koenitz 2023. For a critique of Jordan's approach from the perspective of educational (post)digital storytelling, see also Meyerhofer-Parra et al. 2024.

9 Within the domain of postdigital aesthetics that I would describe as the aesthetic intensification of the digital, a "glitch" can be understood as an "(actual and/or simulated) break from an expected or conventional flow of information or meaning within (digital) communication systems that results in a perceived accident or error" (Menkman 2011, 9). Indeed, it is important to note here that the spectrum of what we can refer to as "glitches" ranges "from complete machine 'spontaneity' in the accident form, to controlled, debuggable or conceptual glitching; to a more conventional realm of glitch design and aesthetics" (Menkman 2011, 65), with the latter having increasingly gained ground "[a]s the error itself has been gentrified" (Menkman 2011, 66). At the same time, "glitches" can also be found beyond the realm of digital media forms. In retracing the trajectories of "[g]litch aesthetics, corruption artefacts, [and] retro 8-bit graphics" in the context of the "new aesthetic," Paul and Levy note that "[t]he terms 'glitch' and 'corruption artefacts' in the broadest sense refer to images and objects that have been tampered with; their creation relates to the core of the media apparatuses used to store, produce and relay information" (2015, 31), and Betancourt states even more bluntly that, while "[i]t is specifically the result of aberrant and apparent 'abnormal' renderings by digital technology that are of interest" (2017, 3) to him, "[g]litch is not necessarily a new or specifically digital form" (2017, 21). Hence, the domain of postdigital aesthetics that I would describe as the aesthetic intensification of the digital should not be conflated with "glitches," as it not only includes broader aesthetic strategies that evoke, simulate, or remediate the materiality of digital media forms such as "pixel art" or "8-bit sound" (see, e.g., Braguinski 2018; Lee 2020; as well as Beil 2011; Meikle 2016) but also excludes "glitches" that evoke, simulate, or remediate the materiality of nondigital media forms such as traces

of dust, hairs, or scratches on (supposedly) nondigital film (see, e.g., Church 2015 on what he describes as "grindhouse nostalgia"). That said, "glitches" are still an important part of the "aesthetic vocabulary" of postdigital aesthetics across media (see also, e.g., Lohmeyer 2021 for a more detailed discussion of videogame-specific "glitches," though these are not necessarily as salient here as the arguably more transmedially relevant forms of "glitches" discussed by Betancourt 2017; Kane 2019; or Menkman 2011). In any case, however, it seems clear that the aesthetic intensification of the digital is not about the "smooth," "glossy," and (interestingly) largely "blue" kind of digital aesthetics that dominated the 1990s anymore (see Cramer 2015; as well as, e.g., Bolz 1991; and the contributions in Rötzer 1991a for further discussion).

10 Bridle's specification of the "new aesthetic" remains programmatically vague and the extraordinary discursive success of the term is likely at least in part caused by its openness. Not coincidentally, the connection between the "new aesthetic" and postdigital aesthetics seems to mainly hail back to Berry and Dieter's influential essay collection *Postdigital Aesthetics* (see Berry and Dieter 2015a), which not only contains a notable number of chapters that focus on the "new aesthetic" (see, e.g., Kwastek 2015; Paul and Levy 2015), but was originally meant to be titled *New Aesthetics/Digital Aesthetics* (see Kwastek 2015, 82n1). One way or another, the "new aesthetic" entails not only a range of cases that can be located in the domain of postdigital aesthetics that I would describe as the aesthetic intensification of the digital (not least in the context of so-called operative or operational images; see Farocki 2004; as well as, e.g., Hoel 2018; Hoelz and Marie 2015, 81–110; Pantenburg 2016; Parikka 2023) but also broadly refers to "eruptions of the digital into the physical world" (Kwastek 2015, 74) that can be located in the domain of postdigital aesthetics that I would describe as the aesthetic transfer from the digital to the nondigital. Here, the "new aesthetic" is no longer just about digital images that foreground their own materiality and mediality as "poor images" *sensu* Steyerl (2009) or as otherwise aestheticized operative or operational images, but increasingly also about processes of remediation which evoke a supposedly digital aesthetics in nondigital objects (see also the more detailed discussion of Bolter and Grusin's [1996; 1999] theory of remediation in the next section). The domain of postdigital aesthetics that I would describe as the aesthetic transfer from the digital to the nondigital thus ranges from the ubiquitous use of "pixel patterns" in fashion and architecture via "glitch sculptures" by artists such as Ferruccio Laviani or Kohei Nawa (see also, once more, Contreras-Koterbay and Mirocha 2016) to various other artistic (or, rather, aesthetic) practices involving the integration of digital technology and aesthetic forms that are conventionally recognized as digital into nondigital physical spaces (see also the more detailed discussion of aesthetic form and aesthetic practice[s] in the next section).

11 Examples of this would include music lovers preferring vinyl records or audio cassettes, even though digital recordings would be more easily available; photographers or filmmakers using nondigital cameras and nondigital film material, even though digital cameras would be more easily available; or graphic designers using nondigital printing processes, even though digital printing processes would be more easily available. While it may go without saying that the borders between the domains of the postdigital that I propose to heuristically distinguish here are likely to blur in actual aesthetic practice(s), it is still noteworthy that Cramer also already identifies the dedicated use of nondigital technologies as central to his conceptualization of the postdigital when he notes that (during the early 2010s in the Netherlands at least) "contemporary young artists and designers clearly prefer working with non-electronic media" and that "digital media are often dismissed as commercial and mainstream by art students" (2015, 14). Against this

background, Cramer argues, "the term 'post-digital' usefully describes 'new media'-cultural approaches to working with so-called 'old media'" (2015, 21). It is also interesting that Cascone himself has since renounced the use of digital technology in music production and instead has "gone back to simpler technologies of magnets, vacuum tubes and the electric guitar," suggesting that "[t]he only critique possible now, if one could call it that, is a 'backgrounding' of digital technology" (Cascone and Jandrić 2021, 568).

12 Research exploring the domain of postdigital aesthetics that I would describe as the aesthetic transfer from the nondigital to the digital certainly exists, but the focus here tends to be on what could be described as *intra*medial references of the current version of a media form to its precursors. The existing research also tends to frame these references of digital to nondigital photography (see, e.g., Caoduro 2014; Schrey 2015), of digital to nondigital film (see, e.g., Baschiera and Caoduro 2015; Church 2015), or of current to older videogames (see, e.g., Braguinski 2018; Garda 2013) in terms of media nostalgia (or a more general "yearning for the past"; see also, e.g., Niemeyer 2014; Schrey 2017), which would seem to be an overly narrow, monocausal explanation for a rather more diverse set of aesthetic practices. In highlighting these particular kinds of processes of remediation, I want to underscore that postdigital aesthetics also often entail what Rajewsky describes as *inter*medial references, which need to generate a "perceptible medial difference" (2005, 62) between the media form *to which* and the media form *in which* reference is made, and which thereby arguably foreground both the mediality of the former and that of the latter (though this applies to *intra*medial references across the digital/nondigital divide as well). Not coincidentally, Schröter similarly emphasizes digital media forms' capability to "produce[] forms that are not only transmedial, but transmaterial" (2023, 5), elaborating that, "while transmedial forms [...] cannot be attributed to any medium in particular, transmaterial forms emphatically refer to the respective specific materiality [...] of a medium, but in a different context" (2023, 5; see also Schröter 2019 for the initial English-language version of this conceptualization of transmateriality, which includes further reflections on media aesthetics). Both Rajewsky and Schröter thus doubtlessly offer productive perspectives on the domain of postdigital aesthetics that I would describe as the aesthetic transfer from the nondigital to the digital, yet they neither connect their discussion to the notion of the postdigital, nor do they provide detailed case studies of the intermedial references and/or processes of transmaterialization in question.

13 This is worth emphasizing not only because (analytic) philosophical aesthetics has kept rather busy trying to "define" art during the second half of the 20th century (see, e.g., the "functionalist" definitions proposed by Beardsley 1982; Schlesinger 1979; the "institutional" definitions proposed by Danto 1981; Dickie 1974; the "historical" definitions proposed by Levinson 1979; Stecker 1994; the "cluster" approach proposed by Gaut 2000; and the extensive survey in Davies 1991) but also because (analytic) philosophers usually employ the term "aesthetic properties" in ways that are much more specific than those in which it might be employed, say, in the broader field of research on the postdigital (if, for example, Contreras-Koterbay and Mirocha mention the "aesthetic properties [...] of digital media" [2016, 36] in passing or Hoy explores the difference between the "analog aesthetic properties" and the "digital aesthetic properties" [2017, 175] of [post]digital works of art). In contradistinction to this more general usage, a nuanced philosophical discussion has followed from Sibley's (1959; 1965; 1968; 1974) influential distinction between "aesthetic" and "nonaesthetic properties" (as well as "terms" or "concepts" that refer to such "qualities" or "features"), with the former (such as being "graceful, dainty, or garish [...], balanced, moving, or powerful" [Sibley 1965, 135]) requiring "the exercise of taste, perceptiveness, or sensitivity, of aesthetic discrimination or appreciation"

(Sibley 1959, 421), while the latter (such as being "large, circular, green, slow, or monosyllabic" [Sibley 1965, 135]) do not. Unsurprisingly, there is quite a bit of theoretical as well as terminological complexity to be found here, with the discussion being defined by longstanding (and closely interrelated) disagreements about whether "property talk" (Bender 1996, 374; Matravers 2005, 208) is particularly helpful for understanding, say, aesthetic experience or aesthetic appreciation (see also, e.g., Irvin 2014) as well as about the ontological status of aesthetic properties (see already Sibley 1968; as well as, e.g., the various arguments in favor of "aesthetic realism" in Eaton 2001; Zangwill 2001; and "aesthetic antirealism" in Goldman 1995; Young 1997), their relation to nonaesthetic properties (see already Sibley 1965; as well as, e.g., Bender 1987; Currie 1990; Levinson 1984; Zangwill 2001 on the supposed "supervenience" of aesthetic properties), and the question whether (some) aesthetic properties are (merely) descriptive or (all) aesthetic properties are (indivisibly) evaluative (see already Sibley 1974; as well as, e.g., Levinson 2001; 2005; Zangwill 2001 vs. De Clercq 2002; 2008; Goldman 1995 for different positions regarding the "evaluative nature" of aesthetic properties). Against this background, Nanay's proposal to focus on "aesthetically relevant properties" (2016, 67; see also, e.g., Budd 1995, 4; Goldman 1995, 148; Zangwill 2001, 100 for some previous uses of the term) may seem like a helpful way to sidestep the theoretical and terminological thicket surrounding aesthetic properties. More specifically, Nanay argues that "properties are aesthetically relevant if attending to them makes an aesthetic difference," but also stresses that "[t]his 'making an aesthetic difference' can mean many things: attending to aesthetically relevant properties may alter our general aesthetic evaluation of the artwork, strengthen (or weaken) our identification with a fictional character, trigger an aesthetic experience of a [Proustian] nature, make us appreciate a narrative twist, and so on" (2016, 67). Yet, despite Nanay's insistence that "aesthetically relevant properties can clearly be non-evaluative" (2016, 82), it would seem that his "working definition" of "aesthetically relevant properties" as those properties that "change[] the *valence* of one's experience" (2016, 72; original emphasis) if one attends to them still preserves at least some "evaluative component," albeit a rather subjective or at least context-dependent one. Nanay's conceptualization of "aesthetically relevant properties" (2016, 67) thus also does not seem too far removed from, say, Eaton's conceptualization of "aesthetic properties" as any "intrinsic propert[ies]" of "an object or event" that are "culturally identified as [...] propert[ies] worthy of attention (i.e., of perception and reflection)" (2001, 11), though the former more explicitly includes what others would describe as "base properties" (Bender 1996, 371; Goldman 1995, 45), while the latter stresses that aesthetic properties "get constructed socially as repaying perception and reflection" (Eaton 2001, 18). In any case, despite my accepting that matters of "taste" play an important role in aesthetics and furthermore suspecting that the attribution of a (specific kind of) postdigital aesthetics to a medial artifact could indeed be understood as the attribution of an aesthetic property, I would maintain that the analysis of postdigital aesthetics should not focus on questions of aesthetic judgment, nor indeed on "evaluative aesthetic properties" (Goldman 1995, 12), "evaluatively laden aesthetic properties" (Levinson 2001, 76), "inherently evaluative [...] aesthetic properties" (De Clercq 2002, 172), and the like.

14 It is, of course, quite common to emphasize the connection between aesthetics and perception. In philosophical aesthetics (see, e.g., Böhme 2001; Nanay 2016; Rancière 2011; Seel 2005) as well as in the broader research on media and postdigital aesthetics (see, e.g., Contreras-Koterbay and Mirocha 2016; Cramer 2015; Hausken 2013; Marchiori 2013), establishing this connection often entails not only more or less well-founded reminders that the term "'[a]esthetics' goes back to the Greek word class *aisthesis*, *aisthanesthai* and *aisthetos* [...,] designat[ing] sensation and perception in general, prior

to any artistic meaning" (Welsch 1995, 1), but also more or less detailed references to the 18th-century origins of the term "aesthetics" in Baumgarten's *Aesthetica* (1750/58) and Kant's *Critik der Urtheilskraft* (1790). I will not offer a more detailed engagement with either Baumgarten or Kant despite their lasting impact on modern philosophical aesthetics, but the more recent conflation of *aisthesis* with *aesthetic* perception in the context of media aesthetics as well as the various resulting proposals to reconceptualize *ae*sthetics as *ai*sthetics need to be unpacked in at least slightly more detail. Welsch in particular has made a sustained effort to connect his early reconstruction of Aristotle's "project of an aisthetics" that ended up as a (mere) "aisthesiology" (Welsch 1987, 29; my translation) with a rather sweeping diagnosis of a "globalized aestheticization" (Welsch 1995, 5) of contemporary culture and a demand for "aesthetics as a field of research which comprises all kinds of questions concerning *aisthesis*" (Welsch 1995, 19–20; see also, e.g., Welsch 1990; 1993; 1996; 1997). While Welsch's work has thus also helped to pave the way for an increased interest in everyday aesthetics (see, e.g., Leddy 2012; Mandoki 2007; Ngai 2015; Saito 2012), I am here mainly concerned with its connection to how the aesthetics of digital media have been theorized during the 1990s. An early German-language collection on digital aesthetics edited by Rötzer (1991a), for example, has explored the ways in which (then) recent developments within computer technology "are relevant for the transformation of modes of perception and aesthetic forms" (Rötzer 1991b, 15; my translation) and the editors of another German-language collection (see Barck et al. 1993a) that aims to present (original as well as translated) "perspectives on another aesthetics" likewise follow the usual pattern in emphasizing that "perception, Greek for 'aisthesis', [...] should not be conflated with aesthetics as the system of fine arts" (Barck et al. 1993b, 445; my translation), before explicitly suggesting a reconceptualization of "aesthetics" as referring to the "perception of a world that becomes more artificial" (Barck et al. 1993b, 446; my translation). Despite the fact that these observations still connect quite closely to Welsch's "aestheticization" thesis, there are also rather more pronounced versions of this kind of argument to be found within the (then) emerging field of media aesthetics. Bolz, for example, confidently (and incorrectly) claims not only that the "term media aesthetics [...] reflects on the original meaning of *aisthesis*" (1990, 7) but also that "aesthetics" in general "is not a theory of (fine) art anymore," instead entailing (only) "a theory of *aisthesis* (media theory)" and "a technology of digital image production (computer graphics)" (1991, 7; my translation). I certainly agree that "[t]he *aesthetics* of media aesthetics" should not be "viewed as a philosophy of art" (Hausken 2013, 30; original emphasis) and would further note that the shift of focus suggested by Hausken and others also provides an important counter-weight to overly narrow approaches to the aesthetic form of media (see, e.g., Manovich 2017 for a brief survey; as well as the influential version of "applied media aesthetics" presented in Zettl 2016), but simply equaling media aesthetics with the "theory of culturally and historically embedded sensation and perception, conceptually developed from the original Greek sense of the term, as *aisthesis* or sense perception" (Hausken 2013, 30; see also, e.g., Rancière 2011) seems yet again too broad. So, instead of accepting the supposed "indistinguishability of aisthetic and aesthetic perception" (Kliche 1998, 485; my translation) that often seems to be at least implied in the field of media aesthetics, I will follow Seel (1993; 1997) and others in resisting the "'de-differentiation' of the terms 'aisthesis' and 'aesthetics'" (Ehrenspeck 1996, 202; my translation) that resulted from Welsch's works in particular, instead insisting on a "precise conceptual distinction between sense perception as *aisthesis* in general, and aesthetic practice in particular" (Reckwitz 2016, 60), which in turn also means that "aisthetics [as the study of the former; JNT] comes before any philosophical 'aesthetics' [...and] hence should not be conflated with the latter" (Seel 1993, 32n1; my translation).

15 Other accounts of aesthetic as opposed to nonaesthetic, functional, or pragmatic perception are available (see, e.g., Nanay's account of "aesthetic attention as distributed attention" [2016, 26]), but I find Seel's conceptualization of the former as a "sensing self-awareness" (2005, 31) that is saliently defined by its process-orientedness (*Vollzugsorientiertheit*) and self-referentiality (*Selbstbezüglichkeit*) particularly convincing (see also, again, Seel 1993; 1997 on this specification). It is also worth noting here that Seel consistently emphasizes that "this sensing has not yet anything to do with a *reflexive* self-referentiality, although this is often the case here too, especially in the context of art" (2005, 31; original emphasis). Incidentally, while I consider Schröter's (2019; 2023) aforementioned work on transmaterialization to provide a rather productive perspective on the domain of postdigital aesthetics that I would describe as the aesthetic transfer from the nondigital to the digital, I am not entirely convinced by his proposal to solve the tension between what he considers a "strong" conceptualization of "media aesthetics as 'aisthesis'" (Schröter 2019, n.pag.) *sensu* Bolz (1990; 1991) and a "weak" conceptualization of media aesthetics connected to "a specific use of the medium for the purpose of aesthetic perception" (Schröter 2019, n.pag.) *sensu* Seel (1993; 1997) by proposing a "medium kind of media aesthetics" that is (exclusively) "concerned with an aesthetics, even aisthetics, of predigital media, which become visible (and audible) once more through their transposed digital repetition" (Schröter 2019, n.pag.). Not only do I perhaps read Seel differently than Schröter seems to have done (in that I think Seel's conceptualization of aesthetic perception does not necessarily "adhere[] to a traditional, modernist concept of media reflexivity" [Schröter 2019, n.pag.]) but also would I suggest that Schröter's exclusive focus on transmaterialization vis-à-vis a media aesthetics of digital media at least slightly overemphasizes the domain of postdigital aesthetics that I would describe as the aesthetic transfer from the nondigital to the digital while ignoring (or at least deemphasizing) the domain of postdigital aesthetics that I would describe as the aesthetic intensification of the digital (both of which I would consider important aspects of the aesthetic form of digital medial artifacts across a range of conventionally distinct media forms, whereas the domain of postdigital aesthetics that I would describe as the aesthetic transfer from the digital to the nondigital and the domain of postdigital aesthetics that I would describe as the aesthetic intensification of the nondigital will mainly manifest themselves in nondigital medial artifacts that Schröter is not concerned with here). Moving beyond the distinction between aesthetic and nonaesthetic, functional, or pragmatic perception, I also occasionally refer to aesthetic *experience* here and in the following, which has been variously understood (in modern philosophical aesthetics) not just as the experience of beauty or, more generally, "the experience of aesthetic properties" (De Clercq 2002, 174; but see also Eaton 2001 and the more detailed discussion in note 13 on what this may mean) but also, for example, rather more broadly as "an integrated complete experience on its own account" (Dewey 1980, 55) that is characterized by the "thorough incorporation" of "desire and thought [...] into perceptual experience" (Dewey 1980, 254), as a "unified experience" within which "the percepts are integrated with affects of various kinds" (Beardsley 1981, lxi), as "including emotional and cognitive engagement along with perception of form" (Goldman 2013, 331), or as "*involving aesthetic perception of some object, grounded in aesthetic attention to the object*" as well as "*a positive hedonic, affective, or evaluative response to the perception itself or the content of that perception*" (Levinson 2016, 39; original emphases). So, there are many different kinds of aesthetic experience, and these different kinds of aesthetic experience (or aesthetic appreciation) can also be conceptualized differently, though perhaps not quite as broadly as "any strong (or intense, or emotionally significant) experience that we have in an aesthetic context"

(Nanay 2016, 12). It might indeed be better "to avoid talking vaguely of aesthetic experience" (Zangwill 2001, 29n10), then, yet my primary reason for (occasionally) using the term is precisely that it arguably serves to emphasize that recipients' engagement with medial artifacts (or other aesthetic objects) entails not only perceptual but also affective (or emotional) and imaginative (particularly quasi-perceptual) processes (a position which, not coincidentally, also seems to be broadly compatible with Seel's account of "aesthetic consciousness" as including "aesthetic perception" and "aesthetic imagination," albeit with the latter remaining "characterized by an imagined sensuous *presence* of what is envisaged" [2005, 73; original emphasis]).

16 In stating that the term "aesthetic form" here refers to the external *Gestalt* of medial artifacts (or other aesthetic objects) that is accessible to perception, I do not mean to suggest that the aesthetic form of such artifacts (or objects) should necessarily be understood as a "singular" *Gestalt*, let alone that it cannot be analyzed more precisely in terms of its constitutive components and their interrelations. Notwithstanding the fact that *Gestalt* psychology (see, e.g., Koffka 1935; Köhler 1929; von Ehrenfels 1890; Wertheimer 1925) has been made somewhat productive in phenomenology (see, e.g., Merleau-Ponty 1945; Wiese 2017) as well as in (broadly) psychological aesthetics (see, e.g., Arnheim 1954; Verstegen 2018), my point here is less about the "configuration of perception(s)" than it is about the "configuration of form(s)." Yet, while some philosophers may hold that "[t]here is no deep analytical problem in specifying what form [as opposed to representation and expression; JNT] in artworks is" (Goldman 1995, 82) and that "form" can thus unproblematically be defined as, say, "consist[ing] in relations among elements of works," which in turn "constitut[e] some intelligible order of these elements" (Goldman 1995, 83), it is worth noting here that "form has never belonged only to the discourse of aesthetics" (Levine 2015, 2) and that the term therefore (once more) has a rather complex conceptual history. That said, most if not "all the historical uses of the term" do seem to share a common conceptual core in that "'form' always indicates *an arrangement of elements*" that could also be described as "*an ordering, patterning, or shaping*" (Levine 2015, 3; original emphases) and that, again, becomes *aesthetic* if it is (in some way) accessible to perception. In any case, from the perspective of philosophical aesthetics, there may well be good reasons to privilege a "*phenomenological* account of aesthetic properties (or their descriptive components)" that understands such properties as "a unitary impression—a look, feel, or appearance—that an object is fitted to afford" over a "*structural* account" that understands their "descriptive components" as "a plurality of combinations of non-aesthetic features that an object might possess" (Levinson 2001, 68; original emphases), but independently of the (controversial) question of whether or not "aesthetic properties" are best conceptualized as "*higher-order ways of appearing*" that "arise out of the lower-order ways of appearing on which they depend in a holistic or emergent manner" (Levinson 2005, 218; original emphasis), it seems clear that the "overall phenomenal impression" (Levinson 2001, 69) afforded by medial artifacts (or other aesthetic objects) should not be the exclusive focus of the analysis of media aesthetics in general and postdigital aesthetics in particular. It is also worth noting again here that, in the broader aesthetic discourse within media studies and research on the postdigital, talk about "the forms of media artifacts" (Manovich 2017, 9) or, indeed, their "formal properties" (Corner 2019, 103) usually does not refer to "aesthetic properties" in the comparatively narrow sense in which that term is employed within (analytic) philosophical aesthetics (see note 13). Yet, even in that latter context, it seems reasonably safe to say that *some* of the formal properties "that attach closely to an object's perceivable form" (Levinson 2005, 224) should be considered to be aesthetic properties or "aesthetically relevant properties" (Nanay 2016, 67), while others should "merely" be considered to be the

kind of "narrow nonaesthetic properties" (Zangwill 2001, 57) that are also described as "perceptual qualities" (Sibley 1959, 438), "lower-order perceptual properties" (Levinson 2001, 61), or "the basest [...] of the base properties" (Goldman 1995, 82). Even if the focus of an analysis of a (specific kind of) postdigital aesthetics that can be attributed to a medial artifact (which may or may not be a medial representation; see note 18) will thus primarily be on the latter's ("aesthetic" as well as "nonaesthetic") formal or at least "semi-formal properties" (Nanay 2016, 99) as opposed to its representational or expressive properties (see also, e.g., Budd 1995; Eaton 2001; Goldman 1995), which some might take as a symptom of at least a mild case of formalism (see, e.g., Curtin on "pure" and "mixed formalism" [1982, 321], Wollheim's distinction between "Normative Formalism," "Analytic Formalism," "Manifest Formalism," and "Latent Formalism" [2001, 127], Zangwill's defense of a "moderate formalism" [2001, 55], Thomson-Jones discussion of the resurgence of "[s]ophisticated formalism" [2005, 375], and Nanay's argument for what he calls "semi-formalism" [2016, 97]), I moreover want to highlight not only the importance of the "(formal) relation between form and content" (Devereaux 1998, 245), which goes well beyond the evaluative aesthetic property of the "aptness of form to content" (Goldman 1990, 32) or "the ability [of works of art; JNT] to satisfy us in virtue of the appropriateness of their forms to their contents" (Eldridge 1985, 315), but also the notion that the representational content of a medial artifact that fulfills representational functions has a "form" of its own.

17 Of course, the concept of aesthetic practice(s) as a whole cannot be reduced to such "localized practices of artefactual construction" (Corner 2019, 108) that are also variously described as (a broad range of) "creative practices" (Andrews 2013, 256), "art and design practices" (Berry and Dieter 2015b, 2), "cultural and artistic practice[s]" (Paul and Levy 2015, 27), or "media practice[s]" (Betancourt 2017, 49) within and beyond research on the postdigital. In fact, aesthetic practice(s) are no less commonly conceptualized as being constituted by "[t]he encounter and the process of exchange between artefact and recipient" (Nielsen 2005, 64) or, indeed, as "practices of self-referential perception" (Reckwitz 2016, 63) *sensu* Seel (1993, 1997; 2005). Seel himself conceptualizes the "aesthetic practice of art as a *local* practice" (amongst other kinds of aesthetic practice) that entails "all human activities of perception- or production-oriented engagement with art" (1993, 31; original emphasis; my translation), while also emphasizing that "aesthetic reception and aesthetic production are categorially different things" (1993, 32; my translation). Yet, just as aesthetic production *also* involves perception, so can aesthetic reception not be reduced to perception or experience. Instead, it should be conceptualized as (also) entailing discursive practice(s). Eaton, for example, notes that, when "people [...] do any of the ordinary and extraordinary things that people do when they describe themselves or others as being engaged in artistic activity, they interact with an artifact, consciously paying attention to intrinsic properties of that artifact that their culture has identified as worthy of perception and reflection" (2001, 5), yet also emphasizes that, "[w]hen personal pleasure leads individuals to invite others to attend to those properties, communal practices and institutions that generate and regenerate attention develop" (2001, 203). While I thus happily accept that both aesthetic practice in general and particular aesthetic practic*es* may entail the creation or production as well as the perception or experience of medial artifacts (or other aesthetic objects) and indeed the broad range of "aesthetic discourse" (Sibley 1965, 136; as well as, e.g., De Clercq 2002, 168; Eaton 2001, 13; Goldman 1995, 25; Levinson 2001, 62) or other follow-up communication that the latter may give rise to (and, not coincidentally, would also acknowledge that these distinctions are not always easily drawn within actual aesthetic practice[s], let alone in the context of our so-called participatory [media] culture; see,

e.g., Bruns 2008; Jenkins 2006; Jenkins et al. 2013; Schäfer 2011), my terminological emphasis on aesthetic *production* practices rather than aesthetic *reception* practices is primarily designed to highlight the need to include the former in any comprehensive analysis of postdigital aesthetics as well. The observation that the analysis of postdigital aesthetics will profit from the inclusion of a praxeological perspective also suggests a methodological stance that aims to combine the detailed analysis of the aesthetic form of specific medial artifacts (or other aesthetic objects) with an expanded analysis of related articulations not only of aesthetic perception or experience but also of aesthetic (production) practices in various paratexts (with the latter term here referring to an expanded conceptualization that has become influential in film and television studies [see, e.g., Gray 2010] as well as in game studies [see, e.g., Švelch 2020] and beyond [see, e.g., Brookey and Gray 2017], leading to *media* paratexts now usually being understood as including trailers and other PR materials, interviews with or other kinds of statements from creators, "making of" documentaries and postmortems, professional and non-professional reviews, Let's Plays and other forms of streaming, as well as other kinds of critical discussions, and hence at least potentially allowing paratextual analysis to offer insights into aesthetic production practices *as well as* aesthetic reception practices).

18 I have, thus far, usually referred to medial artifacts and other aesthetic objects, emphasizing the distinction between aesthetic objects that are human-made and those that are not. That said, my focus is indeed not merely on medial artifacts but rather on the kind of medial artifacts that fulfill representational functions and can therefore be described as (external) medial representations (distinguishing them from internal mental representations), many (though perhaps not all) of which can further be specified as narrative representations (see note 7). Needless to say, the question how medial and/or narrative representations represent what they represent (i.e., their representational content) is yet again quite complex. Walton, for example, treats (human-made and thus artefactual) representations as "props in games of make-believe" (1990, 12), within which their primary function is to mandate the imagining of "fictional truths" (1990, 35) following certain "principles of generation" (1990, 38). Broadly similar conceptualizations of narrative representations are available within transmedial narratology, though those tend to more directly connect their accounts of how recipients comprehend narrative representations to cognitive theory (see, once more, Herman 2009; Ryan 2006; as well as Thon 2016b; 2017). As important as these comprehensive theories of representation are for understanding medial and, indeed, narrative representations, however, I am here mainly interested in the question of different "levels" of representation (see note 38) as well as in how the interplay between Walton's "Reality Principle" or "Mutual Belief Principle" (1990, 144), which Ryan has influentially reformulated as the "principle of minimal departure" (1991, 51), and a more or less medium-specific "principle of charity" (Walton 1990, 183) is realized in the context of videogames, whose interactive gameplay and potentially nonlinear narrative structures arguably lead to rather complex forms of "representational correspondence" (Currie 2010, 59) that regularly include more or less strongly foregrounded tensions between the representation of a videogame's gameplay and its storyworld or storyworlds (see, e.g., Thon 2015; 2016a).

19 As the other chapters in the present volume will have sufficiently illustrated, this transmedial conceptualization of metareference can be specified not only with regard to literary texts, comics, animation, photography, films, and series but also with regard to videogames and other "interactive" media forms. Yet, whether we conceptualize the phenomena in question as (more or less) videogame-specific forms of "metareference" (see, e.g., Krampe 2023; 2025; Krampe et al. 2022) or employ videogame-specific terms such as "metagames" (see, e.g., Waszkiewicz 2024), "metaludicity" (see, e.g., Ensslin 2014),

or "metaproceduralism" (see, e.g., Fest 2016), the kind of foregrounding of the mediality, materiality, or aesthetic form of videogames that constitutes a core aspect of the comprehensive conceptualization of postdigital aesthetics proposed in this chapter evidently only encompasses a comparatively small part of the sum total of metareferential phenomena within and beyond the area of videogames in general and indie games in particular.

20 Indeed, the relation between transparency and opacity has received considerable attention in philosophical aesthetics, semiotics, and media theory well beyond Bolter and Grusin's (1996; 1999) distinction between a logic of (transparent) immediacy and a logic of (opaque) hypermediacy. This includes not just long-standing discussions around the supposed transparency of photographic (and other) pictures (see, e.g., Gaut 2008; Lopes 1996; Walton 1984; Wollheim 1968) and various attempts to conceptualize opacity as a salient aspect of an "aesthetics of the surface" (see, e.g., Bruno 2014; Rathe 2020; Shusterman 2002; and the contributions in Rautzenberg and Wolfsteiner 2010; as well as Nanay's "semi-formalist" discussion of the "surface properties" [2016, 94] of pictures) but also various more specific proposals to come to terms with those aspects of the materiality, mediality, or aesthetic form of semiotic artifacts that "resist" processes of meaning making (for a selection of different approaches, see, e.g., Barthes 1977 on the "obtuse meaning" of photographs; Thompson 1977 on "cinematic excess"; Mersch 2002 on pictures' [material] "presence" as opposed to their [semiotic] "representation"; or Böhme 2016 on how "materiality" shapes "atmospheres"). In this context, it is also worth noting that, while the discussion around formalism in philosophical aesthetics has primarily focused on pictures in general and (modernist) painting in particular (see also note 16), there is of course also a broader "formalist" discourse in literary, cultural, and media studies that often seems to be particularly interested in so-called Russian Formalism. Perhaps most saliently, Shklovsky's (2012) concept of *ostranenie* (or "making strange"), which is often seen as strikingly similar to Brecht's (1964) concept of the *Verfremdungseffekt* (or "alienation effect"), has been made productive not only for media art in general (see Benthien et al. 2019, which also includes a detailed conceptual history) but also for a specific kind of formal analysis of videogames (see Mitchell and van Vught 2023).

21 Thinking about literary texts, comics, animation, photography, films, series, and games in this way presupposes a conceptualization of media as conventionally (rather than "merely" technologically and/or semiotically) distinct (see, e.g., Rajewsky 2010; Ryan 2006; Thon 2016b; Wolf 1999). Rajewsky's aforementioned observation that intermedial references need to be foregrounded in a way that establishes a "perceptible medial difference" (2005, 62) also yet again allows us to connect the concept of postdigital aesthetics to Lev Manovich's program of "postmedia aesthetics," which proposes "substituting the concept of medium by [sic] new concepts from computer and net culture" (2014, 37), but ultimately seems to overemphasize the degree to which (the perception of) media borders actually disappear(s). From the point of view of intermediality studies and transmedial narratology, it is clear that contemporary media cultures still very much operate with conventionally distinct media (or, more precisely, with media forms that are perceived as being conventionally distinct), but the aesthetics of digital media forms such as digital literature, webcomics, digital films and series, or videogames are not defined by their material-technological foundation anymore, which is a core condition for processes of transmaterialization *sensu* Schröter (2019; 2023) and, thus, for what I would describe as the aesthetic transfer from the nondigital to the digital.

22 During the past decade, the interdisciplinary field of game studies has increasingly begun to explore the production, aesthetics, and reception of so-called indie games, often also acknowledging that the term itself is not entirely unproblematic (see, e.g., Garda and Grabarczyk 2016; Juul 2019; O'Donnell 2014; Styhre 2020; as well as the contributions

in Clarke and Wang 2020; Ruffino 2021; and my own attempts to come to theoretical and methodological terms with indie games and their diverse aesthetics in Backe and Thon 2019; Bódi and Thon 2020; Krampe et al. 2022; Thon 2019a; 2020; 2023; 2025). Garda and Grabarczyk, for example, note that we can attribute a greater or lesser degree of financial, creative, and publishing independence to any given videogame, yet still argue that the term "indie game" or " 'indie' functions as a label for a specific kind of independent games that emerged around the mid-2000s," when "indie games became so prominent and so distinct that they started to be easily identifiable via a set of contingent properties" (2016, n.pag.) that include, for example, the expectation that such videogames are developed with a comparatively small budget (and a correspondingly small team), are (primarily or exclusively) distributed digitally, and are more likely than mainstream videogames to engage in aesthetic "experimentation." Drawing slightly different distinctions that fold Garda and Grabarczyk's publishing independence into the category of financial independence while breaking down further their notion of creative independence, Juul (2019) has also examined the discursive construction of what he describes as indie games' financial, aesthetic, and cultural independence in some detail. Garda and Grabarczyk as well as Juul rightly emphasize that this multidimensional "logic of distinction" (see Jahn-Sudmann 2008) is best understood as referring to a discursive construct rather than to a set of properties (aesthetic, aesthetically relevant, or otherwise) that would somehow be inherent in all indie games, which becomes even clearer if we remember not only that some indie games (such as *Hellblade: Senua's Sacrifice* [2017]) are produced with comparatively large budgets and high production values but also that some videogames that are decidedly not "indie" (such as Ubisoft's *Child of Light* [2014]) still "co-opt" a recognizably "independent style" (see also, e.g., Lipkin 2012 on these now fairly widespread processes of "co-optation"). No less importantly, the publishing situation of indie games is also often more complex than Garda and Grabarcyk's or Juul's categories might initially suggest, which is not least illustrated by the fact that the publisher Annapurna Interactive now specializes in publishing indie games (see, e.g., Parker 2021).

23 For previous explorations of videogames through the lens of the postdigital, see also, e.g., Aarseth 2006; Apperley 2015; Thibault 2016, with the latter in particular focusing on the kinds of indie games and "indie" aesthetics that I am also primarily interested in here, albeit with a somewhat different theoretical framing. I would not, for example, follow Thibault in his argument that what he calls "the analogue aesthetics" of (some) indie games leads to their "digital nature" being "hidden—almost denied—while the fictitious nature of the game is brought to the foreground" (2016, 12). Thibault is not alone in confusing the representationality of videogames with their fictionality or, perhaps, their "fictitiousness" (see, e.g., Juul 2005 for an influential discussion of videogames' representationality-as-fictionality; as well as the brief critique in Thon 2016a; 2016b, 104–122), but, to the extent that some indie games' postdigital aesthetics are defined by what I would describe as an aesthetic transfer from the nondigital to the digital, I would argue that they foreground (rather than "hide" or even "deny") not only the remediated materiality, mediality, and aesthetic form of *nondigital* (or not primarily digital) media forms but also their own materiality, mediality, and aesthetic form as *digital* videogames.

24 Hence, I have previously suggested operating within a theoretical framework that systematically distinguishes between the audiovisual, ludic, and narrative aesthetics of indie games (see, e.g., Thon 2019a; 2020; 2023 for a more detailed discussion of what these dimensions of indie aesthetics entail; see also, e.g., Feige 2015; Kirkpatrick 2011; Sharp 2015 for more general discussions of the complex and contested relation between videogames and aesthetic theory, broadly conceived). It may go without saying that this is an analytical distinction of aspects of the aesthetics of videogames in general and

indie games in particular that are in actual practice often quite closely interrelated. It is, for example, commonly the case that visual and auditive signals allow players to orient themselves within the gameplay; that narrative elements such as cutscenes or scripted events are used to frame the interactive gameplay and to communicate pertinent information about game rules or game goals; and that the audiovisually represented, rule-governed gameplay also contributes to the unfolding story of a videogame at least to some extent. Yet, it is precisely the drawing of a distinction between the audiovisual, ludic, and narrative aesthetics of indie games that allows for the in-depth analysis of such interrelations—and, arguably, also of specific instantiations of the postdigital aesthetics of indie games. Indeed, the foregrounding of indie games' mediality, materiality, or aesthetic form that follows the logic of hypermediacy can be realized in many different ways and may also include those videogames' ludic and narrative aesthetics, with *Armello* (2015) or *Card Hunter* (2015), for example, remediating the aesthetics of nondigital "ludic objects" such as game boards, cards, or dice, while *Pyre* (2017) and *Pentiment* (2022) remediate books as arguably the most prototypical of nondigital "narrative objects."

25 Not coincidentally, Juul explicitly draws on Bolter and Grusin's (1999) concept of remediation (which is not particularly unusual in game studies; see, e.g., Ivănescu 2019, 29–74; Kirkland 2011; Sloan 2015), noting not only that the latter "make the broad claim that new media tend to *remediate*—that is, simulate—earlier media forms" and that indie games using an "independent style" can thus be said to "*remediate* earlier styles to create something new and contemporary" (Juul 2019, 31; original emphases) but also underscoring Bolter and Grusin's (1999) argument "that each new medium promises us a more immediate—transparent—experience, while pointing to itself as a medium in the process" (Juul 2019, 38). Yet, despite Juul evidently being aware of Bolter and Grusin's "double logic of remediation" (1999, 31) and, hence, also of the concepts of immediacy and hypermediacy that they develop, he is careful not to employ these terms, instead arguing that the use of "independent style" functions as a marker for a different kind of immediacy in that it "signal[s] that a game with this style is more immediate, authentic, and honest than are big-budget titles with high-end, three-dimensional graphics" (Juul 2019, 38). It might also be worth noting here that, whereas I have intentionally not focused on the concept of "style" in my discussion of postdigital aesthetics (since I prioritize the arguably broader concept of "aesthetic form"), "style" has of course been a very influential (and, perhaps unsurprisingly, notably iridescent) concept not just in game studies but also in literary studies (see, e.g., the various contributions in Burke 2014), comics studies (see, e.g., Etter 2021), film studies (see, e.g., Bordwell et al. 1985), television studies (see, e.g., Butler 2010), and (more recently) critical AI studies (see, e.g., Meyer 2023).

26 As one might expect, the terminology here is somewhat contested, with terms such as "digital games," "computer games," "videogames" (as well as "video games"), or indeed just "games" being used more or less interchangeably in the field of game studies despite various attempts to establish more specific conceptualizations or terminological distinctions (see, e.g., Arjoranta 2019 for a recent survey). Although I will use the term "videogame" throughout, that usage is not meant to mark a conceptual difference to terms such as "digital games," "computer games," or indeed "video games." That said, I would maintain that the more general term "game" should be used to refer to both digital and nondigital games (see also, e.g., Deterding and Zagal 2018; Torner et al. 2016; Wake and Germaine 2023), while the term "indie game" as it is used in the present chapter refers to a subset of videogames that is perceived and positioned as "indie" in terms of their production, distribution, financing, and aesthetics (see also, once more, Garda and Grabarczyk 2016; Juul 2019; as well as note 22).

27 Again, the question which aesthetic practices and aesthetic forms are more or less likely to be perceived as following the logic of hypermediacy as opposed to the logic of immediacy (and, thus, are perhaps also more likely to instigate aesthetic perception) cannot be answered in an "ahistoric vacuum." As Bolter and Grusin note, "[a]lthough the logic of immediacy has manifested itself from the Renaissance to the present day, each manifestation in each age may be significantly different, and immediacy may mean one thing to theorists, another to practicing artists or designers, and a third to viewers. The diversity is even greater for hypermediacy, which seems always to offer a number of different reactions to the contemporary logic of immediacy. Remediation always operates under the current cultural assumptions about immediacy and hypermediacy" (1999, 21). Against this background, an argument could be made not only that the (comparatively) "low resolution" graphics, sound, and music to be found in videogames of the 1960s, 1970s, and 1980s still primarily aimed at following the logic of immediacy rather than that of hypermediacy but also that the increasing conventionalization of "pixelated" graphics and supposedly 8-bit sound and music within what Juul describes as indie games' "independent style" (2019, 38) works to reduce the potential of these aesthetic practices to generate pronounced "hypermediacy effects." That said, I would maintain that some indie games are still able to foreground the relevant processes of remediation in ways that primarily follow the logic of hypermediacy rather than that of immediacy and that the associated aesthetic practices are also still commonly seen as establishing a "logic of distinction" (see Jahn-Sudmann 2008) in the surrounding discourse.

28 When they first started to coalesce as a genre during the first half of the 2010s, walking simulators did break with established conventions of mainstream videogame design to such a large extent that they were not considered to be videogames at all by some players and professional critics (see, e.g., Consalvo and Paul 2019, 109–130; Juul 2019, 187–210; Kagen 2022, 1–28; Montembeault and Deslongchamps-Gagnon 2019; Muscat et al. 2016; van Nuenen 2024, 51–69; Zimmerman and Huberts 2019 for more detailed reconstructions of the relevant discussions; see also Thon 2025 for an exploration of the aesthetics of walking simulators as affording their players experiences of *otium*). While Juul rightly notes that "[w]alking simulators are a prime example of *aesthetic* independence" in that they are "rejecting conventions, giving us new experiences, making us do new things" (2019, 187; original emphasis), this defensive stance toward the emerging genre on the part of some players (and critics) seems to have been closely connected to walking simulators' cultural independence as well, since many walking simulators chose to represent characters and explore themes around gender and queerness that were (and continue to be) comparatively "unusual" in mainstream videogames. Not coincidentally, despite the fact that the term "walking simulator" was initially used derogatorily, it has since been "reclaimed" as a genre label and will be used here and in the following instead of alternative genre labels such as "narrative exploration game." In any case, although discussions around whether or not walking simulators "are" videogames may be more broadly interesting because they shed light on what different discourse participants do or do not consider a videogame and also allow us to explore the question of "what happens when something is deemed *not* a game or not a *real* game" (Consalvo and Paul 2019, xx; original emphases), there still can be little doubt that the digital medial artifacts we would readily describe as walking simulators are commonly positioned and perceived as videogames and, more specifically, as indie games.

29 While using "procedural content generation either to generate terrain, resources, or both" (Bódi 2023, 173; see also the more detailed and critical discussion of "generative methods" in Compton et al. 2013) has been quite common in survival-crafting games

(including *Terraria* and *Minecraft* as well as indie games not using "pixelated" graphics, such as *Astroneer* [2016] or *No Man's Sky* [2016]) for some time now, it remains exceedingly rare in walking simulators. It is also worth noting here that, even if the game spaces in *Proteus* are procedurally generated, the objects they consist of are not (or at least do not seem to be), meaning that procedural generation in *Proteus* is largely a matter of arranging (rather than generating) the objects constituting the game spaces (which is, however, true for both *Terraria* and *Minecraft* as well). Finally, although I cannot unpack the complex question of videogames' narrativity in more detail here, the procedurally generated game spaces of *Proteus* (as well as those of *Terraria* and *Minecraft*) seem to focus on "dramatic" rather than "narrative agency," affording the "players opportunities to 'heighten' the narrativity of the gameplay without relying primarily on predetermined narrative events" (Bódi and Thon 2020, 165; see also Bódi 2023).

30 Just like all other generic or videogame-specific conventions, the use of the W key (for moving forward), the A key (for strafing left), the S key (for moving backward), and the D key (for strafing right) in combination with a mouse or trackpad (for changing both the visual and the spatial orientation of the player-controlled character) is not an ahistorical constant of videogame design. That said, while early first-person shooters (that were not called first-person shooters yet) such as *Wolfenstein 3D* (1992) or *Doom* (1993) used a different default key mapping focusing on the arrow keys, the WASD key mapping was well established by 2013.

31 It would go beyond the scope of this chapter to discuss the question of videogame space in any detail, but it might still be helpful to distinguish between a videogame's game spaces (that the players can interact with), the narrative spaces of a videogame's storyworld (to the extent that the videogame in question does represent one or several storyworlds), and the social spaces that are constructed through the interaction between a videogame's players and/or their avatars (which are mostly, though not exclusively, relevant in the case of multiplayer games) as well as between different "representational types" of game spaces (see, e.g., Thon 2006; 2008 for a more detailed discussion of the former; as well as Egenfeldt-Nielsen 2020, 121–155, for a broad survey of the latter). In any case, it seems clear that the aesthetic form of a videogame employing a first-person perspective to represent 3D game spaces is quite different from that of a videogame using (a) single-screen 2D game space(s). Yet, *Proteus* is noteworthy in its combination of a first-person perspective with flat colors that lead to the representation of 3D game spaces that still look comparatively "two-dimensional."

32 It is worth noting here that many so-called walking simulators do not actually simulate "walking" in a particularly specific way, but the spatial position of the player-controlled character in *Proteus* and the fact that they can traverse the surface of the ocean in exactly the same way as they can traverse the surface of the island arguably still highlights the lack of specificity in *Proteus*'s simulation of the player-controlled character's movement. In contradistinction, the player-controlled character in *Dear Esther* (2012) swiftly drowns (albeit not permanently) when they enter the Sea of the Hebrides that surrounds the (different and very differently represented) island at the center of that walking simulator's gameplay.

33 Time may manifest in different ways in many videogames and it will thus not come as a surprise that different approaches to the analysis of videogame time have been developed (see, e.g., Alvarez Igarzábal 2019; Hanson 2018; Juul 2005; Zagal and Mateas 2010). That said, thinking about time in videogames evidently requires acknowledging different "temporal frames," which may include (but are not limited to) the frame of "[r]eal-world time" that "is established by the set of events taking place in the physical world around the player," the frame of "[g]ameworld time" that "is established by the set of

events taking place within the represented gameworld," the frame of "[c]oordination time" that "is established by the set of events that coordinate the actions of multiple players (human or artificial intelligence) and possibly in-game agents," and the frame of "[f]ictive time" that is established through the application of sociocultural labels [such as "days" or "years"; JNT] to a subset of events" (Zagal and Mateas 2010, 852) and might alternatively be described as "storyworld time." While *Proteus*'s gameplay largely seems to collapse the frames of "real-world time" and "gameworld time," one day/night cycle within the frame of "fictive time" equals 15 minutes within the frame of "real-world time" (though this can be changed in the options menu once the players have completed their first playthrough). No less importantly, however, the seasons of spring, summer, and fall do not end after a set number of days and nights within the frame of "fictive time" (or within a set number of day/night cycles within the frame of "gameworld time"), but rather require the player-controlled character to stand in a stone circle (specific to each season) at night, which then "triggers" the beginning of the next season the following morning. Once spring has passed to summer, summer has passed to fall, and fall has passed to winter in this way, the players can either make the player-controlled character stand in the "winter stone circle" during the night or wait for the next morning. In either case, the player-controlled character will then float toward heaven until the island is out of sight and they close their eyes again. Even if there *are* game goals in *Proteus*, then, it seems clear that the aesthetic experience it affords its players is not focused on reaching these game goals as effectively as possible. Instead, *Proteus* invites its players to have the player-controlled character explore the "sights and sounds" of the island and its different seasons at a rather more leisurely pace.

34 Even if we acknowledge that abstract paintings are not necessarily nonrepresentational, comparing *Proteus* to Turrell's work (and arguably not just his installations) still seems more fitting than comparing it to Kandinsky's (see, e.g., Adcock 1990; Düchting 2000), but the observations that both these comparisons are made is evidently relevant in and of itself.

35 The commonly drawn distinction between "sound," "music," and "speech" is certainly already problematic in theoretical terms and videogames like *Proteus* further remind us of the blurred boundaries between ("mere") sound and ("artfully arranged") music in particular, but these distinctions are still largely established within game studies (or the subfield of game studies that is sometimes called ludomusicology; see, e.g., Collins 2008; 2016; Summers 2016; 2024). Here and in the following, I will employ Egenfeldt-Nielsen and colleagues' rather basic distinction between "vocalization" as referring to "the voices of characters in a game (including voice-over speech and other off-screen elements," "sound effects" as referring to "sounds made by in-game objects," "ambient effects" as referring to "nonspecific sounds contributing to the game atmosphere," and "music" as referring to "the soundtrack to the game" (2020, 145), though I will also use additional distinctions proposed by Collins (2008) between "diegetic" vs. "nondiegetic," "linear" vs. "nonlinear," and "dynamic" vs. "nondynamic" sound.

36 While I was not able to access all of the material in question myself at the time of this writing, it is also worth noting here that O'Hara not only analyzes *Proteus*'s soundscape and musical composition in considerable detail but also engages with Kanaga's theoretical reflections on videogame music and music composition more generally. Among other interesting observations, Kanaga stresses that "[v]ideogames are musical interfaces. And, being dynamic, they're of particular interest, re: fluidity. [...] When a soundtrack is subject to the variability of a game's mechanics, the music itself becomes a mechanic, an instrument—music to be played. And the fluid space that houses this mechanic becomes a space for the play of instruments, a composition—again, music to be played. Spaces hold other spaces which in turn hold others, and so the hierarchical relationship between

instrument and composition which says that the former is a component object used in the latter can be dissolved, reversed" (as quoted in O'Hara 2020, 45). In a sense, then, *Proteus* presents as a successful experiment in a practice-as-research context.

37 Not coincidentally, *Pony Island* is the first "full" indie game developed and published by Daniel Mullins, who later developed and published both *The Hex* and *Inscryption*, thus arguably having been particularly influential in terms of how indie games employ "glitches" toward the aesthetic intensification of the digital (see also the chapter by Hennig as well as the chapters by Caracciolo and Thorne in this volume). Yet, even if it seems plausible that Daniel Mullins "was always trying to think of subversions of typical game expectations" (Daniel Mullins in Kapron 2021, n.pag.) when designing *Pony Island*, it is also worth noting that the latter can be located in a broader generic trend of "glitch horror" or "metareferential horror" (see, e.g., Allan 2023; Gass 2024; Holmes 2010; Prevas 2023; Schlarb 2019; Zawacki 2024; as well as the chapters by Krampe and Waszkiewicz in this volume).

38 In the narratological terminology established by Genette (1983), Bal (1997), and others, the actual indie game *Pony Island* thus can be analyzed as representing a primary, diegetic storyworld level within which the player-controlled character and the fictional Pony Island are located, while the latter represents a secondary, metadiegetic or hypodiegetic storyworld level that is ontologically distinct from the primary, diegetic storyworld level (see also Thon 2015; 2016b for more detailed discussions of this terminology). That said, the borders between the storyworld levels are considerably blurred in *Pony Island*, both because of its tendency to use forms of metalepsis that include the actual players' actual operating systems and actual program files in their supposedly paradoxical ontological transgressions (see also, once more, the chapter by Krampe in this volume) and because another diabolic entity, Baphomet, suggests during a series of brief encounters that the player-controlled character was a 13th-century crusader named Theodore, who was killed at Jerusalem's wall and whose soul is now trapped in limbo, which takes the form of an arcade that includes many more arcade machines than those the player-controlled character ends up playing and the supernatural nature of which allows for a plausibilization of the kind of ontological transgressions between storyworld levels that might initially seem downright paradoxical.

39 In fact, the apparent finality of this radical last step is not only subverted by an alternative ending that sees the player-controlled character pitted in a fight against the Hopeless Soul, which "continues [...] until the player makes a decision to close and exit" (Waszkiewicz 2024, 69) the program, but also hides yet another of the many secret branches of the narrative that *Pony Island* allows its players to explore. As Edrei notes, "if the player delves into the game's registry key [...] and restarts the game rather than delete it, an extra line of dialogue from Lucifer will utterly transform the meaning and context of the Hopeless Soul's request," in that Lucifer is claiming that he sometimes "like[s] to talk in different voices" and thus "suggesting that the antagonist of the game and the player's ally are in fact the same entity" (2018, 118). That said, I would still not agree that *Pony Island*'s extensive use of ontological (rather than rhetorical) metalepses can appropriately be understood as an "attempt[] to imply that it is the player themselves that has become another lost soul trapped in the confines of the arcade cabinet" (Barkman 2021, 12), nor that releasing the Hopeless Soul by deleting the actual *Pony Island* can (or should) actually be described as "releasing Satan to the extra-fictional world" (Waszkiewicz 2024, 69).

40 Although it would perhaps be misleading to describe *Cuphead* as a nonlinear game, its players *do* have the option to make Cuphead and Mugman join the Devil instead of fighting him, thus skipping the final boss fight as well as the standard concluding picturebook cutscene. Instead, a briefer alternative cutscene then represents diabolic versions of Cuphead and Mugman standing at the side of the Devil, and if the players

fast-forward through the following credits, the barbershop quartet tune accompanying the title menu is now played backward.

41 That said, *Cuphead* does also employ various diegetized nondigital objects, including the old phonograph and the "magic inkwell" in Elder Kettle's house as well as, for example, the "soul contracts" that the Devil initially asks Cuphead and Mugman to collect and the various "upgrade cards" available from Porkrind's emporium. Still, while some of these diegetized nondigital objects evidently fulfill important ludic functions, their narrative functions arguably remain quite limited and they certainly do not act as narrative "framing devices" that would be in any way comparable to the picturebook from the opening and closing cutscenes.

42 It is also worth mentioning there that other "unlockable filters" are available: specifically, the "two-strip mode" that remediates early versions of the Technicolor process (and is unlocked by defeating 15 bosses with an A-grade or higher) and the "vintage mode" that adds a "sound filter" remediating the decidedly "echoing" audio quality of many older animated films (and is automatically unlocked once players unlock one of the other available visual filters).

43 Incidentally, McGowan not only suggests that "[t]he playful conceit within *Cuphead* [...] is that players are experiencing and somehow manipulating footage from a lost franchise of the 1930s" (2019, 16) but also notes that the actual "*Cuphead* franchise has already extended beyond just the game, including the release of a deluxe vinyl edition of the title's soundtrack and deals with the toy company Funko to offer action figures and plush dolls in the likeness of characters such as Cuphead and Mugman" (2019, 21). However, the "*Cuphead* franchise" has expanded considerably since 2019 and now includes a significantly broader range of merchandise as well as various tie-in novels, graphic novels, the Netflix animated series *The Cuphead Show!* (2022), and the extensive DLC *Cuphead: The Delicious Last Course* (2022), making it a full-fledged character-centered transmedia franchise (see also, e.g., Jenkins 2006; Johnson 2013; Thon 2019b; Tosca and Klastrup 2020 for further discussions of transmedia franchises, transmedia storytelling, transmedia characters, and transmedia[l] worlds).

44 It might be worth noting that I here use "narrating" in a comparatively broad sense as including both narrative objects that employ a narrator-as-narrating-character and those that do not (see also Thon 2015; 2016b, 123–166, for further discussion of this conceptualization of narrators). Whereas most of the "narrating objects" in *What Remains of Edith Finch* (including Edith's journal that her son reads after she has died during childbirth and which acts as the central "framing device") do use a narrator-as-narrating-character to which we can attribute specific segments of narratorial representation, for example, some (such as the photographs that Edith's mother Dawn took of her [Dawn's] father Sam during a hunting trip right before Sam died) only "trigger" voice-over narration that is not represented as being recorded within the "narrating object" itself in some way. Here and throughout this chapter, I also use the comparatively broad term "object" despite the fact that the "narrating objects" in question are not just any kinds of aesthetic objects but rather medial artifacts, or, more specifically, medial representations. Still, these medial artifacts or medial representations are always (aesthetic) objects as well.

45 While the objects within the various game spaces are generally designed with notable attention to detail, the books populating the Finch family home are worth highlighting not only because of their sheer quantity but also because quite a few of them have well-known real-world counterparts and are likely meant to be read as comments on the gameplay's themes.

46 According to Ian Dallas, *What Remains of Edith Finch*'s "modular" narrative structure also mirrors the overall design process. He explains that "a lot of the individual stories were finished piecemeal" (Ian Dallas in Espineli 2017, n.pag.), yet also stresses that "the Edith story didn't solidify until the last couple of months," when the team "had a better

sense of what that overarching narrative with Edith actually needed to do, and what questions players would have after certain stories, and where they would be emotionally" (Ian Dallas in gamer_152 2018, n.pag.). One might argue, then, that it is precisely *What Remains of Edith Finch*'s "modular" narrative structure that allowed Giant Sparrow to include an unusually broad range of different aesthetic strategies and remediated nondigital "narrating objects" throughout the various "vignettes." No less importantly, though, the "framing device" of Edith's journal also exhibits a particularly foregrounded form of postdigital aesthetics, both because Edith's written verbal narration from the journal is the first segment of narratorial representation that is translated into spoken voice-over narration as well as into floating segments of text that appear as if they were part of the game spaces and because it contains what appears to be a decidedly handdrawn "family tree" to which Edith seems to add portraits of her various family members once she has encountered the "narrating objects" representing their respective deaths.

47 *What Remains of Edith Finch* uses the nonnarratorial gameplay to illustrate and "fill in the gaps" of the framing verbal narration, offering often quite subjective and occasionally metaphorical versions of the family members' deaths. Yet, even if there are plenty of players insisting that "[w]e can't know any answers of what truly happened to any of these characters, because of the wonderful ambiguity in their stories" (Kuyatt 2023, n.pag.), and there are indeed many open questions regarding the supposed "family curse" and other elements of magical realism in *What Remains of Edith Finch*, most deaths are represented in such a way that players will be able to come up with a plausible explanation for what at first glance might be represented as fantastical events. The main exception to this seems to be Milton's flipbook that represents a flipbook representing his disappearance into a painting. What is particularly interesting here is that the players are not offered any information that would contradict the interpretation that Milton has in fact stepped into one of his paintings, never to return. Rather, the interpretation of the flipbook as a largely accurate documentation (of a documentation) of what happened also seems to be shared by Ian Dallas, who has repeatedly stated that Milton did indeed step into one of his paintings and became the king in Giant Sparrow's first game, *The Unfinished Swan* (2012), which is further supported by various objects in and around Milton's room that refer to the latter, suggesting that the two storyworlds of these two videogames might be a single transtextual storyworld (see, e.g., Espineli 2017).

48 That is not to say that this is the only "vignette" that is interesting in terms of postdigital aesthetics. On the contrary, many of the other "vignettes" also exhibit a more or less foregrounded remediation of the mediality, materiality, and aesthetic form of decidedly nondigital objects. Incidentally, although *What Remains of Edith Finch* clearly privileges the domain of postdigital aesthetics that I would describe as the aesthetic transfer from the nondigital to the digital, it is worth noting that the "vignette" representing how Lewis "loses himself" in the increasingly elaborate fantasy world he imagines in order to "escape" from his monotonous job at a local fish cannery (and how he eventually dies by suicide in the factory's automated fish guillotine) also includes at least some elements that move it closer to the domain of postdigital aesthetics that I would describe as the aesthetic intensification of the digital. As with the other "vignettes," this is already prepared by the clutter of objects in Lewis's room, which include a computer with several screens, a dedicated videogame console, and various other gaming paraphernalia, as well as by Edith's voice-over narration noting that they used to play videogames together and that Lewis "died a lot" during these gaming sessions. More importantly, however, while the gameplay segment that fuses the representation of the hypo-hypodiegetic tertiary storyworld level of Lewis working at the fish cannery with the representation of

the hypo-hypo-hypodiegetic quarternary storyworld level of Lewis's increasingly elaborate fantasy world that could be described as a particularly ambitious form of "quasi-perceptual overlay" (Thon 2016b, 261) remediates the mediality and materiality of paper in general and books in particular, the (mildly nonlinear) representation of the hypo-hypo-hypodiegetic quarternary storyworld level of Lewis's fantasy world with its constantly evolving use of different types of perspectives and ever more detailed and colorful graphics could also be analyzed as remediating key stages of the history of videogames.

Works Cited

Aarseth, Espen. 2006. "How We Became Postdigital: From CyberStudies to Game Studies." In *Critical Cyberculture Studies*, edited by David Silver and Adrienne Massanari, 37–46. New York: New York University Press.

Abblitt, Stephen. 2018. "A Postdigital Paradigm in Literary Studies." *Higher Education Research & Development* 38 (1): 97–109.

Adcock, Craig. 1990. *James Turrell: The Art of Light and Space*. Berkeley: University of California Press.

Allan, Matthew. 2023. "Doki Doki Subversion Club! Gothic Ghosts, Uncanny Glitches, and Abject Boundaries." *Press Start* 9 (1): 39–57.

Alvarez Igarzábal, Federico. 2019. *Time and Space in Video Games: A Cognitive-Formalist Approach*. Bielefeld: transcript.

Al-Yagout, Ghada, and Maria Nikolajeva. 2017. "Digital Picturebooks." In *The Routledge Companion to Picturebooks*, edited by Bettina Kümmerling-Meibauer, 270–278. New York: Routledge.

Among Ashes. 2024. Rat Cliff Games. Microsoft Windows.

Anderson, Craig G., and Amanda L.L. Cullen. 2023. "Failing to See a Difference: Closing a Gender Gap in a Challenging Video Game." *Games and Culture* 19 (3): 267–285.

Andrews, Ian. 2013. "Post-Digital Aesthetics and the Function of Process." In *ISEA2013: Proceedings of the 19th International Symposium of Electronic Art*, edited by Kathy Cleland, Laura Fisher, and Ross Harley, 256–258. Sidney: Sidney University/ISEA International, 2013.

And Yet It Moves. 2009. Broken Rules Interactive Media. Microsoft Windows.

Apperley, Thomas. 2015. "Glitch Sorting: *Minecraft*, Curation and the Postdigital." In *Postdigital Aesthetics: Art, Computation and Design*, edited by David M. Berry and Michael Dieter, 232–244. Basingstoke: Palgrave Macmillan.

Apprich, Clemens, Josephine Berry Slater, Anthony Iles, and Oliver Lerone Schultz, eds. 2013. *Provocative Alloys: A Post-Media Anthology*. Berlin: Mute.

Archimedes. 2016. Joshua Hughes. Microsoft Windows.

Arjoranta, Jonne. 2019. "How to Define Games and Why We Need to." *The Computer Games Journal* 8: 109–120.

Armello. 2015. League of Geeks. Microsoft Windows.

Arndt, Sonja, et al. 2019. "Between the Blabbering Noise of Individuals or the Silent Dialogue of Many: A Collective Response to 'Postdigital Science and Education' (Jandrić et al. 2018)." *Postdigital Science and Education* 1: 446–474.

Arnheim, Rudolf. 1954. *Art and Visual Perception: A Psychology of the Creative Eye*. Berkeley: University of California Press.

Arnold, Gordon B. 2017. *Animation and the American Imagination: A Brief History*. Santa Barbara: Praeger.

Astroneer. 2016. System Era Softworks. Microsoft Windows.

Axiom Verge. 2015. Thomas Happ Games. Microsoft Windows.

Backe, Hans-Joachim, and Jan-Noël Thon. 2019. "Playing with Identity: Authors, Narrators, Avatars, and Players in *The Stanley Parable* and *The Beginner's Guide*." *DIEGESIS: Interdisciplinary E-Journal for Narrative Research* 8 (2): 1–25.

Bal, Mieke. 1997. *Narratology: Introduction to the Theory of Narrative*. 2nd ed. Toronto: University of Toronto Press.

Balbi, Gabriele, and Paolo Magaudda. 2018. *A History of Digital Media: An Intermedia and Global Perspective*. New York: Routledge.

Balduzzi, Samuele. 2024. "Literary and Ludic Mise-en-Abyme in *What Remains of Edith Finch*." *Play/Write Student Journal* 4: 38–46.

Barck, Karlheinz, Peter Gente, Heidi Paris, and Stefan Richter, eds. 1993a. *Aisthesis: Wahrnehmung heute oder Perspektiven einer anderen Ästhetik*. Leipzig: Reclam.

Barck, Karlheinz, Peter Gente, Heidi Paris, and Stefan Richter. 1993b. "Statt eines Nachworts." In *Aisthesis: Wahrnehmung heute oder Perspektiven einer anderen Ästhetik*, edited by Karlheinz Barck, Peter Gente, Heidi Paris, and Stefan Richter, 445–468. Leipzig: Reclam.

Barkman, Cassandra. 2021. "'There's No Point in Saving Anymore': Diegesis and Interactional Metalepsis in *Pony Island* and *Doki Doki Literature Club*." *Journal of Games Criticism* 5 (1): 1–22.

Barthes, Roland. 1977. "The Third Meaning: Research Notes on Some Eisenstein Stills." In *Image Music Text*, essays selected and translated by Stephen Heath, 52–68. London: Fontana Press.

Baschiera, Stefano, and Elena Caoduro. 2015. "Retro, Faux-Vintage, and Anachronism: When Cinema Looks Back." *NECSUS: European Journal of Media Studies* 4 (2): 143–163.

Beardsley, Monroe C. 1981. *Aesthetics: Problems in the Philosophy of Criticism*. 2nd ed. Indianapolis: Hackett.

Beardsley, Monroe C. 1982. "Redefining Art." In *The Aesthetic Point of View: Selected Essays*, edited by Michael J. Wreen and Donald M. Callen, 298–315. Ithaca, NY: Cornell University Press.

Beil, Benjamin. 2010. *First Person Perspectives: Point of View und figurenzentrierte Erzählformen im Film und im Computerspiel*. Münster: LIT.

Beil, Benjamin. 2011. "8-Bit-High-Definition: Zu verpixelten Bildern in hochaufgelösten Filmen und Computerspielen." *Navigationen: Zeitschrift für Medien- und Kulturwissenschaften* 11 (1): 83–105.

Beil, Benjamin. 2017. "Film Aesthetics and Interactive Representations of Subjectivity in Video Games." In *Subjectivity across Media: Interdisciplinary and Transmedial Perspectives*, edited by Maike Sarah Reinerth and Jan-Noël Thon, 183–195. New York: Routledge.

Bender, John W. 1987. "Supervenience and the Justification of Aesthetic Judgments." *The Journal of Aesthetics and Art Criticism* 46 (1): 31–40.

Bender, John W. 1996. "Realism, Supervenience, and Irresolvable Disputes." *The Journal of Aesthetics and Art Criticism* 54 (4): 371–381.

Benthien, Claudia, Jordis Lau, and Maraike M. Marxsen. 2019. *The Literariness of Media Art*. New York: Routledge.

Berry, David M. 2014. "Post-Digital Humanities: Computation and Cultural Critique in the Arts and Humanities." *Educause* 49 (3): 22–26.

Berry, David M. 2015. "The Postdigital Constellation." In *Postdigital Aesthetics: Art, Computation and Design*, edited by David M. Berry and Michael Dieter, 44–57. Basingstoke: Palgrave Macmillan.

Berry, David M., and Michael Dieter, eds. 2015a. *Postdigital Aesthetics: Art, Computation and Design*. Basingstoke: Palgrave Macmillan.

Berry, David M., and Michael Dieter. 2015b. "Thinking Postdigital Aesthetics: Art, Computation and Design." In *Postdigital Aesthetics: Art, Computation and Design*, edited by David M. Berry and Michael Dieter, 1–11. Basingstoke: Palgrave Macmillan.

Betancourt, Michael. 2017. *Glitch Art in Theory and Practice: Critical Failures and Post-Digital Aesthetics*. New York: Routledge.

Bimbo's Initiation. 1931. Director Dave Fleischer. USA: Fleischer Studios.

Bishop, Ryan, Kristoffer Gansing, Jussi Parikka, and Elvia Wilk, eds. 2016. *Across and Beyond: A Transmediale Reader on Post-Digital Practices, Concepts, and Institutions*. London: Sternberg Press.

Blamey, Courtney. 2021. "*Cuphead*." In *Encyclopedia of Video Games: The Culture, Technology, and Art of Gaming*, edited by Mark J.P. Wolf, 227–228. New York: Routledge.

Blasphemous. 2019. The Game Kitchen/Team17. Microsoft Windows.

Bódi, Bettina. 2023. *Videogames and Agency*. New York: Routledge.

Bódi, Bettina, and Jan-Noël Thon. 2020. "Playing Stories? Narrative-Dramatic Agency in *Disco Elysium* (2019) and *Astroneer* (2019)." *Frontiers of Narrative Studies* 6 (2): 157–190.

Böhme, Gernot. 2001. *Aisthetik: Vorlesungen über Ästhetik als allgemeine Wahrnehmungslehre*. Munich: Fink.

Böhme, Gernot. 2016. *The Aesthetics of Atmospheres*, edited by Jean Paul Thibaud. New York: Routledge.

Bohunicky, Kira, and Chloe Anna Milligan. 2019. "Reading, Writing, Lexigraphing: Active Passivity as Queer Play in Walking Simulators." *Press Start* 5 (2): 51–71.

Bolter, J. David, and Richard Grusin. 1996. "Remediation." *Configurations* 4 (3): 311–358.

Bolter, J. David, and Richard Grusin. 1999. *Remediation: Understanding New Media*. Cambridge, MA: MIT Press.

Bolz, Norbert. 1990. *Theorie der neuen Medien*. Munich: Raben.

Bolz, Norbert. 1991. *Eine kurze Geschichte des Scheins*. Munich: Fink.

Bordwell, David, Janet Staiger, and Kristin Thompson. 1985. *The Classical Hollywood Cinema: Film Style and Mode of Production to 1960*. New York: Columbia University Press.

Bozdog, Mona, and Dayna Galloway. 2020. "Worlds at Our Fingertips: Reading (in) *What Remains of Edith Finch*." *Games and Culture* 15 (7): 789–808.

Braguinski, Nikita. 2018. "The Resolution of Sound: Understanding Retro Game Audio Beyond the '8-Bit' Horizon." *NECSUS: European Journal of Media Studies* 7 (1): 105–121.

Braid. 2008. Number None. Microsoft Windows.

Break the Game. 2019. Simon Fredholm. Microsoft Windows.

Brecht, Bertold. 1964. *Brecht on Theatre: The Development of an Aesthetics*, translated and edited by John Willet. New York: Hill and Wang.

Bridle, James. 2011. "About." *The New Aesthetic*. https://new-aesthetic.tumblr.com/about.

Bridle, James. 2012. "#sxaesthetic." *booktwo.org*, March 15, 2012. http://booktwo.org/notebook/sxaesthetic/.

Bridle, James. 2013. "The New Aesthetic and Its Politics." *booktwo.org*, June 12, 2013. http://booktwo.org/notebook/new-aesthetic-politics/.

Brookey, Robert, and Jonathan Gray. 2017. "'Not Merely Para': Continuing Steps in Paratextual Research." *Critical Studies in Media Communication* 34 (2): 101–110.

Bruno, Giuliana. 2014. *Surface: Matters of Aesthetics, Materiality, and Media*. Chicago: University of Chicago Press.

Bruns, Axel. 2008. *Blogs, Wikipedia, Second Life, and Beyond: From Production to Produsage*. New York: Peter Lang.

Budd, Malcom. 1995. *Values of Art: Pictures, Poetry and Music*. London: Penguin.
Burke, Michael, ed. 2014. *The Routledge Handbook of Stylistics*. New York: Routledge.
Butler, Jeremy G. 2010. *Television Style*. New York: Routledge.
Caoduro, Elena. 2014. "Photo Filter Apps: Understanding Analogue Nostalgia in the New Media Ecology." *Networking Knowledge* 7 (2): 67–82
Card Hunter. 2015. Blue Manchu. Microsoft Windows.
Cascone, Kim. 2000. "The Aesthetics of Failure: 'Post-Digital' Tendencies in Contemporary Computer Music." *Computer Music Journal* 24 (4): 12–18.
Cascone, Kim, and Petar Jandrić. 2021. "The Failure of Failure: Postdigital Aesthetics against Techno-Mystification." *Postdigital Science and Education* 3: 566–574.
Causey, Matthew. 2016. "Postdigital Performance." *Theatre Journal* 68 (3): 427–441.
Celeste. 2018. Matt Makes Games. Microsoft Windows.
Child of Light. 2014. Ubisoft Montreal/Ubisoft. Microsoft Windows.
Church, David. 2015. *Grindhouse Nostalgia: Memory, Home Video and Exploitation Film Fandom*. Edinburgh: Edinburgh University Press.
Clarke, Bruce. 2020. *Gaian Systems: Lynn Margulis, Neocybernetics, and the End of the Anthropocene*. Minneapolis: University of Minnesota Press.
Clarke, M.J., and Cynthia Wang, eds. 2020. *Indie Games in the Digital Age*. New York: Bloomsbury.
Coleman, I. 2016. "REVIEW: *Pony Island*." *Medium*, February 11, 2016. https://medium.com/@yeetzchak/review-pony-island-85fc3b533ae6.
Collins, Karen. 2008. *Game Sound: An Introduction to the History, Theory, and Practice of Video Game Music and Sound Design*. Cambridge, MA: MIT Press.
Collins, Karen. 2016. *Playing with Sound: A Theory of Interacting with Sound and Music in Video Games*. Cambridge, MA: MIT Press.
Compton, Kate, Joseph C. Osborn, and Michael Mateas. 2013. Generative Methods. In *FDG 2013: Proceedings of the Foundations of Digital Games Conference/4th Workshop on Procedural Content Generation in Games*, n.pag.
Consalvo, Mia, and Christopher A. Paul. 2019. *Real Games: What's Legitimate and What's Not in Contemporary Videogames*. Cambridge, MA: MIT Press.
Contra. 1987. ZX Spectrum. Arcade.
Contreras-Koterbay, Scott, and Łukasz Mirocha. 2016. *The New Aesthetic and Art: Constellations of the Postdigital*. Amsterdam: Institute of Network Cultures.
Cormier, Dave, Petar Jandrić, Mark Childd, et al.. 2019. "Ten Years of the Postdigital in the 52group: Reflections and Developments 2009–2019." *Postdigital Science and Education* 1: 475–506.
Corner, John. 2019. "Aesthetics within Media Inquiry." *Media Theory* 3 (2): 103–116.
Cramer, Florian. 2015. "What Is 'Post-Digital'?" In *Postdigital Aesthetics: Art, Computation and Design*, edited by David M. Berry and Michael Dieter, 12–26. Basingstoke: Palgrave Macmillan.
Cramer, Florian, and Petar Jandrić. 2021. "Postdigital: A Term That Sucks But Is Useful." *Postdigital Science and Education* 3: 966–989.
Crayon Chronicles. 2015. Outer Grid Games. Microsoft Windows.
Crayon Physics Deluxe. 2009. Kloonigames. Microsoft Windows.
CrossCode. 2018. Radical Fish Games/Deck 13 Interactive. Microsoft Windows.
Cubitt, Sean. 2006. "Analogue and Digital." *Theory, Culture & Society* 23 (2–3): 250–251.
Cuphead. 2017. StudioMDHR. Microsoft Windows.
The Cuphead Show! 2022. Creator Dave Wasson. Netflix.
Cuphead: The Delicious Last Course. 2022. StudioMDHR. Microsoft Windows.

Currie, Gregory. 1990. "Supervenience, Essentialism and Aesthetic Properties." *Philosophical Studies: An International Journal for Philosophy in the Analytic Tradition* 58 (3): 243–257.

Currie, Gregory. 2010. *Narratives and Narrators: A Philosophy of Stories*. Oxford: Oxford University Press.

The Cursèd Pickle of Shireton. 2020. Hanon Ondricek. Microsoft Windows.

Curtin, Deane W. 1982. "Varities of Aesthetic Formalism." *The Journal of Aesthetics and Art Criticism* 40 (3): 315–326.

Dammers, Ben, Anne Krichel, and Michael Staiger, eds. 2022. *Das Bilderbuch: Theoretische Grundlagen und analytische Zugänge*. Stuttgart: Metzler.

Danto, Arthur. 1981. *The Transfiguration of the Commonplace: A Philosophy of Art*. Cambridge, MA: Harvard University Press.

David.. 2014. Fermenter Games. Microsoft Windows.

Davies, Stephen. 1991. *Definitions of Art*. Ithaca, NY: Cornell University Press.

Day, Katherine. 2024. *Children's Digital Picture Books: Readers and Publishers*. New York: Routledge.

Dear Esther. 2012. Thechineseroom. Microsoft Windows.

De Clercq, Rafael. 2002. "The Concept of an Aesthetic Property." *The Journal of Aesthetics and Art Criticism* 60 (2): 167–176.

De Clercq, Rafael. 2008. "The Structure of Aesthetic Properties." *Philosophy Compass* 3 (5): 894–909.

Denson, Shane, and Julia Leyda, eds. 2016. *Post-Cinema: Theorizing 21st-Century Film*. Falmer: Reframe Books.

Deterding, Sebastian, and José P. Zagal. 2018. "The Many Faces of Role-Playing Game Studies." In *Role-Playing Game Studies*, edited by José P. Zagal and Sebastian Deterding, 1–16. New York: Routledge.

Devereaux, Mary. 1998. "Beauty and Evil: The Case of Leni Riefenstahl's *Triumph of the Will*." In *Aesthetics and Ethics: Essays at the Intersection*, edited by Jerrold Levinson, 227–256. Cambridge: Cambridge University Press.

Dewey, John. 1980. *Art as Experience*. New York: Wideview/Perigee.

Dickie, George. 1974. *Art and the Aesthetic: An Institutional Analysis*. Ithaca, NY: Cornell University Press.

Diecke, Josephine, Bregt Lameris, and Laura Niebling. 2022. "On #Materiality." *NECSUS: European Journal of Media Studies* 11 (2): 5–23.

Disco Elysium. 2019. ZA/UM Studio. Microsoft Windows.

Doki Doki Literature Club! 2017. Team Salvato. Microsoft Windows.

Domsch, Sebastian. 2013. *Storyplaying: Agency and Narrative in Video Games*. Berlin: De Gruyter.

Doom. 1993. id Software. DOS.

Dordogne. 2023. Un Je Ne Sais Quoi/Umanimation. Microsoft Windows.

Düchting, Hajo. 2000. *Wassily Kandinsky 1866–1944: A Revolution in Painting*. Cologne: Taschen.

Eaton, Marcia M. 2001. *Merit, Aesthetic and Ethical*. Oxford: Oxford University Press.

Edrei, Shawn. 2018. "The World That Wasn't There: Interstitial Ontological Spaces in Contemporary Video Games." *Frontiers of Narrative Studies* 4 (1): 112–122.

Egenfeldt-Nielsen, Simon, Jonas Heide Smith, and Susana Tosca. 2020. *Understanding Video Games: The Essential Introduction*. 4th ed. New York: Routledge.

Ehrenspeck, Yvonne. 1996. "Aisthesis und Ästhetik: Überlegungen zu einer problematischen Entdifferenzierung." In *Aisthesis/Ästhetik: Zwischen Wahrnehmung und Bewußtsein*, edited by Klaus Mollenhauer and Christoph Wulf, 201–230. Weinheim: Deutscher Studien Verlag.

Eldridge, Richard. 1985. "Form and Content: An Aesthetic Theory of Art." *British Journal of Aesthetics* 25 (4): 303–316.

Ensslin, Astrid. 2014. *Literary Gaming*. Cambridge, MA: MIT Press.

Ensslin, Astrid, and Alice Bell. 2021. *Digital Fiction and the Unnatural: Transmedial Narrative Theory, Method, and Analysis*. Columbus: Ohio State University Press.

The Escapists. 2015. Mouldy Toof Studios/Team17. Microsoft Windows.

Espineli, Matt. 2017. "*What Remains of Edith Finch* Dev Discusses the Game's Ending." *GameSpot*, May 7, 2017. www.gamespot.com/articles/what-remains-of-edith-finch-dev-discusses-the-game/1100-6449846/.

Etter, Lukas. 2021. *Distinctive Styles and Authorship in Alternative Comics*. Berlin: De Gruyter.

Evoland. 2013. Shiro Games. Microsoft Windows.

Farocki, Harun. 2004. "Phantom Images." *Public* 29: 12–22.

Fazi, M. Beatrice. 2019. "Digital Aesthetics: The Discrete and the Continuous." *Theory, Culture & Society* 36 (1): 3–26.

Feige, Daniel Martin. 2015. *Computerspiele: Eine Ästhetik*. Berlin: Suhrkamp.

Fernández-Vara, Clara. 2011. "Game Spaces Speak Volumes: Indexical Storytelling." In *Proceedings of DiGRA 2011: Think Design Play*, n.pag.

Fest, Bradley J. 2016. "Metaproceduralism: *The Stanley Parable* and the Legacies of Postmodern Metafiction." *Wide Screen* 6 (1): 1–23.

Fez. 2012. Polytron Corporation/Trapdoor. Xbox 360.

Forceville, Charles, Elisabeth El Refaie, and Gert Meesters. 2014. "Stylistics and Comics." In *The Routledge Handbook of Stylistics*, edited by Michael Burke, 485–499. New York: Routledge.

Ford, Derek R. 2023. "Postdigital Soundscapes: Sonics, Pedagogies, Technologies." *Postdigital Science and Education* 5: 265–276.

The Fresh Vegetable Mystery. 1939. Director Dave Fleischer. USA: Fleischer Studios.

Frigerio, Aldo, Alessandro Giordani, and Luca Mari. 2013. "On Representing Information: A Characterization of the Analog/Digital Distinction." *Dialectica* 67 (4): 455–483.

Galas, Marjorie. 2017. "Music for Games: Composer Jeff Russo Describes Scoring *What Remains of Edith Finch*." *LA411*, April 14, 2017. https://la411.com/blog/post/fargo-composer-jeff-russo-scores-what-remains-of-edith-finch.

gamer_152. 2018. "Interview: Ian Dallas, Creative Director of *What Remains of Edith Finch*." *Giant Bomb*, December 15, 2018. www.giantbomb.com/profile/gamer_152/blog/interview-ian-dallas-creative-director-of-what-rem/120070/.

GameSpot. 2017. "How *Cuphead*'s Devs Gambled On A Dream | The Making of *Cuphead*." *YouTube*, November 11, 2017. www.youtube.com/watch?v=ujkFlNkXMu4.

Gamespot Staff. 2013. "*Proteus* Review." *GameSpot*, January 30, 2013. www.gamespot.com/reviews/proteus-review/1900-6403756/.

Garda, Maria B. 2013. "Nostalgia in Retro Games." In *Proceedings of DiGRA 2013: DeFragging Game Studies*, n.pag.

Garda, Maria B., and Paweł Grabarczyk. 2016. "Is Every Indie Game Independent? Towards the Concept of Independent Game." *Game Studies: The International Journal of Computer Game Research* 16 (1): n.pag.

Gass, Arianna (Ari). 2024. "Glitch as a Trans Representational Mode in Video Games." *Media-N: The Journal of the New Media Caucus* 20 (1): 5–27.

Gaut, Berys. 2000. "'Art' as a Cluster Concept." In *Theories of Art Today*, edited by Noël Carroll, 25–44. Madison: University of Wisconsin Press.

Gaut, Berys. 2008. "Opaque Pictures." *Revue internationale de philosophie* 246 (4): 381–396.

Genette, Gérard. 1983. *Narrative Discourse: An Essay in Method.* Ithaca, NY: Cornell University Press.

Genner, Sarah. 2017. *On | Off: Risks and Rewards of the Anytime-Anywhere Internet.* Zurich: vdf.

Gilyadov, Alex. 2017. "'We Quit Our Jobs, Remortgaged Our Houses': How Relentless Passion Made *Cuphead* a Reality." *GamesRadar+*, June 29, 2017. www.gamesradar.com/we-quit-our-jobs-remortgaged-our-houses-how-relentless-passion-made-cuphead-a-reality/.

Gitelman, Lisa. 2006. *Always Already New: Media, History, and the Data of Culture.* Cambridge, MA: MIT Press.

Glitched. Forthcoming. En House Digital/Digerati. Microsoft Windows.

Golding, Daniel. 2013. "Listening to *Proteus.*" *Meanjin* 72 (2): 108–115.

Goldman, Alan H. 1990. "Aesthetic Qualities and Aesthetic Value." *The Journal of Philosophy* 87 (1): 23–37.

Goldman, Alan H. 1995. *Aesthetic Value.* Boulder: Westview Press.

Goldman, Alan H. 2013. "The Broad View of Aesthetic Experience." *The Journal of Aesthetics and Art Criticism* 71 (4): 323–333.

Gone Home. 2013. Fullbright Company. Microsoft Windows.

Gormley, Michael J. 2021. *The End of the Anthropocene: Ecocriticism, the Universal Ecosystem, and the Astropocene.* Lanham: Lexington Books.

Gray, Jonathan. 2010. *Show Sold Separately: Promos, Spoilers, and Other Media Paratexts.* New York: New York University Press.

Grayson, Nathan. 2013. "*Proteus* Review: A Virtual Vacation in More Ways Than One." *IGN*, February 9, 2013. www.ign.com/articles/2013/02/09/proteus-review.

Gris. 2018. Nomada Studio/Devolver Digital. Microsoft Windows.

Guattari, Felix. 1990. "Vers une ère post-média." *Terminal* 51: 43.

Gunstar Heroes. 1993. Sega. Arcade.

Hagener, Malte, Vinzenz Hediger, and Alena Strohmaier, eds. 2016. *The State of Post-Cinema: Tracing the Moving Image in the Age of Digital Dissemination.* London: Palgrave Macmillan.

Halloween. 1978. Director John Carpenter. USA: Compass International Pictures.

Hansen, Mark B.N. 2004. *New Philosophy for New Media.* Cambridge, MA: MIT Press.

Hanson, Christopher. 2018. *Game Time: Understanding Temporality in Video Games.* Bloomington: Indiana University Press.

Hausken, Liv. 2013. "Introduction." In *Thinking Media Aesthetics: Media Studies, Film Studies and the Arts*, edited by Liv Hausken, 29–50. Berlin: Peter Lang.

Hayes, Sarah. 2021. *Postdigital Positionality: Developing Powerful Inclusive Narratives for Learning, Teaching, Research and Policy in Higher Education.* Leiden: Brill.

Hellblade: Senua's Sacrifice. 2017. Ninja Theory. Microsoft Windows.

Herman, David. 2009. *Basic Elements of Narrative.* Chichester: Wiley-Blackwell.

The Hex. 2018. Daniel Mullins Games. Microsoft Windows.

Hjarvard, Stig. 2013. *The Mediatization of Culture and Society.* New York: Routledge.

Hodgson, Justin. 2019. *Post-Digital Rhetoric and the New Aesthetic.* Columbus: Ohio State University Press.

Hoel, Aud Sissel. 2018. "Operative Images: Inroads to a New Paradigm of Media Theory." In *Image – Action – Space: Situating the Screen in Visual Practice*, edited by Luisa Feiersinger, Kathrin Friedrich, and Moritz Queisner, 11–27. Berlin: De Gruyter.

Hoelzl, Ingrid, and Rémi Marie. 2015. *Softimage: Towards a New Theory of the Digital Image.* Bristol: Intellect.

Holloway, Travis. 2022. *How to Live at the End of the World.* Stanford: Stanford University Press.

Holmes, Eben G. 2010. "Strange Reality: On Glitches and Uncanny Play." *Eludamos: Journal for Computer Game Culture* 4 (2): 255–276.
Hoy, Meredith. 2017. *From Point to Pixel: A Geneology of Digital Aesthetics*. Hanover, NH: Dartmouth College Press.
Imscared: A Pixelated Nightmare. 2016. Ivan Zanotti's MyMadnessWorks. Microsoft Windows.
Inscryption. 2021. Daniel Mullins Games/Devolver Digital. Microsoft Windows.
Irvin, Sherri. 2014. "Is Aesthetic Experience Possible?" In *Aesthetics and the Sciences of the Mind*, edited by Greg Currie, Matthew Kieran, Aaron Meskin, and Jon Robson, 37–56. Oxford: Oxford University Press.
Ivănescu, Andra. 2019. *Popular Music in the Nostalgia Video Game: The Way It Never Sounded*. Cham: Palgrave Macmillan.
Jahn-Sudmann, Andreas. 2008. "Innovation NOT Opposition: The Logic of Distinction of Independent Games." *Eludamos: Journal for Computer Game Culture* 2 (1): 5–10.
Jandrić, Petar, Jeremy Knox, Tina Besley, Thomas Ryberg, Juha Suoranta, and Sarah Hayes. 2018. "Postdigital Science and Education." *Educational Philosophy and Theory* 50 (10): 893–899.
Järvenpää, Hanna. 2021. "The Playful Affordances of Picture Book Apps for Children." *Eludamos: Journal for Computer Game Culture* 12 (1): 149–167.
Järvinen, Aki. 2002. "Gran Stylissimo: The Audiovisual Elements and Styles in Computer and Video Games." In *Proceedings of Computer Games and Digital Cultures Conference*, edited by Frans Mäyrä, 113–128. Tampere: Tampere University Press.
Jenkins, Henry. 2004. "Game Design as Narrative Architecture." In *FirstPerson: New Media as Story, Performance, and Game*, edited by Noah Wardrip-Fruin and Pat Harrigan, 118–130. Cambridge, MA: MIT Press.
Jenkins, Henry. 2006. *Convergence Culture: Where Old and New Media Collide*. New York: New York University Press.
Jenkins, Henry, Sam Ford, and Joshua Green. 2013. *Spreadable Media: Creating Value and Meaning in a Networked Culture*. New York: New York University Press.
Jensen, Klaus Bruhn. 2010. *Media Convergence: The Three Degrees of Network, Mass, and Interpersonal Communication*. New York: Routledge.
Johnson, Derek. 2013. *Media Franchising: Creative License and Collaboration in the Culture Industries*. New York: New York University Press.
Johnson, John "J.J." 2009. *Cheap Tricks and Class Acts: Special Effects, Makeup and Stunts from the Films of the Fantastic Fifties*. Jefferson: McFarland.
Jordan, Spencer. 2020. *Postdigital Storytelling: Poetics, Praxis, Research*. New York: Routledge.
Jung, Tristan. 2017. "*Cuphead* Review." *Medium*, November 16, 2017. https://medium.com/@3stan/cuphead-review-d62d57ce5528.
Juul, Jesper. 2005. *Half-Real: Video Games between Real Rules and Fictional Worlds*. Cambridge, MA: MIT Press.
Juul, Jesper. 2014. "High-Tech Low-Tech Authenticity: The Creation of Independent Style at the Independent Games Festival." In *Proceedings of the 9th International Conference on the Foundations of Digital Games*, n.pag.
Juul, Jesper. 2019. *Handmade Pixels: Independent Video Games and the Quest for Authenticity*. Cambridge, MA: MIT Press.
Kagen, Melissa. 2020. "Archival Adventuring." *Convergence: The International Journal of Research into New Media Technologies* 26 (4): 1007–1020
Kagen, Melissa. 2022. *Wandering Games*. Cambridge, MA: MIT Press.

Kane, Carolyn L. 2019. *High-Tech Trash: Glitch, Noise, and Aesthetic Failure*. Oakland: University of California Press.

Kapron, Nicola Jean. 2021. "*Inscryption* Interview: Developer Daniel Mullins on Bringing New Life to 3D Retro Horror Games." *Game Rant*, October 28, 2021. https://gamerant.com/inscryption-interview-developer-daniel-mullins-3d-retro-horror-games/.

Kim, Matt. 2017. "An Interview with Composer Jeff Russo of *What Remains of Edith Finch*." *Paste*, May 26, 2017. www.pastemagazine.com/games/what-remains-of-edith-finch/an-interview-with-composer-jeff-russo-of-what-rema.

King Neptune. 1932. Director Burt Gillett. USA: Walt Disney Productions.

Kirkland, Ewan. 2011. "Remediation, Analogue Corruption and the Signification of Evil in Digital Games." In *Promoting and Producing Evil*, edited by Nancy Billias, 227–245. 2nd ed. Amsterdam: Rodopi.

Kirkland, Ewan. 2020. "'He Died a Lot': The Gothic Gameplay of *What Remains of Edith Finch*." In *Death, Culture and Leisure: Playing Dead*, edited by Matt Coward-Gibbs, 95–107. Leeds: Emerald Publishing Limited.

Kirkpatrick, Graeme. 2011. *Aesthetic Theory and the Video Game*. Manchester: Manchester University Press.

Kliche, Dieter. 1998. "Ästhetik und Aisthesis: Zur Begriffs- und Problemgeschichte des Ästhetischen." *Weimarer Beiträge: Zeitschrift für Literaturwissenschaft, Ästhetik und Kulturwissenschaften* 44 (4): 485–505.

Koenitz, Hartmut. 2023. *Understanding Interactive Digital Narrative: Immersive Expressions for a Complex Time*. New York: Routledge.

Koffka, Kurt. 1935. *Principles of Gestalt Psychology*. New York: Hartcourt Brace & Co.

Köhler, Wolfgang. 1929. *Gestalt Psychology*. New York: Horace Liveright.

Kouvaras, Linda Ioanna. 2016. *Loading the Silence: Australian Sound Art in the Post-Digital Age*. New York: Routledge.

Krampe, Theresa. 2023. "Rewriting Rules, Changing Worlds: Diegetic and Ludic Forms of Metareference in *The Magic Circle*." *Frontiers of Narrative Studies* 9 (1): 137–157.

Krampe, Theresa. 2025. *Metareference in Videogames*. New York: Routledge.

Krampe, Theresa, Stephanie Lotzow, and Jan-Noël Thon. 2022. "Playful Poetics: Metareferential Interfaces in Recent Indie Games." *Poetics Today* 43 (4): 729–771.

Kümmerling-Meibauer, Bettina, ed. 2017. *The Routledge Companion to Picturebooks*. New York: Routledge.

Kuyatt, Meg Eden. 2017. "*What Remains of Edith Finch*, and Why We Tell Stories." *Why Now Gaming*, July 17, 2017. https://whynowgaming.com/what-remains-of-edith-finch-and-why-we-tell-stories/.

Kuzminski, Adriane. 2017. "Behind the Delightfully Vintage Sound of *Cuphead*—with Samuel Justice." *A Sound Effect*, October 11, 2017. www.asoundeffect.com/cuphead-sound/.

Kwastek, Katja. 2015. "How to Be Theorized: A Tediously Academic Essay on the *New Aesthetic*." In *Postdigital Aesthetics: Art, Computation and Design*, edited by David M. Berry and Michael Dieter, 72–85. Basingstoke: Palgrave Macmillan.

Leddy, Thomas. 2012. *The Extraordinary in the Ordinary: The Aesthetics of Everyday Life*. Peterborough: Broadview Press.

Lee, Cindy. 2020. "Best Practices for Pixel Art." In *The Digital Gaming Handbook*, edited by Roberto Dillon, 275–286. Boca Raton: CRC Press.

Levine, Caroline. 2015. *Forms: Whole, Rhythm, Hierarchy, Network*. Princeton: Princeton University Press.

Levinson, Jerrold. 1979. "Defining Art Historically." *The British Journal of Aesthetics* 19 (3): 232–250.

Levinson, Jerrold. 1984. "Aesthetic Supervenience." *The Southern Journal of Philosophy* 22 (S1): 93–110.

Levinson, Jerrold. 2001. "Aesthetic Properties, Evaluative Force, and Differences of Sensibility." In *Aesthetic Concepts: Essays after Sibley*, edited by Emily Brady and Jerrold Levinson, 61–80. Oxford: Oxford University Press.

Levinson, Jerrold. 2005. "Aesthetic Properties." *Proceedings of the Aristotelian Society, Supplementary Volumes* 79: 211–227.

Levinson, Jerrold. 2016. *Aesthetic Pursuits: Essays in the Philosophy of Art*. Oxford: Oxford University Press.

Levinson, Paul. 2015. *New New Media*. 2nd ed. London: Pearson.

Lipkin, Nadav. 2013. "Examining Indie's Independence: The Meaning of 'Indie' Games, the Politics of Production, and Mainstream Cooptation." *Loading…: The Journal of the Canadian Game Studies Association* 7 (11): 8–24.

Lohmeyer, Eddie. 2021. *Unstable Aesthetics: Game Engines and the Strangeness of Modding*. New York: Bloomsbury.

Lopes, Dominic McIver. 1996. *Understanding Pictures*. Oxford: Oxford University Press.

Ludovico, Alessandro. 2012. *Post-Digital Print: The Mutation of Publishing since 1984*. Eindhoven: Onomatopee.

Lumino City. 2013. State of Play Games. Microsoft Windows.

MacCormack, Patricia. 2020. *The Ahuman Manifesto: Activism for the End of the Anthropocene*. New York: Bloomsbury.

The Magic Circle. 2015. Question. Microsoft Windows.

Makai, Péter Kristóf. 2018. "Video Games as Objects and Vehicles of Nostalgia." *Humanities* 7 (4): 123: 1–14.

Maley, Corey J. 2011. "Analog and Digital, Continuous and Discrete." *Philosophical Studies* 155: 117–131.

Maley, Corey J. 2023. "Analogue Computation and Representation." *The British Journal for the Philosophy of Science* 74 (3): 739–769.

Mandoki, Katya. 2007. *Everyday Aesthetics: Prosaics, the Play of Culture and Social Identities*. New York: Routledge.

Manovich, Lev. 2001. *The Language of New Media*. Cambridge, MA: MIT Press.

Manovich, Lev. 2014. "Postmedia Aesthetics." In *Transmedia Frictions: The Digital, the Arts, and the Humanities*, edited by Marsha Kinder and Tara McPherson, 34–44. Oakland: University of California Press.

Manovich, Lev. 2017. "Aesthetics." In *Keywords for Media Studies*, edited by Laurie Ouellette and Jonathan Gray, 9–11. New York: New York University Press.

Marchiori, Dario. 2013. "Media Aesthetics." In *Preserving and Exhibiting Media Art: Challenges and Perspectives*, edited by Julia Noordegraaf, Cosetta G. Saba, Barbara Le Maître, and Vinzenz Hediger, 81–99. Amsterdam: Amsterdam University Press.

Mathier, Marion. 2023. *Postdigital Disconnects: The Discursive Formation of Technology in Education*. New York: Routledge.

Matravers, Derek. 2005. "Aesthetic Properties." *Proceedings of the Aristotelian Society, Supplementary Volumes* 79: 191–210.

McGowan, David. 2019. "*Cuphead*: Animation, the Public Domain, and Home Video Remediation." *The Journal of Popular Culture* 52 (1): 10–34.

McLuhan, Marshall. 1964. *Understanding Media: The Extensions of Man*. New York: McGraw-Hill.

McMillan, Emily. 2017. "Kristofer Maddigan Interview: A Jazzy, Ragtimey, Big-Band Score." *VGMO*, October 9, 2017. www.vgmonline.net/kristofer-maddigan-interview/.

Mega Man. 1987. Capcom. SNES.

Meikle, Kyle. 2016. “8-Bit Goes to the Movies.” *Wide Screen* 6 (1): 1–16.

Menkman, Rosa. 2011. *The Glitch Moment(um)*. Amsterdam: Institute of Network Cultures.

Merleau-Ponty, Maurice. 1945. *Phénoménologie de la perception*. Paris: Gallimard.

Mersch, Dieter. 2002. *Was sich zeigt: Materialität, Präsenz, Ereignis*. Munich: Fink.

Mészáros, Tímea. 2022. “The Book as Framing Device in Exploration Games: *Myst* (1993) and *What Remains of Edith Finch* (2017).” In *Buch-Aisthesis: Philologie und Gestaltungsdiskurs*, edited by Christopher Busch und Oliver Ruf, 103–118. Bielefeld: transcript.

Metal Slug. 1996. Nazca/SNK. Arcade.

Meyer, Roland. 2023. “The New Value of the Archive: AI Image Generation and the Visual Economy of ‘Style’.” *IMAGE: The Interdisciplinary Journal of Image Sciences* 37 (1): 100–111.

Meyerhofer-Parra, Rafel, Juan González-Martínez, and Marta Peracaula-Bosch. 2024. “Postdigital Storytelling: Storytelling (within or across) the Digital and Transmedia Field.” *Postdigital Science and Education* 6: 886–901.

Minecraft. 2011. Mojang Studios. Microsoft Windows.

Mitchell, Alex, and Jasper van Vught. 2023. *Videogame Formalism: On Form, Aesthetic Experience and Methodology*. Amsterdam: Amsterdam University Press.

Mitchell, William J. 1992. *The Reconfigured Eye: Visual Truth in the Post-Photographic Era*. Cambridge, MA: MIT Press.

Montembeault, Hugo, and Maxime Deslongchamps-Gagnon. 2019. “The Walking Simulator’s Generic Experiences.” *Press Start* 5 (2): 1–28.

Montfort, Nick, and Ian Bogost. 2009. *Racing the Beam: The Atari Video Computer System*. Cambridge, MA: MIT Press.

Morrison, Angus. 2016. “*Pony Island* Review.” *PC Gamer*, January 22, 2016. www.pcgamer.com/pony-island-review/.

Müller, Christian. 2022. “Digitales Bilderbuch.” In *Das Bilderbuch: Theoretische Grundlagen und analytische Zugänge*, edited by Ben Dammers, Anne Krichel, and Michael Staiger, 137–150. Stuttgart: Metzler.

Murray, Sarah. 2020. “Postdigital Cultural Studies.” *International Journal of Cultural Studies* 23 (4): 441–450.

Muscat, Alexander, William Goddard, Jonathan Duckworth, and Jussi Holopainen. 2016. “First-Person Walkers: Understanding the Walker Experience through Four Design Themes.” In *Proceedings of 1st International Joint Conference of DiGRA and FDG 2016*, 1–15.

Nanay, Bence. 2016. *Aesthetics as Philosophy of Perception*. Oxford: Oxford University Press.

Negroponte, Nicholas. 1998. “Beyond Digital.” *Wired*, December 1, 1998. www.wired.com/1998/12/negroponte-55/.

Neverending Nightmares. 2014. Infinitap Games. Microsoft Windows.

Ngai, Sianne. 2015. *Our Aesthetic Categories: Zany, Cute, Interesting*. Cambridge, MA: Harvard University Press.

Nielsen, Henrik Kaare. 2005. “Totalizing Aesthetics? Aesthetic Theory and the Aestheticization of Everyday Life.” *Nordisk estetisk tidskrift* 17 (32): 60–75.

Niemeyer, Katharina, ed. 2014. *Media and Nostalgia: Yearning for the Past, Present and Future*. New York: Palgrave Macmillan.

No Man’s Sky. 2016. Hello Games. Microsoft Windows.

O’Donnell, Casey. 2014. *Developer’s Dilemma: The Secret World of Videogame Creators*. Cambridge, MA: MIT Press.

O'Hara, William. 2020 "Mapping Sound: Play, Performance, and Analysis in *Proteus*." *Journal of Sound and Music in Games* 1 (3): 35–67.

Ohmer, Susan. 2019. "Classical Hollywood, 1928–1946." In *Animation*, edited by Scott Curtis, 48–74. New Brunswick: Rutgers University Press.

Olson, Marisa. 2011. "Postinternet: Art after the Internet." *Foam Magazine* 29: 59–63.

Pantenburg, Volker. 2016. "Working Images: Harun Farocki and the Operational Image." In *Image Operations: Visual Media and Political Conflict*, edited by Jens Eder and Charlotte Klonk, 49–62. Manchester: Manchester University Press.

Papagiannouli, Christina. 2022. "A Postdigital Response: Experiential Dramaturgies of Online Theatre, Cyberformance, and Digital Texts." In *Experiential Theatres: Praxis-Based Approaches to Training 21st Century Theatre Artists*, edited by William W. Lewis and Sean Bartley, 175–181. New York: Routledge.

Papetura. 2021. Petums/Feardemic. Microsoft Windows.

Parikka, Juri. 2023. *Operational Images: From the Visual to the Invisual*. Minneapolis: University of Minnesota Press.

Parker, Felan. 2021. "Boutique Indie: Annapurna Interactive and Contemporary Independent Game Development." In *Independent Videogames: Cultures, Networks, Techniques and Politics*, edited by Paulo Ruffino, 129–147. New York: Routledge.

Parkin, Simon. 2017. "*Cuphead* Review: Hanna-Barbaric." *Eurogamer*, October 2, 2017. www.eurogamer.net/cuphead-review.

Paul, Christiane. 2016. "Introduction: From Digital to Post-Digital—Evolutions of an Art Form." In *A Companion to Digital Art*, edited by Christiane Paul, 1–19. Malden: Wiley-Blackwell.

Paul, Christiane, and Malcolm Levy. 2015. "Genealogies of the New Aesthetic." In *Postdigital Aesthetics: Art, Computation and Design*, edited by David M. Berry and Michael Dieter, 27–43. Basingstoke: Palgrave Macmillan.

Pax Pamir: Second Edition. 2019. Wehrlegig Games. Board Game.

Peckham, Matt. 2016. "Exclusive: See How *Cuphead*'s Incredible Cartoon Graphics Are Made." *Time*, April 12, 2016. https://time.com/4123150/cuphead-preview/.

Pedroza, Jason. 2017. "*Cuphead* Review." *Merry-Go-Round Magazine*, October 11, 2017. https://merrygoroundmagazine.com/cuphead-review/.

Pentiment. 2022. Obsidian Entertainment/Xbox Game Studios. Microsoft Windows.

Pepperell, Robert, and Michael Punt. 2000. *The Postdigital Membrane: Imagination, Technology and Desire*. Bristol: Intellect.

A Picnic Panic. 1935. Directors Burt Gillett and Tom Palmer. USA: Van Beuren Studios.

Pinocchio. 1940. Directors Ben Sharpsteen and Hamilton Luske. USA: Walt Disney Productions.

Pixel Tactics Deluxe. 2015. Level 99 Games. Card Game.

The Plucky Squire. 2024. All Possible Futures/Devolver Digital. Microsoft Windows.

Pony Island. 2016. Daniel Mullins Games. Microsoft Windows.

Poor Cinderella. 1934. Directors Dave Fleischer and Seymour Kneitel. USA: Fleischer Studios.

Popeye the Sailor Meets Sindbad the Sailor. 1936. Director Dave Fleischer. USA: Fleischer Studios.

Prevas, Christine. 2023. "Unlocked Doors: The Trans Glitch in Kitty Horrorshow's *Anatomy*." *Communication, Culture and Critique* 16 (3): 134–140.

Proteus. 2013. Ed Key and David Kanaga. Microsoft Windows.

Punday, Daniel. 2019. *Playing at Narratology: Digital Media as Narrative Theory*. Columbus: Ohio State University Press.

Pyre. 2017. Supergiant Games. Microsoft Windows.

Rajewsky, Irina O. 2005. "Intermediality, Intertextuality, and Remediation: A Literary Perspective on Intermediality." *Intermédialités / Intermediality* 6: 43–64.

Rajewsky, Irina O. 2010. "Border Talks: The Problematic Status of Media Borders in the Current Debate about Intermediality." In *Media Borders, Multimodality and Intermediality*, edited by Lars Elleström, 51–68. Basingstoke: Palgrave Macmillan.

Rancière, Jacques. 2011. *Aisthesis: Scènes du régime esthétique de l'art*. Paris: Galilée.

Rathe, Clemens. 2020. *Die Philosophie der Oberfläche: Medien- und kulturwissenschaftliche Perspektiven auf Äußerlichkeiten und ihre tiefere Bedeutung*. Bielefeld: transcript.

Rautzenberg, Markus, and Andreas Wolfsteiner, eds. 2010. *Hide and Seek: Das Spiel von Transparenz und Opazität*. Munich: Fink.

Reckwitz, Andreas. 2016. "How the Senses Organize the Social." In *Praxeological Political Analysis*, edited by Michael Jonas and Beate Littig, 56–66. Abingdon: Routledge.

Roche, David. 2014. *Making and Remaking Horror in the 1970s and 2000s: Why Don't They Do It Like They Used To?* Jackson: University Press of Mississippi.

Rothwell, Ian. 2024. *Postinternet Art and Its Afterlives*. New York: Routledge.

Rötzer, Florian, ed. 1991a. *Digitaler Schein: Ästhetik der elektronischen Medien*. Frankfurt am Main: Suhrkamp.

Rötzer, Florian. 1991b. "Mediales und Digitales: Zerstreute Bemerkungen und Hinweise eines irritierten informationsverarbeitenden Systems." In *Digitaler Schein: Ästhetik der elektronischen Medien*, edited by Florian Rötzer, 9–78. Frankfurt am Main: Suhrkamp.

Ruffino, Paolo, ed. 2021. *Independent Videogames: Cultures, Networks, Techniques and Politics*. New York: Routledge.

Ruhland, Perry. 2016. "Literally Developed By Satan: A *Pony Island* Interview." *TechRaptor*, January 18, 2016. https://techraptor.net/gaming/interview/literally-developed-by-satan-pony-island-interview.

Ryan, Marie-Laure. 1991. *Possible Worlds, Artificial Intelligence, and Narrative Theory*. Bloomington: Indiana University Press.

Ryan, Marie-Laure. 2006. *Avatars of Story*. Minneapolis: University of Minnesota Press.

Saito, Yuriko. 2012. *Everyday Aesthetics*. Oxford: Oxford University Press

Schäfer, Mirko Tobias. 2011. *Bastard Culture! How User Participation Transforms Cultural Production*. Amsterdam: Amsterdam University Press.

Schlarb, Damien B. 2019. "Narrative Glitches: Action Adventure Games and Metaleptic Convergence." In *Playing the Field: Video Games and American Studies*, edited by Sascha Pöhlmann, 195–210. Berlin: De Gruyter.

Schlesinger, George. 1979. "Aesthetic Experience and the Definition of Art." *The British Journal of Aesthetics* 19 (2): 167–176.

Schoppmeier, Sören. 2018. "Breaking the Habitual: *Pony Island* as Countergaming." In *Modernities and Modernization in North America*, edited by Ilka Brasch and Ruth Mayer, 427–448. Heidelberg: Winter.

Schrey, Dominik. 2015. "Retrofotografie: Die Wiederverzauberung der digitalen Welt." *MEDIENwissenschaft: Rezensionen | Reviews* 32 (1): 9–26.

Schrey, Dominik. 2017. *Analoge Nostalgie in der Digitalen Medienkultur*. Berlin: Kadmos.

Schröter, Jens. 2004. "Analog/Digital – Opposition oder Kontinuum?" In *Analog/Digital – Opposition oder Kontinuum? Zur Theorie und Geschichte einer Unterscheidung*, edited by Jens Schröter and Alexander Böhnke, 7–30. Bielefeld: transcript.

Schröter, Jens. 2019. "Media Aesthetics, Simulation, and the New Media." *MediArXiv Preprints*, March 29, 2019. https://osf.io/preprints/mediarxiv/bs2zu.

Schröter, Jens. 2023. "Intermediality and Computer Simulation." In *The Palgrave Handbook of Intermediality*, edited by Jørgen Bruhn, Asunción López-Varela, and Miriam de Paiva Vieira, 1–12. Cham: Palgrave Macmillan.

Scoggin, Lisa. 2023. "The Pseudo-1930s World of *Cuphead*." In *The Intersection of Animation, Video Games, and Music: Making Movement Sing*, edited by Lisa Scoggin and Dana Plank, 62–75. New York: Routledge.

Scolari, Carlos A. 2023. *On the Evolution of Media: Understanding Media Change*. New York: Routledge.

ScourgeBringer. 2020. Flying Oak Games/Dear Villagers. Microsoft Windows.

Sea of Stars. 2023. Sabotage Studios. Microsoft Windows.

Seel, Martin. 1993. "Zur ästhetischen Praxis der Kunst." *Deutsche Zeitschrift für Philosophie* 41 (1): 31–43.

Seel, Martin. 1997. "Ästhetik und Aisthetik: Über einige Besonderheiten ästhetischer Wahrnehmung." In *Bild und Reflexion: Paradigmen und Perspektiven gegenwärtiger Ästhetik*, edited by Birgit Recki and Lambert Wiesing, 17–38. Munich: Fink.

Seel, Martin. 2005. *Aesthetics of Appearing*. Stanford: Stanford University Press.

Senior, Tom. 2013. "*Proteus* Review." *PC Gamer*, March 5, 2013. www.pcgamer.com/proteus-review/.

Sharp, John. 2015. *Works of Game: On the Aesthetics of Games and Art*. Cambridge, MA: MIT Press.

Shea, Cam. 2017. "*Pony Island* Review: The Devil Is in the Details." *IGN*, May 1, 2017. www.ign.com/articles/2016/01/19/pony-island-review.

The Shivers. 2022. Pop Fiction Games. Board Game.

Shklovsky, Viktor. 2012. "Art as Technique." In *Russian Formalist Criticism: Four Essays*, edited by Lee T. Lemon and Marion J. Reis, 21–34. 2nd ed. Lincoln: University of Nebraska Press.

Shore, Robert. 2014. *Post-Photography: The Artist with a Camera*. London: Laurence King Publishing.

Shusterman, Richard. 2002. *Surface and Depth: Dialectics of Criticism and Culture*. Ithaca, NY: Cornell University Press.

Sibley, Frank. 1959. "Aesthetic Concepts." *The Philosophical Review* 68 (4): 421–450.

Sibley, Frank. 1965. "Aesthetic and Nonaesthetic." *The Philosophical Review* 74 (2): 135–159.

Sibley, Frank. 1968. "Objectivity and Aesthetics." *Proceedings of the Aristotelian Society, Supplementary Volumes* 42: 31–72.

Sibley, Frank. 1974. "Particularity, Art and Evaluation." *Proceedings of the Aristotelian Society, Supplementary Volumes* 48: 1–21.

Slay the Princess. 2023. Black Tabby Games. Microsoft Windows.

Sloan, Robin J.S. 2015. "Videogames as Remediated Memories: Commodified Nostalgia and Hyperreality in *Far Cry 3: Blood Dragon* and *Gone Home*." *Games and Culture* 10 (6): 525–550.

Snow-White. 1933. Director Dave Fleischer. USA: Fleischer Studios.

Snow White and the Seven Dwarves. 1937. Director David Hand. USA: Walt Disney Productions.

Stardew Valley. 2016. Chucklefish/Concerned Ape. Microsoft Windows.

Stecker, Robert. 1994. "Historical Functionalism or the Four Factor Theory." *The British Journal of Aesthetics* 34 (3): 255–265.

Steyerl, Hito. 2009. "In Defense of the Poor Image." *e-flux Journal* 10: n.pag.

Stuart, Keith. 2013. "*Proteus*—Review." *The Guardian*, February 4, 2013. www.theguardian.com/technology/gamesblog/2013/feb/04/proteus-review.

Styhre, Alexander. 2020. *Indie Video Game Development Work: Innovation in the Creative Economy*. Basingstoke: Palgrave Macmillan.

Sullivan, Lucas. 2017. "*Cuphead* Review: 'Stands Tall Among the Best 2D Shooters of All Time.'" *GamesRadar+*, September 29, 2017. www.gamesradar.com/cuphead-review/.

Summers, Tim. 2016. *Understanding Video Game Music*. Foreword by James Hannigan. Cambridge: Cambridge University Press.

Summers, Tim. 2024. *Pixel Soundtracks: Exploring Video Game Music through Twenty Games*. Foreword by Jason Graves. London: Rowman & Littlefield.

Švelch, Jan. 2020. "Paratextuality in Game Studies: A Theoretical Review and Citation Analysis." *Game Studies: The International Journal of Computer Game Research* 20 (2): n.pag.

Swing You Sinners! 1930. Director Dave Fleischer. USA: Fleischer Studios.

Taffel, Sy. 2016. "Perspectives on the Postdigital: Beyond Rhetorics of Progress and Novelty." *Convergence: The International Journal of Research into New Media Technologies* 22 (3): 324–338.

Terraria. 2011. Re-Logic. Microsoft Windows.

There Is No Game: Wrong Dimension. 2020. Draw Me a Pixel. Microsoft Windows.

Thibault, Mattia. 2016. "Post-Digital Games: The Influence of Nostalgia in Indie Games' Graphic Regimes." *Gamevironments* 4: 1–24.

Thimbleweed Park. 2017. Terrible Toybox. Microsoft Windows.

Thompson, Kristin. 1977. "The Concept of Cinematic Excess." *Ciné-Tracts* 1 (2): 54–63.

Thomson-Jones, Katherine. 2005. "Inseparable Insight: Reconciling Cognitivism and Formalism in Aesthetics." *The Journal of Aesthetics and Art Criticism* 63 (4): 375–384.

Thon, Jan-Noël. 2006. "Unendliche Weiten? Schauplätze, fiktionale Welten und soziale Räume heutiger Computerspiele." *Hamburger Hefte zur Medienkultur* 5: 29–60.

Thon, Jan-Noël. 2008. "Immersion Revisited: On the Value of a Contested Concept." In *Extending Experiences: Structure, Analysis and Design of Computer Game Player Experience*, edited by Amyris Fernandez, Olli Leino, and Hanna Wirman, 29–43. Rovaniemi: Lapland University Press.

Thon, Jan-Noël. 2009. "Perspective in Contemporary Computer Games." *In Point of View, Perspective, and Focalization: Modeling Mediation in Narrative*, edited by Peter Hühn, Wolf Schmid, and Jörg Schönert, 279–299. Berlin: De Gruyter.

Thon, Jan-Noël. 2015. "Game Studies und Narratologie." In *Game Studies: Aktuelle Ansätze der Computerspielforschung*, edited by Klaus Sachs-Hombach and Jan-Noël Thon, 104–164. Cologne: Halem.

Thon, Jan-Noël. 2016a. "Narrative Comprehension and Video Game Storyworlds." In *Video Games and the Mind: Essays on Cognition, Affect and Emotion*, edited by Bernard Perron and Felix Schröter, 15–31. Jefferson: McFarland.

Thon, Jan-Noël. 2016b. *Transmedial Narratology and Contemporary Media Culture*. Lincoln: University of Nebraska Press.

Thon, Jan-Noël. 2017. "Transmedial Narratology Revisited: On the Intersubjective Construction of Storyworlds and the Problem of Representational Correspondence in Films, Comics, and Video Games." *Narrative* 25 (3): 285–320.

Thon, Jan-Noël. 2019a. "Playing with Fear: The Aesthetics of Horror in Recent Indie Games." *Eludamos: Journal for Computer Game Culture* 10 (1): 197–231.

Thon, Jan-Noël. 2019b. "Transmedia Characters: Theory and Analysis." *Frontiers of Narrative Studies* 5 (2): 176–199.

Thon, Jan-Noël. 2020. "Analyzing Indie Aesthetics." In Proceedings of *DiGRA 2020: Play Everywhere*, n.pag.

Thon, Jan-Noël. 2021. "Comics Narratology." In *Handbook of Comics and Graphic Novels*, edited by Sebastian Domsch, Dan Hassler-Forest, and Dirk Vanderbeke, 99–120. Berlin: De Gruyter.

Thon, Jan-Noël. 2023. "Bildmedium Computerspiel? Zur ästhetischen Komplexität aktueller Indie Games." In *Bildmedien: Materialität – Semiotik – Ästhetik*, edited by Frauke Berndt and Jan-Noël Thon, 441–462. Berlin: De Gruyter.

Thon, Jan-Noël. 2025. "Playing with *Otium*? On the Aesthetics of Walking Simulators." *Narrative* 33 (3).

Torner, Evan, Aaron Trammel, and Emma Leigh Waldron. 2016. "Reinventing Analog Game Studies: Introductory Manifesto." In *Analog Game Studies: Volume 1*, edited by Evan Torner, Aaron Trammel, and Emma Leigh Waldron, 1–5. Pittsburg, PA: ETC Press.

Tosca, Susana, and Lisbeth Klastrup. 2020. *Transmedial Worlds in Everyday Life: Networked Reception, Social Media, and Fictional Worlds*. New York: Routledge.

To the Death! 2019. Brian Garber. Card Game.

To the Moon. 2011. Freebird Games. Microsoft Windows.

Trials of Fire. 2021. Whatboy Games. Microsoft Windows.

Turkle, Sherry. 2008. "Always-On/Always-On-You: The Tethered Self." In *Handbook of Mobile Communication Studies*, edited by James E. Katz, 121–137. Cambridge, MA: MIT Press.

Undertale. 2015. Toby Fox. Microsoft Windows.

The Unfinished Swan. 2012. Giant Sparrow/Annapurna Interactive. Microsoft Windows.

van Nuenen, Tom. 2024. *Traveling through Video Games*. New York: Routledge.

Vella, Daniel. 2013. "'The Wanderer in the Wilderness: Being in the Virtual Landscape in *Minecraft* and *Proteus*." In *The Philosophy of Computer Games Conference Proceedings 2013*, 1–16.

Verstegen, Ian. 2018. *Arnheim, Gestalt and Media: An Ontological Theory*. Cham: Springer.

von Ehrenfels, Christian. 1890. "Über 'Gestaltqualitäten'." *Vierteljahrsschrift für wissenschaftliche Philosophie* 14: 249–292.

VVVVVV. 2010. Terry Cavanagh. Microsoft Windows.

Wake, Paul, and Chloé Germaine. 2023. "Introduction: Material Game Studies." In *Material Game Studies: A Philosophy of Analogue Play*, edited by Paul Wake and Chloé Germaine, 1–18. New York: Bloomsbury.

Walker, John. 2016. "Wot I Think: *Pony Island*—The Smartest Game of 2016: Asmodeus Ex." *Rock Paper Shotgun*, January 5, 2016. www.rockpapershotgun.com/wot-i-think-pony-island-the-smartest-game-of-2016.

Walton, Kendall L. 1984. "Transparent Pictures: On the Nature of Photographic Realism." *Critical Inquiry* 11: 246–277.

Walton, Kendall L. 1990. *Mimesis as Make-Believe: On the Foundations of the Representational Arts*. Cambridge: Harvard University Press.

Waszkiewicz, Agata. 2024. *Metagames: Games about Games*. New York: Routledge.

Welsch, Wolfgang. 1987. *Aisthesis: Grundzüge und Perspektiven der Aristotelischen Sinneslehre*. Stuttgart: Klett-Kotta.

Welsch, Wolfgang. 1990. *Ästhetisches Denken*. Stuttgart: Reclam.

Welsch, Wolfgang, ed. 1993. *Die Aktualität des Ästhetischen*. Munich: Fink.

Welsch, Wolfgang. 1995. "Aesthetics beyond Aesthetics: Regarding the Contemporary Relevance of the Aesthetic and Recharting the Field of Aesthetics." *Journal of Contemporary Literature and Aesthetics* 18 (1–2): 1–23.

Welsch, Wolfgang. 1996. *Grenzgänge der Ästhetik*. Stuttgart: Reclam.
Welsch, Wolfgang. 1997. *Undoing Aesthetics*. London: Sage.
Wertheimer, Max. 1925. *Drei Abhandlungen zur Gestalttheorie*. Erlangen: Verlag der Philosophischen Akademie.
What Remains of Edith Finch. 2017. Giant Sparrow/Annapurna Interactive. Microsoft Windows.
Whitted, Qiana. 2019. *EC Comics: Race, Shock, and Social Protest*. New Brunswick: Rutgers University Press.
Wiese, Wanja. 2017. *Experienced Wholeness: Integrating Insights from Gestalt Theory, Cognitive Neuroscience, and Predictive Processing*. Cambridge, MA: MIT Press.
Wildermyth. 2019. Worldwalker Games. Microsoft Windows.
Wolf, Mark J.P., ed. 2019. *The Routledge Companion to Media Technology and Obsolescence*. New York: Routledge.
Wolf, Werner. 1999. *The Musicalization of Fiction: A Study in the Theory and History of Intermediality*. Amsterdam: Rodopi.
Wolf, Werner. 2009. "Metareference across Media: The Concept, Its Transmedial Potentials and Problems, Main Forms and Functions." In *Metareference across Media: Theory and Case Studies*, edited by Werner Wolf, 1–85. Amsterdam: Rodopi.
Wolfenstein 3D. 1992. id Software/Apogee Software. DOS.
Wollheim, Richard. 1968. *Art and Its Objects: An Introduction to Aesthetics*. New York: Harper & Row.
Wollheim, Richard. 2001. "On Formalism and Pictorial Organization." *The Journal of Aesthetics and Art Criticism* 59 (2): 127–137.
Wood, Andrew, and Adam Summerville. 2019. "Understanding Boss Battles: A Case Study of *Cuphead*." https://exagworkshop.institutedigitalgames.com/archive/wood2019battles.pdf.
Yanes, Nicholas. 2021. "EC Comics." In *Keywords for Comics*, edited by Ramzi Fawaz, Deborah Whaley, and Shelley Streeby, 85–89. New York: New York University Press.
Young, James O. 1997. "Aesthetic Antirealism." *The Southern Journal of Philosophy* 35 (1): 119–134.
Zagal, José P., and Michael Mateas. 2010. "Time in Video Games: A Survey and Analysis." *Simulation & Gaming* 41 (6): 844–868.
Zangwill, Nick. 2001. *The Metaphysics of Beauty*. Ithaca, NY: Cornell University Press.
Zawacki, Alexander J. 2024. "Glitches and Ghosts: The Digital Uncanny in Video Games and Creepypasta." *Horror Studies* 15 (1): 83–98.
Zettl, Herbert. 2016. *Sight, Sound, Motion: Applied Media Aesthetics*. 8th ed. Boston: Cengage Learning.
Zimmerman, Felix, and Christian Huberts. 2019. "From Walking Simulator to Ambience Action Game: A Philosophical Approach to a Misunderstood Genre." *Press Start* 5 (2): 29–50.

Index

Made in the USA
Las Vegas, NV
19 August 2026

16debd3d-666a-48a2-98b4-beca15a86875R01